I0814300

HISTORICAL GLOSS AND FOREIGN AFFAIRS

HISTORICAL GLOSS AND FOREIGN AFFAIRS

CONSTITUTIONAL AUTHORITY IN PRACTICE

CURTIS A. BRADLEY

Harvard University Press
Cambridge, Massachusetts
London, England
2024

Printed in the United States of America
First printing

Publication of this book has been supported through the generous provisions of the Maurice and Lula Bradley Smith Memorial Fund.

Library of Congress Cataloging-in-Publication Data

Names: Bradley, Curtis A., author.
Title: Historical gloss and foreign affairs : constitutional authority in practice / Curtis A. Bradley.
Other titles: Constitutional authority in practice
Description: Cambridge, Massachusetts ; London, England : Harvard University Press, 2024. | Includes bibliographical references and index.
Identifiers: LCCN 2023057415 | ISBN 9780674292055 (cloth)
Subjects: LCSH: United States. Congress—History. | United States. Executive Office of the President. | Constitutional law—United States. | Constitutional history—United States. | Executive power—United States—History. | United States—Foreign relations. | United States—Foreign relations—Law and legislation. | United States—Foreign relations administration.
Classification: LCC E183.7 .B6924 2024 | DDC 342.7302/9—dc23
=/eng/20240215
LC record available at https://lccn.loc.gov/2023057415

To Kathy, David, and Liana

Contents

HISTORICAL GLOSS AND FOREIGN AFFAIRS

INTRODUCTION

> Upon this point a page of history is worth a volume of logic.
>
> —New York Trust Co. v. Eisner, 256 U.S. 345, 349 (1921) (Holmes, J.)

THE UNITED STATES HAS ONE OF THE OLDEST CONSTITUTIONS IN THE world, developed when the country was a new and weak nation, and it is extremely difficult to amend. Yet in the more than 230 years since the Constitution took effect, the United States has changed in fundamental ways, as have the challenges and threats that it faces. The constitutional law governing the United States' conduct of foreign affairs has evolved with the nation, but not through formal amendments to the text. Rather, this law has been shaped and defined by the accretion of governmental practice. This book provides an account of the influence of such practice on issues ranging from the recognition of foreign governments to the making and termination of treaties and the use of military force.

In some areas of constitutional law, such as those related to individual rights, courts have played a central and often controversial role in developing the law in lieu of formal amendments to the text. But courts have played much less of a role in the foreign affairs area, especially in the modern era. In part this is because foreign affairs disputes often do not arise in a posture that satisfies traditional requirements for judicial review, such as requirements relating to standing to sue. But it is also because courts perceive that they lack sufficient expertise and information to mediate the disputes that arise. As a result, constitutional understandings relating to foreign affairs authority have often been developed through the practices of Congress and the executive branch, at times cooperatively and at other times through conflict. To take just one example, even though the text of the Constitution specifies only one process for making treaties—a process that requires the approval of two-thirds of the Senate—the U.S. government almost never uses that process anymore and instead concludes the vast majority of U.S. international agreements through less-demanding "executive agreement" procedures.

As this and other examples will illustrate, it is impossible to understand our modern foreign affairs Constitution without understanding the evolution of governmental practice. This practice has had the effect, the book will argue, of "glossing" the meaning of the Constitution. As the word "gloss" implies, governmental practice is not typically treated as a freestanding source of constitutional law. Instead, it is used to help interpret other constitutional materials, most notably the constitutional text and structural inferences from the text, when those materials are thought to be unclear or incomplete. As will be discussed more fully in subsequent chapters, governmental practices are credited as gloss when they have persisted and become stable. Sometimes these practices have existed since the early post-Founding period, and other times they developed later. Crediting gloss means giving weight to these practices, which are a form of nonjudicial precedent, when interpreting the Constitution's distributions of authority.

Appeals to history are common in constitutional interpretation, but gloss involves an appeal to a particular type of history arising from the actions and interactions of Congress and the executive branch. This practice can flesh out the meaning of the Constitution's text and fill in its gaps and, in doing so, allow the Constitution to better adapt to changed circumstances. Reliance on gloss is especially common with respect to issues relating to the separation of powers, where the textual allocations of authority are often unclear, judicial review tends to be infrequent, and the political branches bargain over matters of governance. These separation of powers issues concern not only the Constitution's distribution of authority among Congress, the executive branch, and the judiciary, but also its distribution of authority within Congress between the House of Representatives and the Senate.

The idea of historical gloss informing constitutional meaning is most famously associated with Justice Felix Frankfurter's concurrence in the *Youngstown* case from the early 1950s. In that case, President Truman had directed the government's seizure of the nation's steel mills during the Korean War in an effort to avoid a labor stoppage. In support of this action, Truman claimed that a halt in steel production would be a direct threat to U.S. national security. "If steel production stops," he said, "we will have to stop making the shells and bombs that are going directly to our soldiers at the front in Korea."[1] Despite this claim, the Supreme Court held that Truman had acted unlawfully. Justice Black's majority opinion explained that "the President's power, if any, to issue the order must stem either from an act of Congress or from the Constitution itself."[2] The Court found no express or implied statutory authorization. As for the Constitution, the Court rejected the argument that Truman's Commander in Chief power was sufficient to sustain the order, reasoning that a foreign war does not give the president "the ultimate power as such to take possession of private property in order to keep labor disputes from stopping production." Nor did the Court think the Constitution's conferral of executive power on the president was sufficient: the Court implied that overriding private property rights is legislative in character and said that "the President's power to see that the laws are faithfully executed refutes the idea that he is to be a lawmaker."

Frankfurter agreed with the majority that Truman had acted unlawfully, but he thought that the issue was more complicated than Black's discussion suggested.[3] He began by emphasizing that "the Framers . . . did not make the judiciary the overseer of our government." While acknowledging that courts "may . . . have to intervene in determining where authority lies as between the democratic forces in our scheme of government," he thought that in doing so they "should be wary and humble." With this general perspective in mind, Frankfurter argued that when courts consider the scope of governmental authority, they should take account of historical governmental practice. "Deeply embedded traditional ways of conducting government cannot supplant the Constitution or legislation," he said, "but they give meaning to the words of a text or supply them." In his view, it was "an inadmissibly narrow conception of American constitutional law to confine it to the words of the Constitution and to disregard the gloss which life has written upon them." After reviewing the practice of executive seizure of property, however, Frankfurter found it insufficient to sustain Truman's action.

In his better-known concurrence in the case, Justice Robert Jackson outlined what has become a canonical framework for assessing presidential power, and this framework implicitly invites a consideration of historical practice.[4] "Presidential powers," Jackson argued, "are not fixed but fluctuate depending upon their disjunction or conjunction with those of Congress." He then proceeded to set out what he acknowledged was "a somewhat over-simplified grouping of practical situations in which a President may doubt, or others may challenge, his powers":

1. When the President acts pursuant to an express or implied authorization of Congress, his authority is at its maximum, for it includes all that he possesses in his own right plus all that Congress can delegate. . . .
2. When the President acts in absence of either a congressional grant or denial of authority, he can only rely upon his own independent powers, but there is a zone of twilight in which he and Congress may have concurrent authority, or in which its distribution is uncertain. . . .

3. When the President takes measures incompatible with the expressed or implied will of Congress, his power is at its lowest ebb, for then he can rely only upon his own constitutional powers minus any constitutional powers of Congress over the matter.

Applying that framework, Jackson concluded that the case fell into the third category because Congress had regulated the seizure of property in ways that were inconsistent with Truman's action. Truman could win under that category, Jackson explained, only if the "seizure of such strike-bound industries is within his domain and beyond control by Congress," which Jackson concluded was not the case.

Historical practice is relevant to Jackson's framework in several ways. First, the framework takes note of *implied* congressional approval or disapproval, and congressional and executive practice can potentially provide a basis for such inferences.[5] Second, the middle tier of the framework envisions situations in which the text of the Constitution is unclear about a distribution of authority, something that necessitates a consideration of nontextual materials, including, potentially, historical practice. Such practice can include congressional inaction in the face of executive branch assertions of authority. Indeed, Jackson noted that in the middle tier, "congressional inertia, indifference or quiescence may sometimes, at least, as a practical matter, enable, if not invite, measures on independent presidential responsibility."[6] Finally, Jackson's framework envisions that, although Congress should generally prevail in the third, "lowest ebb," category, there will be situations in which the president is exercising authority that cannot be circumscribed by Congress. The text of the Constitution, however, does not clearly specify these situations, which may necessitate a consideration of how the two branches have interacted over time.[7]

Despite its association with *Youngstown,* reliance on gloss has a much longer history. This is apparent even when we are looking just at judicial decisions, but it is especially clear once we shift our gaze away from the courts. From nearly the beginning of the country, the executive branch and Congress have looked to historical practice to inform their understandings of the constitutional law of foreign affairs. As William Howard Taft observed after his presidency, "precedents from previous administrations and from previous Congresses create an historical construction of the extent and limitations of their respective powers."[8] Even when they have disagreed about issues of authority, Congress and the executive branch have often framed their disagreements in terms of claims about the practice rather than about the text or original understandings. The judiciary has played a relatively modest role in this area, but on the occasions that it has addressed issues of foreign affairs authority, including in decisions long before *Youngstown,* it has often given significant weight to established practices.

The examples in this book all involve important exercises of foreign affairs authority that have been developed and refined through practice. For some examples, the practice has generally moved in one direction, although with extensions and, at times, accelerations and consolidations. This is true, for example, of the power over recognition, the rise of executive agreements, and some of the gloss-based powers of Congress (including Congress's power to delegate its authority). For other examples in the book, such as treaty termination and to some extent war powers, there have been significant shifts over time in the nature or direction of the practice. For all the examples, the model of constitutional development involves the accumulation of nonjudicial precedent. While some events have been more important than others, the practice-based gloss recounted herein has developed over time, akin to the development of the common law (that is, the law developed by courts through their interpretations and extensions of judicial precedent).

Whether from accretion or shifts in practice, presidential power over foreign affairs has expanded significantly since the Founding.[9] This book documents this expansion across a range of issues. The account here is largely a functional one: as the United States assumed a greater presence in the world after the Spanish-American War, presidents perceived that they needed more authority in foreign affairs to promote U.S. national interests, and Congress generally accepted this fact but pushed back in select instances because of policy disputes or a desire to protect particular institutional interests. Consistent with this book's claims, when presidents sought to extend their authority, they reasoned from precedent to help justify the extensions. Like any precedent-based approach, these efforts were subject to debate about whether the new precedents were consistent with the past ones or were reasonable extensions of them in light of new circumstances.

Despite the rise of presidential power, Congress has also benefited from gloss. Although Congress has a much broader array of textual provisions in the Constitution to draw from than the president has, some of its exercises of authority cannot easily be grounded in the text (over immigration, for example) but are unquestioned because of longstanding legislative practice. Moreover, it is difficult to think of areas of foreign relations law today that Congress does not regulate at least to an extent, whether directly or indirectly. Although it is common to refer to an "imperial presidency" in foreign affairs, in many respects we have a *statutory* foreign affairs presidency. To be sure, Congress often chooses to delegate broad authority to the executive branch, but what is delegated can be cabined or withdrawn.

Gloss also helps Congress defeat claims of exclusive presidential authority. Justice Jackson, while accepting in *Youngstown* that there are pockets of such exclusive authority, suggested that presidential claims to such authority "must be scrutinized with caution, for what is at stake is the equilibrium established by our constitutional system."[10] As will be seen, historical gloss rarely can establish such exclusivity, which means that support for it usually must be found elsewhere, typically in structural and functional considerations. Congress, meanwhile, has substantial authority to disrupt claims of exclusive executive authority by legislating in contested areas, and—contrary to the imperial presidency narrative—it often does so. Modern presidents sometimes protest in signing statements, but this merely leaves the matter (at most) disputed rather than settled in the president's favor.[11] In presenting this account of congressional power, the book critiques some of the claims of exclusivity that have been made by the executive branch, including by the Justice Department's Office of Legal Counsel.

The gloss-based nature of our constitutional law of foreign affairs is not well captured by existing constitutional theories. Professor Philip Bobbitt famously listed six "modalities" of constitutional reasoning: historical, textual, structural, doctrinal, ethical, and prudential.[12] Although Bobbitt referred to history as a modality, he defined that category as focused only on the intentions or understandings of the constitutional framers and ratifiers. Reliance on gloss is a different type of historical modality, focused on post-Founding governmental practice. One of the goals of this book is to confirm gloss's status as one of the important modalities of constitutional interpretation.

In addition, part of the argument in this book is that accounts of our constitutional law should bear some resemblance to the way in which this law has long been practiced and applied by political actors. This book therefore adds to a scholarly literature that focuses on the Constitution outside the courts.[13] It is also related to recent efforts to describe the positive law of American constitutionalism—that is, the law as it is actually understood and practiced.[14] This book will show that our constitutional law of foreign relations is, and always has been, gloss based. This is easier to see once we look beyond the judiciary. Debates over constitutional theory tend to obsessively focus on the Supreme Court; a focus on foreign relations law, an area of constitutional law that is less court centered, helps counter this tendency.[15]

This book is also a call for realism about our Constitution in a more general sense. The original Constitution was drafted more than two centuries ago, during a hot summer in Philadelphia.[16] The drafters could only know the time in which they lived and (to some extent) the events that had preceded it, and there are many aspects of our modern society, government, and world that they could not have reasonably foreseen. Even if one credits the enormous talent and intellect of some members of this Founding generation, they were only human. They made some good choices and some bad choices, and often they made no choices at all on important issues because of the need for compromise, the constraints of time, and the limits of imagination.

Another recurring theme of the book is that there has been an interactive relationship between the evolution of the U.S. constitutional law relating to foreign affairs and international law. Congress and the executive branch exercise foreign affairs authority against the backdrop of international law, and claims about their authority have often been linked, at least rhetorically, with international legal doctrines. Conversely, how the United States engages with international law is often affected by domestic understandings of how foreign affairs authority is to be exercised. Focusing on this interactive relationship reveals something that is usually overlooked, which is that international law has often been invoked in support of expansions of presidential power in foreign affairs. It is sometimes suggested that greater emphasis on international law will help constrain executive power,[17] but in practice the outcome has often been the reverse.[18]

* * *

Chapter 1 explains the nature of historical gloss, its relationship to the constitutional text and other interpretive materials, and its place within debates over constitutional theory. "Gloss," as the word implies, is used to help interpret other constitutional materials, most notably the constitutional text and structural inferences from the text, when those materials are thought to be unclear. Gloss does not purport to override clear constitutional text, although perceptions of textual clarity are themselves likely affected by the practice. While the book's primary focus is on the actions and reasoning of the executive branch and Congress, this chapter shows that when the Supreme Court has addressed separation of powers issues, including those relating to the conduct of foreign affairs, it, too, has often relied on historical gloss.

Chapter 2 describes the laconic nature of the constitutional text as it relates to foreign affairs. Many important issues of foreign affairs authority are not addressed, at least specifically, in the text. This is especially true of issues relating to executive power, given the sparse nature of the grants of authority in Article II of the Constitution. Nor, except in a few instances, does the text explain how the respective foreign affairs powers of Congress and the president interrelate. Although various theories have been developed to resolve these uncertainties, none of them seems satisfactory or complete. The chapter also explains that, because of various limiting doctrines, the courts have played only a modest role in addressing issues of foreign affairs authority. All of this makes foreign affairs a fertile ground for the development of historical gloss.

Chapter 3 addresses the power to recognize foreign governments and their territories. There is no "recognition power" listed in the Constitution, but presidents from early in U.S. history have exercised this power. At times in the nineteenth century, Congress attempted to assert its own views relating to recognition policy, sometimes producing constitutional conflict. By the twentieth century, however, Congress largely accepted that the executive branch would manage issues of recognition, although conflicts still sometimes arose. For most of U.S. history, the Supreme Court treated political branch recognition decisions as binding on the courts, without attempting to sort out the relationship between congressional and executive authority. That changed in 2015, when the Court held in *Zivotofsky v. Kerry* that recognition decisions are exclusively the province of the executive branch, in part on the basis of what the Court described as "the weight of historical evidence."

Chapter 4 describes the rise of "executive agreements" in lieu of treaties. Although the text of the Constitution mentions only one process by which the national government can make international agreements—a process that requires approval by two-thirds of the Senate—presidents have long concluded agreements in other ways. While these executive agreements were relatively rare early in U.S. history, the phenomenon grew over time and especially accelerated in the 1930s and 1940s. For the most part, the Senate has acquiesced in the shift, although it has tried to hold on to some pockets of authority. When the Supreme Court has considered cases involving executive agreements, it has upheld them, in large part because of longstanding historical practice.

Chapter 5 discusses the power to terminate treaties and other international agreements. Here, the story is one of not only an accretion of practice but also an eventual shift in the direction of the practice. In the nineteenth century, Congress was generally involved in treaty terminations, and presidents appeared to believe that this was necessary. In the twentieth century, however, presidents shifted to unilateral exercises of termination authority, a phenomenon that accelerated during the Franklin Roosevelt administration. This development did not produce much constitutional controversy until the 1970s, when some members of Congress objected to President Carter's termination of a mutual defense treaty with Taiwan. The Supreme Court declined to intervene in that dispute, and since then presidents have terminated dozens of treaties, usually without triggering constitutional controversy. Executive branch lawyers in the Trump administration argued not only that the president has the authority to terminate treaties but that Congress lacks the authority to limit presidential terminations. This claim, however, is not supported by historical gloss.

Chapter 6 addresses the authority to use military force. Although the Constitution gives Congress the power to declare war, there were uncertainties from almost the beginning about the nature and scope of this power. Although there appears to have been a general understanding that offensive military operations required congressional approval, there were often questions about the line between offense and defense, especially as the United States developed a broader naval presence. By the early twentieth century, presidents routinely engaged in limited military operations without congressional authorization, on the theory that they were "police" actions rather than the initiation of war. Since World War II, extensive ground campaigns have generally been authorized by Congress (with the Korean War being a major exception), but short-term and aerial campaigns have often been conducted by presidents unilaterally. Congress has acquiesced at least to an extent in this practice, including in its 1973 War Powers Resolution.

Chapter 7 provides examples of congressional (and senatorial) powers over foreign affairs that have been enhanced by gloss, even when these powers intersect with areas of executive authority. These examples include such matters as the conditional consent to treaties, the regulation of passports, conditions on foreign aid, U.S. participation in international institutions, the termination of military conflicts, and the treatment of prisoners of war. The chapter also explains why a longstanding congressional practice, even if contested, will tend to defeat gloss-based claims of exclusive executive authority. A central theme of this book is that Congress can usually have the last word, even in foreign relations.

Finally, Chapter 8 considers the relevance of gloss to the constitutionality of delegations of foreign affairs authority from Congress to the executive branch. Some Supreme Court justices today seem to favor a revival of "nondelegation" constraints on Congress's ability to vest discretionary authority in the executive branch, while also accepting that it may be appropriate for Congress to grant more discretion to the executive branch in the foreign affairs area. This chapter shows that broad delegations have existed in this area since the Founding, across a wide range of issues, including trade restrictions, responses to emergencies, the exclusion of immigrants, and uses of force. Nondelegation objections have sometimes been raised against these grants of authority, but inconsistently and usually unsuccessfully. The Supreme Court has repeatedly deferred to this practice, including most famously in a 1936 decision, *United States v. Curtiss-Wright Export Corporation,* when it upheld a delegation of authority to the president to ban arms sales to countries involved in a conflict in Latin America.

In terms of methodology, the book draws upon and supplements the extensive collections of practice compiled over the years by the State Department and its lawyers, including most notably in the *Digests of Practice in International Law* that date back to the late nineteenth century;[19] similar collections that have been compiled at various times in Congress, including by the Senate Foreign Relations Committee and the Congressional Research Service; legal opinions prepared by the Justice Department, including its Office of Legal Counsel, many of which have extensive recitations of practice; and compilations of materials put together by scholars. All of the practices described in the book have occurred publicly and thus have been subject to potential objection by affected institutional actors, although the book also sometimes describes the internal reasoning of the executive branch to provide a sense of how it has understood the practice. It also recounts debates in Congress to provide a sense of the range of views held by its members and the constitutional understandings that these members do and do not seem to be taking for granted. Each chapter except for Chapter 2 begins by recounting an event that illustrates the important role played by historical gloss for that issue. All of the chapters highlight the relevant constitutional text before turning to the practice.

1

HISTORICAL GLOSS AND CONSTITUTIONAL INTERPRETATION

IN EARLY 2014, THE SUPREME COURT HEARD ORAL ARGUMENTS IN *National Labor Relations Board v. Noel Canning.* At issue in the case was the validity of appointments made by President Obama to the National Labor Relations Board (NLRB). The NLRB, which adjudicates charges of unfair labor practices, consists of five members, each of whom serves a five-year term and is to be appointed by the president with the advice and consent of the Senate. To have a quorum, the NLRB needs to have at least three members in place. When the Board's membership fell to two in early 2012, Obama appointed three new members during a several-week Senate break, a period in which the Senate held some pro forma sessions but did not conduct business. Obama did so without obtaining the Senate's advice and consent for the appointments, on the understanding that the individuals would, like past recess appointees, serve only until the end of the next congressional session unless confirmed by the Senate in the meantime.

The Court had to decide whether Obama's appointments were authorized by the Constitution's Recess Appointments Clause, which provides that the president "shall have Power to fill up all Vacancies that may happen during the Recess of the Senate, by granting Commissions which shall expire at the End of their next Session."[1] The two principal questions were whether the phrase "the Recess" in this clause refers only to breaks *between* congressional sessions or also includes breaks *during* the session (like the Senate break in this case) and whether the positions filled under this clause must have become vacant during the recess (unlike in this case). A third question was whether there was a sufficiently long break here to qualify as a recess, given the existence of the pro form sessions.

Donald Verrilli, the Solicitor General, argued the case on behalf of the NLRB. Early in the argument, Justice Scalia asked him a pointed question: Assuming for the sake of argument that the Court concluded that the text of the Constitution clearly limits recess appointments to vacancies that occur during a recess but that the Court also found that there was longstanding practice to the contrary, what should the Court hold? "What do you do," asked Scalia, "when there is a practice that—that flatly contradicts a clear text of the Constitution? Which of the two prevails?"[2] Verrilli repeatedly tried to resist this question, noting that it is unlikely that we would see a conflict develop between clear constitutional text and longstanding practice. But when Scalia continued to press him, Verrilli replied that when there is "a practice going back to the founding of the Republic, the practice should govern."[3]

Ultimately, a majority of the Court decided that it need not address the question posed to Verrilli because it concluded that the text of the Recess Appointments Clause was not clear with respect to the questions at issue.[4] As a result, the Court said that it was appropriate to "put significant weight upon historical practice," something that it insisted was "neither new nor controversial." Scalia, writing what was in effect a dissent on behalf of himself and three other justices, saw matters differently.[5] He acknowledged that "where a governmental practice has been open, widespread, and unchallenged since the early days of the Republic, the practice should guide our interpretation of an ambiguous constitutional provision." But he contended that "the majority casts aside the plain, original meaning of the constitutional text in deference to late-arising historical practices that are ambiguous at best." The debate among the justices, in other words, was over when, not whether, it was appropriate to credit historical practice in constitutional interpretation.

This chapter describes the nature of "historical gloss" and considers its place within constitutional theory.[6] It also explains why it makes sense under certain conditions for courts and other actors to credit gloss when interpreting the Constitution, especially when addressing issues relating to the separation of powers. It then outlines the general requirements for crediting gloss. Finally, the chapter addresses one of the most common objections to relying on gloss in constitutional interpretation: that it unduly favors executive authority. One of the key takeaways from the chapter is that although gloss will often support presidential foreign affairs actions in the face of congressional silence, it generally will not disempower Congress from acting.

Historical Gloss and Its Justifications

Historical gloss arises from the longstanding practices of government institutions. Crediting gloss means giving weight to these practices when interpreting the Constitution. As the name "gloss" implies, it is not typically treated as a freestanding source of constitutional law. Instead, it is used to help interpret other constitutional materials, most notably the constitutional text and structural inferences from the text, when those materials are thought to be unclear.[7]

There are a number of reasons why it can make sense for courts and other actors to give weight to historical gloss in constitutional interpretation.[8] These reasons can be grouped into three basic categories: "Burkean" justifications (named after the eighteenth-century Anglo-Irish statesman and philosopher Edmund Burke), comparative institutional competence, and constitutional effectiveness and legitimacy.

Burkean Justifications

One of the Burkean justifications for crediting gloss concerns *presumptive workability*. This rationale is similar to Burke's notion that longstanding traditions merit deference because they reflect the judgments of many people who have come before us.[9] As applied to gloss, the idea is that longstanding practices of government institutions—disciplined by regular elections—are indicative of what works reasonably well, or at least better than anything the judiciary is likely to impose. This point should not be overstated: some practices may persist because of path dependence or institutional dysfunction. But deference along these lines can still make sense as a general rule of thumb, and many institutions (including the law schools that I have had the privilege of teaching at) give some weight to their own past practices on precisely this ground.

A related Burkean reason concerns the *value of settlement*. Under this rationale, deferring to gloss protects reliance interests and promotes the stability of governance.[10] It also avoids the danger of unforeseen consequences, given that longstanding practices are likely to be embedded within a broader array of understandings and institutional behavior.[11] Invalidating a longstanding governmental practice, this rationale suggests, is likely to undermine other practices in ways that may be difficult to predict.

Finally, if a particular type of authority has been exercised repeatedly in the past without significant controversy, its use the next time is less likely to be an opportunistic power grab than if it is unprecedented. Conversely, if similar situations have arisen in the past without the authority being invoked, it is harder to claim that the authority is necessary for governance. This does not mean that novel claims of authority are automatically disallowed, just that they are more likely to be viewed with suspicion than those with a historic pedigree.[12]

Comparative Institutional Competence

The comparative institutional competence reasons for deferring to gloss include *decisional capacity*. Courts and other interpreters sometimes rely on practice because other constitutional materials are perceived to offer insufficient guidance. This may be especially likely with respect to questions of executive power, given the limited textual guidance in Article II of the Constitution as well as the substantial changes since the Founding in the nature of the presidential office and international affairs. For such issues, relying on practice may offer the best option for a reasoned disposition of the case that seeks to avoid appealing simply to the interpreter's own policy assessment. This rationale is similar to one of the justifications for deeming some issues to be "political questions" that cannot be resolved by the courts: a lack of "judicially discoverable and manageable standards."[13] Indeed, as discussed in Chapter 2, reliance on historical gloss overlaps with the political question doctrine: under both approaches, the judiciary places the constitutional answer substantially in the hands of the political branches.

A related reason for crediting gloss concerns *institutional deference.* Courts do not have a monopoly on constitutional interpretation, and for reasons of expertise and majoritarianism, it can make sense for them to defer to other departments of the government about some aspects of the Constitution. Other governmental actors are sworn to uphold the Constitution, and they must by necessity interpret it as part of their duties. Moreover, with respect to separation of powers issues, political branch actors are likely to have a better understanding than courts of the practical consequences of particular constitutional interpretations.[14] Judicial deference to political branch understandings, which may be reflected in historical practice, can also reduce "countermajoritarian" concerns associated with constitutional judicial review, concerns that are especially strong when both political branches share a view that is different from the judiciary's view and have held that view for a long time.

Constitutional Effectiveness and Legitimacy

A constitutional effectiveness reason for crediting gloss is that doing so allows for needed *constitutional updating.* The U.S. Constitution is over 230 years old. The country and the challenges it faces are substantially different from those at the Founding. Making formal amendments to the text of the Constitution to take account of the changed conditions, however, is exceedingly difficult.[15] Reliance on gloss allows for common-law-style development of the Constitution. Indeed, one way of understanding the role of gloss in the U.S. constitutional system is as preserving in the United States an element of British constitutionalism. As historian Jonathan Gienapp has noted, the U.S. constitutional Founders understood the British constitution as both immutable *and* as changing: "Because the [British] constitution could be deciphered only through the method of the common law, it could be both fixed and yet perpetually changing."[16] Gloss allows for a similar dynamic in U.S. constitutionalism, albeit through a nonjudicial form of common-law development.[17]

Another general constitutional reason for crediting gloss involves *descriptive fit*. To the extent that past practice predicts the future behavior of governmental actors, it should arguably inform legal analysis because descriptions of what the law is should have some correspondence to operational reality. Especially in areas where the prospect of judicial review is remote, descriptions of the law or a legal system that ignore longstanding institutional practice are likely to fail on descriptive grounds. Moreover, if in fact government actors look to past practice to inform their understanding of—and to shape their claims about—the law, legal philosophers working in the tradition of H. L. A. Hart would treat that second-order practice as itself a fundamental feature of the legal order.[18] In the same way that entrenched judicial precedents form part of what the law is even if there is reason to believe that they might have been wrongly decided, it can be argued that any account of executive and legislative power must take account of how the branches have actually acted and reasoned over time.[19]

Although these justifications are analytically distinct, they overlap. For example, limits on judicial capacity can be a reason both for deferring to political branch interpretations and also for the risk aversion associated with the Burkean justifications. Moreover, the justifications are not mutually exclusive: it would not be inconsistent for an interpreter to invoke more than one justification—or even all of them—to justify resort to gloss.

Gloss's Domain

The arguments for relying on historical gloss are especially strong in the area of separation of powers—that is, for issues concerning the distribution of authority among the branches of the federal government (and between the House and Senate in Congress).[20] This is in part due to the fact that separation of powers disputes are less likely than federalism or individual rights disputes to meet the requirements for judicial review (such as having plaintiffs with standing to sue), which means that there are fewer judicial precedents to guide the relevant actors. In the absence of judicial precedents, institutional actors coordinate around the nonjudicial precedent.

Moreover, when courts do address issues relating to constitutional structure, they are less likely to have strong intuitions about what should be permissible than they have with respect to other issues, especially individual rights issues, and thus more likely to defer to practice. Chief Justice Marshall made this point in *McCulloch v. Maryland*, a famous early Supreme Court decision upholding

Congress's authority to create a national bank.[21] As Marshall explained, for uncertain questions concerning the authority of government institutions, "the decision of which the great principles of liberty are not concerned, but the respective powers of those who are equally the representatives of the people, are to be adjusted," the resolution of the questions, "if not put at rest by the practice of the Government, ought to receive a considerable impression from that practice."[22]

The settlement and institutional deference justifications for gloss also apply more readily in the separation of powers context. At least as a general matter, the political branches are likely to have a better sense than the courts of what works well in matters of governance, especially in the face of substantially changed conditions.[23] Moreover, because those branches routinely interact and bargain with each other, their practices are likely to reflect reciprocal arrangements that may be difficult to disentangle when examining particular constitutional issues in isolation.

This is not to suggest that appeals to historical practice are irrelevant outside the separation of powers context. History intersects in a wide variety of ways with constitutional interpretation.[24] For example, arguments from "tradition" are common, and sometimes highly controversial, in individual rights controversies.[25] In the separation of powers area, however, the focus is solely on governmental practices, not general social practices or beliefs. Moreover, relying on past practice in this area does not typically raise concerns about the oppression of minorities or other disadvantaged groups, or at least not to the same extent that it does in some individual rights areas.[26] Governmental actors in the rights context typically interact with those who possess far less power than the government to push back or advance contrary understandings. As a result, the settlement and institutional deference justifications for relying on practice are weaker in that context.[27]

That said, the line between separation of powers issues and other issues is not always clear, and some separation of powers issues intersect with individual rights. In those situations, courts tend to be more actively involved and thus more likely to disrupt the development of gloss. Most of the examples in this book, by contrast, are of the "purer" separation of powers variety, where courts have a lower profile. In any event, the lack of perfectly neat divisions does not preclude rough generalizations about where the arguments for using gloss are stronger or weaker, and the point here is simply that the arguments tend to be stronger in the separation of powers context.

Gloss and the Supreme Court

As this book will document, both Congress and the executive branch routinely invoke gloss when interpreting and arguing about the Constitution's distributions of authority. The Supreme Court, too, looks to gloss. As discussed in the Introduction, the most prominent judicial endorsement of gloss before the *Noel Canning* decision was Justice Felix Frankfurter's concurrence in the 1952 *Youngstown* steel seizure case.[28]

Although Frankfurter's analysis is a noteworthy endorsement of gloss, the Supreme Court's reliance on historical practice in discerning the scope of governmental authority long predates *Youngstown.* As already noted, it was an important component of the Court's 1819 decision in *McCulloch v. Maryland.* In a 1915 decision, *United States v. Midwest Oil Co.*,[29] the Court rejected a challenge to President Taft's decision to temporarily withdraw certain public lands from private development, emphasizing the "long continued practice [of making] orders like the one here involved." Similarly, in a 1925 decision, in concluding that the president's pardon power extends to a conviction for contempt of court, the Court reasoned that "long practice under the pardoning power and acquiescence in it strongly sustains the construction it is based on."[30] A few years later, the Court emphasized longstanding practice when considering the circumstances under which the president's "pocket veto"—that is, failure to sign a bill before Congress recesses—should be deemed to operate.[31]

The Court has also emphasized longstanding practice in upholding broad delegations of authority from Congress to the president. In an 1892 decision, *Field v. Clark,* the Court rejected a constitutional challenge to a delegation of tariff-adjustment authority to the president, emphasizing that the statute in question had "the sanction of many precedents in legislation."[32] In its 1936 decision in *United States v. Curtiss-Wright Export Corporation,* the Court upheld a delegation of arms embargo authority, reasoning that it was supported by "uniform, long-continued and undisputed legislative practice," which the Court did "not feel at liberty at this late day to disturb."[33]

The Court has also continued to invoke historical practice in constitutional interpretation after *Youngstown.* As discussed more fully in Chapter 4, the Court in a 1981 decision, *Dames & Moore v. Regan,* upheld executive orders transferring billions of dollars in claims to an international tribunal in The Hague, as part of the resolution of the Iranian hostage crisis, in large part because of the history of presidential settlement of claims.[34] In doing so, the Court expressly invoked Justice Frankfurter's discussion of historical gloss and concluded that "such longstanding practice is present here."

The Court again invoked Frankfurter's concurrence in *Mistretta v. United States,* in upholding the constitutionality of the U.S. Sentencing Commission, an independent body created within the judiciary to establish sentencing guidelines.[35] In response to the objection that the creation of the Commission violated the separation of powers because judges serving on the Commission were performing nonjudicial duties, the Court emphasized that throughout history there were many examples of judges performing such duties. Citing Frankfurter's *Youngstown* concurrence, the Court observed that "our 200-year tradition of extrajudicial service is additional evidence that the doctrine of separated powers does not prohibit judicial participation in certain extrajudicial activity."

As noted at the outset of this chapter, the Court placed particular emphasis on historical practice in its 2014 decision in *Noel Canning,* in construing the scope of the president's authority to make recess appointments. The following year, in *Zivotofsky v. Kerry,* the Court again emphasized historical practice, this time in concluding that the president has an exclusive authority to recognize foreign governments and their territories that cannot be limited by Congress.[36] Citing *Noel Canning,* the Court in *Zivotofsky* said that, "having examined the Constitution's text and this Court's precedent, it is appropriate to turn to accepted understandings and practice."

To be sure, the Court has not always credited historical practice relating to the separation of powers. Probably the most famous case in which it did not do so is *INS v. Chadha.*[37] There, the Court held that a "legislative veto" provision enacted by Congress was invalid because it allowed Congress to engage in a legislative act (overturning exercises of the attorney general's statutorily delegated authority to suspend deportations) without resort to the bicameralism and presentment process for legislation specified in Article I of the Constitution. The Court reached this conclusion even though, as Justice White pointed out in dissent, Congress had enacted hundreds of legislative veto provisions since the 1930s. Believing that the unconstitutionality of the provision was clear, the Court dismissed the historical practice, saying that its "inquiry is sharpened rather than blunted by the fact that congressional veto provisions are appearing with increasing frequency in statutes which delegate authority to executive and independent agencies." The Court also noted, however, that numerous presidents had expressed constitutional concerns about the legislative veto—suggesting that there had not been executive acquiescence.[38]

Gloss and Constitutional Theory

The central debate within constitutional theory is between "originalist" and "nonoriginalist" approaches to constitutional interpretation.[39] There are many versions of both originalism and nonoriginalism, but each has certain core elements. In particular, originalists tend to insist that the meaning of the Constitution became fixed at the time that its text was ratified and that interpreters are bound by that original meaning.[40] By contrast, nonoriginalists tend to accept that constitutional meaning can change even absent formal amendments to the text and that it can be appropriate for interpreters to apply the changed meaning.

Because reliance on gloss may add to or even change constitutional meaning from what existed at the Founding, it is likely to have more appeal to nonoriginalists. Nevertheless, it may be compatible with at least some forms of originalism. Strict originalists, for example, may be willing to credit historical practice in the early years of the nation on the theory that it may provide evidence of what was understood or settled by the Founding generation, but they may resist relying on later practices, especially if those practices depart from what would otherwise appear to be the understandings of those involved in the Constitution's ratification.[41]

That said, there are practice-based arguments that might appeal to some originalists even when the practice is not traced to the early post-Founding period. For example, such arguments are consistent with the idea of "constitutional construction" that has been articulated by some originalist theorists, which envisions that interpreters can draw on various materials to resolve constitutional meaning "when the Constitution as written cannot in good faith be said to provide a determinate answer to a given question."[42] Similarly, Professor Jack Balkin's idea of "framework originalism," which "views the Constitution as an initial framework for governance that sets politics in motion and must be filled out over time through constitutional construction," is compatible with reliance on historical practice.[43] As discussed below, some originalists are also open to the idea of the "liquidation" of constitutional meaning through post-Founding practice, a concept that overlaps with that of gloss.

Gloss might also appeal to some originalists as a form of precedent. Even many originalists acknowledge that there should be some deference to *judicial* precedent, regardless of whether it is consistent with the original understanding.[44] And many of the standard values associated with deference to such precedent—such as consistency, predictability, reliance, and transparency—can support deference to nonjudicial precedent as well.[45]

Even if some versions of originalism are compatible with practice-based arguments, various nonoriginalist approaches are likely to be more receptive to such arguments. Many nonoriginalists are "pluralist" in that they are willing to credit a range of materials, including history of various types.[46] Historical gloss can be part of those materials.

More specific nonoriginalist theories also tend to be compatible with a consideration of historical practice. Given its emphasis on tradition, the gloss approach fits well with Burkean approaches to constitutional law. Reliance on historical practice also fits well with the somewhat related idea of "common law constitutionalism," which involves an incremental interpretation of the Constitution in light of both judicial precedent and tradition.[47] Like Burkeanism, this approach is deferential to the "accumulated wisdom of many generations" and to judgments that "have been tested over time, in a variety of circumstances, and have been found to be at least good enough."[48] Both of these approaches also allow for the possibility that constitutional law can adapt over time to changing circumstances.[49]

Similarly, a focus on the historical practice of the political branches is consistent with the scholarly emphasis in recent years on constitutional law developed outside the courts.[50] Parts of that literature focus on "popular constitutionalism"—that is, the constitutional views of "the people," including social movements organized around political, social, and cultural ideas expressed in constitutional terms.[51] But other parts, more relevant here, stress the importance of governmental practices to constitutional meaning and development.[52]

Historical practice-based arguments also overlap with approaches to constitutional law that emphasize particularly decisive moments in history, such as Professor Bruce Ackerman's account of constitutional "moments" and Professors Eric Posner and Adrian Vermeule's account of "constitutional showdowns."[53] These descriptions of constitutional law are similar to practice-based arguments in that both place special weight on the actions of the political branches. However, these types of accounts tend to focus on critical turning points, whereas invocations of the historical gloss method tend to emphasize longer-term accretions of practice. Indeed, the Burkean values associated with gloss stem in part from its more gradual and evolutionary nature. This is not to suggest that gloss-based developments are always slow; sometimes practices and views change fairly quickly, but the gloss approach still requires the perspective of a longer time horizon to know whether the practices have become established.

Distinct from "Liquidation"?

Some originalist scholars have invoked a different term to describe the potential relevance of post-Founding practice to constitutional interpretation: "liquidation."[54] Drawing on references to that term by James Madison and certain other members of the Founding generation, those commentators have outlined the conditions under which post-Founding practice can potentially "liquidate" indeterminate constitutional meaning such that it becomes "fixed."[55] (The word "liquidate" is used here to signify essentially the opposite of the principal modern connotation; instead of signifying dissolution, as in a "liquidation sale," it signifies making something more determinate, as in "liquidated damages.") The Supreme Court, too, has sometimes invoked the idea of "fixing" constitutional meaning when referring to the relevance of historical practice to constitutional interpretation.[56]

In part because the concepts of gloss and liquidation have only recently begun to receive sustained academic attention, it is not clear whether and to what extent they do or should differ from each other. In *Noel Canning*, the Court seemed to assume that liquidation and gloss were the same phenomenon. After quoting a reference to liquidation by Madison, the Court said that "our cases have continually confirmed Madison's view."[57] In the decisions it cited in support of this proposition, however, the Court included a number of decisions typically associated with historical gloss, including Frankfurter's concurrence in *Youngstown*.

Whether liquidation is different from gloss depends on how it is defined.[58] A narrow version of the liquidation concept might look only to early post-Founding practice and might insist that, once liquidated, constitutional meaning can never be reliquidated. A broad version, by contrast, might be open to considering later practices and might allow for the possibility that an initial liquidation could be undone through subsequent practice.

The narrow version of the liquidation concept is distinct from gloss, but the differences appear to make liquidation less normatively attractive than gloss. The theory behind liquidation is that the Founders expected that indeterminacies in constitutional meaning would be resolved by subsequent governmental actors.[59] But it is not clear why it would have made sense to have constitutional meaning determined dispositively by whatever political alignment happened to exist whenever the issue first arose. In attempting to determine constitutional meaning, the initial generations of political actors would likely be no less self-serving, partisan, and potentially short-sighted than later generations, and they would have much less experience in assessing the needs of American governance. Yet the narrow version of liquidation would license earlier generations of politicians to bind more experienced successors through simple majoritarian politics.

If anything, the settlement, decisional capacity, and deference justifications for gloss, outlined above, suggest that durable modern practices should be privileged over earlier ones—because, for example, those who have engaged in the modern practices are closer to contemporary conditions and problems. The net effect of the narrow version of the liquidation idea would be a regime that possesses many of the "dead hand" disadvantages of originalism but few of the theory's asserted upsides—namely, preventing constitutional change outside the demanding supermajoritarian process specified in Article V of the Constitution and conferring democratic legitimacy upon the institution of judicial review by limiting it to enforcement of the original supermajoritarian act of higher law-making. For what it is worth, the Court in *Noel Canning* seemed to reject the narrow version of liquidation, noting that "this Court has treated practice as an important interpretive factor even when the nature or longevity of that practice is subject to dispute, and even when that practice began after the founding era."[60]

The broad version of liquidation is similar to historical gloss and might even be identical to it, depending on how it is framed. Professor Will Baude has advanced a broad version of liquidation that would still be distinct from gloss in at least two respects.[61] First, Baude's approach would require that the course of practice be the product of *constitutional deliberation* by the political branches about the question at issue. If that is indeed a prerequisite for liquidation, it would be somewhat narrower than gloss, at least as a matter of theory. As discussed above, although such deliberation is certainly relevant when assessing and crediting patterns of practice, gloss can additionally or alternatively rest on risk-averse Burkean arguments about what has worked tolerably well, about stability and reliance interests, and about decisional capacity. Such considerations may exist even when it is not clear that the practices are the product of constitutional deliberation, as opposed to deliberation about (for example) what is practically needed. Nevertheless, this distinction between gloss and liquidation is relatively insignificant with respect to the examples discussed in this book, which are characterized by repeated constitutional deliberations in both Congress and the executive branch.

Baude also suggests a second requirement for liquidation that would further distinguish it from gloss: that the liquidation process is not complete until *the public* directly or indirectly approves a proposed political settlement. Baude does not explain what counts as direct or indirect public approval or how to discern it, but that requirement is distinct from accounts of historical gloss, which focus exclusively on the actions, inactions, and decisions of government officials, not on the approval of the general public. In any event, this requirement, even more than the first one, seems to make liquidation less appealing than gloss. It is hard enough to use historical practice in a principled fashion when focusing only on the conduct and arguments of government officials. Discerning when "the public" has blessed the settlement seems like an impossible task: even when constitutional issues do attract public attention, the engaged public will rarely reach consensus on a given question, and the requisite percentage of the public that needs to sanction a settlement is unclear. Requiring public approval is also hard to justify with respect to the many constitutional issues regarding which the mass public will not be directly informed or engaged. The issues of foreign affairs discussed in this book are prime examples.

Again, these just happen to be limitations on liquidation suggested by one commentator. To the extent that other supporters of liquidation offer a different account, it is possible that the gap between gloss and liquidation could be narrowed or even eliminated.

Relationship to the Constitutional Text

Although ostensibly just one of a number of constitutional modalities, the constitutional text plays a central role in U.S. constitutional discourse. As a result, few interpreters would assert, as the Solicitor General did in *Noel Canning,* that gloss can supersede clear text.[62] In fact (as the Solicitor General emphasized), the situation will rarely arise, because gloss is unlikely to develop in a manner that is acknowledged to be inconsistent with clear text. To take one example, the Constitution specifies that each state is to elect two senators, and even though this provision is often criticized today as inconsistent with democratic governance, we are unlikely to see practice develop to the contrary absent a formal amendment of the text. As this example illustrates, when a constitutional provision's meaning is broadly viewed as clear as a matter of its plain text, that clear meaning is likely to serve as a focal point for the practice.[63]

Instead of purporting to supersede the text, therefore, gloss is typically invoked to resolve ambiguities and omissions in the text. The extent to which interpreters credit gloss therefore depends in part on the perceived clarity of the text. Importantly, however, whether the text is perceived to be clear or unclear *is itself likely affected by practice.* As will be evident throughout this book, interpreters, whatever their methodology, often work to align their understandings of the text with the practice, rather than the other way around. As a result, some practices that seem supported by the text likely seem that way only because of the practice.[64]

Consider, for example, one of the least controversial aspects of presidential foreign affairs authority addressed in this book: the power to recognize foreign governments and their territories (addressed in Chapter 3). It may seem obvious that presidents can exercise this authority, given their textually assigned roles in negotiating treaties and receiving foreign diplomats, but that is because this authority has been worked out and settled through longstanding practice. There is no recognition clause in the Constitution, so the power must be inferred, and practice is an important factor in discerning when such inferences are persuasive.[65] If our longstanding practice had been for presidents to obtain congressional approval for recognition decisions, we would likely read the text differently today with respect to that issue.[66]

The effect of gloss on textual understandings is often even stronger than with the recognition example. Consider, for example, the requirement in Article II of the Constitution that presidents obtain the "advice and consent" of the Senate to conclude treaties. The word "advice" might suggest that the Senate was supposed to be consulted about the negotiation of treaties, and that is how President George Washington initially interpreted the provision. For practical reasons, however, Washington and other presidents moved away from allowing the Senate a formal advice role and instead mainly just sought its consent once treaties had been negotiated.[67] The Senate accepted this development, although not necessarily because it thought that it reflected the best reading of the text. In return, the Senate insisted on being able to condition its consent on "reservations" that modified or deleted particular treaty provisions, something that at that point was unprecedented in international relations. Presidents accepted this development as well, but not because they necessarily thought that it was the best reading of the text. These practices now have more than 200 years of history and are taken for granted by all branches of the government.

Even for more controversial examples, some matters that might have seemed clear from the text are no longer viewed that way. For example, if one looked only at the text of the Constitution, the best reading of the Treaty Clause might be that the president must obtain the consent of two-thirds of the Senate before concluding international agreements. This reading becomes less clear, however, when one realizes that more than 90 percent of the international agreements concluded by presidents since the 1930s have not involved such consent and that some of these nontreaty agreements were being concluded shortly after the Founding. Similarly, the Constitution's assignment to Congress of the power to declare war might suggest that the president must obtain congressional authorization before initiating military operations. But the implications of Congress's power to declare war become cloudier when one realizes that Congress has neither declared war since World War II nor expressly authorized numerous military operations since then (including the Korean War).

It may be that an interpreter's methodology will also affect the likelihood that they will perceive the text to be clear or unclear. In particular, it may be that textualists and originalists are more likely to find the constitutional text to be determinate than interpreters applying a different interpretive methodology.[68] If so, such interpreters may perceive a narrower space for the operation of gloss than those applying a different methodology. This might help explain the Supreme Court's decision in *INS v. Chadha,* in which the Court discounted decades of legislative practice concerning the legislative veto: the majority, applying a largely formal analysis, thought the relevant text was clear, whereas the dissent, applying a more functional approach, thought otherwise.[69]

Relationship to Judicial Review

As a general matter, gloss is more likely to thrive and be consulted in areas of law where judicial interventions are infrequent. Part of the reason is that when they have the choice, courts tend to prioritize their own precedents and reasoning over nonjudicial materials. In addition, when there is frequent judicial review, political actors tend to coordinate around the judicial decisions, so such decisions are likely to disrupt the ongoing development of practice that is required for gloss. It is no coincidence that Justice Frankfurter, who supported deference to historical gloss, was also a proponent of limited judicial review.[70]

As a result, a judicial decision crediting practice has the potential to freeze the practice in place, thereby undermining gloss's ability to evolve in response to new circumstances, which is one of its potential advantages. That possibility might counsel courts to pursue an approach that Professor Cass Sunstein has called "judicial minimalism" when they engage with customary practice, particularly where it appears that the practice is still in flux.[71] Such judicial minimalism would involve deciding cases through narrow reasoning that is just enough to resolve a particular dispute. Decisions based heavily on practice should also be subject to reconsideration if the practice later shifts.[72]

In some instances, the danger of unduly hampering the evolution of practice might suggest judicial abstention altogether—through, for example, the political question doctrine. The danger of judicial entrenchment is also a reason for courts to be especially cautious before treating historical practice as evidence of presidential power that is immune from congressional regulation, because such a decision can chill further interbranch negotiation and accommodation. This is a theme that will be highlighted by a number of the examples in this book.

As discussed in Chapter 2, one of the factors that makes the foreign relations law area especially suited for historical gloss is the relative infrequency of judicial review. In other areas of constitutional law, Supreme Court decisions have tended to take center stage, and modern debates over constitutional theory have tended to focus, therefore, on the proper role of the Court and the weight that should be given to judicial precedent. The judicial supremacy model, however, never became the dominant approach in foreign relations law, leaving intact a more robust role for historical gloss.

Requirements for Crediting Gloss

There is no canonical account of the historical gloss approach to constitutional interpretation. A review of the ways in which it has typically been invoked by courts and other interpreters suggests three general requirements: (1) governmental practice (2) that is longstanding and (3) concerning which the affected branch of government has acquiesced. To illustrate these three requirements, I borrow in part from the Supreme Court's decision in *Noel Canning,* which reflects the Supreme Court's most extensive consideration of the gloss approach to constitutional interpretation.

There is no specific threshold of the density or longevity of the practice or the degree to which there must be interbranch agreement about its validity. Instead, these factors affect the weight that is to be given to the practice in the constitutional analysis.[73] Gloss is simply a mode of constitutional interpretation, to be considered with other materials, and thus need not have an on-off switch. Moreover, because gloss-based changes are not permanently locked in, the requirements need not be as demanding as those for permanent constitutional amendments.

Gloss, it should be emphasized, is focused on *governmental practice*—that is, the actions and inactions of government institutions, whether executive, legislative, or judicial. Gloss is not focused on historical traditions or events in general or on public or social attitudes. It is also distinct from the general mass of nonbinding norms that inform the exercise of government discretion, in that it is treated as relevant to the interpretation of binding constitutional law.[74] In addition, more weight is generally placed on the actual behavior of institutions than on their stated views, for the obvious reason that talk can be cheap in politics. Nonetheless, governmental statements and reasoning are still relevant because, among other things, they can provide insights into how participants in a practice understand the practice and its scope. In *Noel Canning,* for example, the Supreme Court reviewed in detail the history of presidential recess appointments and the Senate's responses to them, and it looked to executive branch memoranda in large part as confirmation that "upset[ting] this traditional practice . . . would seriously shrink the authority that Presidents have believed existed and have exercised for so long."[75]

That is not to say, of course, that appeals to practice are straightforward. One inevitable complication is the need to determine the level of generality at which to describe the practice. If the current action is precisely analogous to past practice and if the past practice is supported by consensus, disputes are unlikely to arise. But when there are disputes, they are likely to focus on how to characterize the practice in question.[76] Difficult as those questions may be, they are not unique to arguments based on past governmental practice. Any practice-based or precedent-based approach naturally must confront questions about how to specify the scope of the past practice or precedent. Resolving these questions may require an evaluation of whether the new actions implicate different policy trade-offs or have a materially different impact than the past practices.

Unlike what exists for judicial decisions, however, there is no standard collection of the relevant precedent.[77] Lawyers and historians must do the work of collecting them and assessing the context in which they arose. But the challenges here are no more daunting than in any other area of constitutional law that turns in part on historical assessments (which, in fact, is much of constitutional law). Indeed, the challenges may be less daunting, given that the gloss approach focuses on a discrete set of materials that emanate from the government and are publicly known. In any event, there are a number of detailed and well-organized collections of U.S. foreign relations practice, in the *Digests of Practice* compiled over the years by State Department lawyers, compilations prepared at various times by Congress (including through its research arm, the Congressional Research Service), and scholarly accounts. This book draws upon (and supplements) those existing sources.[78]

Moreover, some aspects of the practice can be objectively determined—when treaties have been terminated, when the United States has concluded agreements or used military force, and the like. In any event, because the norms here are primarily administered by the political branches, they can be less precise than if they were administered by courts, which are expected to issue reasoned and consistent decisions and to provide guidance to potential litigants. To take two examples considered in this book, there might be a general sense that some significant agreements require the Senate's advice and consent or that some significant uses of force require congressional authorization, without a clear understanding of (or agreement about) the precise threshold.

As for the *duration* of the practice, there is no magic number of years, but the case for gloss is strongest when the practice has continued over numerous presidential administrations and has enjoyed the support of both major political parties, because such practices are less likely to be the product of mere transient partisan politics. Nor is there a magic number in terms of the frequency of the practice over time, something that will vary depending on how often the issue tends to arise and the nature and context of the events in question. If the practice has been very infrequent, however, there are likely to be questions about whether there is in fact a settled approach.

Importantly, the practice need not date to or near the Founding period, and modern practice can potentially qualify as gloss even if it differs from earlier practice. In *Noel Canning*, for example, although the Court found the pre–Civil War history not to be useful in resolving whether the president had the authority to make "intra-session" recess appointments, the Court emphasized that modern practice was sufficient to establish gloss. The Court explained that "three-quarters of a century of settled practice is long enough to entitle a practice to 'great weight in a proper interpretation' of the constitutional provision."

Whenever it develops, gloss is not necessarily permanent. At least in theory, what is glossed can be reglossed.[79] This is most likely to happen when conditions have changed and, in response, an institution starts asserting new authority. In the early stages of this development, there is obviously no *gloss-based* reason for deferring to the new practice. But if the new practice continues and becomes stable in that it is not subject to continued interbranch contestation, it will eventually acquire the status of gloss. This book does not attempt to determine the precise causal factors that produce such reglossing, which are likely to be issue specific and include a mix of political and functional considerations.

The most debated element of the three requirements for gloss concerns *acquiescence*. According to many accounts of how historical practice relates to the separation of powers, a practice by one branch of government that implicates the prerogatives of another branch gains constitutional legitimacy only if the other branch can be deemed to have "acquiesced" in the practice over time.[80] Acquiescence can be seen as serving any one of several functions. Some accounts treat it as reflecting an agreement on the part of the acquiescing branch that the actions of the other branch are lawful.[81] On other accounts, acquiescence is treated as evidence that the political branches have settled on an institutional arrangement that they both deem desirable or at least practically workable and acceptable.[82] Another approach treats acquiescence as a kind of waiver of the affected branch's institutional prerogatives, which may in turn generate reliance interests.[83]

In his concurrence in *Youngstown,* Frankfurter gave as an example a scenario that, if adopted as a general requirement for acquiescence, would sharply limit gloss's relevance: "A systematic, unbroken, executive practice, long pursued to the knowledge of the Congress and never before questioned, engaged in by Presidents who have also sworn to uphold the Constitution, making as it were such exercise of power part of the structure of our government, may be treated as a gloss on 'executive Power' vested in the President by § 1 of Art. II."

In reality, neither courts nor other interpreters have required that a practice have "never before [been] questioned" before being credited as gloss, presumably because very few practices would qualify as gloss if subjected to such a demanding test. From context, it seems unlikely that Frankfurter meant this observation to define the scope of gloss, and he did not seem to treat it as a test when evaluating the presidential action at issue in *Youngstown.* In that case, he found only three instances of presidential action arguably similar to the one at issue, and they all had occurred in a six-month period at the outset of U.S. involvement in World War II. "It suffices to say," noted Frankfurter, "that these three isolated instances do not add up, either in number, scope, duration or contemporaneous legal justification, to the kind of executive construction of the Constitution" that the Court had previously credited.

At a minimum, the acquiescence requirement means that, to qualify as gloss, the practice must have become reasonably stable over time. That is, the practice must have operated for a significant amount of time without generating continued interbranch contestation. Stability does not necessarily require that the relevant institutions have reached an agreement about the meaning of the Constitution, although if there is such an agreement the case for gloss is stronger because the likelihood of stability is higher. In *Noel Canning*, for example, the Court emphasized that although the Senate had been hostile at times to recess appointments made to fill vacancies that predated the recess, "the Senate subsequently abandoned its hostility" and, in addressing issues relating to recess appointments in the twentieth century, had not argued that the presidential practice was unconstitutional. The fact that "the Senate as a body has not countered this practice for nearly three-quarters of a century, perhaps longer," gave the practice enough stability to qualify as gloss.

It is sometimes suggested by commentators that the third requirement for gloss should be more demanding than stability—in particular, that the affected branch must have *actually agreed* that the practice is constitutional.[84] Among the justifications for crediting gloss discussed above, however, only the institutional deference justification potentially requires an interbranch agreement about the meaning of the Constitution. And even some variants of the deference idea do not depend on a showing of agreement at the level of constitutional interpretation. In particular, if one branch has long articulated a constitutional view about the separation of powers and the other branch has been silent, it may not be clear whether there is any agreement between the branches. Nevertheless, the views of the branch that has maintained the position may still be entitled to some deference, especially if those views have been consistent and have reflected the positions of elected officials of both major political parties. After all, as Justice Frankfurter observed in *Youngstown*, longstanding executive practice is "engaged in by Presidents who have also sworn to uphold the Constitution." Similarly, in *Noel Canning*, the Supreme Court gave weight to the fact that "the publicly available opinions of Presidential legal advisers that we have found are nearly unanimous in determining that the [Recess Appointments] Clause authorizes" appointments during intrasession breaks.

The other justifications for gloss have an even weaker connection to any requirement of agreement with respect to constitutional meaning. For example, the Burkean considerations of settlement and presumptive workability can support attention to historical practice even absent any evidence of such agreement, because of, for example, the risks of institutional disruption.[85] Similarly, limits on decisional capacity can suggest deferring to practice even if it does not clearly reflect a common constitutional understanding of the political branches, because the practice can still provide a type of precedent external to an interpreter's preferences or values.

In sum, under the historical gloss approach, when the Constitution is perceived to be unclear or indeterminate as it relates to the separation of powers, longstanding governmental practices that have become stable are consulted to inform constitutional interpretation. Those practices need not date to the early post-Founding period, and they can still qualify as gloss even if they differ from earlier practices. An interbranch agreement about constitutional meaning is not required for gloss, although evidence of such an agreement will bolster the case for deferring to the practice.

Favors the Executive?

Probably the most common objection to relying on gloss when interpreting the separation of powers is that it will tend to favor expansions of executive authority.[86] This is because it is easier for the executive branch to act than it is for Congress to do so.[87] The executive branch is led by a single figure elected from one party and thus does not face the same collective action and partisan limitations that Congress confronts when it seeks to take action. While Congress could in theory pass legislation to override a unilateral presidential action, such an override faces the difficult task of overcoming a potential presidential veto, and this fact will tend to discourage members of Congress even from trying. In addition, because Congress is a collective, members have less incentive than the president to protect the prerogatives of their institution.

Justice Scalia expressed concern about this asymmetry in his concurrence in *Noel Canning,* noting that "in any controversy between the political branches over a separation-of-powers question, staking out a position and defending it over time is far easier for the Executive Branch than for the Legislative Branch."[88] As a result, Scalia contended, the majority's heavy reliance on historical practice "all but guarantees the continuing aggrandizement of the Executive Branch." Justice Jackson had expressed similar concerns about the structural advantages of the executive branch in his concurrence in *Youngstown,* while also soberly noting that he had "no illusion that any decision by this Court can keep power in the hands of Congress if it is not wise and timely in meeting its problems."[89]

The observation about asymmetry is valid, but it is difficult to know how much to be concerned about it. A core problem is that there is no clear baseline against which to measure whether the executive branch is acquiring too much authority. It has become a sort of dogma that the president is too powerful today, but this dogma is usually just assumed rather than defended. The presidency was much weaker in the early years of U.S. history, but it is doubtful that anyone wants the presidency *that* weak. The presidency that probably saw the greatest single expansion of executive authority was Franklin Roosevelt's, but most observers applaud the fact that Roosevelt was able to address the severe problems associated with both the Great Depression and World War II. As the Roosevelt example shows, views about presidential power often depend on whether the observer agrees with the presidential action. As I write this book, for example, many observers who were critical of President Trump's exercises of unilateral authority support President's Biden's many unilateral actions to address the war in Ukraine.

It is easy, of course, to think of modern abuses of authority by presidents, such as the Watergate scandal in the Nixon administration, the Iran-Contra scandal in the Reagan administration, and the effort by President Trump to pressure Ukraine to dig up (or manufacture) dirt relating to a political opponent. But most of these abuses had little to do with historical gloss. Indeed, the fact that they were done in secret shows that the officials involved did not think they could rely on established practices to justify their actions. It is also easy to think of significant foreign policy mistakes made by some modern presidents. Again, though, gloss is not responsible for unwise presidential decision-making, and some of what are regarded as the most significant modern mistakes (such as the Vietnam War and the 2003 Iraq War) were authorized by Congress. Some gloss-based presidential actions, moreover, are regarded as positive achievements—the general shift by presidents to using congressional-executive agreements in lieu of formal treaties after World War II, for example (as discussed in Chapter 4).[90]

Some critics of historical gloss have compared it to the doctrine of "adverse possession" in property law.[91] Under that doctrine, someone who occupies someone else's property for a certain amount of time can acquire rights regarding the property. When the analogy is applied to gloss, the argument is that the president is being allowed to take Congress's authority merely by exercising it. This analogy, however, has a number of flaws.[92] Among other things, the property law doctrine imagines a clear assignment of property rights and then asks whether adverse possession can change the allocation. For many separation of powers issues, however, there is no clear allocation of authority. That is why gloss is considered a mode of constitutional interpretation: it helps determine which institution has the authority when the textual assignments are unclear. In addition, whereas adverse possession can result in a loss of property rights, gloss often results only in a sharing of authority. Even when historical gloss favors presidential authority, it does not tend to show that this authority is unregulable by Congress; usually it just supports presidential power under the middle category of Justice Jackson's framework from *Youngstown*—the so-called "zone of twilight" in which Congress has not acted to the contrary.[93] In other words, gloss in the separation of powers area tends not to disable majoritarian politics.

Nevertheless, when interpreters credit gloss, they should be attentive to the danger of executive aggrandizement. As will become evident at times in this book, the executive branch tends to overclaim about the nature and implications of past precedent, so its claims should be considered carefully. Moreover, precisely because it is difficult for Congress to express its opposition to practice in the form of statutes, interpreters should consider congressional "soft law," such as House and Senate resolutions and committee reports, in discerning whether a practice is sufficiently settled.[94] The Supreme Court in *Noel Canning* may have given a nudge to such consideration in noting that "neither the Senate considered as a body *nor its committees,* despite opportunities to express opposition to the practice of intra-session recess appointments, have done so."[95] Conversely, because it is easier for the executive branch to protect its institutional prerogatives, its silence in the face of repeated congressional practice should merit particular weight when courts discern whether Congress has the authority to regulate in an area.[96] Indeed, as will be discussed in Chapter 7, congressional practice is often given this weight, even when it intersects with core executive powers.[97]

Finally, those who worry that gloss tends to facilitate executive aggrandizement of power are often unclear about what should take gloss's place. Usually, these critics seem to have in mind greater judicial review, but that assumes that courts will limit executive authority, which is far from clear, especially when it comes to foreign affairs. Sometimes when courts have intervened in this area, as in *Zivotofsky v. Kerry,* they have simply entrenched greater executive authority. Even if courts do not look to gloss, they may be influenced by functional considerations about what will work best for the conduct of U.S. foreign relations (something that was a significant factor in the analysis in *Zivotofsky*), but such considerations are even more likely to favor the executive. Courts could of course try to rely purely on originalism, but it is not clear that such an approach would be more determinate than gloss, and it would be much less attuned to modern needs and conditions. Attempting to impose a strictly originalist approach would also be radically disruptive, given that (as subsequent chapters will show) much of our modern constitutional law of foreign relations is based on gloss.

Conclusion

Appeals to historical gloss involve appeals to a particular type of history—governmental practice. As will become evident throughout the book, appeals to such practice have long played a central role in constitutional interpretation relating to U.S. foreign relations. Congress and the executive branch have created bodies of nonjudicial precedent that they, and the courts, have treated as having significant weight in constitutional interpretation and debate, sometimes in ways that alter earlier constitutional understandings. The next chapter explains why the foreign affairs area has been an especially fertile ground for gloss.

2

THE LACONIC FOREIGN AFFAIRS CONSTITUTION

MANY ISSUES OF FOREIGN AFFAIRS AUTHORITY ARE NOT ADDRESSED specifically in the constitutional text. This is especially true of issues relating to executive power, given the sparse nature of the grants of authority in Article II of the Constitution (which addresses the presidency). Nor, except in a few instances, does the text specify how the respective foreign affairs powers of Congress and the president interrelate. Various theories have been developed to address these uncertainties—concerning, for example, the "Vesting Clause" in Article II, the idea of "sovereignty-based" powers, and the purported role of the president as the "sole organ" for the United States in foreign affairs—but none of these theories provides a satisfying or complete account. This chapter explains that, because of various limiting doctrines, the courts have played only a modest role in addressing issues of foreign affairs authority. Both the laconic nature of the text and the limited scope of judicial review have meant that there has been significant room for the development and evolution of governmental practice relating to foreign affairs.

Limited Textual Guidance

Before the United States adopted its Constitution, it operated for years with a weak central government that had no independent executive branch and no national court system.[1] In the *Federalist Papers*, Alexander Hamilton observed that as a result the United States had no "respectability in the eyes of foreign powers."[2] The "imbecility of our government even forbids them to treat with us," he noted, and "our ambassadors abroad are the mere pageants of mimic sovereignty." One of the chief goals of the Founders of the Constitution was to strengthen the national government so that it could operate more effectively in foreign affairs.[3] Not surprisingly, therefore, the Constitution includes a number of features designed to serve this purpose. Most notably, it creates a separate executive branch headed by a president. As Hamilton explained, having a single figure at the top of the executive branch would allow for "decision, activity, secrecy, and d[i]spatch."[4] The resulting "energy," Hamilton claimed, would be the "bulwark of the national security."

Despite the importance of the Constitution's creation of an executive branch, most of the foreign affairs powers mentioned in the Constitution are allocated to Congress, not the president. Article I of the Constitution, which addresses congressional authority, lists an array of congressional foreign affairs powers, including the ability to regulate commerce with foreign countries, determine the standards under which immigrants can become citizens, declare war, make rules for the governance of the armed forces, and "define and punish Piracies and Felonies committed on the high Seas, and Offenses against the Law of Nations." Congress also was given broad authority over monetary matters, including the government's collection of taxes, borrowing of money, and authorization of expenditures, all of which are relevant to the conduct of foreign affairs. In addition, Article I gives Congress the power to pass laws that are "necessary and proper" to carry into execution not only its own powers but also those of the other branches of government. The Supreme Court early on construed this necessary and proper authority broadly to encompass all measures that are "calculated to effect any of the objects intrusted to the Government."[5] Other articles of the Constitution give Congress additional authority that is relevant to foreign affairs, including the authority to dispose of and regulate U.S. territory and property.[6]

By comparison, the grants of foreign affairs authority to the president in Article II of the Constitution seem sparse. The president is made the Commander in Chief of the armed forces, a role that Hamilton described as entailing "nothing more than the supreme command and direction of the military and naval forces."[7] Presidents have of course asserted much broader authority than that at times, sometimes controversially. As Justice Jackson noted in *Youngstown,* the words of the Commander in Chief Clause "have given rise to some of the most persistent controversies in our constitutional history," and "just what authority goes with the name [Commander in Chief] has plagued presidential advisers who would not waive or narrow it by nonassertion, yet cannot say where it begins or ends."[8]

The president is also given the power to make treaties, but Article II requires that the president obtain the advice and consent of two-thirds of the Senate before ratifying them, which is a difficult hurdle. Appointments of officials, including ambassadors, need to be approved by a majority of the Senate. The president is to "receive Ambassadors and other public Ministers," but this sounds more like a functionary duty than a source of authority.

Article II also states that the president is to "take Care that the Laws be faithfully executed." Although written as a duty, this Take Care Clause can reasonably be construed to give the president some authority to take actions designed to effectuate federal laws, including laws relating to foreign affairs.[9] There has long been debate, however, about the scope of this authority.

In a late nineteenth-century decision, *In re Neagle*, the Supreme Court broadly reasoned that the president's duty to execute the laws is not "limited to the enforcement of acts of Congress or of treaties of the United States according to their express terms" but also includes "the rights, duties, and obligations growing out of the Constitution itself, our international relations, and all the protection implied by the nature of the government under the Constitution."[10] That case, however, did not involve foreign affairs; rather, it involved the Attorney General's assignment of a federal marshal to protect a Supreme Court justice. And, in more recent decisions (including in cases involving foreign affairs), the Supreme Court has emphasized that the Take Care Clause does not give the president the authority to make law.[11] In any event, the key point is that the extent to which the president can claim authority based on the Take Care Clause is unclear.

Some scholars have argued that the first sentence of Article II conveys foreign affairs authority to the president.[12] This Vesting Clause states that "the executive Power shall be vested in a President of the United States of America." It has been argued that, because the Founders would have viewed the conduct of foreign affairs as traditionally an executive function, the vesting of executive authority in presidents implicitly gave them all foreign affairs authority not expressly assigned to Congress. This "Vesting Clause thesis" has been criticized (including by the present author) on textual and historical grounds.[13] Among other things, critics have pointed out that there is no direct evidence that this is how the clause was understood during the drafting and ratification of the Constitution, and they have noted that it is hard to understand why the Founders made certain specific grants of authority to the president if they had this theory in mind. It is also unlikely that the Founders would have had a clear and agreed-upon conception of what powers are, and are not, executive in nature.[14]

In his influential concurrence in the *Youngstown* steel seizure case, Justice Jackson dismissed the Vesting Clause thesis, noting that, "if that be true, it is difficult to see why the forefathers bothered to add several specific items, including some trifling ones."[15] He also more generally expressed doubt about the usefulness of attempting to discern original Founding understandings concerning executive power, observing that "just what our forefathers did envision, or would have envisioned had they foreseen modern conditions, must be divined from materials almost as enigmatic as the dreams Joseph was called upon to interpret for Pharaoh." At the same time, Jackson emphasized that just "because the President does not enjoy unmentioned powers" does not mean that the ones that are mentioned should be construed narrowly. "Some clauses could be made almost unworkable, as well as immutable," he noted, "by refusal to indulge some latitude of interpretation for changing times." He thus suggested that judges should "give to the enumerated powers the scope and elasticity afforded by what seem to be reasonable, practical implications."

In more recent decisions, the Supreme Court has not shown any inclination to adopt the Vesting Clause thesis. For example, in its 2015 decision in *Zivotofsky v. Kerry*, concerning the president's recognition power, the Court expressly avoided relying on the Vesting Clause and "declin[ed] to acknowledge" "that the President has broad, undefined powers over foreign affairs."[16] (This decision is discussed in more detail in Chapter 3.)

Whatever one's views about the implications of the Article II Vesting Clause, it is at least fair to say that many foreign affairs powers are not addressed specifically in the text.[17] The following powers, for example, have long been taken for granted but are not mentioned: managing diplomacy, declaring neutrality, issuing passports, recognizing foreign governments, acquiring territory, concluding non-treaty international agreements, withdrawing from treaties, waging undeclared war, and regulating immigration. These powers presumably must lie somewhere in the national government, but the text of the Constitution does not say precisely where.[18]

Nor, except in a few instances, does the text explain how the respective foreign affairs powers of Congress and the president interrelate.[19] It is unclear from the text, for example, how Congress's power to declare war relates to the president's Commander in Chief power or how Congress's control over commerce and appropriations relates to the president's (implied) authority to conduct diplomacy. Nor is it clear how Congress's understandable desire to oversee the executive branch's foreign policy initiatives relates to the executive branch's ability to maintain the confidentiality needed for candid deliberations and negotiations. Because of these and other uncertainties, the eminent constitutional law scholar Edward Corwin famously described the Constitution as "an invitation to struggle for the privilege of directing American foreign policy."[20]

Example of the Neutrality Controversy

An early constitutional debate highlighted some of the uncertainties concerning the distribution of foreign relations authority. In 1793, four years after the United States had begun to operate under its Constitution, France had undergone a revolution and was waging war against a number of other European powers. The United States had treaty commitments with France, but the Washington administration wanted to avoid getting drawn into France's conflicts. One immediate issue, discussed in Chapter 3, was whether to receive an ambassador from France's revolutionary government. Washington's decision to do so became an early precedent in support of a presidential power over the recognition of foreign governments. Another issue was whether to declare that the United States was neutral, a status that would require that the United States and its citizens avoid taking certain actions favoring either side in the European war.[21]

Washington decided to issue a proclamation of neutrality, stating that "the duty and interest of the United States require, that they should with sincerity and good faith adopt and pursue a conduct friendly and impartial towards the belligerent Powers."[22] This triggered a public debate between Alexander Hamilton and James Madison over the constitutionality of this action. The Constitution does not mention a "neutrality power," so the debate was over the proper inferences that should be drawn from the constitutional text and structure.

Hamilton, writing as "Pacificus," contended that the issuance of a proclamation of neutrality naturally fell to the president because under the Constitution he is the "organ of intercourse" with foreign nations.[23] In support of this claim, Hamilton relied heavily on the Vesting Clause in Article II, which he described as a "comprehensive grant" of executive power.[24] But he also invoked more specific sources of authority, including the president's authority to take care that treaties and other international law obligations of the United States are faithfully implemented, which he suggested "might alone have been relied upon."[25] Hamilton contended that "the Executive is charged with the execution of all laws, the laws of Nations as well as the Municipal law, which recognises and adopts those laws." Finally, Hamilton claimed that the president's power to declare neutrality did not intrude on Congress's authority to declare war, reasoning that it was "the duty of the Executive to preserve Peace till war is declared."

In response, Madison—who is sometimes called the "father of the Constitution" for his significant role in its drafting—argued that Washington had violated the separation of powers.[26] Writing as "Helvidius," Madison contended that the powers of making war and concluding treaties are legislative by nature and thus do not fall to the president. Although the executive branch "may be a convenient organ of preliminary communications with foreign governments" on these subjects, "it can have no pretensions," he argued, "to that essential agency which gives validity to such determinations." In other words, Madison claimed that the president's role is to communicate U.S. positions with respect to war and treaties, not to unilaterally make those positions. In asserting broader authority for the president, suggested Madison, Hamilton was attributing the monarchial prerogatives of the British Crown to the president. Madison also objected to the idea that the Constitution granted overlapping authority to Congress and the president concerning war, contending that "a concurrent authority in two independent departments to perform the same function with respect to the same thing, would be as awkward in practice, as it is unnatural in theory."[27]

Hamilton accepted, it should be noted, that Congress could legislate on the subject of neutrality. And, in fact, at the Washington administration's urging, Congress passed a Neutrality Act the following year.[28] This statute regulated the issue and delegated enforcement authority to the president. As will be discussed in other chapters, both Washington's action and Congress's action created early precedents that have been treated as relevant to constitutional interpretation.[29]

Regardless of whether one thinks that Hamilton or Madison had the stronger arguments, the debate highlighted—early on in U.S. history—that there were deep uncertainties about the Constitution's distribution of foreign affairs authority.[30] Such uncertainties would continue to surface, and they would be resolved through practice.

Sovereignty as a Possible Source of Authority

Most scholars view the source of the national government's foreign relations powers, as with its domestic powers, to be the Constitution. If so, then the question simply becomes how to interpret the Constitution, and there are of course a range of views on that topic, including about the extent to which historical practice should inform that interpretation. But another way of finding "missing" foreign affairs powers would be to look outside the Constitution. And, indeed, the Supreme Court has suggested at times that the government may derive at least some foreign relations power from the very fact that the United States is a sovereign in the international community.

This sovereign authority idea was most expansively developed by Justice George Sutherland in his 1936 decision for the Court in *United States v. Curtiss-Wright Export Corporation.*[31] In that case (which will be referenced a number of times in this book), the Court considered the constitutionality of a grant of authority from Congress to the president to restrict arms sales to countries involved in a conflict in Latin America. Ranging far beyond the issue at hand, Sutherland drew a sharp distinction between the domestic and foreign affairs powers of the national government, reflecting views that he had earlier developed in an article (when he was a senator) and then in a series of lectures that resulted in a book.[32]

The government's domestic powers, said Sutherland, were "carve[d] from the general mass of legislative powers then possessed by the states." By contrast, he contended that, "since the states severally never possessed international powers," these powers "were transmitted to the United States from some other source." This source, he claimed, was the British Crown: "When, therefore, the external sovereignty of Great Britain in respect of the colonies ceased, it immediately passed to the Union." This meant, according to Sutherland, that the government's powers over "external sovereignty" do not depend on the grants of authority in the Constitution. Rather, "as a member of the family of nations, the right and power of the United States in that field are equal to the right and power of the other members of the international family." Under this view, foreign affairs powers such as "the power to acquire territory by discovery and occupation, the power to expel undesirable aliens, the power to make such international agreements as do not constitute treaties in the constitutional sense, none of which is expressly affirmed by the Constitution, nevertheless exist as inherently inseparable from the conception of nationality."

In *Curtiss-Wright,* Justice Sutherland was, as one commentator put it, "in the happy position of being able to give [his] writings and speeches the status of law."[33] Sutherland's theory of extraconstitutional foreign affairs authority has, however, been heavily criticized by scholars on structural and historical grounds.[34] Among other things, the theory appears to require, as Professor Louis Henkin noted, "that a panoply of important powers be deduced from unwritten, uncertain, changing concepts in international law and practice, developed and growing outside our constitutional tradition and our particular heritage."[35] It also seems inconsistent with the oft-repeated idea that the Constitution established a government of enumerated powers.[36]

The 1952 *Youngstown* steel seizure decision, discussed in Chapter 1, can be read as a repudiation of Sutherland's theory. After all, despite the foreign affairs backdrop of the case, the Court said that Truman's authority had to come from either a statute or the Constitution. And Justice Jackson noted in his concurrence that he "did not suppose, and [was] not persuaded, that history leaves it open to question, at least in the courts, that the executive branch, like the Federal Government as a whole, possesses only delegated powers."[37] That said, the presidential action in *Youngstown* involved something regarded by the Court as domestic in nature and implicitly disallowed by Congress, and the Court's analysis might not speak to exercises of foreign affairs authority not involving those circumstances. In any event, as Justice Jackson observed in his concurrence in *Youngstown,* it is arguable that "much of the Court's opinion [in *Curtiss-Wright*] is *dictum*"—that is, not essential to the decision.[38] The source of the national government's foreign affairs authority was not directly relevant to the questions in that case about whether and to what extent Congress could delegate foreign affairs authority (whatever its source) to the president.

Despite these reasons for skepticism, the sovereign authority idea reflected in *Curtiss-Wright* has been invoked in other contexts. The Supreme Court has, for example, grounded Congress's power to regulate immigration in notions of external sovereignty that are similar to what Sutherland suggested. The Constitution assigns to Congress the authority to "establish a uniform Rule of Naturalization," which is a process by which noncitizens can become citizens.[39] But the Constitution contains no general authority to regulate the entrance and deportation of noncitizens. Congress, however, has long regulated these issues.[40] Initially, the Supreme Court grounded Congress's authority to do so in the Commerce Clause.[41] But the Court subsequently reasoned that, by establishing a sovereign in international affairs, the Constitution implicitly gave the national government the powers of a sovereign, including most notably the power to control its borders.[42] This view, it should be noted, still differs from Justice Sutherland's theory, in that it treats the Constitution as the ultimate (albeit implicit) source of the sovereign authority. As a result, it is easier to justify constitutional *limitations* on the exercise of this authority than under Sutherland's approach.

Sovereignty reasoning also appears in *Missouri v. Holland,* a much-discussed 1920 decision concerning the scope of the treaty power.[43] In that case, the Court upheld statutory restrictions on the hunting and capturing of migratory birds that were enacted to implement a treaty, reasoning that even if this legislation would have exceeded Congress's authority if enacted in the absence of the treaty, the existence of the treaty supplied sufficient authority. The Court relied in part on the sovereignty idea, observing that "it is not lightly to be assumed that, in matters requiring national action, 'a power which must belong to and somewhere reside in every civilized government' is not to be found."[44] Judicial interpretations of other governmental powers, such as Congress's authority to regulate foreign commerce, have also been influenced by sovereignty considerations.[45]

The Louisiana Purchase, concluded in 1803 by President Thomas Jefferson through a treaty with France, was also defended by some in sovereign-power terms. Under the treaty, the United States acquired a vast new territory (over 800,000 square miles), which, according to the treaty, was to be "incorporated into the Union of the United States." But the Constitution does not specifically give the federal government authority to acquire territory, let alone to incorporate it into the Union. As a result, Jefferson initially thought that a constitutional amendment would be needed to accomplish these actions, reasoning that "the general government has no power but such as the constitution has given it."[46]

Ultimately, though, he suppressed his constitutional doubts and moved forward with the purchase. Others thought that the purchase was constitutional on grounds relating to national sovereignty. For example, Jefferson's Treasury Secretary, Albert Gallatin, maintained that "the existence of the United States as a nation presupposes the power enjoyed by every nation of extending their territory by treaties."[47]

Decades later, the Supreme Court similarly reasoned that "the Constitution confers absolutely on the government of the Union, the powers of making war, and of making treaties; consequently, that government possesses the power of acquiring territory, either by conquest or by treaty."[48] And, in the late nineteenth and early twentieth centuries, the Court relied in part on notions of sovereignty as a basis for congressional regulation of acquired territories.[49] The Supreme Court has also suggested that the national government's authority to regulate Indian tribes has a sovereignty source that gives it more power than is contained merely in specific textual grants of authority (such as in the Indian Commerce Clause).[50]

Importantly, though, even if one accepts that some foreign affairs powers are derived from extraconstitutional or sovereignty-based sources, that by itself would not tell us which branch of the U.S. government has the authority to exercise those powers or which branch should prevail in the event of a conflict between them. It might well be that many of these powers would properly rest with Congress rather than with the President. As a prominent lower court judge observed in a 1921 opinion concerning the authority to regulate the laying of submarine cables off the U.S. coast, even if "the United States [as] a sovereign nation . . . must be deemed to have all customary national powers . . . it does not follow that the Executive has the necessary authority."[51] Again, historical practice can potentially resolve this uncertainty.

The President as "Sole Organ"

The executive branch often refers to the president as the "sole organ" for the United States in foreign affairs, and the Supreme Court also sometimes uses that label, including in *Curtiss-Wright*.[52] The "sole organ" reference originated in a speech given in 1800 by John Marshall while he was a member of the House of Representatives, about a year before he was appointed as Chief Justice of the Supreme Court.[53] The speech was a defense of President John Adams's decision to extradite a criminal suspect from the United States to Great Britain, pursuant to a treaty between the two countries. The suspect—Thomas Nash, alias Jonathan Robbins—was alleged to have committed murder during a mutiny on a

British ship. The extradition was controversial because some believed that Robbins was a U.S. citizen who had been impressed into naval service by the British.

A federal district court judge presiding over the case initially declined to turn Robbins over to British authorities in response to their request under the treaty, apparently because he believed that he needed executive authorization. The Adams administration then communicated to the court its "advice and request" that the suspect be extradited pursuant to the terms of the treaty. The court subsequently held a hearing and concluded that there was sufficient evidence that Robbins had committed murder and that the court was therefore bound by the terms of the treaty to deliver him to British authorities.[54] Robbins was transferred to British custody, tried by a court-martial, and executed.

Adams was criticized by Republicans in the House for having intervened in the judicial process, and they introduced a resolution condemning him for "a dangerous interference of the Executive with Judicial decisions."[55] In his speech defending Adams, Marshall argued that there was nothing improper about a president seeking to carry out the terms of a treaty. He explained:

> The President is the sole organ of the nation in its external relations, and its sole representative with foreign nations. Of consequence, the demand of a foreign nation can only be made on him. He possesses the whole Executive power. He holds and directs the force of the nation. Of consequence, any act to be performed by the force of the nation is to be performed through him. He is charged to execute the laws. A treaty is declared to be a law. He must execute a treaty where he, and he alone, possesses the means of executing it.[56]

In context, in using the "sole organ" characterization, Marshall was not claiming broad substantive authority for the president; rather, he was making the claim that in diplomacy the United States acts through its president. At least today, this is not a controversial proposition.[57] Indeed, it was not a novel proposition even when articulated by Marshall: Thomas Jefferson had made a similar point years earlier when explaining why it was not proper for a foreign nation to communicate directly with Congress.[58] Moreover, in defending Adams's effort to carry out the treaty obligation, Marshall was arguing only for presidential authority *in the absence of congressional action* (what we would today classify as the middle category of Justice Jackson's framework from *Youngstown*). Indeed, Marshall proceeded to observe that "Congress, unquestionably, may prescribe the mode [of executing a treaty obligation], and Congress may devolve on others the whole execution of the contract," but he said that "till this be done, it seems the duty of the Executive department to execute the contract by any means it possesses."[59]

As will become evident in later chapters, the executive branch often invokes the "sole organ" characterization for claims of authority that far exceed the circumstances surrounding Marshall's statement. As Professor Harold Koh has noted, the executive branch likes to say, in essence, "*Curtiss-Wright,* so I'm right."[60] Despite this tendency by the executive to exaggerate its "sole organ" role, even under a narrow interpretation the president is the formal spokesperson for the United States, a role that carries with it substantial ability to influence U.S. relations with other countries, at least in the absence of a contrary directive from Congress. Think, for example, of the many "doctrines" announced by presidents that commit the United States to important foreign policy positions, such as, most famously, the Monroe Doctrine (which will be discussed in subsequent chapters). Moreover, historical practices like these are likely to inform how we understand the nature of the "sole organ" role of the presidency.

"Sole organ" reasoning is also part of a more general tendency of courts in foreign relations cases to take into account functional considerations in their interpretation of the Constitution and statutes.[61] Indeed, even when the courts adopt formal rules and doctrines in foreign affairs cases, they often do so in part on the basis of functional considerations.[62] These considerations tend to favor the executive branch, precisely because of the capacity of the presidency, as Hamilton put it, for "decision, activity, secrecy, and dispatch." Nevertheless, some functional considerations, such as deliberation by representatives who reflect a wide variety of interests, may favor Congress, and in any event, there will sometimes be value in having two political institutions consider an important issue rather than just one. The bottom line is that simply labeling the president the "sole organ" does not by itself resolve many of the difficult constitutional issues relating to foreign affairs authority.

Limitations on Judicial Review

In theory, the courts could resolve the uncertainties about the Constitution's distributions of foreign affairs authority, but in practice, they have played only a modest role. The Supreme Court has observed that "matters intimately related to foreign policy and national security are rarely proper subjects for judicial intervention."[63] This is an overstatement, but it is true that judicial review is more circumscribed with respect to foreign affairs than with respect to domestic matters. To sue in federal court, a plaintiff must have standing, which requires that they show that they are concretely injured by what the defendant has done.[64]

Many foreign affairs actions, however, do not have that sort of individualized effect. If a president acts to withdraw the United States from a mutual defense treaty, for example, it is unlikely that any private citizen will be injured in a way that would suffice for standing. It may be that some members of Congress will perceive that such an action invades their constitutional prerogatives, but the Supreme Court has sharply limited the circumstances under which such members may challenge presidential actions.[65]

In addition, the courts apply a "political question doctrine," pursuant to which some issues are deemed to be inappropriate for judicial resolution. The modern version of the doctrine is generally traced to the Court's 1962 decision in *Baker v. Carr,* a case that did not involve foreign affairs.[66] The Court there held that the judiciary could adjudicate claims that unequal-sized voting districts violated the Constitution's Equal Protection Clause. In concluding that these claims did not present political questions, Justice Brennan's opinion reviewed the Court's past decisions applying the political question doctrine, many of which involved foreign affairs. The Court acknowledged that the political question doctrine had particular relevance to the foreign affairs context, given "the necessity of the country's speaking with one voice in such matters" as well as the frequent lack of a "standard ascertainable by settled judicial experience or process by reference to which a political decision affecting the question at issue between the parties can be judged." In its decisions before *Baker,* the Court had held that a variety of foreign affairs issues, concerning, for example, the application of treaties and the extent of the United States' and other countries' sovereign territory, raised political questions.[67]

Since *Baker,* a majority of the Supreme Court has applied the doctrine as a basis for dismissal in only a few decisions, and never in a foreign affairs case. However, in a 1979 decision, *Goldwater v. Carter,* a plurality of four justices reasoned that a constitutional challenge to President Carter's termination of a treaty with Taiwan presented a political question. Those justices explained that, "in light of the absence of any constitutional provision governing the termination of a treaty, and the fact that different termination procedures may be appropriate for different treaties," the dispute turned on political considerations. They also noted that, unlike in *Youngstown,* they were being "asked to settle a dispute between coequal branches of our Government, each of which has resources available to protect and assert its interests, resources not available to private litigants outside the judicial forum."

In a later foreign affairs decision, *Zivotofsky v. Clinton,* a majority of the Court appeared to evince a more limited view of the doctrine, describing it as a "narrow exception" to the judiciary's general duty to decide cases.[68] That case involved a challenge to the executive branch's disregard of a statutory mandate to list "Israel" in the passports of U.S. citizens born in Jerusalem, a mandate that the executive claimed invaded its authority over recognizing foreign states and their territories. The Court noted that, although politically sensitive, "resolution of [the case] demands careful examination of the textual, structural, and historical evidence," which "is what courts do."

Zivotofsky involved a direct confrontation between Congress and the executive branch and probably does not signal a change from the Court's usual diffidence in foreign affairs cases that do not involve such a confrontation. For example, in a subsequent decision disallowing a private damage remedy for an alleged constitutional violation that implicated foreign affairs, the Court emphasized that "the political branches, not the Judiciary, have the responsibility and institutional capacity to weigh foreign-policy concerns."[69]

In any event, the political question doctrine has had a more active life in the lower federal courts in the years since *Baker,* including most notably in cases relating to foreign affairs.[70] Applying the doctrine, lower courts have declined to adjudicate separation of powers disputes relating to issues such as the recognition of foreign governments, the use of executive agreements in lieu of treaties, the termination of international agreements, and the use of military force. They have also applied the doctrine as a basis for dismissing tort claims against the U.S. government, and sometimes its contractors, for military and covert operations abroad.

Some lower courts also apply an institutional ripeness doctrine, pursuant to which they will not adjudicate separation of powers disputes unless there is an actual confrontation between the branches.[71] This doctrine was suggested by Justice Lewis Powell in a concurrence in *Goldwater.* Although Powell did not think the treaty termination issue there presented a political question, he agreed that the Court should abstain from adjudicating the dispute given that Congress had not attempted to stop the presidential action: "If the Congress chooses not to confront the President, it is not our task to do so."[72]

Even when courts do hear foreign affairs disputes, they often give deference to the views of the executive branch, on the theory that the executive has greater expertise and information concerning the international environment. Indeed, the Court has said that it follows a "customary policy of deference to the President in matters of foreign affairs."[73] This includes, for example, giving "great weight" to the executive branch's interpretation of treaties.[74] The grounds for deference are even stronger when Congress and the executive branch are in agreement on a foreign affairs issue. When courts credit historical gloss, this can be seen as a form of judicial deference to the political branches.

Debates over "Foreign Affairs Exceptionalism"

Debates over the proper role of the courts in the foreign affairs area intersect with debates over what has been called "foreign affairs exceptionalism"—that is, the differential treatment by courts of foreign affairs issues as compared with domestic legal issues.[75] In these debates, it is not always clear what qualifies as "exceptional."[76] Everyone agrees that only cases that are similar should be treated the same, but the extent to which foreign affairs cases are similar to domestic cases is contested. Moreover, while it is true that structural constitutional limitations have been applied less strictly in foreign affairs than in domestic affairs, whether that distinction is correct ultimately depends on how one interprets the Constitution.

Although some scholars have suggested that courts are moving away from distinguishing between foreign and domestic affairs in their legal analysis,[77] there is little to support the claim. Indeed, a number of Supreme Court decisions in recent years, concerning matters such as human rights litigation, constitutional tort claims, and immigration regulation, have drawn expressly on the distinction.[78]

To the extent that scholars are claiming as a normative matter that courts *should* treat foreign affairs cases more like they treat domestic affairs cases, one immediately runs into difficult questions about what it would mean to do so. What scholars usually mean is that courts should abstain less and hold against the executive more, but those two propositions need not travel together: by abstaining less, the courts might actually hold for the executive more. In *Zivotofsky*, for example, the Court declined to abstain from resolving a separation of powers dispute between Congress and the executive and then proceeded to hold for the executive.

Although critiques of exceptionalism are not directly relevant to the focus of this book, some of these critiques may be at least indirectly relevant. In particular, doctrines of foreign affairs deference and abstention, which have been targets of the critiques, have helped create space for the development of historical gloss. If these doctrines had been narrower, there might have been less accretion of practice in some areas. However, some non-exceptionalist doctrines, such as the requirement of standing to sue, would still have limited the number of judicial interventions. In any event, the historical gloss method is not by its terms exceptionalist: courts and other interpreters do not claim that historical practice is only relevant in the foreign affairs context. Indeed, as the example at the beginning of Chapter 1 illustrated, the Supreme Court's most extensive endorsement of the use of historical gloss came in a non–foreign affairs context (concerning recess appointments). It is also worth noting that the exceptionalism debate is chiefly focused on the role of the judiciary, whereas much of the focus of this book is on constitutional reasoning by nonjudicial actors.

Conclusion

The constitutional text addresses some issues of foreign affairs authority, such as which branch of government has the authority to declare war (Congress) and which branch is to receive foreign ambassadors (the executive). But many issues are not addressed specifically in the text, and courts have played only a modest role in resolving those issues. Faced with limited textual and judicial guidance, Congress and the executive branch have adopted practices that reflect their own interpretations of the Constitution, sometimes cooperatively and sometimes in conflict. That is, they have developed historical gloss. The rest of the book provides illustrations of this phenomenon.

3

THE RECOGNITION POWER

IN 2017, PRESIDENT DONALD TRUMP REVERSED DECADES OF EXECUTIVE branch policy by announcing that the United States was recognizing the city of Jerusalem as the capital of Israel.[1] Consistent with that announcement, he directed that the U.S. embassy in Israel be moved from Tel Aviv to Jerusalem, something that Congress had unsuccessfully been trying to force presidents to do since the 1990s. Two years later, in 2019, Trump announced that the United States was also recognizing Israeli sovereignty over the Golan Heights, territory that Israel had seized from Syria during their 1967 war.[2] These actions were controversial and potentially inconsistent with international law, but unlike other steps that Trump took as president, they generated little constitutional debate. Although the Constitution does not mention a power to recognize foreign governments and their territories, presidents have from the beginning of U.S. history exercised a "recognition power." The bounds and implications of this power have been worked out through practice, and occasionally through judicial decisions.[3]

As with other issues of presidential authority considered in this book, the most difficult question concerning the recognition power is the extent to which it can be regulated by Congress. In 2015, the Supreme Court provided an answer to that question, in *Zivotofsky v. Kerry*.[4] Relying in part on what it described as "the weight of historical evidence," the Court concluded that the recognition power is exclusive to the president and thus that Congress cannot "alter the President's statements on matters of recognition or force him to contradict them." The executive branch has since invoked *Zivotofsky* to argue that another presidential power considered in this book—treaty termination—is also exclusive and cannot be limited by Congress.[5]

This chapter recounts some of the key historical episodes concerning the power over recognition, and it considers the extent to which this history supports the Supreme Court's conclusion that the president's recognition power is exclusive. It also suggests some reasons for concluding that, in any event, *Zivotofsky* should be read narrowly.

Recognition and the Constitutional Text

Acts of recognition are an important part of diplomacy. These acts can involve the acknowledgment of a particular territory as an independent foreign state, the acceptance of a particular government as the ruling body of a state, or a determination of the extent of another nation's sovereign territory.[6] Recognition issues often arise after dramatic developments such as a coup, civil war, revolution, or territorial dissolution. The United States itself sought recognition during its Revolutionary War against Great Britain; indeed, obtaining that recognition was a central purpose of the Declaration of Independence.[7] Recognition can be implied rather than express—for example, by sending diplomats to a regime, receiving their diplomats, or concluding a treaty with the regime.[8]

As the Supreme Court has observed, "legal consequences follow formal recognition."[9] For example, a regime that is not recognized by the United States may be disallowed from suing in U.S. courts and may not be able to access state property located in the United States.[10] Recognition decisions also can determine whether a foreign government and its representatives receive immunity in U.S. litigation.[11] The application of the "act of state" doctrine, pursuant to which U.S. courts will presume the validity of acts by foreign governments taken within their own territory, also may depend on recognition.[12] The acceptance by U.S. courts of territorial claims by foreign states are also dependent on recognition of those claims by the political branches of the government. And the Supreme Court has said that "recognition is retroactive in effect and validates all the actions and the conduct of the government so recognized."[13] In addition to these domestic effects, decisions about recognition can implicate rights under international law—for example, the right to send an ambassador or to invoke preexisting treaties made by the state.[14]

Despite its importance, there is no "recognition power" listed in the Constitution. That power instead has been inferred from other sources of authority. Most notably, Article II, Section 3, of the Constitution states that the president "shall receive Ambassadors and other public Ministers," and this Receptions Clause has long been construed as implicitly conveying to the president some authority over recognition.[15] The basic idea is that, when deciding whether to receive particular foreign representatives, the president necessarily has to decide whether to recognize the government that is sending them. Indeed, under the international law at the time of the Founding, an unqualified reception of a foreign ambassador would itself constitute an official recognition of the ambassador's government.[16]

Similar judgments about who represents the foreign state are sometimes required when the president negotiates or implements treaties since, again, the president may need to determine which treaty negotiator properly represents the state. Presidential control over recognition can also potentially be implied from other sources of authority. For example, as discussed in Chapter 2, the president has long been viewed as the formal organ of communication between the United States and foreign nations, and this role might naturally include the articulation of U.S. positions about recognition. In addition, although the president normally needs to obtain Senate consent for the appointment of ambassadors, the president has the power to appoint ambassadors on his own during a Senate recess, and such appointments may constitute acts of recognition.[17] In addition, it has long been accepted that as part of their control over the executive branch, presidents have the authority to recall ambassadors, which might signal a break in diplomatic relations with a regime. Similarly, the president's power to receive foreign ambassadors has long been thought to include the power to expel them—again, an action that may be connected to recognition and derecognition.[18] Another means of recognition would be the grant of an "exequatur" to a foreign official to exercise consular functions in the United States, and from the earliest days of the nation, presidents have exercised the authority to grant them.[19]

It could also be argued that, since the recognition power was a traditionally executive function at the time of the Founding and was not expressly assigned to Congress, it falls within the authority conveyed by the Vesting Clause of Article II, which states that "the executive Power shall be vested in a President of the United States of America."[20] As discussed in Chapter 2, construing the Vesting Clause as conveying unspecified substantive powers is controversial. In any event, debates between Congress and the executive branch over the recognition power have not tended to focus on the Vesting Clause. Nor has the Supreme Court relied on the clause in its decisions concerning recognition.[21]

Whatever its source, there has been little dispute that the president has a recognition power. The more difficult question has been whether this power is subject to congressional limitation—that is, whether it is exclusive to the president or concurrent with congressional power. A number of congressional powers at least intersect with the recognition power. Recognition decisions have the potential to lead to military conflict, and this was especially true early in U.S. history, which means that the recognition power potentially intersects with Congress's authority to declare war. Congress also has the power to regulate international commerce, and in exercising that power, Congress can affect issues relating to recognition—for example, by authorizing or disallowing trade with a particular regime. In addition, recognition decisions can have monetary consequences, creating, for example, the need to fund new diplomatic posts, embassies, and consulates, thus potentially implicating Congress's authority over appropriations. Moreover, the president's appointment of "ambassadors, other public ministers and consuls" requires approval by the Senate, which potentially gives that body a role in connection with decisions to recognize particular regimes. The president's treaty power, which, as noted, will sometimes implicate questions of recognition, is also shared with the Senate.

Even though recognition decisions implicate issues of international law and not just matters of policy, the judiciary has not played much of an independent role in this area. Instead, at least in the absence of interbranch conflict, courts have deferred to political branch determinations relating to recognition.[22] Indeed, these deferential decisions are an important historical strand of the political question doctrine discussed in Chapter 2.[23]

The Neutrality Controversy of 1793

The United States' first major foreign policy crisis, which prompted the debate between Hamilton and Madison recounted in the last chapter, involved issues of recognition. In 1789, a revolution began in France, and the revolutionary regime soon was at war with a number of European countries. The United States had treaties with France that could be construed as requiring the United States to assist that country in its conflicts. The United States was a new and weak nation, however, and thus had good reasons to avoid getting pulled into war. As George Washington noted, "unwise should we be in the extreme to involve ourselves in the contests of European Nations, where our weight could be but small; tho' the loss to ourselves would be certain."[24]

In 1793, after a new government was in place in France, the United States had to decide whether to recognize that government for purposes of diplomatic relations.[25] Secretary of State Jefferson and President Washington, without consulting Congress, authorized the American ambassador in Paris to resume relations with the new regime.[26] Soon thereafter, the new French government sent an ambassador, Edmond Genet, to the United States. Washington's cabinet understood that receiving Genet would be viewed as an act of recognition. After some debate, they decided to receive him without qualification and without consulting Congress.[27] This action did not trigger constitutional controversy. Nor did the administration's subsequent decision to ask France for Genet's recall, after Genet had engaged in a variety of actions that undermined U.S. neutrality in the conflict.

During deliberations over whether to recognize the revolutionary French government, Jefferson advocated a position that became the official U.S. policy until at least the Civil War.[28] That policy was one of "de facto recognition," whereby the United States would recognize whatever regime had control of governmental authority and reflected the "will of the nation," regardless of what form it took or how it came into being.[29] The "will of the nation" component of this approach, moreover, was often deemphasized or ignored.[30] The de facto approach, which ostensibly was mandated by international law,[31] allowed the United States to maintain that it was simply taking account of facts on the ground and not endorsing the legitimacy of regimes that it recognized, although in practice U.S. leaders also considered U.S. foreign policy interests in deciding whether and when to recognize particular regimes. The de facto approach also ostensibly reduced separation of powers concerns because it purportedly meant that, when making recognition decisions, the president was simply noting a fact and implementing international law obligations, not adopting his own policy for the nation. As is true for many examples in this book, international law and presidential power were viewed as mutually reinforcing.

Haiti

In 1791, slaves in Saint-Domingue (present-day Haiti)—then a French colony on the western portion of the island of Hispaniola—began a series of revolts against France. Under the initial leadership of Toussaint L'Ouverture (who was captured in 1802 and died in 1803), the Haitians succeeded in achieving independence in 1804. This was a momentous development in world history: Haiti became the first independent nation in Latin America, the first postcolonial Black-led nation in the world, the second republic in the Americas (after the United States), and the only nation whose independence was gained as a result of a successful slave rebellion.

The United States provided a variety of forms of assistance to the independence movement. But the developments were viewed with alarm by Southern plantation owners in the United States, who successfully pressured the U.S. government not to recognize Haitian independence.[32] In fact, despite the United States' purportedly de facto approach to recognition, it would not recognize Haiti until 1862, after the Southern states had seceded from the Union.

Importantly, U.S. policy toward Haiti in the early 1800s was determined by Congress as much as by the executive branch. During part of the time that the conflict was raging in Haiti, the United States was engaged in a naval war against France. As discussed in Chapter 6, this war was managed by Congress, which among other things sharply restricted trade with France. In 1800, although not directly addressing the situation in Haiti, Congress declared that "the whole of the island of Hispaniola shall for the purposes of this act [restricting trade] be considered as a dependency of the French Republic."[33] In 1806, when the United States was no longer at war with France, Congress prohibited commerce with "any person or persons resident within any part of the island of St. Domingo, not in possession, and under the acknowledged government of France," undoing President Jefferson's policy of permitting trade with Haiti.[34] During this period, Jefferson was not seeking to recognize Haiti as an independent nation, so the 1800 and 1806 statutes were not contradicting presidential recognition policy. But the fact remains that Congress acted on its own initiative rather than simply leaving the matter to the executive branch.

The courts, meanwhile, deferred to the political branches and did not attempt to apply international law relating to recognition. In *Rose v. Himely*, for example, the Supreme Court rejected the argument that it should simply consult the law of nations (as articulated by Vattel) to determine Haiti's status.[35] Vattel, reasoned the Court, "addresses himself to sovereigns, not to courts." "It is for governments to decide," said the Court, "whether they will consider St. Domingo as an independent nation; and till such decision is made, or France shall relinquish her claim, courts must consider the ancient state of things as remaining unaltered, and the sovereign power of France over the colony as still subsisting."[36]

South America

In the early 1800s, people living in South America in areas colonized by Spain began rising up and declaring independence. By 1811, Venezuela had declared its independence, and other provinces were in a state of revolution. Late that year, a House committee proposed a congressional resolution that would have declared that "when those provinces shall have attained the condition of nations by the just exercise of their rights, the Senate and House of Representatives will unite with the Executive in establishing with them, as sovereign and independent states, such amicable relations and commercial intercourse as may require their legislative authority."[37] No action was taken on the resolution, however, perhaps because of the onset of the War of 1812. In any event, Spanish troops soon retook Venezuela, squelching the revolutionary movement.

By 1816, more South American provinces were seeking recognition. A group of these former colonies, including Buenos Aires and Chile, called themselves the "United Provinces of Rio de la Plata" and declared independence. President Monroe was sympathetic to the independence movement but acted cautiously, seeking to avoid any action that might prompt European intervention. He also seemed uncertain, at least at first, about the scope of his constitutional authority over recognition, asking his cabinet, for example, whether he had "power to acknowledge the independence of new states whose independence has not been acknowledged by the parent country, and between which parties a war actually exists on that account."[38]

Henry Clay, the Speaker of the House, favored immediate recognition of the provinces. Mounting what John Quincy Adams critically called his "South American great horse," Clay proposed that Congress "appropriate the sum of eighteen thousand dollars as the outfit and one year's salary of a Minister to be deputed from the United States to the independent provinces of the River Plata, in South America."[39] Clay defended this proposal at length, arguing that it would be consistent with the U.S. practice of recognizing de facto regimes, citing the Edmond Genet situation as precedent.[40] He also anticipated arguments that recognition was an exclusive executive power, contending that Congress also had authority in this area as a result of its powers over commerce and war.

Clay's proposal prompted significant debate in Congress, including over whether it improperly invaded executive authority,[41] and Clay quickly modified it to state that a minister should be sent to the provinces "whenever the President shall deem it expedient."[42] Even so, the proposal was soundly defeated. Part of the opposition stemmed from constitutional concerns, but there were also international law, policy, and political objections.[43] That same year, the Monroe administration denied an exequatur to the consul general for Buenos Aires, on the understanding that granting it would amount to a recognition of the regime.[44]

The next year, Clay made another motion to recognize the United Provinces, and this time the motion narrowly passed the House. The Monroe administration opposed it, however, because of a concern that it would jeopardize the conclusion of a treaty with Spain in which the United States was seeking to acquire Florida, and the administration asked Congress to defer consideration of the issue.[45] The Senate declined to take up Clay's motion. In 1821, Clay once again put forward his motion for recognition, and it was narrowly defeated in the House.[46] One of his fellow House members, who was otherwise sympathetic to the cause, explained his opposition to the motion: "Why annoy the Executive, session after session, with our opinion and advice, when we know that he does not desire them, and will not conform to them?"[47] Clay did manage to get the House to send a much-watered-down resolution to the president stating that it would "give its Constitutional support to the President of the United States, whenever he may deem it expedient to recognize the sovereignty and independence of any of the said provinces."[48]

Monroe and his cabinet understood that recognition would likely be appropriate at some point, and they discussed how it might be accomplished. Secretary of State John Quincy Adams felt strongly that this was exclusively an executive prerogative. He noted in his memoirs that he "thought the Executive ought carefully to preserve entire[ly] the authority given him by the Constitution, and not weaken it by setting the precedent of making either House of Congress a party to an act which it was his exclusive right and duty to perform."[49] According to Adams, Monroe shared his view but sought to work cooperatively with Congress on the issue.

In 1822, Monroe concluded that it was time to recognize the provinces, and he sought congressional support. In a message to Congress, he explained that it was now clear that the provinces had obtained independence and that recognition was warranted as a matter of international law, pursuant to the de facto approach followed by the United States. He concluded by noting that, if Congress concurred in his judgment, it "will doubtless see the propriety of making the necessary appropriations for carrying it into effect."[50] By this point, Clay had left the House to return to private practice, so he was no longer pressuring the administration.[51]

Congress proceeded to appropriate up to $100,000 to meet the expenses of "such missions to the independent nations on the American continent as the President might deem proper."[52] The president then extended recognition to various states by sending and receiving diplomatic representatives.[53] In response to protests from Spain, the administration invoked the de facto recognition doctrine, insisting that its actions were "the mere acknowledgement of existing facts." The next year, as discussed further in Chapter 6, Monroe announced what has come to be called the Monroe Doctrine, pursuant to which the United States would treat any effort at recolonizing the states in the Western Hemisphere as a threat to its security.[54]

Texas

What is now the state of Texas was once part of Mexico. In 1836, American settlers in Texas declared independence, defeated Mexican forces at the Battle of San Jacinto (after an earlier defeat at the Alamo), and sought American recognition and subsequent annexation. President Andrew Jackson was wary of acting too quickly, however, lest he provoke a war with Mexico. The issue was also fraught politically because annexation would bring another slave state into the Union.[55] Debates about Texas also related more generally to always-controversial (and racially inflected) notions of the United States' "Manifest Destiny"—that is, its supposed destiny of controlling the North American continent.[56]

At this point, the indefatigable Henry Clay was chair of the Senate Foreign Relations Committee. In June 1836, responding to various public appeals for the recognition of Texas, he submitted a report to the Senate on behalf of the committee stating that Texas could be recognized "in various ways": "1st, by treaty; 2d, by the passage of a law regulating commercial intercourse between the two Powers; 3d, by sending a diplomatic agent to Texas, with the usual credentials; or lastly, by the Executive receiving and accrediting a diplomatic representative from Texas, which would be a recognition as far as the Executive only is competent to make it."[57]

The report also expressed the view that, although the president ordinarily should take the initiative on issues of recognition, "he may be quickened in the exercise of his power by the expression of the opinion, or by other acts, of one or both branches of Congress, as was done in relation to the republics formed out of Spanish America." But it made clear that it did not think that the president was tardy in his recognition in this instance, and it merely proposed that there should be recognition whenever there was satisfactory information that Texas "has in successful operation a civil government." Both houses of Congress then passed resolutions expressing that view.

After having an agent investigate the conditions in Texas, Jackson reported back to Congress in December 1836.[58] He expressed uncertainty about the Constitution's distribution of authority over recognition. But he said that, in any event, he was inclined to work with Congress on the issue and did not "consider it necessary to express any opinion as to the strict constitutional right of the Executive, either apart from or in conjunction with the Senate, over the subject." This was especially appropriate, he suggested, given the danger that recognition could lead to war. In such a situation, Jackson said that the submission of the matter to Congress would be "consistent with the spirit of the Constitution" and "would certainly afford the fullest satisfaction to our own country and a perfect guaranty to all other nations of the justice and prudence of the measures which might be adopted."

Jackson made clear that his preference was to act cautiously, consistent with the way the United States had acted in connection with the earlier South American independence movement. Recognition, in his view, should wait "at least until the lapse of time or the course of events shall have proved beyond cavil or dispute the ability of the people of that country to maintain their separate sovereignty and to uphold the Government constituted by them." But he said that if Congress disagreed and thought that the United States should act more quickly, he would acquiesce. As one commentator notes, Jackson seemed to want "to avoid as much as possible the responsibility of initial action."[59]

Congress proceeded to consider the recognition issue and, in March 1837, passed legislation providing "for the outfit and salary of a diplomatic agent to be sent to the Republic of Texas, whenever the President of the United States may receive satisfactory evidence that Texas is an independent power, and shall deem it expedient to appoint such minister."[60] Earlier versions of the proposed legislation would have simply declared that Texas should be recognized, but the provision for a presidential determination was added after John Quincy Adams (now a member of the House) objected that he "was not disposed to set the example of taking the responsibility from the hands of the Executive, where it properly belonged."[61] This approach also allowed Congress a way around its own political division on the recognition question.[62] The Senate, however, passed a separate resolution stating that it was "expedient and proper" to recognize Texas. The day before his successor, Martin Van Buren, took office, Jackson recognized Texas. In a message to the Senate, he said that the appropriations statute and the Senate resolution were "a virtual decision of the question submitted by me to Congress" and that he thought it was his "duty to acquiesce therein."[63] As it had earlier done with respect to Spanish protests over the recognition of the South American states, the United States deflected Mexican protests by emphasizing that it followed a de facto recognition policy that simply turned on the facts on the ground rather than on a policy decision.

As discussed in Chapter 4, some years later the Tyler administration proposed to acquire Texas pursuant to a treaty, but the Senate rejected the treaty. The administration then accomplished annexation through a joint resolution passed by Congress, and Texas entered the Union as the twenty-eighth state in December 1845. The next year, in the Polk administration, the United States and Mexico would be at war, as discussed in Chapter 6.

The Lincoln Administration

The Civil War marked a turning point for U.S. policy on recognition. Up to that point, the executive branch had ostensibly followed a de facto approach, but the U.S. approach became at least sometimes more normative, considering, for example, whether a government had been accepted by its people and whether it had shown a willingness to honor its international obligations and to protect Americans and their property.[64] Not surprisingly, the Lincoln administration did not extend de facto recognition to the Confederate States, and it insisted that European and other powers also avoid such action.[65]

Other recognition issues also arose during Lincoln's presidency. In 1861, Lincoln sought Congress's support for recognizing Haiti and Liberia. He did so in part because it constituted an important change in U.S. policy and also because he needed congressional appropriations for the new diplomatic missions.[66] Charles Sumner, the chair of the Senate Foreign Relations Committee, subsequently introduced legislation in support of recognition. When the measure came up for debate, Sumner asserted that the president could have recognized Haiti and Liberia on his own and said that Congress should cooperate with the president.[67] Congress responded by enacting a statute that provided that the president was "authorized, by and with the advice and consent of the Senate, to appoint diplomatic representatives of the United States to the Republics of Hayti and Liberia, respectively."[68]

Recognition issues arose again after France installed Archduke Maximilian of Austria as emperor of Mexico in 1864, an action at odds with the Monroe Doctrine.[69] The House of Representatives responded by unanimously passing a resolution stating that "it does not accord with the policy of the United States to acknowledge a monarchical government, erected on the ruins of any republican government in America, under the auspices of any European power."[70] The Lincoln administration agreed with this sentiment but did not want to provoke a war with France while fighting the Civil War, so Secretary of State Seward wrote to the minister of France asking him to inform that country that the recognition power in the United States is a "purely executive question."[71]

The House Committee on Foreign Affairs became agitated with Seward's action and demanded the correspondence. It then issued a report strongly disagreeing with Seward's claim of exclusivity.[72] The committee reviewed in detail the history of U.S. recognition decisions, starting with the South American examples, and it said that it was "anxious not to depart from the approved precedents of our history." This history, claimed the committee, showed that "no President has ever claimed such an exclusive authority" and that "all questions of recognition [have] heretofore been debated and considered as grave questions of national policy, on which the will of the people should be expressed in Congress assembled; and the President, as the proper medium of foreign intercourse, has executed that will."

The committee recommended that the House adopt a resolution stating, among other things, that Congress has a "constitutional right to an authoritative voice in declaring and prescribing the foreign policy of the United States, as well in the recognition of new powers as in other matters," and the resolution passed almost unanimously in the House.[73] The Senate did not act on the resolution, however, apparently because, like the Lincoln administration, it did not want to create a conflict with France while the United States was fighting the Civil War.[74]

Indian Tribes

Early in U.S. history, the United States frequently entered into treaties with Indian tribes. In fact, the first treaties concluded after adoption of the Constitution were with tribes. In concluding these treaties, presidents used the senatorial advice and consent process specified in Article II of the Constitution.[75] Eventually, hundreds of treaties with Native tribes would be concluded in this manner. But the House of Representatives began to object to being excluded from the conclusion of these agreements, arguing that the Constitution expressly gives it a role in regulating commerce with Indian tribes and in making necessary appropriations.

In 1867, Congress briefly prohibited further treaty making with Indian tribes, but it repealed the measure a few months later.[76] The next year, the House initially resisted making appropriations to fulfill treaties with tribes that had been approved by the Senate, and when it eventually approved the appropriations, it stated that the legislation should not "be so construed as to ratify or approve any treaty made with any tribes, bands, or parties of Indians since the twentieth day of July, eighteen hundred and sixty-seven."[77] Finally, in 1871, Congress passed a law stating that "hereafter no Indian nation or tribe within the territory of the United States shall be acknowledged or recognized as an independent nation, tribe, or power with whom the United States may contract by treaty."[78] Although the federal government continued to make agreements with Indian tribes, the agreements were no longer concluded through the Article II treaty process.

In instructing the president that he no longer could treat Indian tribes like foreign nations for purposes of treaty making, Congress was arguably addressing an issue that fell within his recognition power (and potentially also his treaty negotiation power).[79] In the debates in Congress over the law, some members of the Senate thought that the provision was unconstitutional for that reason.[80] President Grant, however, raised no objections to it.

Cuba

The next major flash point over recognition concerned Cuba. There were a number of insurgencies in Cuba against Spanish rule during the latter half of the nineteenth century. In 1875, the Grant administration declined to recognize Cuba's independence on the ground that the insurgents did not yet have a "civil organization [that] may be recognized as an independent government capable of performing its international obligations and entitled to be treated as one of the powers of the earth."[81] Another insurgency began in 1895, and resolutions were introduced in Congress to recognize Cuban independence. President Grover Cleveland maintained, however, that conditions did not yet merit recognition. He also expressed concern that recognition would lead to war with Spain, and he cited the precedent of President Jackson's cautious actions concerning Texas.[82]

Cleveland's Secretary of State maintained, moreover, that the executive branch's power over recognition was exclusive and could not be exercised by Congress.[83] This prompted substantial debate in Congress, and much of the focus was on the historical practice up to that point. During these debates, Senator Hale presented the Senate with an extensive memorandum reviewing the practice, which he contended showed that the president's recognition power was indeed exclusive.[84] Among other things, he recounted how presidents had unilaterally determined U.S. recognition policy in over a hundred instances up to that point.[85] But other senators disagreed with his conclusion.

Although Cleveland's successor, President McKinley, sought to avoid a military conflict with Spain, the pressure for the use of force became overwhelming after the sinking of the USS *Maine* in the Havana harbor in February 1898. In April, McKinley requested congressional authorization to use force "to secure a full and final termination of hostilities between the Government of Spain and the people of Cuba, and to secure in the island the establishment of a stable government."[86] At the same time, however, he made clear that he did not think Cuba yet merited recognition as an independent state. McKinley invoked the precedent of Texas, where, he said, Congress had "left the matter of the recognition . . . to the discretion of the Executive, providing merely for the sending of a diplomatic agent when the President should be satisfied that the Republic of Texas had become 'an independent State.'"

Congress subsequently passed a joint resolution demanding that Spain withdraw from Cuba and stating that "the President of the United States be, and he hereby is, directed and empowered to use the entire land and naval forces."[87] In the resolution, Congress stated that the people of Cuba "are, and of right ought to be, free and independent," thereby stopping short of recognizing Cuba as an independent nation. The Senate had wanted the resolution to go further on the recognition issue but compromised with the House on this language.[88]

The Spanish government rejected the U.S. ultimatum and immediately severed diplomatic relations with the United States. McKinley responded by implementing a naval blockade of Cuba. Spain then declared war on the United States, and Congress responded with its own declaration of war. The United States eventually recognized Cuba as an independent nation in 1902, through executive action, after having occupied the island for several years.[89]

Twentieth-Century Practice

During the twentieth century, there were few conflicts between Congress and the executive branch over recognition until President Carter decided in the 1970s to recognize the People's Republic of China as the government of China. Presidents acted unilaterally on a wide range of matters relating to recognition, and Congress did not seriously oppose these actions.[90] The U.S. approach to recognition varied over this period, sometimes reflecting a de facto approach and at other times reflecting more normative considerations.

One of the noteworthy recognition decisions early in the twentieth century was President Theodore Roosevelt's recognition of Panama as independent from Colombia, an action that facilitated the U.S. acquisition of access to the Panama Canal.[91] President Taft subsequently used the recognition power as part of a broader program of "dollar diplomacy" in Latin America, which involved supporting foreign governments that would protect U.S. business and investments. President Wilson continued that policy and also used a normative approach to recognition in an effort to export democracy.[92] In the 1930s, the United States applied the "Stimson Doctrine," pursuant to which it would not recognize regimes established through uses of force in violation of the Kellogg-Briand Pact, in which the parties had renounced war as an instrument of foreign policy.[93] The United States later applied that policy, in the 1940 "Welles Declaration," to avoid recognizing Soviet annexation of the Baltic countries. Also significant were presidential decisions not to recognize particular regimes. For example, presidents declined to recognize the Soviet government for many years after the 1917 Russian Revolution, and presidents declined to recognize the People's Republic of China for many years after that country's 1949 revolution.

There were occasional disputes in the early twentieth century between members of Congress and the executive branch over recognition. In 1913, a joint resolution was introduced in the Senate stating that the United States recognized the Republic of China, which had taken power after a 1912 revolution against the Qing dynasty.[94] The senator who introduced the resolution claimed that recognition actions can be undertaken either by the president acting alone or by Congress and the president acting jointly but that the final authority over the matter rested in the legislative branch. The Secretary of State sharply disagreed with this view, claiming that recognition was exclusively a power of the executive branch. The Secretary quoted from, among other things, Senator Hale's 1897 memorandum.[95]

There was another brief constitutional scuffle in 1919, when the Senate considered a concurrent resolution "request[ing]" that the president "withdraw . . . the recognition" of the Carranza government in Mexico in response to evidence of a plot in Mexico to incite a revolt in the United States.[96] Even though that resolution acknowledged the president's authority over recognition, President Wilson insisted that the executive branch possessed sole recognition authority and that the resolution would "constitute a reversal of our constitutional practice which might lead to very grave confusion in regard to the guidance of our foreign affairs."[97] The Senate immediately dropped the resolution.

Some of the twentieth-century recognition actions by presidents were highly significant. For example, in 1933, President Franklin Roosevelt recognized the Soviet government,[98] and in 1948, President Truman recognized the state of Israel, making the United States the first country to do so.[99] Neither in these instances nor in many others was there serious objection from Congress. When a Senate resolution was introduced in 1935 that would have suggested that recognition of the Soviet government should be withdrawn, Secretary of State Cordell Hull expressed the view that this was a matter "within the exclusive jurisdiction of the President," and the resolution apparently did not proceed further.[100]

Roosevelt's recognition of the Soviet government also highlighted how the president's recognition power could be invoked in support of other executive actions. Roosevelt accomplished recognition through a series of diplomatic notes exchanged with the Soviet Union's commissar of foreign affairs, Maxim Litvinov. In these notes, the two countries resolved outstanding claims, including claims relating to the expropriation of American property. Under what is known as the Roosevelt-Litvinov Agreement, the Soviet Union agreed to transfer to the U.S. government title to Russian-owned property in the United States that the Soviet Union had purported to confiscate (which the U.S. government planned to use to pay off U.S. claimants). The Supreme Court gave effect to this transfer of ownership and held that any contrary state law concerning property ownership was preempted.[101] The Court reasoned that the "power to remove such obstacles to full recognition as settlement of claims of our nationals certainly is a modest implied power of the President who is the 'sole organ of the federal government in the field of international relations.'"[102]

Mainland China and Taiwan

In December 1978, after months of secret negotiations, President Jimmy Carter announced that the United States was recognizing the People's Republic of China (PRC) as the sole legal representative of China and that it was derecognizing the

Republic of China (ROC), which was based on the island of Taiwan. This decision was formalized in a "joint communique" (a type of executive agreement) with mainland China that became effective on January 1, 1979.[103] With respect to Taiwan's status, Carter merely "acknowledge[d] the Chinese position" that "Taiwan is part of China" without accepting the claim. But he announced that he was withdrawing the United States from a mutual defense treaty with the ROC, something that mainland China had insisted was a precondition to normal relations.

Many in Congress objected on policy grounds to Carter's actions, and some of them challenged the constitutionality of his withdrawal from the defense treaty, an issue addressed in Chapter 5 of this book. But Congress did not seriously contest Carter's constitutional authority to decide the recognition questions.[104]

Congress did, however, act to regulate the resulting U.S. relationship with Taiwan. The Taiwan Relations Act, which Congress passed in April 1979 and which is still in effect today, while not formally recognizing Taiwan as an independent nation, treats Taiwan in many respects like one.[105] Pursuant to the Act, many of the privileges under U.S. law that are afforded to recognized nations are extended to Taiwan, and diplomatic relations are conducted under the auspices of an entity called the American Institute of Taiwan. Instead of an "ambassador" to the United States, Taiwan has an "economic and cultural representative" whose office is known as the "Taipei Economic and Cultural Representative Office" rather than an embassy.[106] The Act, it should be noted, was passed with the support of the executive branch, which made clear that it would veto any legislation contradicting the president's recognition decisions.[107]

Despite declining to take a position on the status of Taiwan, for many years the State Department recorded the birthplace of U.S. citizens born in Taiwan as "China," a designation that was consistent with the U.S. acceptance of "one China" (including the ambiguities unresolved by that characterization).[108] But in 1994 Congress passed a law giving U.S. citizens born there the option of having their passports instead read "Taiwan."[109] The executive went along with this change, on the theory that this was a location name, not the recognition of a separate nation from China. As noted below, this precedent came up in the *Zivotofsky* case decided by the Supreme Court in 2015.

Other Contemporary Examples

Since the 1960s, the United States has deemphasized formal recognition of governments, instead focusing on the extent of diplomatic and economic relations that it wishes to have with a regime.[110] As a result, it tends not to make a formal recognition of new governments when they come into power.

But issues of state and territorial recognition continue to arise. To take a few examples: the 1991 breakup of the Soviet Union presented questions concerning which entities assumed the rights and obligations under U.S.-Soviet treaties; the George H. W. Bush administration recognized Slovenia, Croatia, and Bosnia-Herzegovina in 1992 after the post–Cold War breakup of Yugoslavia; the George W. Bush administration recognized Kosovo, which had declared independence from Serbia, in 2008; the Obama administration recognized the new state of South Sudan in 2011; and the Biden administration recognized the Cook Islands, a former New Zealand colony, in 2022. Moreover, in addition to the recognition decisions relating to Israeli territory recounted at the beginning of this chapter, the Trump administration recognized Moroccan sovereignty over the Western Sahara in 2020.[111]

Even governmental recognition issues continue to arise. Contemporary examples include the George H. W. Bush administration's refusal to recognize the Noriega government in Panama in 1989, the Obama administration's derecognition of the Qadhafi regime in Libya in 2011, and the Obama administration's recognition of the government of Somalia in 2013 after more than a decade of transitional governments in that country. In addition, when a recognized government is removed from power, the United States has occasionally continued to recognize it as the lawful "government-in-exile," even if it lacks effective control. This was the U.S. position, for example, toward Jean-Bertrand Aristide following his ouster as Haiti's president in 1991 and toward President Abdrabbuh Mansour Hadi when he was forced to flee Yemen in 2015. It was also the Trump administration's position with respect to the presidency of Juan Guaido in Venezuela in 2019, despite the fact that the Maduro government was effectively in control of the country.[112] The Biden administration deliberated about whether to recognize the Taliban government in Afghanistan and seemed disinclined to do so.[113] Presidents in recent years have declined to recognize Russian sovereignty over territory seized by Russia through its military incursions into Ukraine.

Conflicts over Israeli Policy

Although both Congress and the executive branch have traditionally been strong supporters of Israel, they have differed at times about the depth and nature of that support. In particular, Congress has at times pushed the executive branch to take more pro-Israeli positions than the executive has wanted to take, especially with respect to the competing claims between Israel and the Palestinians.

For decades, a particularly sensitive issue was the status of Jerusalem. Both Israel and the Palestinians have holy sites in that city, and both claim it as their capital. Israel began exercising control over the western portion of the city after its 1948 war and then over the entire city after its 1967 war. The executive branch had long avoided taking a position on the status of Jerusalem, preferring to leave it to be determined through negotiation between Israel and the Palestinians. As part of that policy, the United States (like most countries) maintained its official embassy in Tel Aviv rather than in Jerusalem.

Congress disagreed with the executive branch's approach. In 1995, it enacted the Jerusalem Embassy Act, which stated that "Jerusalem should be recognized as the capital of the State of Israel" and that "the United States Embassy in Israel should be established in Jerusalem no later than May 31, 1999."[114] The Act also tied State Department funding to compliance with the directive about relocating the embassy, although it allowed for a periodic presidential waiver of the provision. When this legislation was being considered without an allowance for presidential waiver, the Justice Department's Office of Legal Counsel concluded that it unconstitutionally interfered with the president's authority over recognition, reasoning that it would "severely impair the President's constitutional authority to determine the form and manner of the Nation's diplomatic relations."[115] The addition of the waiver provision avoided a presidential veto, and Clinton and subsequent presidents consistently invoked the provision.

Congress acted again in 2002. As part of its annual State Department authorization statute, Congress included a section entitled "United States Policy with Respect to Jerusalem as the Capital of Israel."[116] That section provided, among other things, that children of U.S. citizens born in Jerusalem can have the place of birth listed in their passports as Israel. When signing the statute into law, President George W. Bush issued a statement contending that the provisions in this section, "if construed as mandatory rather than advisory, impermissibly interfere with the President's constitutional authority to formulate the position of the United States, speak for the Nation in international affairs, and determine the terms on which recognition is given to foreign states."[117] Both Bush and his successor, Barack Obama, declined to comply with the statute.

The executive branch's failure to comply with the 2002 passport statute was challenged in court. Menachem Binyamin Zivotofsky was born in Jerusalem to American parents, and his mother requested that Israel be listed as the place of birth in his U.S. passport. After the State Department refused, the parents brought suit on his behalf. The litigation was protracted, in part because there were also issues of standing that the courts had to resolve.[118]

The Supreme Court reviewed the case twice. The first time, it held (as discussed in Chapter 2) that resolution of the case was not barred by the political question doctrine.[119] When the case returned to the Supreme Court, the Court held that the 2002 statute was unconstitutional because it infringed on the president's exclusive recognition power.[120] Applying Justice Jackson's framework from the *Youngstown* steel seizure case, the Court concluded that this was a rare case in which the president should prevail in the third category, where he could "rely only upon his own constitutional powers minus any constitutional powers of Congress over the matter."

In holding that the president's recognition power was exclusive, the Court emphasized what it referred to as "functional considerations." The United States needs to act with "one voice" on such issues, reasoned the Court, and it concluded that the president was best situated to exercise this voice, both because he could engage in the "delicate and often secret diplomatic contacts that may lead to a decision on recognition" and because he was "better positioned to take the decisive, unequivocal action necessary to recognize other states at international law."

In addition to these considerations, the Court invoked historical practice. While acknowledging that "history is not all on one side," the Court concluded that "on balance it provides strong support for the conclusion that the recognition power is the President's alone." In considering this issue, the Court discussed a number of the historical examples recounted in this chapter. With respect to the examples in which Congress had appeared to participate in recognition actions, the Court thought that those examples "establish[] no more than that some Presidents have chosen to cooperate with Congress, not that Congress itself has exercised the recognition power." Having determined that the recognition power was exclusive, the Court proceeded to conclude that the 2002 statute infringed on this power by forcing the executive branch to contradict its recognition policy in the passports, which are official government-issued documents.[121]

Exclusive Power?

There is little dispute that historical practice supports a presidential power over recognition.[122] The difficult question is whether, as the Court concluded in *Zivotofsky,* it supports an *exclusive* power that cannot be limited or contradicted by Congress.

As noted above, the Court in *Zivotofsky* claimed that, although "history is not all on one side, . . . on balance it provides strong support for the conclusion that the recognition power is the President's alone." In fact, the history by itself seems inconclusive. In the nineteenth century, the executive branch sometimes did assert an exclusive recognition power, but at other times, it was more diffident. Some members of Congress agreed at times that the president's recognition power was exclusive, but it is difficult to know if that was a majority sentiment. At other times, presidents worked directly with Congress on matters of recognition.

To be sure, recognition decisions have been handled primarily by the executive branch since the dawn of the twentieth century, but that might simply show that the president has a well-settled independent power, not an exclusive one. As the example of Taiwan illustrates, Congress has not always been silent even in the modern era. The most direct modern conflict between Congress and the president over recognition was the one at issue in *Zivotofsky,* but that example merely shows disagreement, not a settled practice.

On the other hand, the historical record is not sharply inconsistent with the Court's finding of exclusivity. In his account of the history of U.S. recognition policy, Professor Robert Reinstein argues that history shows only a concurrent presidential power over recognition, not an exclusive one.[123] In support of this claim, Reinstein contends that there have been a number of instances of Congress "exercising the recognition power." This characterization, however, overstates the case. As we have seen, there have been instances in which Congress has taken action *relating to* recognition, often after pulling back from more directly attempting to address the issue. With the possible exception of the Jerusalem passport statute, Congress has never mandated U.S. recognition or derecognition in the face of executive objection. Moreover, a number of the congressional actions relating to recognition have been at the invitation of the president. It is one thing for a president to invite congressional support—for example, in conjunction with a request for appropriations—and another thing for Congress to force a recognition action without presidential agreement.

It is also worth noting that some prominent commentators throughout history have thought that the president's recognition power was exclusive. This appears to have been Joseph Story's view in his 1833 treatise.[124] Edward Corwin reached the same conclusion in 1917,[125] as did Quincy Wright in 1922.[126] This was also the conclusion of the *Restatement (Third) of Foreign Relations Law,* published in 1987.[127] Dicta in some Supreme Court decisions before *Zivotofsky* also suggested that the power was exclusive.[128]

Nevertheless, it is difficult for history alone to establish exclusive presidential power, on this or any other issue.[129] The evidence that would be most probative of such exclusivity—congressional attempts to regulate that are rebuffed on constitutional grounds—is often absent or ambiguous. There are some historical examples relating to recognition that could be read that way, such as with respect to Cuba, but they are not entirely clear. When Congress backs off or modifies its position, it might be because of political and policy considerations, not a sense that it lacks constitutional authority. And of course Congress did not back off in the statute at issue in *Zivotofsky*.[130] Moreover, Congress has continued to address issues relating to recognition since *Zivotofsky*. For example, in a series of appropriations statutes starting in 2016, Congress has prohibited the use of funds by the Department of Defense for "any activity that recognizes the sovereignty of the Russian Federation over Crimea," although it has allowed for national security waivers of the prohibition.[131]

Whatever the right conclusion on this issue, it is worth bearing in mind that there is far more historical support for the exclusivity of presidential power over recognition than for any other issue of presidential power addressed in this book. That is one reason for caution before applying *Zivotofsky*'s analysis beyond the context of recognition. The Court itself signaled such caution, emphasizing that "the Executive's exclusive power extends no further than his formal recognition decision."[132] General concerns about checks and balances also counsel in favor of a narrow reading of the decision. As Justice Jackson noted in *Youngstown* when commenting on the idea of exclusive presidential authority, a "presidential claim to a power at once so conclusive and preclusive must be scrutinized with caution, for what is at stake is the equilibrium established by our constitutional system."[133]

As the Court also emphasized in *Zivotofsky*, the fact that the recognition power is exclusive does not mean that Congress lacks authority to regulate issues that *relate to* recognition. "Congress' powers, and its central role in making laws," reasoned the Court, "give it substantial authority regarding many of the policy determinations that precede and follow the act of recognition itself." Congress could, for example, cut off trade with a regime recognized by a president, strip the regime of sovereign immunity, mandate economic sanctions, refuse to fund an embassy, and decline to approve ambassadors nominated by the president, just to name a few actions.[134] The Taiwan Relations Act, discussed above, is an especially dramatic example of Congress's ability to regulate matters that are adjacent to the issue of recognition.

Perhaps unsurprisingly, executive branch lawyers are less cautious in making claims of exclusivity than Justice Jackson's admonition would suggest. As Professor Jack Goldsmith has noted, these lawyers have "an institutional predilection to read presidential power broadly" and thus will "tend to construe [the Court's] holding, dicta, and ambiguities in the President's favor."[135] Indeed, consistent with this prediction, in 2020 the Justice Department's Office of Legal Counsel relied on *Zivotofsky* in concluding that the president could disregard statutory limitations on U.S. withdrawal from the Open Skies Treaty, a multilateral agreement that allowed the parties (including the United States and Russia) to conduct unarmed surveillance flights over the other party countries. OLC recited the reasoning in *Zivotofsky* and claimed that "the same conclusion follows here."[136] "Just as the recognition power is an exclusive power of the President arising as an incident to his other constitutional authorities," reasoned OLC, "his power to exercise the United States' right to terminate a treaty is an exclusive power that is part of the President's executive power, treaty-making power, and diplomatic power." I critique that reasoning in Chapter 5. Even if historical gloss supports an exclusive recognition power—a close call, in my view—the support for exclusivity is significantly weaker in the treaty termination context.

Conclusion

Of the examples of presidential power covered in this book, recognition presents the strongest case for an exclusive sphere of authority that cannot be limited by Congress. At times, presidents and their advisers argued for such exclusivity even during the nineteenth century, and in a number of instances, Congress relented from direct efforts to determine recognition. Even for this issue, however, a finding of exclusivity likely depends not only on the history but also on contestable inferences from constitutional structure and functional reasoning.

Regardless of the right legal conclusion, the example of recognition illustrates the significance of the president's control over the channels of diplomacy. Under even the narrowest version of the "sole organ" conception of the presidency, it has long been accepted that formal communications with other nations must be routed through the executive branch. This means that, as a practical matter, the president has a tremendous ability to affect both how and when such communications are made. It is like the adage about possession being nine-tenths of the law—in this case, the possession is of the communicative organ of the United States.

This topic also illustrates how issues of foreign relations law authority are interconnected. Control over one issue, such as recognition, can give the president the practical ability to affect other issues, such as the making and unmaking of international agreements and the conduct of war. Conversely, Congress's control over other foreign relations law issues, such as appropriations and trade and the approval of certain international agreements, can give it the practical ability to affect recognition, as the Court observed in *Zivotofsky*. These interconnections are a key reason why it is important to consider foreign relations powers collectively and not merely in isolation.

The *Zivotofsky* decision also provides an example of how concerns about the "imperial presidency" are not necessarily eliminated by more judicial review. Before that decision, there was uncertainty about the extent to which Congress could regulate issues relating to recognition, and the political branches had to bargain over the issue. After the decision, however, the executive branch now has a judicial trump card to prevent congressional regulation, and it is also using that card in support of other claims of authority. This is an example of how more judicial review, something typically called for by critics of "foreign affairs exceptionalism" (as noted in Chapter 2), might just lead to a greater entrenchment of executive authority. The development of gloss-based presidential power outside the courts, by contrast, is more fluid and subject to revisitation.

Finally, international law is an important part of the story here. It has treated certain actions that indisputably fall within the president's authority, such as receiving ambassadors, as acts of recognition, thus facilitating executive control over the issue. In addition, especially in the early days of U.S. recognition practice, presidents were able to appeal to international law to help deflect not only international objections but also separation of powers concerns about their unilateral actions. If presidents were merely implementing the law of nations and responding to facts on the ground, the argument went, they were not usurping legislative authority. In fact, presidents exercised significant discretion in deciding whether and when to recognize regimes, and they also themselves affected the international law standards.

4

MAKING INTERNATIONAL AGREEMENTS

IN 1993, PRESIDENT BILL CLINTON CONCLUDED A SIGNIFICANT TRADE agreement with Canada and Mexico. In eliminating almost all tariffs and trade restrictions among the three countries, the North American Free Trade Agreement (NAFTA) created the world's largest free-trade zone. In addition to addressing a wide range of trade and other issues such as intellectual property protection, the agreement established a new arbitral institution designed to resolve investor-state disputes as well as a new binational panel system designed to review issues relating to unfair trade practices.

When concluding NAFTA, Clinton did not seek the approval of two-thirds of the Senate, as called for in the Treaty Clause of the Constitution. Instead, he concluded NAFTA as a "congressional-executive agreement," based on the approval of a simple majority in both houses of Congress. The vote in the Senate was 61–38, short of the two-thirds majority in that chamber that would have been required if the agreement had been concluded as a treaty. Although by that point congressional-executive agreements were common in U.S. practice, the use of that process for NAFTA sparked controversy. A trade association sued the U.S. government, arguing that the agreement was unconstitutional, but the case was dismissed under the political question doctrine.[1]

Despite the controversy, Clinton used the process the following year to conclude a global trade agreement, which among other things established a major new international institution, the World Trade Organization. This action, too, generated constitutional criticism. Professor Laurence Tribe, for example, testified in Congress that the importance and nature of the obligations in the agreement made it a treaty requiring supermajority Senate approval. In defending the legality of using the congressional-executive agreement process, the Justice Department's Office of Legal Counsel relied heavily on historical practice, noting that "a significant guide to the interpretation of the Constitution's requirements is the practical construction placed on it by the executive and legislative branches acting together."[2]

This chapter describes the rise of executive agreements—that is, binding international agreements concluded by presidents without the supermajority Senate consent called for by Article II. As will be explained, there are several categories of these agreements, each with a long history. The general pattern here is one of accretion of practice, along with a significant growth in that practice starting in the 1930s. With a few important qualifications, both Congress as a whole and the Senate as a body have acquiesced in this development. The constitutional dispute over NAFTA was unusual, and subsequent agreements concluded in that fashion have not generated controversy. Most of the recent controversies have instead centered on agreements that have been concluded without any formal congressional involvement.

The Constitutional Text

The Constitution specifies only one process by which the national government can conclude international agreements. Article II provides that the president has the power to make treaties "by and with the advice and consent of the Senate . . . provided two thirds of the Senators present concur." In practice, this has mainly meant only consent and not advice; as early as the George Washington administration, presidents stopped routinely seeking the Senate's negotiation advice and instead merely sought its approval of treaties after the treaties were finalized.[3] Nevertheless, Article II appears to require that all treaties that are ratified by the United States receive the approval of a supermajority of the Senate.

There is, however, another provision in the Constitution that might suggest that the Article II process is not required for *all* agreements with foreign nations. Article I, Section 10, prohibits U.S. states from entering into "any treaty, alliance, or confederation," but it says that they may enter into an "agreement or compact . . . with a foreign power" if they have "the consent of Congress." If Congress can authorize *the states* to make some agreements with foreign powers, it might be reasonable to conclude that it can also authorize *the president* to do so.

The international law at the time of the Founding might also support this conclusion, at least to an extent. International law theorists like Emmerich Vattel, who were well known to and often invoked by the Founders, distinguished between "treaties" and "compacts, agreements, or conventions." Whereas treaties, in Vattel's classification, are "executory in character and the acts called for must continue as long as the treaty exists," for other agreements "the act in question is performed [and] these pacts are executed once and for all."[4] Treaties, in other words, might have been a term for ongoing as opposed to one-time commitments. It has been argued that Vattel's classification underlies the Constitution's distinction between treaties and agreements/compacts for purposes of state agreement making,[5] and perhaps the same is true for executive agreement making. Even if so, however, this distinction might suggest a fairly narrow scope for the executive agreement power since many international agreements call for ongoing execution and thus would be considered treaties under Vattel's classification.

In addition to this possible inference from Article I, some of the president's independent powers might also be interpreted as entailing an ability to conclude agreements to effectuate the exercise of these powers. The president is the Commander in Chief of the armed forces and the spokesperson for the United States in international relations and (as discussed in Chapter 3) has the power to decide whether to recognize foreign governments. The president also has the obligation to take care that the laws are faithfully executed. These sources of authority, it might be argued, carry with them some ability to conclude agreements to effectuate their exercise.

General Growth in Executive Agreements

The conclusion of executive agreements was relatively rare early in U.S. history. According to one widely cited calculation, in the first fifty years after the adoption of the Constitution, the federal government concluded 60 Article II treaties and only 27 executive agreements.[6] By contrast, in the fifty-year period from 1939 to 1989, there were, according to a State Department calculation, 702 Article II treaties and 11,698 executive agreements.[7] In other words, executive agreements constituted almost 95 percent of the overall international agreements during that period.

This trend has continued during the last several decades.[8] In fact, in recent years the use of the Article II treaty process has slowed to a trickle,[9] so almost all binding international agreements concluded by the United States have been executive agreements. The Clinton administration submitted around twenty-three treaties to the Senate per year; the George W. Bush administration submitted around twelve treaties per year; the Obama administration submitted only around five treaties per year; and the Trump administration submitted only five treaties to the Senate during Trump's entire four-year term. At the time this book went to press in 2024, the Biden administration had submitted only a few treaties to the Senate. When the United States makes binding international agreements today, it almost never uses the Article II process.

In considering the historic growth in executive agreements, it is useful to divide them into several categories, although actual practice is more complicated than these categories might suggest. First is the category of "treaty-based executive agreements"—that is, executive agreements made pursuant to authorization (express or implied) in a prior Article II treaty. Second is the category of "congressional-executive agreements"—that is, agreements concluded with the approval of a majority of Congress. This category can be subdivided into ex ante congressional-executive agreements authorized in advance by Congress and ex post congressional-executive agreements approved by Congress after they are negotiated. Most executive agreements are congressional-executive agreements, and the vast majority of them are of the ex ante variety, which means that they are not voted on by Congress after they are negotiated. Third is the category of "sole executive agreements"—that is, agreements concluded by the executive branch without treaty-based or statutory authorization or approval. This category probably constitutes a relatively small fraction of the overall number of agreements.[10]

Treaty-Based Executive Agreements

It has long been accepted that an Article II treaty can delegate authority to the president to make executive agreements relating to the treaty. In part because a supermajority of the Senate is involved in making the delegation, this category of executive agreements has generally been uncontroversial.[11]

Administrative details about how treaty obligations are to be implemented—for example, about where and how payments under a treaty are to be made—have often been handled through executive agreements.[12] Treaties establishing a process for the determination of an international boundary have sometimes been followed by executive agreements accepting the outcome of the treaty process.[13] Treaties establishing U.S. military bases sometimes delegate authority to the president to conclude "status of forces" agreements concerning (among other things) the conduct and trial of U.S. service personnel stationed there.[14]

A recent, high-profile example of an executive agreement that was made pursuant to a treaty is the Paris Agreement on climate change. The Obama administration concluded the agreement in part on the basis of authority conferred in an earlier treaty—the UN Framework Convention on Climate Change, which the United States had ratified in 1992.[15] As discussed below, a core provision of the Paris Agreement was probably not authorized by the Framework Convention, but it was made nonbinding and thus, the Obama administration maintained, did not need to be authorized.

Although this category of executive agreements has not typically provoked controversy, there were debates in the nineteenth and early twentieth centuries about delegations of authority in arbitration treaties.[16] Under the treaties, the parties were supposed to refer their future disputes to international arbitration if such disputes could not be resolved through diplomacy. The actual referral would occur at the time of the dispute and would require an agreement by the parties about the nature and scope of the issue to be arbitrated. The Senate repeatedly insisted, as a condition of consenting to these treaties, that the president would need to obtain the additional advice and consent of the Senate before making any referrals of U.S. disputes under the treaties.[17] The Theodore Roosevelt administration initially found this condition to be unacceptable and declined to move forward on the treaties, but it later changed its mind and agreed to the condition. The Senate continued to successfully insist on this condition for arbitration treaties all the way into the 1930s.

These delegation concerns eventually receded. At the end of World War II, the United States agreed by treaty to the establishment of the International Court of Justice (ICJ), which can hear international disputes between consenting states, including when the states jointly make a referral of a dispute, and the Senate did not insist on approving executive branch referrals. In the ensuing decades, the Senate approved many treaties that allowed for future disputes under the treaties to be resolved by the ICJ—again, without requiring Senate consent for each case.[18] The United States now generally avoids committing to such provisions and has withdrawn from some of them, but this is due to policy concerns rather than constitutional objections.

Occasionally, disputes have arisen over whether a particular agreement is in fact authorized by a treaty. In 1971, for example, the Nixon administration concluded an agreement with Portugal concerning the stationing of U.S. forces at an air base in the Azores, which called for the United States to provide over $400 million in credits and assistance to Portugal. The State Department contended that the agreement was based on authority provided by the NATO treaty, but the Senate Foreign Relations Committee disagreed.[19]

Congressional-Executive Agreements

Congress has authorized the executive branch to conclude international agreements since the early days of the nation. In 1792, for example, Congress authorized the postmaster general to "make arrangements with the postmasters in any foreign country for the reciprocal receipt and delivery of letters and packets, through the post-offices."[20] Soon thereafter, the Washington administration concluded a postal convention with Canada, and most postal agreements concluded by the United States since that time have been done as executive agreements rather than as Senate-approved treaties.[21] In arguing many years later that the postal agreements were constitutional, then Solicitor General William Howard Taft reasoned that, "where long usage, dating back to a period contemporary with the adoption of the Constitution, sanctions an interpretation of that instrument different from that which would be reached by the ordinary rules of construction were the question a new one, the usage will be followed."[22]

The United States' acquisitions of both Texas (in 1845) and Hawaii (in 1898) were accomplished through statutes, after the Senate failed to give its consent to treaties that would have annexed these territories. For Texas, the legislation set forth conditions for annexation, which Texas then accepted (and the president then reported this back to Congress), and for Hawaii, the legislation accepted an agreement that the executive branch had made with Hawaii.[23] As discussed in Chapter 3, at Congress's insistence, all agreements with Indian tribes since 1871 have been concluded as congressional-executive agreements rather than as Article II treaties. Before that time, hundreds of Article II treaties were concluded with tribes, including the very first treaty concluded after the Constitution took effect.[24]

Congress also has long authorized presidents to conclude agreements relating to the amount of duties and tariffs to be paid on imports. As early as 1815, Congress passed laws delegating authority to the president to repeal discriminatory duties on imports if the importing countries did the same for U.S. goods.[25] While this could be accomplished merely by parallel action, presidents often chose to memorialize these reciprocity conditions in agreements.[26] Similarly, the 1890 McKinley Tariff Act allowed the president to impose duties on imports whenever, in his judgment, the duties imposed by the importing country were "reciprocally unequal or unreasonable." Presidents relied on this statute as the basis for securing reciprocal commercial agreements with a number of countries. Later statutes, such as the Dingley Tariff Act of 1897, expressly delegated to the president agreement-making authority relating to tariffs on specified products, in order to secure "reciprocal and equivalent concessions."[27]

In a 7–2 decision, the Supreme Court upheld the constitutionality of the 1890 tariff delegation in *Field v. Clark*.[28] Relying heavily on historical practice, the Court noted: "If we find that Congress has frequently, from the organization of the government to the present time, conferred upon the President powers, with reference to trade and commerce . . . that fact is entitled to great weight in determining the question before us." The Supreme Court also referenced the phenomenon of executive agreements in a 1912 decision, *B. Altman & Co. v. United States*, in which it construed the term "treaty" in a jurisdictional provision as including an agreement made under the authority of the Dingley Tariff Act.[29]

Many other statutory delegations of agreement-making authority followed. The Panama Canal Act of 1912 authorized agreements with Panama to establish wireless telegraph installations.[30] During World War I, Congress enacted the Liberty Loan Act, which authorized the executive branch to enter into agreements with U.S. allies to purchase their foreign bonds.[31] After the war, the Coolidge administration negotiated debt relief agreements with European countries that were subject to the approval of Congress rather than a supermajority of the Senate.[32]

By the 1930s, Congress was delegating even more general authority to the executive branch to negotiate trade-related executive agreements. For example, in the 1934 Reciprocal Trade Agreements Act, Congress provided that "the President, whenever he finds as a fact that any existing duties or other import restrictions of the United States or any foreign country are unduly burdening and restricting the foreign trade of the United States . . . is authorized from time to time—to enter into foreign trade agreements with foreign governments and instrumentalities thereof."[33] In defending the constitutionality of the 1934 statute, the State Department Legal Adviser noted that, since 1928, the government had concluded "no less than seventy-eight executive agreements" on a wide range of topics.[34]

The United States also started joining international institutions by means of congressional-executive agreements. It did so in 1934, for example, when joining the International Labour Organization.[35] In defending the constitutionality of this process, Secretary of State Cordell Hull emphasized that "there exists a long line of instances where the President of the United States has entered into international engagements on behalf of this Government in pursuance of Joint Resolutions or Acts of Congress."[36] Some commentators at this point began arguing for complete interchangeability of Article II treaties and congressional-executive agreements.[37]

World War II, unsurprisingly, saw more delegations of agreement-making authority. The 1941 Lend-Lease Act, which authorized the president to enter into arrangements with foreign governments to lend or lease military supplies when the president "deem[ed] it in the interest of national defense," served as the basis for a number of agreements. In 1944, Congress authorized the president, "by such means as he finds appropriate," to acquire military bases "he may deem necessary for the mutual protection of the Philippine Islands and of the United States," and President Truman subsequently used this authority to enter into a ninety-nine-year military base agreement with the Philippines. The executive branch later negotiated a supplemental agreement with the Philippines providing for preferential hiring of Filipino citizens at the bases.[38]

As these examples illustrate, there was a tremendous growth in the number of executive agreements during the Franklin Roosevelt administration.[39] Sometimes this triggered controversy. For example, Roosevelt in 1942 sought congressional rather than senatorial support for an agreement transferring lands and facilities to Panama. Congress gave its approval the next year, but only after significant debate, including over whether the administration was improperly undermining the Senate's authority over treaties. During the debates, Senator Robert Taft complained that "no treaties of any importance have been submitted to the Senate since I have been a member of the body."[40]

In 1943, the Roosevelt administration indicated that it planned to join the new United Nations Relief and Rehabilitation Administration on its own authority. Some senators expressed concerns, and the Senate directed its Foreign Relations Committee to determine whether the agreement should be submitted to the Senate for approval as a treaty. Ultimately, a compromise was reached whereby a draft of the agreement was submitted to the committee, which made revisions that were accepted by the State Department, and the administration then joined the agreement after the other parties to the agreement accepted the revisions. The agreement was then incorporated into a joint resolution approved by both houses of Congress.[41]

In the face of these developments, the Senate sought to preserve some of its institutional authority. Discussions were underway to establish an international organization that would help maintain international peace and security after the war, and in September 1943, the House of Representatives passed the Fulbright Resolution, stating that it "favor[ed] the creation of appropriate international machinery with power adequate to establish and to maintain a just and lasting peace, among the nations of the world, and as favoring participation by the United States therein through its constitutional processes."[42] The House passed this as a concurrent resolution in the hope that the Senate might join in it. Instead, the Senate passed what is known as the Connally Resolution, stating that it "recognizes the necessity of there being established at the earliest practicable date a general international organization . . . for the maintenance of international peace and security" but that "any treaty made to effect the purposes of this resolution . . . shall be made only by and with the advice and consent of the Senate of the United States, provided two-thirds of the Senators present concur."[43]

Debates in the 1940s

There was significant debate in the 1940s—among scholars, politicians, and the public—over the proper scope of executive agreements, and in particular over whether congressional-executive agreements were completely interchangeable with Article II treaties. Looming over the debates was the memory of the Senate's rejection after World War I of the Versailles Treaty, something that President Wilson had said "broke the heart of the world." With efforts underway to rebuild the international order after yet another world war, many observers viewed the Constitution's requirement of supermajority Senate consent for treaties as detrimental to U.S. foreign policy interests. Members of the House were also pushing for a role in the treaty process.

A number of prominent scholars at this point began arguing for complete interchangeability between treaties and congressional-executive agreements.[44] The chief academic critic of this argument was Edwin Borchard, a professor at Yale Law School.[45] Drawing on the distinction set forth by Vattel (described above), he suggested that minor and short-term matters are appropriate for executive agreements but that important and long-term commitments need to be approved as Article II treaties. "It is only agreements of a more important character, involving future commitments," he maintained, "that encroach upon the treaty-making power of the Senate." He claimed that historical practice was at least roughly consistent with this conclusion.

In response, Myres McDougal and Asher Lans published a lengthy article that, among other things, described a wide array of executive agreements that had been made throughout history.[46] They claimed that "the practices of successive administrations, supported by the Congress and by numerous court decisions, have for all practical purposes made the Congressional-Executive agreement authorized or sanctioned by both houses of Congress interchangeable with the agreements ratified under the treaty clause by two-thirds of the Senate." Both sides in the debate, it should be noted, accepted the importance of historical gloss; they simply construed the practice differently.

There was also increasing public support for shifting to majority congressional approval for international agreements, and Congress began considering proposed constitutional amendments that would allow for this. In 1945, one of these proposals passed the House by a wide margin.[47] The Senate, not surprisingly, was less enthusiastic, and it never voted on the amendment. But there was nevertheless substantial political support at this point for making greater use of congressional-executive agreements.

Post–World War II

The end of World War II, the establishment of the United Nations, and decolonization all contributed to a substantial increase in the number of international agreements. The United States also emerged from the war as a superpower, with interests that spanned the globe. There was at this point a corresponding growth in the use by the United States of executive agreements, including for some very important commitments.

Although the United Nations Charter was (consistent with the Connally Resolution) approved as an Article II treaty, the Headquarters Agreement for the United Nations was concluded as a congressional-executive agreement.[48] So were the Bretton Woods agreements through which the United States joined the World Bank and International Monetary Fund.[49] The same was true of U.S. membership in various other international bodies such as the World Health Organization and the United Nations Educational, Scientific and Cultural Organization (UNESCO). And in 1947, the Truman administration joined the original General Agreement on Tariffs and Trade (GATT) on the basis of authority delegated in the 1934 Reciprocal Trade Agreements Act.[50]

In addition to its endorsements of particular executive agreements, Congress began enacting more general authorizations, many of which continue to provide authority for executive agreements today. For example, in the 1954 Agriculture Trade Development and Assistance Act, Congress gave the president authority to "negotiate and carry out agreements with friendly nations or organizations of friendly nations to provide for the sale of surplus agricultural commodities for foreign currencies."[51] And in the Foreign Assistance Act of 1961, Congress authorized the president to enter into agreements with foreign countries for both development assistance and military assistance.[52]

The growth in executive agreements continued to prompt debate, especially in the Senate. The validity of these agreements was one of the issues discussed in the "Bricker Amendment" debates during the 1950s over whether to limit the treaty power through a constitutional amendment. Although there were a number of variants of the proposed amendment, the effort is named after their chief sponsor, Senator John Bricker of Ohio.[53] A central target of the effort was the Supreme Court's 1920 decision in *Missouri v. Holland,* which (as discussed in Chapter 2) held that treaties could regulate domestic matters that Congress could not otherwise regulate under its Article I authority. But early versions of the Bricker Amendment also would have included a provision stating that "executive agreements could not be made in lieu of treaties." Later versions of the amendment, however, merely would have required congressional implementation of executive agreements. No version of the Bricker Amendment was ever adopted, although one of the later versions came within one vote of receiving the needed two-thirds support in the Senate. The controversy ultimately died down, in part because of assurances from the Eisenhower administration that it had no intention of using the treaty power to regulate purely domestic matters or of joining the then-emerging human rights treaties (which some senators viewed as posing particular federalism concerns).[54]

During this period, the State Department also adopted an internal process, known as "C-175," for determining which type of pathway to use when concluding international agreements. The relevant State Department guidance for this process lists eight factors to be considered. These factors are open ended and discretionary, but they include "past U.S. practice as to similar agreements" and "the preference of the Congress as to a particular type of agreement."[55]

Interchangeability?

The debate today concerning congressional-executive agreements is not over whether they are constitutional as a general matter but rather over the extent to which they are freely interchangeable with Article II treaties. The nonbinding but influential *Restatement (Third) of the Foreign Relations Law of the United States* suggested in 1987 that they were completely interchangeable, and some scholars have agreed.[56] Other scholars, however, have questioned this claim, in part on the basis of historical practice. As they note, for some topics it does not appear that presidents perceive themselves to have complete discretion to pursue a congressional-executive agreement in lieu of an Article II treaty, and this appears to be due in part to Senate opposition to such substitution.

One area in which the Senate has resisted interchangeability is arms control. Although the 1972 Strategic Arms Limitation Talks (SALT I) agreement with the Soviet Union was concluded as a congressional-executive agreement, it was intended only as an interim measure, and every other major arms control treaty since World War II has been concluded through the Article II process.[57] This pattern appears to stem at least in part from Senate insistence. When giving its advice and consent to a number of arms control treaties, the Senate has included a declaration stating that agreements "that would obligate the United States to reduce or limit the Armed Forces or armaments of the United States in a militarily significant manner [should be concluded] only pursuant to the Treaty Power as set forth in Article II, Section 2, Clause 2 of the Constitution."[58]

Presidents have repeatedly acquiesced in the Senate's insistence on using the treaty process for arms control agreements. In the late 1970s, President Carter considered submitting the SALT II agreement as a congressional-executive agreement but relented in the face of senatorial protests.[59] In 1997, President Clinton responded to Senate pressure by agreeing to submit an update of the Treaty on Armed Conventional Forces in Europe to the Senate for its advice and consent, thereby abandoning an earlier decision to seek only majority congressional approval for the agreement.[60] Clinton also sought (unsuccessfully) the Senate's advice and consent for the Comprehensive Nuclear Test Ban Treaty and did not appear to contemplate concluding it as a congressional-executive agreement. When President Obama sought later to resurrect this agreement, he also went back to the Article II process.[61]

George W. Bush, after initially suggesting that he might conclude a nuclear weapons reduction agreement with Russia through some sort of executive agreement, decided to submit the reduction agreement to the Senate for its advice and consent. He did so after senior Democratic and Republican members of the Senate Foreign Relations Committee told the Secretary of State that, because the agreement "would most likely include significant obligations by the United States regarding deployed U.S. strategic nuclear warheads," they were "convinced that such an agreement would constitute a treaty subject to the advice and consent of the Senate."[62] President Obama sought and obtained the Senate's advice and consent for the New START (Strategic Arms Reduction Treaty) with Russia in 2010.[63]

Another subject area that has been dominated by Article II treaties is human rights. For many years, the United States avoided joining human rights treaties, in part because of opposition in the Senate. As noted above, the Eisenhower administration, in an effort to quell debates over the Bricker Amendment, indicated that it had no intention of joining human rights treaties. When the United States finally did start joining these treaties in the late 1980s and early 1990s, it did so only through the Article II process. This is true even though the requirement of supermajority Senate consent has proved to be a formidable obstacle. President Obama tried twice, for example, to obtain Senate approval of the UN Convention on Persons with Disabilities, and he failed each time.[64] Other human rights treaties, like the Convention on the Elimination of Discrimination Against Women, have also languished, despite presidential support, because of the difficulty of obtaining Senate consent.

For the most part, extradition agreements have also been concluded only as Article II treaties. The one exception is the extradition agreements that the United States made with the ad hoc criminal tribunals for Yugoslavia and Rwanda in the 1990s, which were concluded as congressional-executive agreements.[65] That context was unusual, involving trials by international institutions rather than other nations and the use of international criminal law rather than domestic law. As the use of the Article II process has dropped off sharply in recent years, extradition treaties continue to be submitted to the Senate (and approved). Of course, the very fact that extradition treaties tend to be approved by the Senate reduces the incentive of the executive branch to try to conclude them through some other process.[66]

In short, there are a few discernible categories where, at least for significant agreements, the Article II treaty process is used instead of the congressional-executive agreement process.[67] Presidents, moreover, seem constrained by this customary practice, feeling obligated to use the Senate process even if this makes it more difficult or even impossible for them to conclude the agreements. This is not to suggest that the categories are either fully consistent or analytically sensible. But the need for consistency and coherence may be lower in this context than for legal regimes administered by the courts, given that political actors, unlike courts, do not need to provide a reasoned explanation of why the distinctions are being drawn as they are.

Sole Executive Agreements

Sole executive agreements are concluded without authorization or approval from Congress and thus are based solely on the president's own constitutional authority. These, too, date back to early in U.S. history. It may be useful to divide these into four categories: settlement of claims, war and military affairs, recognition-related issues, and modi vivendi. This is not a comprehensive list, but it captures the most prominent areas of practice.

Settlement of Claims

The most well-recognized category of sole executive agreements concerns the settlement of the claims of American citizens against foreign governments. One of the earliest such agreements was concluded by the John Adams administration with the Netherlands in 1799. The settlement concerned claims of American citizens arising out of a seizure of the cargo of a U.S. schooner, the *Wilmington Packet,* by a Dutch privateer during a war between the Netherlands and France.[68]

There have been many subsequent examples of sole executive agreements being used to settle American claims against foreign governments.[69] Thus, for example, in 1825 the John Quincy Adams administration negotiated a settlement of claims with Colombia concerning the seizure of U.S. schooners and their cargo. In 1832, the Andrew Jackson administration entered into an agreement with Portugal to settle claims arising out of American ships lost in a Portuguese blockade. Skipping ahead to the late nineteenth century, the executive branch made an agreement with Great Britain in 1881 to settle the claims of American fishermen concerning operations off the coast of Newfoundland. Using a sole executive agreement for such settlements was thought to be especially appropriate in situations in which the claims were small and the U.S. claimants supported the settlement.[70]

Some of the settlement agreements, rather than specifying a dollar amount, referred disputes for arbitration.[71] In a memorandum written in 1909, the State Department reasoned that, as long as the United States was the claimant in these arbitrations, there was no danger that the United States would have to appropriate money to satisfy a judgment, in which case no congressional approval was needed.[72] In fact, though, the executive branch often agreed to arbitrate even claims against the United States without seeking Senate consent.[73]

One scholar calculated that, during the period from 1817 to 1917, "no fewer than eighty executive agreements were entered into by the United States looking toward the liquidation of claims of its citizens."[74] Occasionally, such agreements have been submitted to the Senate, but this has been the exception rather than the rule, especially since World War II.[75] In 1860, President Buchanan submitted a settlement agreement with Venezuela to the Senate for its advice and consent while noting that "usually it is not deemed necessary to consult the Senate in regard to similar instruments relating to private claims of small amount when the aggrieved parties are satisfied with the terms."[76]

In a 1983 decision, *Dames & Moore v. Regan,* the Supreme Court endorsed the president's authority to conclude settlement agreements.[77] In that case, President Carter entered into an agreement with Iran, known as the Algiers Accords, to settle the Iranian hostage crisis. Under the agreement, the United States agreed to suspend billions of dollars of pending claims against Iran and have them adjudicated in a new international tribunal to be established in The Hague in return for Iran's release of the hostages. While concluding that the president lacked specific statutory authorization for this action, the Court noted that there was "a longstanding practice" of presidential settlement of claims and that Congress had been supportive of this practice.

The scope of the president's power to settle American claims is not clear. The Court in *Dames & Moore* emphasized the "narrowness" of its decision, noting that the case involved a settlement that was "a necessary incident to the resolution of a major foreign policy dispute between our country and another, and where, as here, we can conclude that Congress acquiesced in the President's action." And the Court said that it was not deciding whether the president possesses "plenary power to settle claims, even as against foreign governmental entities."

In a 2003 decision, *American Insurance Association v. Garamendi,* the Court gave preemptive effect to executive agreements that President Clinton made with several countries for the settlement of Holocaust-related claims against private companies.[78] In its 5–4 decision, the Court broadly noted that "our cases have recognized that the President has authority to make 'executive agreements' with other countries, requiring no ratification by the Senate or approval by Congress, this power having been exercised since the early years of the Republic." And it said that "making executive agreements to settle claims of American nationals against foreign governments is a particularly longstanding practice."[79] Although disagreeing with the finding of preemption, the dissenting justices in *Garamendi* agreed with the majority's general claim about the power to settle claims by executive agreement.[80]

But in a 2008 decision, *Medellin v. Texas,* the Court described the executive branch's authority to settle claims in narrower terms.[81] In that case, the president attempted to reopen state criminal cases by issuing a memorandum directing compliance with a decision by the International Court of Justice. Even though this action would have resolved a dispute with Mexico, the Court reasoned that it was not supported by the historical practice of claims settlement. "The claims-settlement cases," the Court said, "involve a narrow set of circumstances: the making of executive agreements to settle civil claims between American citizens and foreign governments or foreign nationals." The Court explained that this presidential authority had been approved because it was supported by "particularly longstanding practice," something not true of the unilateral executive action in this case.

War and Military Affairs

Another category of sole executive agreements concerns the conduct of war and military affairs. It appears to have long been understood that, as Commander in Chief, the president has authority to make some agreements relating to this role. During the War of 1812, for example, President Madison made an agreement with Great Britain concerning the exchange of prisoners and their treatment.[82] Another, more complicated example is the Rush-Bagot agreement concluded by President Monroe in 1817, pursuant to which the United States and Great Britain agreed to limit naval armaments on the Great Lakes.[83] Monroe was unsure of whether this agreement required Senate approval. Nearly a year after concluding it, he sent it to the Senate, stating: "I submit it to the consideration of the Senate, whether this is such an arrangement as the Executive is competent to enter into, by the powers vested in it by the Constitution, or is such a one as requires the advice and consent of the Senate."[84] The Senate then approved the agreement, after it had already come into force.[85] The example is further complicated by the fact that, although Congress had not specifically authorized Monroe to make the agreement, it had previously authorized him to dismantle or sell armed vessels on the Great Lakes.[86]

In 1882, the executive branch made a sole executive agreement with Mexico to allow for the cross-border movement of troops in pursuit of hostile Indians, and it renewed this agreement in subsequent years. Later commenting on the agreement, the Supreme Court noted that, "while no act of Congress authorizes the executive department to permit the introduction of foreign troops, the power to give such permission without legislative assent was probably assumed to exist from the authority of the President as commander-in-chief of the military and naval forces of the United States."[87] More generally, presidents have often relied on their Commander in Chief authority as the basis for agreements with other nations concerning joint military exercises and operations.[88]

Presidents have also relied on their Commander in Chief authority to conclude armistice agreements. President McKinley did so, for example, at the end of the Spanish-American War. The terms of the agreement, which included Spain's relinquishment of sovereignty over Cuba and the cession of Puerto Rico to the United States, were later incorporated into a treaty agreed to by the Senate.[89] Fighting in World War I was brought to an end with armistice agreements concluded by the executive branch. A peace treaty was subsequently developed, but when the Senate failed to consent to it, a majority of Congress simply adopted a joint resolution declaring the war at an end.[90] The Nixon administration ended the Vietnam War in 1973 through a sole executive agreement.[91] The Biden administration ended the U.S. war in Afghanistan in 2021 through a nonbinding agreement that was not submitted to the Senate or to Congress.[92]

Some war-related agreements relate to the settlement of claims and thus overlap with that category of sole executive agreements. An example is the Boxer Indemnity Protocol, which the McKinley administration concluded (along with a number of other nations) in 1901 to resolve issues relating to the Boxer uprising in China, including China's payment of indemnity. A few years later, a commentator described this agreement as "probably the broadest exercise of executive authority in foreign affairs matters without the concurrence of the Senate."[93]

In 1940, the Franklin Roosevelt administration concluded the Hull-Lothian Agreement with Great Britain, pursuant to which the United States gave Britain fifty overage destroyers in return for long-term leases on British bases in the Western Hemisphere. In an opinion defending the agreement, Attorney General Robert Jackson acknowledged that "some negotiations involve commitments as to the future which carry an obligation to exercise powers vested in the Congress."[94] But he concluded that this agreement was constitutional, in part because it did not impose on the United States continuing obligations. He further noted that, although his analysis did not depend solely on the president's Commander in Chief power, that power "places upon [the president] a responsibility to use all constitutional authority which he may possess to provide adequate bases and stations for the utilization of the naval and air weapons of the United States at their highest efficiency in our defense."[95] Congress subsequently appropriated money for the construction of the bases.

Some of the agreements in this category have triggered controversy. In 1975, for example, the Senate's Office of Legislative Counsel objected to the defense and other commitments that the Ford administration made in agreements with Israel and Egypt, arguing that the commitments were sufficiently important that they should have been submitted to the Senate as treaties.[96] In response, the State Department Legal Adviser contended that "the choice of treaty or executive agreement is not amenable to precise rules of law."[97] This does not mean that the president's choice is "totally unfettered," the Legal Adviser insisted, because the president "is expected to adhere to the customs and practices which have developed since the conclusion of the first executive agreements in the early years of the Republic." But he resisted the suggestion that all "important" agreements had to be concluded as Article II treaties, noting that, "from the early days of the Republic, executive agreements have been concluded on matters of great national importance."

Recognition-Related Agreements

As discussed in Chapter 3, presidents have long exercised the power to recognize (or decline to recognize) foreign governments and their territories. These recognition decisions are sometimes accompanied by sole executive agreements that, for example, resolve outstanding claims between the United States and the recognized country. An especially noteworthy example is Franklin Roosevelt's recognition of the Soviet Union in 1933, which was reflected in a series of diplomatic notes known as the Roosevelt-Litvinov Agreement. In these notes, it was agreed that the Soviet Union would assign to the U.S. government its claims to property currently held by American nationals.[98]

The Supreme Court gave domestic legal effect to this agreement in *United States v. Belmont.*[99] In that case, a Russian company had deposited money with a private banker in New York before the Russian Revolution. The Soviet Union later purported to nationalize the worldwide assets of the company, including the money in New York. As a result of the Roosevelt-Litvinov Agreement, the U.S. government now sought to claim the money (which it intended to distribute to U.S. claimants). The banker's heirs argued, however, that the Soviet nationalization decree amounted to an unlawful confiscation of property and should not, as a matter of New York state law, be recognized by the courts. And if the Soviet Union did not have a valid claim to the money, the heirs contended, it could not have transferred ownership of the money to the U.S. government.

In rejecting this argument, the Court in *Belmont* first reasoned that the agreement implicitly "validat[ed], so far as this country is concerned, all acts of the Soviet Government here involved from the commencement of its existence." The Court also said that it "may not be doubted" that the president had the power to make the agreement, noting that "the Executive had authority to speak as the sole organ of [the U.S.] government." Emphasizing historical practice, the Court further explained that not all international agreements need to go through the Article II process: "An international compact, as this was, is not always a treaty which requires the participation of the Senate. There are many such compacts, of which a protocol, a *modus vivendi*, a postal convention, and agreements like that now under consideration are illustrations." Finally, the Court reasoned that a valid international agreement, regardless of whether it is an Article II treaty, preempts inconsistent state law in the United States.[100]

Modi Vivendi

Presidents have often concluded agreements, referred to as modi vivendi, that are designed to freeze a state of affairs in place pending further negotiation, arbitral resolution, or senatorial or congressional approval. For example, in 1860, the Fillmore administration made an agreement with Great Britain concerning the joint occupation of San Juan Island pending a final adjustment of the international boundary through arbitration. The Supreme Court of the Territory of Washington held that this agreement was proper, reasoning that "the power to make and enforce such a temporary convention respecting its own territory is a necessary incident to every national government, and inheres where the executive power is vested," and that Congress had "tacitly acquiesced" in the agreement.[101] In the late nineteenth and early twentieth centuries, the executive branch entered into various agreements with Great Britain concerning fishing rights, pending further negotiation.[102] In 1899, the executive branch entered into a modus vivendi with Great Britain concerning the Alaskan boundary, an agreement that lasted for four years, until there was a final determination by a joint commission that was established pursuant to a treaty.[103]

The precise scope of this modi vivendi category is uncertain, and it has not always been clear whether these agreements have been viewed as legally binding. In 1905, President Theodore Roosevelt made an agreement with the Dominican Republic to take over its customs houses so that European creditors would not seize them after it had defaulted on loans. When the Senate failed to promptly give its consent, he proceeded to administer it as a sole executive agreement.[104] Two years later, the Senate finally gave its approval. Meanwhile, there was an intense debate in the Senate over the constitutionality of Roosevelt's action.[105] Roosevelt's Secretary of War William Howard Taft also made agreements with Panama concerning details of the boundaries and operation of the canal zone there, arrangements that Congress eventually endorsed by statute. Taft later noted that this approach "was attacked vigorously in the Senate as a usurpation of the treaty-making power . . . but the *modus vivendi* continues as the practical arrangement."[106]

Executive Agreements "Plus"?

Sometimes the executive branch has suggested that it has the authority to conclude executive agreements to facilitate statutory enactments even if it is not specifically authorized to do so by such enactments. If so, these agreements might fall somewhere between sole executive agreements and congressional-executive agreements. The textual hook for such agreements might be the Take Care Clause, the idea being that making agreements is part of the authority that the president has in taking care that statutes are faithfully executed. Professors Dan Bodansky and Peter Spiro have labeled this category "executive agreements plus."[107]

It seems likely that the executive branch has relied on this theory in concluding some agreements, perhaps many of them. But it is difficult to know because the executive branch rarely if ever identifies when it is relying on the theory. As a result, it is difficult to discern the level of Congress's awareness of the practice, let alone its acceptance of it. The case for a gloss-based expansion of executive agreement authority along these lines is therefore thin. In part for this reason, Bodansky and Spiro describe the executive agreements plus practice as "in its nascency" and acknowledge that it is "not yet constitutionally entrenched."[108]

In 2010, a controversy arose that touched on this issue and showed that the matter was far from settled. The Obama administration announced that it was concluding a controversial multilateral agreement designed to enhance intellectual property enforcement—the Anti-Counterfeiting Trade Agreement Act (ACTA). The U.S. Trade Representative initially suggested that ACTA could be concluded as a sole executive agreement because it did not require changes in U.S. laws. In response, Senator Ron Wyden sent a letter to President Obama insisting that "regardless of whether the agreement requires changes in U.S. law . . . the executive branch lacks constitutional authority to *enter* a binding international agreement covering issues delegated by the Constitution to Congress' authority, absent congressional approval."[109]

State Department Legal Adviser Harold Koh responded to Wyden with a somewhat different rationale. Without specifying precisely what type of executive agreement it was, Koh emphasized that a 2008 statute, the Prioritizing Resources and Organization for Intellectual Property Act, had directed the executive branch to prepare a "joint strategic plan" detailing how the administration was "working with other countries to establish international standards and policies for the effective protection and enforcement of intellectual property rights."[110] ACTA, claimed Koh, "helps to answer that legislative call." A group of over fifty scholars contested this rationale in a letter to the Senate Finance Committee.[111] Wyden was also unpersuaded.[112] ACTA never took effect, so the claim was never tested.

Koh subsequently explained in a published lecture that the Legal Adviser's Office had "surveyed how the political branches have dealt with similar agreements in the past and found that Congress's call for executive action to protect intellectual property rights arose against the background of a long series of agreements on the specific question of intellectual property protection done in a similar fashion."[113] This amounted, he suggested, to a "quasi-constitutional custom"—"a widespread and consistent practice of Executive Branch activity that Congress, by its conduct, has essentially accepted." In support of this historical gloss-type claim, he relied heavily on the analysis in *Dames & Moore.* Since leaving government, Koh has argued more broadly, in terms akin to the executive agreements plus idea, that the executive branch can conclude an international agreement whenever it "determine[s] that the negotiated agreement fit[s] within the fabric of existing law, [is] fully consistent with existing law, and [does] not require any further legislation to implement."[114] Regardless of what one thinks of this specific claim, it seems likely that Koh is right that, as a matter of practice, it is too simplistic to think only in terms of three categories of executive agreements.[115]

If accepted, the executive agreements plus idea has the potential to substantially expand the president's unilateral authority to conclude binding international agreements. The broadest version of this idea would mean that presidents could make an agreement anytime they decided that doing so would help promote the policies in an existing statute. Given that there are statutes on almost every conceivable topic, this theory would come close to making the sole executive agreement a complete alternative to the treaty process, a result that would seem to be flatly inconsistent with constitutional text and structure.[116]

At least in its broadest form, the executive agreements plus idea has not been settled by practice. The executive branch has not clearly claimed such authority, and to the extent that it has implicitly relied on it at times, there is no indication that Congress has even been aware of this fact. Two other scholars and I reviewed decades of the executive branch's reporting of agreements to Congress, and we could not find support for even an implicit claim of authority to conclude agreements based merely on consistency with existing law.[117] That said, it does seem to be the case that the executive branch often liberally interprets statutory authority to conclude agreements, as was evident in the ACTA example.

Congressional Concerns and Regulation

In the late 1960s, Congress became concerned about two intersecting issues—unilateral presidential uses of force, and sole executive agreements. The topics were viewed as connected because presidents had made commitments to use force during the Vietnam War pursuant to sole executive agreements, some of which were secret.

In 1969, the Senate approved (by a vote of 70–16) the National Commitments Resolution, which stated that it was the sense of the Senate that a "national commitment" should result "only from affirmative action taken by the Legislative and Executive Branches of the United States Government by means of a treaty, statute, or concurrent resolution of both Houses of Congress specifically providing for such commitment."[118] In its report recommending adoption of the resolution, the Senate Foreign Relations Committee complained that "the traditional distinction between the treaty as the appropriate means of making significant political commitments and the executive agreement as the appropriate instrument for routine, nonpolitical agreements has substantially broken down."[119]

Concerns about the proliferation of executive agreements also surfaced in connection with the Nixon administration's effort to obtain the Senate's advice and consent to the Vienna Convention on the Law of Treaties. The convention addresses a wide range of issues concerning the formation, interpretation, and termination of international agreements and is generally consistent with U.S. practice on these issues. The Senate Foreign Relations Committee was concerned, however, about Article 46 of the Convention, which says that a party "may not invoke the fact that its consent to be bound by a treaty has been expressed in violation of a provision of its internal law regarding competence to conclude treaties as invalidating its consent unless that violation was manifest and concerned a rule of its internal law of fundamental importance." Fearing that this provision would further legitimize using executive agreements in lieu of treaties, the committee suggested that the United States include with its ratification an "understanding and interpretation" making clear that the U.S. Constitution's requirement of two-thirds Senate consent is a rule of internal law of fundamental importance. The executive branch objected to this formulation on the ground that it would needlessly call into question the commitments that the United States often makes through executive agreements, and the dispute was never resolved.[120] As a result, even though the convention has now been ratified by well over one hundred countries, the United States is not one of them.

The Senate again became agitated upon learning that the executive branch had concluded military base agreements with Portugal and Bahrain. The Senate passed a resolution urging the Nixon administration to submit the agreements to the Senate for its advice and consent,[121] but the administration declined to do so, noting that the agreements had already been concluded.

To address what it viewed as a lack of transparency in the conclusion of executive agreements, Congress in 1972 enacted the Case-Zablocki Act.[122] The act required that the executive branch transmit to Congress all nontreaty agreements within sixty days after they take effect. Although the act only mandated transparency and did not attempt to curtail the use of executive agreements, it was clear from the hearings that some senators perceived that their constitutional prerogatives were being undermined. As Senator Sam Ervin observed at the outset of the hearings, "the use of executive agreements as a substitute for treaties has spiraled in recent years, giving rise to increasing concern which has been voiced in Senate hearing rooms, on the Senate floor, and in the national press."[123]

The executive branch has since reported thousands of agreements to Congress pursuant to the Case-Zablocki Act. The reporting has often been late and incomplete, however, and Congress has amended this statute a number of times in an effort to improve compliance.[124] In 2022, Congress adopted more sweeping reforms that require faster and more detailed reporting and more comprehensive publication of executive agreements, as well as greater coordination within the executive branch.[125] Occasionally, Congress has imposed additional requirements for particular types of executive agreements, such as "report-and-wait" periods that allow Congress time to review the agreements before they take effect or requirements relating to the content of the agreements.[126]

Nonbinding Agreements

The Case-Zablocki Act, which requires the reporting of executive agreements to Congress, was long interpreted by the executive branch to apply only to agreements that are binding on the United States under international law. For a variety of reasons, however, the executive branch often concludes agreements with foreign nations that it does not consider binding. These agreements take many forms, including mutual declarations, joint communiques, and memoranda of understanding. It appears that the use of such nonbinding agreements has been growing in recent years and that they are increasingly being used in place of binding treaties and executive agreements.[127] Responding to this trend, Congress in 2022 amended the Case-Zablocki Act to require reporting and publication of nonbinding agreements that "could reasonably be expected to have a significant impact on the foreign policy of the United States."[128]

Discerning the history of nonbinding agreements is challenging. They are less likely than binding agreements to have been publicly reported. Moreover, the line between binding and nonbinding agreements is not always clear and sometimes is purposefully ambiguous. Given that there is often a lack of centralized enforcement of international agreements, it can be very difficult for observers to determine which ones are viewed as binding absent specific statements to that effect by the parties. Even determining the universe of "agreements" is challenging, given that diplomatic exchanges often involve informal understandings and promises.

There does not appear to have been much focus on executive authority to make nonbinding agreements until the early twentieth century. In 1899–1900, Secretary of State John Hay obtained agreements with France, Germany, Great Britain, Italy, Japan, and Russia concerning an "open door" policy for China and did not appear to conceive of them as legally binding. In 1907–1908, the United States made a "gentleman's agreement" with Japan relating to immigration, which lasted for nearly two decades but appears not to have been viewed as legally binding.

In the early 1900s, presidents sometimes responded to arguments that they had exceeded their authority in concluding agreements by insisting that the agreements were not legally binding or were binding only on them rather than the country. The agreements during the Theodore Roosevelt administration concerning the administration of the customs houses in Santo Domingo and the Panama Canal Zone, described above, were justified on this ground.[129] In 1919, in defending an agreement with Japan concerning certain issues relating to China, Secretary of State Lansing said that the agreement lacked "any binding force" on the United States and was "simply a declaration of . . . the policy of this Government, as long as the President and the State Department want to continue that policy."[130]

Another complication with respect to the line between binding and nonbinding agreements was that agreements concluded on the basis of congressional delegations of authority were sometimes alleged to be terminable at will by Congress, notwithstanding limitations on termination set forth in the agreements. For example, after Congress repealed the McKinley Tariff Act in 1894, the United States summarily terminated a tariff agreement with Brazil that had been concluded on the basis of the act, even though the agreement purported to require three months' notice. In response to complaints from Brazil, the executive branch contended that Brazil should have known that, because the agreement was based on a statutory delegation, it would last only as long as that delegation. The termination clause in the agreement, asserted the executive, should have been viewed "merely as a declaration of the manner in which [the executive] would, in the particular case, exercise the special power conferred on him."[131]

In the 1940s, presidents joined the Atlantic Charter and the Yalta and Potsdam Agreements—which concerned aims and principles relating to World War II and its aftermath—on their own authority. The executive branch suggested that all three were nonbinding under international law, but some countries and scholars disagreed with respect to the latter two.[132] In 1975, President Ford joined the Helsinki Accords, a Cold War agreement between Western and Soviet Bloc nations that included commitments to respect human rights, to pursue peaceful dispute resolution, and to avoid interfering in the internal affairs of other nations. This agreement, too, was described as nonbinding.[133]

In 1977, shortly before the expiration of the SALT I interim arms control agreement with the Soviet Union, the Carter administration made a nonbinding commitment not to take actions inconsistent with the agreement if the Soviet Union did the same.[134] The next day, the Soviet Union made the same commitment. The Carter administration made clear that the agreement was not intended to be legally binding and that, as a result, it did not need congressional approval.[135] In 1978, the United States and a number of other countries issued the Bonn Declaration concerning aircraft hijacking, which the State Department made clear was "not a legally binding commitment."

In 1982, the United States and China issued a joint communique concerning arms sales to Taiwan, which the State Department said was "not a treaty or agreement but a statement of future U.S. policy." In 1989, thirty-five nations, including the United States, issued a nonbinding Vienna Declaration concerning freedom of association, religion, travel, and emigration. Recent examples of important nonbinding high-level agreements include a multilateral agreement known as the Artemis Accords, which concerns the conditions for the safe and peaceful exploration of space; an Organisation for Economic Co-operation and Development/G20 agreement on global tax reform; and the New Atlantic Charter (a United States–United Kingdom agreement for promoting democratic values and institutions).[136]

The Iran Deal and the Paris Agreement

Two agreements concluded during the Obama administration—the Iran nuclear deal and the Paris Agreement on climate change—generated controversy, in part because of the way in which the administration relied on the distinction between binding and nonbinding agreements. In the Iran deal, known as the Joint Comprehensive Plan of Action, the United States and five other nations agreed to lift international and domestic sanctions against Iran in exchange for Iran's dismantling of its nuclear weapons development program. Majorities in the House and Senate appeared to oppose the deal, but President Obama was able to avoid the need for legislative approval by treating the agreement as nonbinding. He was then able to implement the U.S. pledges by exercising domestic authority that Congress had already conferred on the executive branch, both to waive domestic sanctions against Iran for up to a year at a time and to vote in the UN Security Council to lift the international sanctions.

As for the Paris Agreement on climate change, for the most part it was a binding agreement that the administration arguably had the authority to conclude on the basis of an earlier treaty—the United Nations Framework Convention on Climate Change. But the core new pledge in the agreement, for developed countries to undertake "economy-wide emission reduction targets," probably could not be justified by the treaty. Because this provision was made nonbinding—it said "should" rather than "shall"—the administration maintained that it did not need to obtain congressional approval. And then, in a move similar to the exercise of domestic waiver authorities for the Iran deal, the administration relied on regulations under the Clean Air Act and other domestic statutes to reduce greenhouse gas emissions to meet the pledge.

It appears that, as a matter of practice, presidents have essentially unfettered ability to commit the United States to nonbinding agreements (assuming they are genuinely nonbinding). This fact may render some of the constitutional debates discussed in this chapter less important. For example, the precise constitutional limits on sole executive agreements may not matter very much if presidents can accomplish the same thing through nonbinding agreements. As part of its 2022 reforms to the Case-Zablocki Act, noted above, Congress has insisted on transparency for "significant" nonbinding agreements, but it has not attempted to restrict their use.

Conclusion

Part of the reason for the substantial growth in executive agreements, especially after World War II, has been practical necessity: as the United States became a major world power, and as international affairs became more complex, the executive branch needed to conclude many more agreements than could reasonably be considered by the Senate. The House, moreover, insisted on a role in the making of international agreements, as such agreements increasingly addressed matters relating to congressional prerogatives. Both Congress and the executive branch responded by developing alternatives to the Article II treaty process. The institution most affected by this development is the Senate, which has lost some of its historic authority, but it, too, has largely acquiesced.

As with the other examples in this book, international law has tended to facilitate the shift in practice. International law views all binding international agreements made by the United States as "treaties" and does not express a preference for which process is used to conclude them. It is also very difficult to argue under international law that an agreement is invalid because it was concluded through an unconstitutional process. Indeed, as noted earlier in this chapter, this feature of international law is one reason that the Senate has balked at approving the Vienna Convention on the Law of Treaties. Furthermore, the executive branch's shift in recent years to greater use of nonbinding agreements takes advantage of the sharp binding-versus-nonbinding distinction in international law, even though the distinction may not make much of a practical difference in many contexts.

The constitutionality of the modern practice of executive agreements seems firmly entrenched, but it is difficult to defend from the perspective of originalism. Executive agreements are not specifically mentioned in the constitutional text, and they were rare early in U.S. history. Some originalist accounts of the Constitution suggest that executive agreements would have been viewed as constitutional for short-term or minor commitments,[137] but even if so, this does not capture the actual practice of the last 230 years. Many executive agreements have concerned ongoing commitments, and some of the most consequential agreements in modern history have been concluded as executive agreements.

The courts, meanwhile, have shown no inclination to disrupt the arrangements in this area that have been worked out by the political branches. Courts have allowed Congress broad leeway to delegate to the executive branch authority relating to foreign affairs, including with respect to international agreements; they have interpreted statutes against the backdrop of the modern executive agreements practice; and they have given even sole executive agreements preemptive force over state law. On other issues, courts have simply avoided weighing in.[138]

This is not to suggest that there are no constitutional issues surrounding executive agreements. Although it seems settled that congressional-executive agreements are generally constitutional, the practice does not yet support complete interchangeability of these instruments with Article II treaties. In addition, although it seems settled that presidents have some authority to conclude sole executive agreements—to resolve American claims against foreign governments, for example—the bounds of this authority are unclear and sometimes contested, and practice does not suggest anything like full interchangeability of these agreements with Article II treaties. Instead, these agreements likely need to be connected in some way to the president's independent constitutional authority, such as over recognition, military affairs, the settlement of claims, and the like.

Whatever the precise scope of the president's independent authority to conclude agreements, historical practice does not suggest that this authority is generally *exclusive*—that is, unregulable by Congress. As this chapter makes clear, Congress has often regulated executive agreements. To be sure, some agreements might be so bound up with exclusive executive authority that Congress could not validly regulate them—perhaps an agreement to recognize a particular regime, for example. But most agreements will not be like this. Claims settlement agreements, for example, do not appear to fall within the president's exclusive authority (and, indeed, the Court in *Dames & Moore* assumed that they did not). To take another example, even if the president had the independent authority to have the United States join the International Criminal Court (which he probably does not have), Congress could validly prohibit such unilateral action. And, indeed, it has done so.[139]

Professors Bruce Ackerman and David Golove have claimed that the shift to executive agreements occurred as a result of an informal constitutional amendment, the foundations of which they trace to the 1940s, especially the 1944 presidential election.[140] But, as this chapter has shown, the shift is much more longstanding and evolutionary. It is true, as Ackerman and Golove emphasize, that most ex post congressional-executive agreements have been concluded since World War II, but some of these agreements occurred earlier, and in any event, those agreements are a small part of the executive agreement landscape (only about one per year in recent decades).[141] The vast majority of executive agreements today are ex ante congressional-executive agreements, a type of agreement that can trace its lineage back to the 1790s. Moreover, the debates in the 1940s, while an important part of the history, did not in fact settle core issues, such as the extent to which congressional-executive agreements (whether ex ante or ex post) are interchangeable with Article II treaties.[142] Historical gloss provides a better account of constitutional development in this area.

5

TERMINATING TREATIES AND EXECUTIVE AGREEMENTS

AFTER MONTHS OF SECRET NEGOTIATIONS, PRESIDENT JIMMY CARTER announced in December 1978 that the United States would finally recognize the People's Republic of China (PRC), a commitment that was reflected in a joint communique (a type of executive agreement) between the two countries.[1] Separately, Carter announced that he would withdraw the United States from a mutual defense treaty with the Republic of China (ROC), which was based in Taiwan, a step that mainland China had insisted was a precondition for normal relations. Under the treaty, the United States and the ROC had pledged that if there were an attack in the western Pacific against the territory of either of them, they would "act to meet the common danger in accordance with [their] constitutional processes."[2] The treaty provided, however, that it could be terminated by either party after giving one year's notice, and Carter proceeded to give that notice. He did so without consulting with Congress, even though Congress had earlier that year expressed the view that "there should be prior consultation between the Congress and the executive branch" before any policy changes were adopted that would affect the continuation of the treaty.[3]

In large part because of the historical practice described in Chapters 3 and 4, there was little dispute that Carter had the constitutional authority to recognize the PRC and that he could do so through an executive agreement. But it was less clear whether he had the authority to withdraw the United States from the Taiwan treaty, which had been approved by the Senate decades earlier. In support of Carter's action, the State Department's Legal Adviser prepared a memorandum citing twelve purported instances in which presidents had terminated treaties unilaterally, and it included an appendix describing the "History of Treaty Termination by the United States."[4] But the question would get litigated all the way to the Supreme Court without receiving a definitive answer. Congress, meanwhile, passed the Taiwan Relations Act, an extensive statute regulating various aspects of U.S.-Taiwan relations—a statute that continues to play an important role in U.S. foreign policy.[5]

This chapter recounts how, starting in the early twentieth century, historical practice shifted from a shared treaty termination power to one exercised solely by the president.[6] Although this shift has occasionally generated controversy (such as in the Taiwan example), for the most part Congress and the Senate appear to have accepted it. The principal point of controversy is no longer whether the president can act alone but rather whether Congress can (if it wishes) restrict the president from doing so.

Lack of Specific Constitutional Text

The text of the Constitution describes the process for making treaties ("by and with the Advice and Consent of the Senate . . . provided two thirds of the Senators present concur"), but it says nothing about how they are to be terminated.[7] This was not a pressing issue at the Founding: when the Constitution was drafted, the United States was a party to only a handful of treaties, and it was not contemplating withdrawing from any of them. Moreover, although the international law at the time allowed for the termination of treaties under certain circumstances (such as in response to a material breach by the other party), treaties did not typically have discretionary withdrawal provisions akin to the one in the Taiwan defense treaty. Some scholars have argued that the Constitution's general vesting of executive power in the president would have been understood as implicitly conveying treaty termination authority,[8] but there is no direct evidence from the Founding to support this claim, and, as discussed in Chapter 2, reading the Vesting Clause as conveying such unstated powers is controversial.

One might argue that, by setting forth a process for making treaties, the Constitution implicitly requires resort to that process for their unmaking. After all, the Constitution sets forth a process for making statutes (majority approval by both houses of Congress and presentment to the president for signature or an override of the president's veto by a two-thirds vote in both houses), and it is understood that the same process is required for terminating statutes.[9] And treaties, like statutes, are referred to by the Constitution as part of the "Supreme Law of the Land." On the other hand, there are important differences between treaties and statutes. Congress can enact a statute over a president's veto, but it is assumed that no treaty can be concluded by the United States without the president's consent.[10] In addition, treaties, unlike statutes, create not only domestic law but also obligations for the country under international law.[11] Moreover, not all actions that require senatorial or congressional approval for their initiation require that approval for their termination. In particular, the president must obtain senatorial approval to make appointments of federal officers, but it is understood that the president does not need to obtain such approval to terminate such appointments.[12]

The president and Congress each have powers that are potentially relevant to this issue. As noted in Chapter 2, the president acts as the formal organ of communication for the United States, and treaty termination might fit naturally within that role. The president's recognition power, discussed in Chapter 3, also has potential connections to treaty termination—connections that were obvious with Carter's termination of the Taiwan treaty. In addition, the president has the responsibility to take care that the laws are faithfully executed, so when there are potential conflicts between statutes and treaties, it could be argued that terminating a treaty is part of taking care of executing the statute.

That said, the Constitution gives Congress the power to declare war, and this power is potentially relevant to treaty terminations in two respects: some treaty terminations would have been considered a basis for war at the time of the Founding, and war might cause (or provide a legal basis for) some treaties to be suspended or terminated.[13] It has also long been recognized that Congress has the authority to enact statutes that override the domestic effect of treaties; while not precisely the same thing as terminating a treaty, Congress's ability to override the domestic effect of a treaty might be thought to give it some authority over termination.[14] Among other things, the existence of legislation inconsistent with a treaty may prompt the president to withdraw from a treaty to avoid an ongoing breach, and presidents might even view such action as required by their constitutional duty to take care that laws are faithfully executed. Congress could also potentially use its control over appropriations to force a termination—for example, by refusing to fund actions that would be required for implementation of a treaty.

Congressional Involvement

The United States first acted to terminate a treaty in 1798, and it acted pursuant to congressional direction. On the eve of war with France, Congress passed a statute providing that four U.S.-French treaties "shall not henceforth be regarded as legally obligatory on the government or citizens of the United States."[15] Although Thomas Jefferson later cited this example as the proper method of treaty termination,[16] it was the only time in history in which the full Congress acted to terminate a treaty directly. Congress's action in this instance can be seen as connected to its authority to declare war, even though Congress merely authorized naval actions against France and did not formally declare war.

During the nineteenth century, although Congress did not act to directly effectuate treaty terminations, it continued to be involved in them. In 1846, for example, President Polk sought congressional authorization for the termination of a treaty with Great Britain relating to the two countries' joint occupation of the Oregon Territory.[17] In response, Congress passed a joint resolution authorizing Polk "at his discretion" to terminate the treaty.[18] During consideration of the resolution, there was substantial debate in Congress over whether it was proper for the House of Representatives to be involved in the issue.[19] Most of those who spoke seemed to think that it was proper, but several members of the House issued a minority report arguing that, except when a treaty is being terminated pursuant to a declaration of war, authorization of treaty termination properly should come from a supermajority of the Senate, not the full Congress.[20] In any event, after Congress had acted, the Secretary of State informed the U.S. ambassador to Great Britain that "Congress have spoken their will upon the subject, in their joint resolution; and to this it is his (the President's) and your duty to conform."[21] Before the expiration of the notice period, however, the United States and Great Britain negotiated a new treaty to supersede the one that the United States had acted to terminate.[22]

Congress continued to direct treaty terminations without triggering constitutional controversy. In 1865, Congress passed a joint resolution calling for the termination of a treaty with Great Britain concerning trade with Canada and "charging the President with the communication of such notice."[23] The Secretary of State subsequently conveyed the notice.[24] In 1874, Congress passed a joint resolution stating that a commercial treaty with Belgium was no longer in the U.S. interest and should be terminated, and it "authorized" the president to convey that notice to Belgium, which the Grant administration immediately did.[25] In 1883, Congress "directed" the president to terminate various articles in a treaty with Great Britain, and President Arthur subsequently terminated the articles.[26] In 1915, Congress, in the Seaman's Act, "requested and directed" President Wilson to give notice of termination of various treaty obligations inconsistent with the act, and Wilson proceeded to do so.[27]

Occasionally, the Senate, but not the full Congress, was involved in authorizing termination. In 1855, a dispute arose between the United States and Denmark over Denmark's insistence that U.S. vessels pay dues when sailing between the North and Baltic Seas. In response, President Pierce announced that he thought that the United States should withdraw from an 1826 Treaty of Friendship, Commerce, and Navigation with Denmark that allowed the tolls.[28] The

Senate passed a resolution authorizing the president to give notice of termination, and the president did so "in pursuance of the authority conferred by a resolution of the Senate."[29] Some members of Congress objected on the ground that the full Congress should be involved in the termination of treaties, just as it is involved in the termination of statutes. The Senate then asked its Committee on Foreign Relations to consider the matter. The committee concluded that action by the president and Senate was sufficient, at least where, as here, the treaty specifically provided for unilateral withdrawal.[30] "So far as the 'practice of the government' is concerned," said the committee, "there is nothing to question the sufficiency of the notice that has been given to Denmark to terminate the treaty."[31]

In a few instances, congressional directives led to constitutional conflict, but not because treaty termination was thought to be an exclusively presidential function. In 1879, President Hayes vetoed an immigration bill on the ground that it was trying to get him to partially terminate a treaty. In the bill, Congress directed the president to terminate two provisions in a treaty with China relating to Chinese immigration. In his veto message, President Hayes conceded that Congress had the authority to terminate a treaty and in fact said that this was "free from controversy."[32] But he pointed out that the bill called for the abrogation only of *parts* of a treaty and argued that "the power of making new treaties or modifying existing treaties is not lodged by the Constitution in Congress, but in the President, by and with the advice and consent of the Senate."

In 1920, Congress in the Jones Act "authorized and directed" the president to terminate within ninety days various treaty obligations that disallowed the United States from imposing discretionary customs duties and tonnage fees.[33] President Wilson refused to comply with the directive, maintaining that Congress did not have the constitutional authority to compel this action.[34] Like Hayes in the earlier episode, Wilson avoided arguing that Congress could not direct the president to terminate treaties. Rather, his objection was that the Act would have the president partially terminate treaties, whereas the treaties in question did not allow for such partial termination.[35]

Steps toward Unilateralism

On a few occasions in the nineteenth and early twentieth centuries, presidents took what might be viewed as half steps toward unilateral action, without directly challenging the need for congressional involvement. In 1864, President Lincoln sought to terminate the Great Lakes Agreement with Great Britain (also known as the Rush-Bagot Agreement). The Agreement limited the naval military presence of the United States on the lakes, and Lincoln was concerned about Confederate raids from Canada.[36] A resolution that would authorize the termination passed the House but failed in the Senate. Nevertheless, the Lincoln administration gave notice to Britain that the United States was withdrawing from the treaty. Congress then passed a joint resolution "adopt[ing] and ratif[ying]" the termination "as if the same had been authorized by Congress."[37] There was substantial debate, however, over the propriety of Lincoln's action.[38] Ultimately, Lincoln decided to rescind the notice of termination after further negotiation with Great Britain, so it never took effect.

In 1876, President Grant informed Congress that Great Britain was not complying with an extradition provision in a treaty, and he stated that "it is for the wisdom of Congress to determine whether the article of the treaty relating to extradition is to be any longer regarded as obligatory on the Government of the United States or as forming part of the supreme law of the land."[39] In the meantime, he indicated that he would not comply with extradition requests from Great Britain under the treaty "without an expression of the wish of Congress that I should do so." In other words, he acted to suspend the operation of the treaty on his own authority, subject to congressional override. Extradition by the United States under the treaty was then suspended for six months until the dispute with Great Britain was resolved.

Another example of somewhat unilateral presidential action occurred in 1911, when President Taft gave notice to Russia of a termination of a commercial treaty. In response to Russia's mistreatment of American Jews, the House of Representatives had passed a strongly worded resolution demanding termination of the treaty, and the resolution was thought likely to pass in the Senate. Taft, who had been reluctant to terminate the treaty at all, was concerned that the harsh tone of the House resolution would needlessly offend Russia. He therefore quickly communicated his own statement of termination to Russia and submitted that statement to the Senate "with a view to its ratification and approval."[40] The Senate Foreign Relations Committee proposed a resolution stating that the notice of termination was "adopted and ratified," and this resolution was subsequently passed by both houses of Congress (with the vote in the Senate being unanimous).[41] The discussion in Congress primarily concerned whether the Senate or the full Congress should be involved in approving the termination, not whether the president had a unilateral power of termination.

These episodes are closer to presidential unilateralism than situations in which the president obtains advance authorization for a treaty termination. Nevertheless, during the nineteenth century there was a general understanding that congressional or senatorial approval was required for the termination of U.S. treaties.

Congress or the Senate were almost always involved in treaty terminations, and presidents generally acted as if they needed such involvement. Lincoln's initially unilateral action in 1864 was potentially contrary to this understanding, but it was an outlier and generated constitutional criticism in Congress rather than acquiescence. Grant's action in 1876 might have suggested some unilateral authority to *suspend* a treaty obligation, but this action was embedded within an acknowledgment of the need for congressional approval of termination. Tellingly, in the digests of international practice prepared by the executive branch in the late nineteenth century, the materials quoted relating to treaty termination referred only to termination by Congress.[42]

Scholars during this period also generally assumed that presidents did not have a unilateral power of treaty termination. This was uniformly true during the nineteenth century, and it was generally true even during the first two decades of the twentieth century. Charles Butler's highly regarded treatise on the U.S. treaty-making power, published in 1902, noted that treaties could be abrogated "by Congressional action in several different methods" and did not seem to contemplate termination by unilateral presidential action.[43] Similarly, Edward Corwin, in his 1917 book, *The President's Control of Foreign Relations,* stated: "All in all, it appears that legislative precedent, which moreover is generally supported by the attitude of the Executive, sanctions the proposition that the power of terminating the international compacts to which the United States is party belongs, as a prerogative of sovereignty, to Congress alone."[44] And Quincy Wright, in his well-regarded 1922 treatise on foreign relations law, expressed the view that the president "ought not to act without consent either of Congress or of the Senate, except in extraordinary circumstances."[45]

The Rise of Presidential Unilateralism

The first instance in which a president proceeded to terminate treaty provisions without even after-the-fact congressional or senatorial approval appears to have been in 1899, when the McKinley administration terminated clauses in an 1850 commercial treaty with Switzerland.[46] McKinley's action need not be viewed as purely unilateral, however, given that he was responding to a potential conflict between the treaty and a federal statute. As discussed in Chapter 4, the Dingley Tariff Act of 1897 had authorized the president to negotiate reciprocal trade agreements, and, pursuant to the Act, the United States had concluded such an agreement with France. Switzerland contended that it was automatically entitled to the benefit of the concessions granted to France because of most-favored-nation provisions in the 1850 treaty. But granting it such concessions, without obtaining in return concessions similar to the ones given by the French, would have been contrary to longstanding U.S. trade policy, including the policy of Congress reflected in the Tariff Act.[47]

Despite the potentially limited nature of this precedent, presidential treaty termination became the norm during the next several decades. In 1909, at the outset of the Taft administration, the Solicitor for the State Department wrote an internal memorandum suggesting that it was constitutionally permissible for the president to act unilaterally in terminating a treaty.[48] The memorandum stated that, although presidential action pursuant to a congressional directive might be the "most effective and unquestionable method" for terminating a treaty, the president also had the option under U.S. law of acting either in conjunction with the Senate or through "notice given by the President upon his own initiative without either a resolution of the Senate or the joint resolution of the Congress." In support of the last option, the memorandum noted that there had been one instance of unilateral presidential termination of a treaty, namely the 1899 termination of the provisions in the Swiss treaty. The memorandum concluded that the choice of which method to use for terminating a treaty "would seem to depend either upon the importance of the international question or upon the preference of the Executive."

In 1927, the Coolidge administration, without authorization or subsequent approval from Congress or the Senate, withdrew the United States from a convention with Mexico to prevent smuggling. The administration explained that the United States had no commercial treaty with Mexico and that "it is not deemed advisable to continue in effect an arrangement which might in certain contingencies bind the United States to cooperation for the enforcement of laws or decrees relating to the importation of commodities of all sorts into another country with which this Government has no arrangement, by treaty or otherwise, safeguarding American commerce against possible discrimination."[49]

Unilateral presidential terminations subsequently became more common in the administration of Franklin Roosevelt, although some of these terminations, like McKinley's 1899 termination of provisions in the Swiss treaty, were because of potential conflicts with trade legislation. In 1933, the executive branch, without authorization or subsequent approval from Congress or the Senate, withdrew the United States from a convention abolishing import and export restrictions, because of (among other things) alleged conflicts between the convention and the new National Industrial Recovery Act.[50] Also in 1933, Roosevelt unilaterally announced the termination of an extradition treaty with Greece after Greece had refused to extradite Samuel Insull, an American business magnate who was accused of fraud and antitrust violations.[51] After Greece forced Insull to leave the country and negotiated a protocol to the extradition treaty, however, Roosevelt withdrew the notice.

In 1936, the Roosevelt administration withdrew the United States from a commercial treaty with Italy. While acknowledging that "the question as to the authority of the Executive to terminate treaties independently of the Congress or of the Senate is in a somewhat confused state," the State Department observed in a memorandum that "no settled rule or procedure has been followed."[52] It also noted that there was a potential conflict between the treaty with Italy and a 1934 trade statute and that, if the treaty were not terminated, the president could "be placed in the position of having to choose between the execution of the act and observance of the treaty." The memorandum claimed that this situation was "closely analogous" to the termination of provisions in the Swiss treaty in 1899.

Because many of the early twentieth-century presidential terminations were based on potential conflicts with statutes, these actions would not necessarily have been understood as fully unilateral in nature. By the late 1930s, however, the executive branch was increasingly asserting a purely unilateral authority. In 1939, the Roosevelt administration, after resolutions had been introduced in both houses of Congress supporting withdrawal, announced that the United States was terminating a commercial treaty with Japan. In connection with this decision, the State Department argued that the president had unilateral termination authority, reasoning that "the power to denounce a treaty inheres in the President of the United States in his capacity as Chief Executive of a sovereign state."[53] The Department claimed that its conclusion was in accord with "the general spirit" of the Supreme Court's 1936 decision in *United States v. Curtiss-Wright Export Corporation* (discussed in Chapter 2), in which the Court referred to "the very delicate, plenary and exclusive power of the President as the sole organ of the federal government in the field of international relations."

Two years later, Roosevelt suspended, for the duration of World War II, the International Load Lines Convention (which regulated ocean shipping) after his Attorney General, Francis Biddle, advised him that "the convention may be declared inoperative or suspended by the President."[54] Biddle also noted, however, that, since "it is not proposed that the United States denounce the convention under [the withdrawal clause in the treaty], nor that it be otherwise abrogated. . . . action by the Senate or by the Congress is not required." The opinion thus seemed to suggest that a full termination of a treaty, as opposed to a suspension, would require legislative action. Nevertheless, the Roosevelt administration terminated another treaty unilaterally in 1944—a protocol relating to a Latin American trademark treaty—citing the treaty's general ineffectiveness.[55] By the 1940s, there was also increased scholarly support for a unilateral presidential termination authority (often by the same scholars who supported presidential authority to conclude executive agreements in lieu of treaties).[56]

The 1950s saw several additional unilateral presidential terminations, usually in low-profile situations that did not generate much attention, such as the Truman administration's withdrawal of the United States from a whaling convention and the Eisenhower administration's termination of both a convention relating to the classification of merchandise and a Treaty of Friendship, Commerce, and Navigation with El Salvador.[57] The Eisenhower administration also entered into a sole executive agreement in 1958 with Morocco to end a treaty relating to the management of a lighthouse in that country.[58]

A 1958 memorandum from the State Department's Deputy Assistant Legal Adviser for Treaty Affairs, William Whittington, noted that, although "matters of policy or special circumstances may make it appear to be advisable or necessary to obtain the concurrence or support of the Congress or the Senate," in practice treaties have been terminated in a variety of ways, including through unilateral presidential action.[59] The memorandum also asserted that, at least for a self-executing treaty containing a withdrawal clause, "it is now generally considered that . . . it is proper for the Executive acting alone to take the action necessary to terminate or denounce the treaty." Attached to the memorandum were appendices listing the various treaty terminations in U.S. history and the ways they were carried out.

The practice of unilateral terminations continued during the 1960s. In 1962, the Kennedy administration terminated a commercial treaty with Cuba as part of the United States' embargo policy after the Cuban Revolution.[60] In 1965, the Johnson administration gave notice that the United States was withdrawing from the Warsaw Convention, which governs liability for international air carriers, but retracted the withdrawal shortly before the notice period expired.[61]

Terminating the Taiwan Treaty

The presidential treaty termination that has generated the most constitutional controversy is the one mentioned at the outset of this chapter: President Carter's termination of a mutual defense treaty with Taiwan in the late 1970s. Many in Congress, especially Republicans, disagreed with Carter's decision as a matter of policy.

Several resolutions were proposed in Congress, including one sponsored by Senator Harry Byrd that provided that it was "the sense of the Senate that approval of the U.S. Senate is required to terminate any mutual defense treaty between the United States and another nation."[62] The Senate Foreign Relations

Committee rejected the approach of the Byrd Resolution and reported out instead a resolution that would have recognized fourteen grounds for unilateral presidential action to terminate treaty obligations, including the existence of a withdrawal clause like the one in the Taiwan treaty.[63] After it reached the Senate floor, however, the Senate (on a vote of 59–35) substituted for its consideration the original Byrd Resolution, after Byrd's motion for substitution was supported by a number of senators who expressed the view that the president should not have unilateral power over treaty termination.[64] But the Senate never voted on this resolution.

Meanwhile, former Senator Barry Goldwater, along with a group of eight current senators and sixteen members of the House, sued President Carter in the federal district court in Washington, DC, seeking declaratory and injunctive relief to prevent him from terminating the Taiwan treaty. The district court held in favor of the plaintiffs, reasoning that "termination must receive the approval of two-thirds of the United States Senate or a majority of both houses of Congress for it to be effective."[65] But the court of appeals reversed.[66] In addition to emphasizing the president's role as "sole organ" in foreign relations, the court noted that the historical practice was varied and that there was no past instance in which "a treaty [has] been continued in force over the opposition of the President." The court also emphasized that Carter had acted pursuant to a withdrawal clause in the treaty and reasoned that "the President's authority . . . is at its zenith when the Senate has consented to a treaty that expressly provides for termination on one year's notice, and the President's action is the giving of notice of termination." Judge MacKinnon issued a lengthy dissent, focused especially on the history of treaty terminations, contending that "congressional participation in termination has been the overwhelming historical practice."

The plaintiffs appealed to the Supreme Court, but a majority of the Court declined to resolve the dispute. Four justices concluded that the dispute presented a political question, and Justice Powell deemed the suit to be institutionally unripe because Congress had not seriously attempted to stop the termination.[67] The Court's dismissal of the case effectively ended the controversy.[68]

Meanwhile, Congress enacted (and Carter signed into law) the Taiwan Relations Act, which states, among other things, that U.S. laws will continue to apply to Taiwan in the same manner in which they would have applied before Carter's recognition of the PRC and that "Congress approves the continuation in force of all treaties" between the United States and Taiwan "until terminated in accordance with law" (without taking a position on how that might be accomplished).[69] The Act further states that the United States will provide to Taiwan "such defense articles and defense services in such quantity as may be necessary to enable

Taiwan to maintain a sufficient self-defense capability" and that the United States would "consider any effort to determine the future of Taiwan by other than peaceful means . . . a threat to the peace and security of the Western Pacific area and of grave concern to the United States."[70] Since then, instead of a treaty commitment to defend Taiwan in the event that it is attacked by China, the United States has pursued an approach of "strategic ambiguity."[71] Congress has also enacted other laws relating to Taiwan. In 2004, for example, it directed the executive branch to support observer status for Taiwan in the World Health Organization.[72] In 2023, it enacted a law purporting to regulate the negotiation of trade agreements with Taiwan.[73]

Subsequent Treaty Terminations

In the years since the controversy over the termination of the Taiwan treaty, the United States has terminated dozens of treaties, and almost all of these terminations have been accomplished by unilateral presidential action. In 1985, for example, the Reagan administration gave notice of its termination of a Treaty of Friendship, Commerce, and Navigation with Nicaragua, and the treaty terminated the following year.[74] And in 1995, President Clinton gave notice of the termination of a tax treaty with Malta.[75] In 2002, the State Department Legal Adviser's Office listed twenty-three bilateral treaties and seven multilateral treaties that had been terminated by presidential action since termination of the Taiwan treaty.[76] Since then, there have been at least a dozen more such terminations.

Most of these terminations do not appear to have generated controversy. An exception is President George W. Bush's announcement in 2002 that he was withdrawing the United States from the Anti-ballistic Missile (ABM) Treaty with Russia.[77] In an op-ed article, Professor Bruce Ackerman contended that Bush was acting unconstitutionally and asked rhetorically, "If President Bush is allowed to terminate the ABM treaty, what is to stop future presidents from unilaterally taking America out of NATO or the United Nations?"[78] Thirty-two members of Congress brought suit challenging the constitutionality of the termination of the ABM Treaty, but the suit was dismissed for lack of standing and under the political question doctrine.[79] The Justice Department's Office of Legal Counsel (OLC) issued a memorandum concluding that the president had the authority to suspend or terminate the treaty.[80] While acknowledging that Congress and the Senate have sometimes been involved in treaty terminations, the memorandum contended that "these examples represent the workings of practical politics, rather than acquiescence in a constitutional regime."[81]

After that, the Bush administration terminated a protocol to a consular convention in 2005 and a tax treaty with Sweden in 2007.[82] In 2016, the Obama administration unilaterally initiated withdrawal from a multilateral fisheries treaty but rescinded the notice of withdrawal after the treaty was renegotiated.[83]

President Trump was especially aggressive in terminating international agreements, withdrawing or initiating withdrawal from about ten international agreements, including five Senate-approved treaties.[84] He also withdrew the United States from both the Iran nuclear deal and the Paris Agreement on climate change, both of which (as discussed in Chapter 4) were concluded unilaterally by President Obama. But the Biden administration has also acted unilaterally in terminating international agreements. In 2021, it initiated the termination of several asylum cooperation agreements that the Trump administration had concluded as executive agreements with Central American nations.[85] And in 2022, it initiated withdrawal from a tax treaty with Hungary that had been concluded by the Carter administration with the Senate's advice and consent.[86]

Occasionally, Congress has been involved in modern treaty terminations. In 1976, it authorized the Ford administration to renegotiate certain fisheries treaties and expressed the sense of Congress that the United States should withdraw from these treaties if they were not renegotiated within a reasonable time.[87] In 1986, it passed a law, over President Reagan's veto, mandating the termination of an air services agreement and a tax treaty with South Africa because of that country's apartheid practices, as part of a package of U.S. sanctions.[88] The Reagan administration complied and provided the required notice of termination.[89] Nevertheless, most treaty terminations since *Goldwater* have been accomplished through unilateral presidential action.

Terminating Executive Agreements

There seems to be little dispute that presidents can unilaterally withdraw the United States from sole executive agreements. After all, these agreements, as discussed in Chapter 4, are made on the president's own authority. If Congress has no role in making them, it is difficult to argue that it needs to be involved in their unmaking.[90]

For similar reasons, there is little dispute that the president can unilaterally terminate nonbinding agreements. These agreements are made unilaterally by the executive branch and are terminable at will under international law. Moreover, unlike for binding executive agreements, Congress until recently did not even attempt to regulate the reporting and publication of nonbinding agreements.

There was little constitutional dispute, therefore, that President Trump had the authority to withdraw the United States from the Iran nuclear deal, despite the highly consequential nature of this action.[91] As discussed in Chapter 4, the deal had been concluded by the Obama administration as a nonbinding agreement precisely to avoid the need for congressional approval.

But what about congressional-executive agreements—that is, agreements that were concluded on the basis of either ex ante congressional authorization or ex post congressional approval? Is the president's authority to terminate such agreements narrower (or broader) than their authority to terminate Senate-approved treaties? On the international plane, congressional-executive agreements are considered treaties just as much as agreements approved by the Senate. And these agreements, like Senate-approved treaties, often contain withdrawal clauses. All of this might suggest that the president's withdrawal authority is the same for these agreements as it is for Senate-approved treaties.[92]

That said, congressional-executive agreements more closely resemble statutes in terms of their process (two houses of Congress and presidential signature), so it might be argued that, like statutes, they should be terminable only through a new statute. There is also less historical practice of presidential termination of congressional-executive agreements as compared with Senate-approved treaties, so it might be argued that the president has less gloss-based authority for terminating the former.[93] Or, on the other hand, the very fact that the rise of congressional-executive agreements is itself grounded in historical practice (as discussed in Chapter 4) may suggest that there should be even greater constitutional flexibility with respect to withdrawal.

What historical practice there is, which spans many presidential administrations and is bipartisan, tends to favor a unilateral presidential authority to withdraw from congressional-executive agreements. For example, in the 1950s and 1960s, presidents terminated multiple ex ante congressional-executive agreements relating to trade by obtaining the consent of the trading partner but not of Congress.[94] In 1955, President Eisenhower terminated a trade agreement with Ecuador.[95] In 1982, President Reagan terminated a trade agreement with Argentina because of a material breach.[96] In 2004, the Bush administration terminated a textile trade agreement with Japan and an agreement with the European Union on trade in civil aircraft.[97]

In addition, the United States has joined a number of international organizations through ex post congressional-executive agreements, and presidents have sometimes unilaterally withdrawn the United States from the agreements. For example, the United States joined the International Labour Organization in 1934 through a congressional-executive agreement. In 1975, the Ford administration unilaterally withdrew the United States from the organization, and in 1980, the Carter administration unilaterally had the United States rejoin.[98] Similarly, the United States became a member of the United Nations Educational, Scientific and Cultural Organization (UNESCO) through a congressional-executive agreement in 1946, and the Reagan administration unilaterally withdrew the United States in 1984.[99] After the Bush administration rejoined the organization in 2003, the Trump administration once again announced a U.S. withdrawal.[100] Biden, in turn, has taken steps to have the United States rejoin. In 2020, President Trump initiated U.S. withdrawal from the World Health Organization, which the United States had joined in 1948 through a congressional-executive agreement, but President Biden revoked the notice of withdrawal before it took effect.[101]

To be sure, Congress has occasionally played a role in the termination of congressional-executive agreements. In the Payne-Aldrich Tariff Act of 1909, Congress authorized and directed the president to terminate congressional-executive agreements that had been made under the authority of the earlier Dingley Tariff Act of 1897.[102] In 1923, Congress authorized termination of executive agreements relating to the Panama Canal (which had been concluded unilaterally by President Taft and then approved by Congress).[103] In the Trade Agreements Extension Act of 1951, Congress directed the president to "take such action as is necessary to suspend, withdraw or prevent the application of" concessions contained in prior trade agreements regulating imports from the Soviet Union and "any nation or area dominated or controlled by the foreign government or foreign organization controlling the world Communist movement."[104] In the Trade Expansion Act of 1962, Congress mandated that agreements concluded under authority of the Act would be subject to termination upon notice at the end of not more than three years and, if not terminated then, would be subject to termination upon not more than six months' notice.[105] Moreover, one of the agreements with South Africa that Congress directed President Reagan to terminate in the 1980s (as discussed above) was a congressional-executive agreement. But most terminations of congressional-executive agreements have occurred through unilateral presidential action.[106]

Some commentators have argued that congressional-executive agreements relating to trade and commerce cannot be terminated by the president alone because they concern subject areas within the exclusive authority of Congress,[107] but this argument is unpersuasive. There may well be some powers that are exclusive to Congress and thus that cannot be exercised through other means. The most likely example is the power to appropriate money from the Treasury. But the regulation of commerce has never been thought to be exclusive in that way, and, as a result, treaties have regulated commercial matters throughout American history.[108] Relatedly, many presidential treaty terminations have involved commercial treaties.[109]

There was renewed academic debate about this issue after President Trump began suggesting that he might withdraw the United States from the North American Free Trade Agreement (NAFTA).[110] As discussed in Chapter 4, NAFTA was a significant trade agreement between the United States, Canada, and Mexico that President George H. W. Bush had concluded in 1992 as a congressional-executive agreement and that Congress had approved and implemented the following year during the Clinton administration. NAFTA provided that any party could withdraw from the agreement after giving six months' notice.

In 2018, OLC published a memorandum concluding that the president had the authority to invoke the NAFTA withdrawal clause.[111] OLC emphasized the modern historical practice of presidential unilateralism in treaty terminations, and it relied extensively on my scholarship on this topic. It noted that the presidential termination of treaties had become the norm in the modern era and that many of the Senate-approved treaties that presidents have terminated have concerned commercial and trade matters. And it argued that there was no reason to conclude that the president had less authority in this regard for congressional-executive agreements.[112] Ultimately, the question of whether Trump could withdraw the United States from NAFTA was never tested because he managed to negotiate a new agreement with Canada and Mexico that superseded NAFTA (and that was approved by Congress).

Importantly, as OLC has acknowledged, the power to terminate a congressional-executive agreement does not give the president the power to terminate legislation that implements that agreement. As noted earlier, it is settled that a statute can be terminated only through another statute. This does not necessarily mean, however, that a statute implementing an agreement will continue to operate after the agreement is terminated. If Congress has expressly or implicitly made the operation of the statute conditional on the continued operation of the agreement, the statute will cease to have effect upon termination. If Trump had withdrawn the United States from NAFTA, for example, many of the provisions in the implementing legislation (such as certain trade concessions and provisions for dispute resolution) likely would have become inoperative because they were implicitly conditioned on the agreement remaining in effect. For many other trade agreements, the implementing legislation specifically states that it will cease to have effect if the agreement is terminated.[113]

Is This Power Exclusive?

Most debates in this area have concerned whether the president has the authority to act unilaterally in terminating treaties or other agreements. That is, the debates have concerned whether this is an *independent* power of the president that can be exercised without authorization or approval from the Senate or Congress. Because Congress has rarely acted to restrict presidential treaty terminations, the issue of whether a presidential treaty termination power is exclusive has rarely arisen. This changed in 2020.

During his presidency, Donald Trump withdrew the United States from a number of international agreements, and he threatened to withdraw the United States from others. Members of Congress became especially concerned when he began suggesting that he might withdraw the United States from NATO.[114] The United States has been a party to the North Atlantic Treaty that established NATO since 1949, and maintaining this alliance has been a central part of the United States' post–World War II foreign policy. Some members of Congress also became concerned about Trump's contemplated withdrawal from the Open Skies Treaty, a multilateral agreement that allowed for observation flights over the territories of the other parties (including Russia).

In 2019, Congress passed legislation designed to limit withdrawal from both NATO and the Open Skies Treaty. As for NATO, Congress disallowed the use of funds to "suspend, terminate, or provide notice of denunciation of the North Atlantic Treaty."[115] With respect to the Open Skies Treaty, the legislation required the Secretary of State to provide notice to Congress at least 120 days before officially notifying parties to the Open Skies Treaty that the United States intended to withdraw.[116] In signing this legislation, President Trump "reiterate[d] the longstanding understanding of the executive branch that these types of provisions encompass only actions for which such advance certification or notification is feasible and consistent with the President's exclusive constitutional authorities as Commander in Chief and as the sole representative of the Nation in foreign affairs."[117]

In May 2020, the Trump administration announced that it was initiating withdrawal from the Open Skies Treaty, without having first given notice to Congress, and the withdrawal became effective six months later, in November 2020. The following month, OLC released an opinion reasoning that Congress's 120-day notice requirement could be disregarded because it "unconstitutionally interferes with the President's exclusive authority to execute treaties and to conduct diplomacy, a necessary incident of which is the authority to execute a treaty's termination right."[118] OLC contended that the president has control over U.S. diplomacy and that this includes the communication of treaty withdrawals. The president's control over communicating a treaty withdrawal, OLC next asserted, "necessarily includes discretion to determine whether and when he should do so." This conclusion, however, is not compelled by the premise, since it is logically possible to separate policymaking authority from communication authority.[119] OLC relied heavily on the Supreme Court's *Zivotofsky* decision, which, as discussed in Chapter 3, held that the president's authority to recognize foreign sovereigns and their territories is exclusive and thus cannot be limited by Congress.

OLC claimed that its conclusion was "reinforced by the historical practice of the United States' withdrawal from treaties." This claim, however, is questionable. As we have seen, Congress was heavily involved in treaty terminations for over a hundred years and has been intermittently involved since that time. Moreover, before President Trump, presidents had never refused to follow a congressional directive concerning treaty termination. President Reagan followed Congress's directive concerning the termination of agreements with South Africa, for example, despite disagreeing with the directive as a matter of policy.[120] It is difficult to see how that history can support OLC's claim of exclusive presidential authority. Importantly, two years earlier OLC had made no such claim in its opinion concerning the president's authority to withdraw the United States from NAFTA.[121]

In an effort to explain away the substantial history of congressional involvement, OLC characterizes many of the examples as involving mere voluntary interbranch cooperation. As for the situations in which presidents followed congressional directives, OLC contends that "the few examples where the President complied with the directives may further indicate nothing more than that the President agreed with those measures as a matter of policy." None of this comes close to meeting the burden of proof that the executive branch should have to meet to justify disregard of an enacted statute. As Justice Jackson noted in the *Youngstown* steel seizure case, when a president is violating a statute, the presidential action is "most vulnerable to attack and in the least favorable of possible constitutional postures."[122]

The historical picture here, it should be noted, is different than for the issue of recognition that was addressed in *Zivotofsky*. As discussed in Chapter 3, the executive branch had maintained even in the nineteenth century that its recognition power was exclusive, which is not true of treaty termination. Moreover, congressional involvement in treaty terminations has been more persistent and direct, and has generated less historical controversy, than in matters of recognition.[123] As a result, from the perspective of historical gloss, the president's power of treaty termination is best viewed as a concurrent power, falling within Justice Jackson's intermediate "zone of twilight" category.[124] As such, it should be subject to limitation through statute or through reservations attached by the Senate when it gives its advice and consent to treaties.[125] In late 2023, Congress enacted legislation that purported to require either two-thirds senatorial consent or congressional approval for presidential suspension of or withdrawal from the NATO Treaty, and President Biden signed the legislation without objecting to this provision.[126]

Conclusion

As a matter of practice, it seems settled that the president today can act unilaterally in terminating U.S. treaty commitments, at least to the extent that international law allows for such termination. This is how most treaty terminations are now accomplished, and most of them generate little constitutional controversy.[127] This practice is bipartisan and longstanding.[128]

The modern practice, it bears emphasizing, reflects a change in constitutional understandings. Historical practice through at least the late nineteenth century reflected an understanding that congressional or senatorial approval was constitutionally required for the termination of U.S. treaties. Not only was Congress or the Senate almost always involved in treaty terminations but presidents generally acted as if they needed such involvement. The chief debate was simply over whether the full Congress or merely the Senate should be involved in treaty terminations, and historical practice was viewed as relevant to that debate.

Very likely the change in treaty termination practice was driven in part by other changes—such as the increased role of the United States in the world—that were contributing to the enhancement of executive authority across a wide range of issues. Both the growth in treaty making in general and the increasingly widespread inclusion of unilateral withdrawal clauses in treaties also probably were factors. But lawyers, including those within the State Department as well as legal scholars, also appear to have played a role in assessing and influencing the relationship between the constitutional practice and constitutional understandings. While its role was less direct, the Supreme Court also may have helped facilitate the shift, through its increasingly deferential posture toward the executive branch starting in the 1930s.

This historical account presents difficulties for scholars who have attempted to defend a presidential power over treaty termination on originalist grounds, such as under the Vesting Clause thesis (which hypothesizes that the Vesting Clause of Article II of the Constitution implicitly conveys to the president "executive" authority not otherwise listed in Article II). The first century of U.S. practice weighs strongly against a Founding understanding that there was a unilateral presidential power of treaty termination. If the Article II Vesting Clause conveyed to presidents that authority, it is surprising that no one (including presidents and their legal advisers) seemed to be aware of it for a hundred years. Moreover, originalist accounts do not accord with how the constitutional law of treaty termination has actually been discussed and debated throughout American history. That is, they do not describe our actual interpretive practice.

At the same time, the historical account presented here also complicates some nonoriginalist accounts of constitutional change. Most notably, contrary to Professor Ackerman's theory of "constitutional moments," the twentieth-century shift toward a unilateral presidential power of termination was not the result of one particular period of contestation and deliberation, although some periods (such as Franklin Roosevelt's increased unilateralism and the debate over Carter's termination of the Taiwan treaty) were especially important. Nor was the change the product of a dramatic showdown between the branches, although such events naturally can become important precedents.[129] Instead, the shift involved an accretion of actions and claims by the executive branch combined with long periods of inaction by Congress. As can be seen throughout this book, the accretion model is also characteristic of other aspects of the constitutional law of foreign relations.[130]

Another undercurrent of this historical account is that international law has helped facilitate the shift to presidential unilateralism. International law treats notices of treaty termination as authoritative when received from a head of state, and it does not attempt to evaluate the extent of the head of state's actual authority under domestic law. This means that regardless of what U.S. constitutional law has to say about the matter, a presidential notice of treaty termination will be deemed as effective under international law—and thus, for example, will start the clock for any required notice period for withdrawal. OLC has relied on this fact in arguing that an exclusive presidential termination authority is needed for the United States to speak with one voice in foreign affairs. Somewhat relatedly, presidents have invoked international law's allowance of treaty termination as a source of domestic authority, even though there is no necessary connection between the two, a phenomenon that is also evident in Chapter 6, which covers the use of military force.[131]

6

USING MILITARY FORCE

IN THE FALL OF 2013, AFTER A LONG EVENING WALK AROUND THE White House grounds, President Barack Obama changed his mind. On his orders, the U.S. military had been preparing to carry out military strikes against Syria in response to its use of sarin gas to kill over a thousand of its own people during its civil war. The proposed military response would have been consistent with Obama's suggestion the previous year that Syria's use of chemical weapons would cross a "red line" that would prompt U.S. military intervention. But opposition to the proposed military action was brewing in Congress, Obama was having trouble getting support for it among the United States' allies, and there was little appetite among the public for another Middle East conflict.

Obama was also concerned about contradicting his own prior position concerning the president's war authority. In 2007, when he was a candidate for the presidency, he had maintained that "the President does not have power under the Constitution to unilaterally authorize a military attack in a situation that does not involve stopping an actual or imminent threat to the nation."[1] He had already deviated from that position by using force against Libya in 2011, an action that the Justice Department's Office of Legal Counsel (OLC) had defended on the basis of "the 'historical gloss' placed on the Constitution of two centuries of practice."[2] But at least in that instance he had received an endorsement from the UN Security Council, something lacking in connection with Syria. Moreover, the use of force in Libya had been designed to prevent an impending humanitarian crisis and thus arguably required a quick response, whereas it was more feasible to involve Congress in deciding how to respond to something that Syria had already done.

For whatever reason, this time Obama decided at the last minute that he should not act unilaterally, explaining that "it was right, in the absence of a direct or imminent threat to our security, to take this debate to Congress."[3] As it turns out, Congress never decided whether to support the strikes because, with

Russia's help, the Obama administration was able to work out a diplomatic resolution with Syria that involved the alleged removal and destruction of Syria's chemical weapons stockpile. In 2017 and 2018, however, Obama's successor, Donald Trump, ordered air strikes against Syria in response to a series of new uses of chemical weapons, and Trump did not seek congressional authorization. OLC subsequently explained in a memorandum why his actions were constitutional, in an analysis that relied on what it described as "deeply rooted historical practice."[4]

This chapter begins by describing uncertainties that surfaced in the early years of the nation about the Constitution's distribution of war authority and some of the circumstances under which presidents acted unilaterally in using force during the nineteenth century. It then recounts how presidents exercised increasingly broader war authority after the Spanish-American War and how they often invoked international law as support. Finally, the chapter assesses the extent to which historical practice has settled certain aspects of presidential authority to use military force.

The Constitutional Text and the Founding Period

The United States was the product of war, and it became a nation at a time in which war was a common instrument of foreign policy. Not surprisingly, therefore, the Constitution has a great deal to say about war. What may be surprising is that most of what it says concerns Congress, not the president. As Justice Robert Jackson observed, "out of seventeen specific paragraphs of congressional power [listed in the Constitution], eight of them are devoted in whole or in part to specification of powers connected with warfare."[5] Thus, for example, Congress is assigned the powers of declaring war, issuing letters of marque and reprisal (which were authorizations to private parties to engage in acts of hostility), making rules concerning captures on land and water, and raising and supporting an army and navy. Congress also has the power to make appropriations, which will be needed to sustain any protracted military conflict.

To be sure, the Constitution also makes the president the Commander in Chief of the armed forces. But it is not obvious that this command function encompasses the policy decisions associated with initiating hostilities. Indeed, Alexander Hamilton—not known for having a modest view of presidential authority—maintained in *The Federalist Papers* that the Commander in Chief power "amounted to nothing more than the supreme command and direction of the military and naval forces."[6] By contrast, noted Hamilton, the British king's authority extended to the "*declaring* of war and to the *raising* and *regulating* of fleets and armies—all which, by the Constitution under consideration, would appertain to the legislature."[7]

But it is also not obvious that Congress's power to declare war gives that body exclusive control over decisions to use military force. At the time of the constitutional Founding, undeclared wars were common, and they are the norm today. In fact, although the United States has been involved in hundreds of military conflicts in its history, it has declared war in connection with only five of them: the War of 1812, the Mexican-American War, the Spanish-American War, World War I, and World War II.[8] Moreover, at the time of the Founding, declarations of war served particular functions under international law, triggering an array of international law rules concerning matters such as the seizure of vessels, shipment of contraband, and institution of blockades. It might be that Congress was simply given control over triggering these international law consequences, not over the decision whether to initiate hostilities. These consequences are much less relevant today in light of modern international law rules governing the use of force, but that might just mean that one of Congress's powers has become less significant. In any event, it may be that not all acts of hostility will amount to a "war" in the constitutional sense, in which case it can be argued that, as Commander in Chief, the president has some authority to initiate such acts.

As a practical matter, moreover, it seems unlikely that the Founders meant to deprive the president of *all* unilateral war power. In particular, it seems unlikely that they would have wanted to deprive the president of the ability to use force to defend against an attack on the United States, especially since Congress would often have been out of session in the Founding era and would not have had the ability in a time of horse-and-buggy transportation to reassemble quickly in the event of an emergency. This intuition appears to be confirmed by discussions that occurred during the drafting of the Constitution. An initial draft would have given Congress the power to "make" war, but, according to James Madison's notes taken during the drafting process, this word was changed to "declare" so as to "leav[e] to the Executive the power to repel sudden attacks."[9]

That there was uncertainty about the Constitution's distribution of war authority became evident in the country's first foreign relations crisis after the adoption of the Constitution: the neutrality controversy of 1793. As will be recalled from Chapter 2, the issue there was whether the president had the constitutional authority to render the United States a neutral power in connection with a conflict between France and other European countries. In arguing that George Washington had exceeded his authority in issuing a proclamation of neutrality, James Madison noted that the power to declare neutrality was closely related to the power to declare war, which had been assigned to Congress.[10] By contrast, Alexander Hamilton contended that a presidential declaration of neutrality was different from a declaration of war and that nothing Washington had done had taken away Congress's ability to declare war if it chose to do so.[11]

Four decades later, in a eulogy for Madison, John Quincy Adams reflected on Madison's debate with Hamilton.[12] Adams, who by that point had served as Secretary of State for eight years, president for another four, and a member of the House of Representatives for fifteen, observed that "the respective powers of the President and Congress of the United States in the case of war with foreign powers are yet undetermined" and that "perhaps they can never be defined." While acknowledging that Congress was assigned the power of declaring war, Adams pointed out that "war is often made without being declared." Of equal importance, Adams emphasized the country's half century of experience with its Constitution: "However startled we may be by the idea that the Executive Chief Magistrate has the power of involving the nation in war, even without consulting Congress, an experience of fifty years has proved that in numberless cases he has and must have exercised that power." This observation is even more apt today, after more than 230 years of experience.[13]

Offensive versus Defensive Operations

Early presidents seemed to believe that they needed congressional authorization for offensive military actions. George Washington, in response to attacks by Native American tribes along the United States' western frontier, maintained that "the Constitution vests the power of declaring war with Congress, therefore no offensive expedition of importance can be undertaken until after they shall have deliberated upon the subject, and authorized such a measure."[14] John Adams sought and obtained congressional authorization for an undeclared naval war against France at the end of the 1700s, which was the United States' first military conflict against another nation after obtaining independence. France had been seizing U.S. merchant vessels throughout the Atlantic and Caribbean, and, although Adams at one point authorized the arming of these vessels so that they could defend themselves, he otherwise repeatedly asked Congress to consider approving additional measures. After learning of the mistreatment of U.S. negotiators whom Adams had sent to France, Congress finally enacted a series of statutes authorizing military action, including the seizure of French armed vessels.[15] Cases arising out of this "Quasi-War" against France eventually reached the Supreme Court, which held both that Congress did not need to formally declare war to authorize hostilities and that the navy was required to comply with the restrictions that Congress had placed on its authorizations.[16] In one of these cases, the Court observed that "the whole powers of war being, by the constitution of the United States, vested in Congress, the acts of that body can alone be resorted to as our guides in this enquiry."[17]

It is worth keeping in mind, however, that in the early days of the nation presidents had little in the way of standing military forces to draw upon. In 1789, when the United States started operating under its Constitution, there were fewer than a thousand men in the regular armed forces, and the United States had no navy. This meant that, for any significant military operation, presidents were dependent on Congress—to raise troops and obtain arms and ships.

In any event, it quickly became apparent that there was uncertainty about the line between offensive and defensive uses of force. Even though Washington thought he needed congressional authorization to conduct offensive operations, he controversially directed the use of force against the Wabash Tribe in 1790 in retaliation for earlier Native American atrocities.[18] Before Congress began authorizing hostilities against the French, Adams's Secretary of War, James McHenry, asked Hamilton for advice about what instructions it would be proper for the administration to give to the captains of U.S. Navy vessels in the event that they encountered French privateers or warships. Hamilton advised McHenry that, in terms of the president's constitutional authority to use force, Hamilton "was not ready to say that [the President] has any other power than merely to employ the Ships as Convoys with authority to *repel* force by *force,* (but not to capture), and to repress hostilities within our waters including a marine league from our coasts."[19] Any additional use of force, reasoned Hamilton, "must fall under the idea of *reprisals* [and] requires the sanction of that Department which is to declare or make war."

Uncertainty about the scope of the president's defensive war authority surfaced again during Jefferson's presidency, in connection with military action he took against the Barbary pirates (who operated under the control of North African states).[20] Shortly before Jefferson took office, the ruler of Tripoli had issued an ultimatum: either the United States would enter into an agreement to pay substantially more tribute or Tripoli would declare war on the United States. At the conclusion of the naval war with France, Congress had mandated that at least six frigates "be kept in constant service in time of peace."[21] Jefferson decided to send four of these vessels to the Mediterranean on his own authority to protect U.S. shipping. When the squadron arrived, they learned that the ruler of Tripoli had indeed declared war on the United States (by the established custom of chopping down the flagpole at the U.S. consulate). The squadron responded by imposing a blockade against Tripoli, which turned out to be ineffectual. In addition, one of the U.S. vessels engaged in a naval battle with a Tripolitan cruiser off the coast of Malta and defeated it. After doing so, however, the U.S. captain released the ship and her surviving crew.

Jefferson explained to Congress that the Tripolitan cruiser had been released because Congress had not authorized offensive military actions: "Unauthorized by the Constitution, without the sanction of Congress, to go beyond the line of defense, the vessel being disabled from committing further hostilities, was liberated with [its] crew."[22] In response, Hamilton—despite his own cautious advice earlier to McHenry during the Adams administration—attacked Jefferson for his timidity. Writing in the *New York Evening Post* as "Lucius Crassus," Hamilton acknowledged that the Constitution's assignment of the power to declare war to Congress meant that "it is the peculiar and exclusive province of Congress, *when the nation is at peace,* to change that state into a state of war."[23] "But when a foreign nation declares, or openly and avowedly makes war upon the United States," said Hamilton, "they are then by the very fact *already at war,* and any declaration on the part of Congress is nugatory; it is at least unnecessary." In that situation, claimed Hamilton, "the distinction between offensive and defensive war makes no difference." In Hamilton's view, therefore, the president had the constitutional authority to capture the Tripolitan cruiser and its crew.[24] Congress subsequently authorized the use of force to "subdue, seize, and make prize of all vessels, goods and effects, belonging to the Bey of Tripoli, or his subjects."[25]

The difficulty of maintaining a clear dividing line between offensive and defensive uses of force would continue to arise. In 1818, for example, President Monroe sent U.S. forces, led by Andrew Jackson, to the border with Spanish-controlled Florida to stop raids by the Seminole Indians. Monroe explained to Congress that he had authorized U.S. forces to cross into Florida in pursuit of the enemy, if necessary, in light of Spain's failure to stop the Indians from making the raids.[26] He also suggested that a treaty with Spain gave the United States the authority to take this action.[27] Jackson, however, interpreted the instructions more liberally and proceeded to invade the territory and in the process captured Spanish forts, occupied Pensacola, and tried and executed two British tradesmen suspected of inciting the Indians.[28] These actions led to international protests and were the subject of committee investigations in both houses of Congress. A Senate committee report strongly condemned Jackson, accusing him of violating his orders, contravening the Constitution, and "inflicting a wound on the national character."[29] Monroe and most of his cabinet thought that Jackson had exceeded his instructions, and Monroe made clear to Jackson that he had not been authorized to attack Spanish forts, since allowing such action "would authorize war, to which, by the principles of our Constitution, the Executive is incompetent."[30] Secretary of State John Quincy Adams, however, thought that

Jackson's actions were proper because "*defensive* acts of hostility may be authorized by the Executive."[31]

Protecting U.S. Citizens (and Other Interests) Abroad

As the United States developed a broader naval presence, another issue came to the fore: To what extent could the president (and, by extension, military commanders) use defensive war powers to protect Americans living, traveling, or working abroad? There appears to have been a general assumption that the president had some such power, and this justification was frequently invoked as a justification for using and threatening force abroad.[32] But there was significant uncertainty about how far the president (and his agents) could go. An intersecting question was whether and to what extent the president's war powers were broader with respect to unrecognized states and nonstate entities.

In 1831, for example, after the Argentine-appointed commander of the Falkland Islands had directed the seizure of U.S. vessels that were hunting seals, President Jackson explained the matter to Congress and asked it to "clothe the Executive with such authority and means as they may deem necessary for providing a force adequate to the complete protection of our fellow citizens fishing and trading in those seas."[33] But he had already dispatched the USS *Lexington* to the area, and, after failing to obtain redress, the captain sacked the island and seized some of the perpetrators as prisoners, charging them with piracy. Jackson made no reference to the captain's actions in his subsequent annual message to Congress.[34] Jackson also directed the USS *Potomac* to seek restitution in Sumatra after villagers in what is now Kuala Batu had attacked a U.S. merchant vessel that was engaged in the pepper trade, killing several members of its crew. After arriving, the U.S. forces attacked the forts and killed over a hundred Sumatrans. Jackson suggested that the use of force had been proper as a "chastisement" because the villagers were "a band of lawless pirates" rather than "members of a regular government, capable of maintaining the usual relations with foreign nations."[35] Additional clashes between the U.S. Navy and Native populations continued to occur in the Pacific throughout this period.

The limitations of communication also affected the exercise of war powers in this period. The wireless telegraph did not exist until the end of the nineteenth century. Before that, naval commanders could not easily request and receive direction about how to handle particular situations and thus by necessity relied on general instructions and their own judgment.[36]

A relatively uncontroversial example of the exercise of a protection power, this time against a Western state, occurred in 1853 in the Koszta Affair. Martin

Koszta, a Hungarian by birth, had been active in efforts to detach Hungary from the Austro-Hungarian Empire. After emigrating to the United States and initiating a process of naturalization to become a U.S. citizen, he made a business trip to Turkey. While there, he was apprehended by the Austrian military and placed in chains on board an Austrian ship docked in Turkey. A U.S. Navy captain then threatened to open fire on the Austrians if Koszta were not released. After the matter was resolved without force, the Austrians filed a protest with the U.S. government. The Secretary of State defended the actions of the navy captain, explaining that, because Koszta was in the process of becoming a U.S. citizen, the United States "had, therefore, the right, if they chose to exercise it, to extend their protection to him" and that "from international law . . . Austria could derive no authority to obstruct or interfere with the United States in the exercise of this right, in effecting the liberation of Koszta."[37]

Many years later, the Supreme Court referred to the Koszta Affair in *In re Neagle,* in which the Court held that the executive had the inherent authority to assign a federal marshal to protect a Supreme Court justice.[38] Citing the Koszta Affair as an example, the Court reasoned that the president's constitutional responsibility to take care that the laws are faithfully executed is not "limited to the enforcement of acts of Congress or of treaties of the United States according to their express terms" but rather includes "the rights, duties and obligations growing out of the constitution itself, our international relations, and all the protection implied by the nature of the government under the constitution." With some exaggeration, the Court described the Koszta Affair as "one of the most remarkable episodes in the history of our foreign relations."

Shortly after the Koszta Affair, there was a more controversial episode involving the use of force to protect U.S. citizens. In the 1850s, a dispute broke out between a Central American transit company, of which Americans owned a substantial portion of the shares, and the authorities in the port city of Greytown, Nicaragua (now San Juan del Norte), a community that was seeking to establish itself as an independent town. After company property was damaged and the U.S. minister to Central America was injured by a bottle thrown from a mob, the United States demanded reparations and an apology, and it sent a naval warship to the area. After failing to receive satisfaction, the warship bombarded the town, and then U.S. forces came ashore and burned the remaining buildings.[39] Various nations sought reparations from the United States for damage to their citizens' property in Greytown, but the United States denied liability and never made any payments. James Buchanan, serving as minister to the United Kingdom, initially told the British that the navy captain had exceeded his authority. But, consistent with advice from his Secretary of War, William Marcy,

President Pierce decided to defend the captain's actions. In a message to Congress, Pierce described Greytown as a "marauding establishment too dangerous to be disregarded and too guilty to pass unpunished, and yet incapable of being treated in any other way than as a piratical resort of outlaws or a camp of savages."[40] Nevertheless, some members of Congress argued that the executive had acted unconstitutionally.[41] A federal circuit court, in *Durand v. Hollins,* later rejected a damages claim brought against the captain, reasoning that "it is to [the president that] the citizens abroad must look for protection of person and of property."[42] In part because the military action received judicial support, the executive branch has often cited the Greytown incident as precedent for unilateral presidential war powers.[43]

President Buchanan similarly invoked a protective power, approving the U.S. Navy's destruction of four barrier forts in China after U.S. forces landed in Canton to protect American lives and property and a Chinese garrison fired upon the forces and killed the commander.[44] His Secretary of State, Lewis Cass (who earlier as a senator had defended Polk in connection with the Mexican-American War), explained to the British foreign minister that, although "the Executive branch of this government is not the war-making power" and thus could not participate with the British in certain offensive military operations in China, "our naval officers have the right—it is their duty, indeed—to employ the forces under their command, not only in self-defence, but for the protection of the persons and property of our citizens when exposed to acts of lawless outrage."[45]

The idea that presidents had the authority to protect American citizens abroad expanded over time to encompass other purported interests, including most notably commercial interests. For example, in the 1850s, Commodore Matthew Perry "opened" Japan to trade by threatening it with a naval attack.[46] In 1864, the U.S. Navy took part in a military operation designed to ensure continued access to the Shimonoseki Straits in Japan, after a U.S. merchant vessel had been fired upon the previous year.[47] In 1871, the U.S. military conducted a military campaign in Korea, designed in part to open up trade relations, that resulted in hundreds of Korean casualties.[48] None of these operations were authorized by Congress.

One American interest, the protection of which provoked particular controversy, was foreign territory that the United States was seeking to acquire. This had already been an issue when the Tyler administration was negotiating with the Republic of Texas in the 1840s to conclude a treaty of annexation and Tyler assured the Republic that he would use military force to protect it from Mexico in the interim.[49]

A similar scenario unfolded in 1871, when President Grant sent a naval force to protect Santo Domingo (as the Dominican Republic was then called) against both internal insurrection and a potential attack by Haiti. He did so on the theory that the administration was attempting to conclude a treaty of annexation with the government of Santo Domingo and that he was therefore protecting potential U.S. territory. The theory became especially strained when Grant kept forces there after the Senate's rejection of the treaty. During the ensuing debate, Senator Sumner proposed a resolution stating that a presidential use of force either against a friendly nation or as part of an intervention in another nation's internal affairs was "a usurpation of power not conferred on the President."[50] As the Senate considered this and other proposed resolutions, there was substantial discussion of the scope of the president's defensive war authority and his authority to protect U.S. citizens abroad, with extensive focus on historical practice. The central defender of Grant's actions was Senator Harlan, who cited a variety of historical examples, including the bombardment of Greytown and the use of force in Japan. Others joined Sumner in criticism. Senator Schurz, for example, expressed concern that Congress's control over the initiation of war could be evaded if presidents could act unilaterally in seeking to defend inchoate treaty interests. Ultimately, the resolutions were tabled and never voted on.[51]

Presidential Inducement of War

Another issue that arose in the post-Founding period and that would continue resurfacing throughout American history concerned the possibility that presidents could use their nonwar powers in a way that would in effect pull the United States into war. Such actions might include verbal threats as part of U.S. diplomacy, the recognition of one regime over another, or the positioning of U.S. forces in a way that would create a likelihood of conflict. As a leading nineteenth-century scholar of constitutional law observed, "the intercourse with foreign nations, the direction of the military and naval power, being confided to the president, his errors or misconduct may draw hostilities upon us."[52]

Consider, for example, the famous Monroe Doctrine. In 1823, in an annual message to Congress, President Monroe declared that any effort by European powers to interfere with the independence of countries in the Western Hemisphere would be viewed by the United States as "dangerous to our peace and safety" and as "the manifestation of an unfriendly disposition toward the United States."[53] The not very implicit threat was that the United States would be prepared to use military force to prevent such action by the European powers.[54]

The Monroe Doctrine was not controversial domestically when announced, but controversy about it developed in the next administration in connection with a proposal by President John Quincy Adams to send a delegation to the "Panama Congress" being organized by Simon Bolivar, a leader of the independence movement in Latin America.[55] Some members of Congress objected that attending the event would, especially in light of the policy announced by Monroe, risk drawing the United States into war with Spain.[56] There was also broader debate about the constitutionality of Monroe's policy, with some senators contending that it had unconstitutionally committed the United States to use military force. In response, Adams transmitted to Congress a letter from his Secretary of State, Henry Clay, arguing that Monroe had not in fact made any such promise.[57] Ultimately, Congress appropriated funds for the proposed delegation, and the Senate approved the appointment of the two delegates, but the delegation did not arrive in time for the sessions (one of them died of yellow fever en route, and the other arrived after the sessions were concluded).

Near the middle of the nineteenth century, a prominent example arose that illustrated the potential for a president to use his control over the military to pull the United States into war. In 1846, President Polk directed U.S. troops to occupy a disputed area near the border with Mexico, and this action unsurprisingly resulted in hostilities between Mexican and U.S. forces.[58] Polk then informed Congress that Mexico "has passed the boundary of the United States, has invaded our territory and shed American blood upon the American soil," and he asked Congress to "recognize the existence of the war, and to place at the disposition of the Executive the means of prosecuting the war with vigor."[59] Congress did so overwhelmingly, but there was a telling exchange in the Senate over the issue. Senator Calhoun insisted that, regardless of what Mexico had done, "there could be no state of war—no declaration of its existence made, but by the constitutional authority—the Congress of the United States."[60] Senator Cass disagreed, contending that although "it is certain that Congress alone has the right to declare war," this simply means that "no authority but Congress can commence an aggressive war."[61]

Near the end of the war, the Whig majority in the House of Representatives supported an amendment to a resolution honoring General Zachary Taylor that would have characterized the war as "unnecessarily and unconstitutionally begun by the President of the United States," but the amendment was later dropped by the Senate.[62] A young Whig representative in the House, Abraham Lincoln, voted in support of the amendment. "Allow the president to invade a neighboring nation, whenever *he* shall deem it necessary to repel an invasion," Lincoln explained to his former law partner, "and you allow him to do so, *whenever he may choose to say* he deems it necessary for such purpose—and you allow him to make war at pleasure."[63]

Greater Presidential Unilateralism

Despite the uncertainties and qualifications, it was still generally assumed at the middle of the nineteenth century—as it had been assumed shortly after the Founding—that the power to initiate war remained with Congress. In 1851, for example, Secretary of State Daniel Webster explained to the U.S. commissioner to the Kingdom of Hawaii that, as much as it might like to do so, the executive branch could not use military force to stop French interference with Hawaii's independence. The instruction came after the kingdom unilaterally proclaimed that, because of French aggression, it was placing itself under the protection of the United States. Webster sent an official letter to the U.S. commissioner in Hawaii, intended to be shared with the French, stating that the United States would not permit a foreign power to acquire Hawaii and that the navy was ready to do what was necessary to protect the islands. At the same time, Webster sent the commissioner a confidential letter making clear that "the war-making power in this Government rests entirely with Congress" and that the executive branch "has no power to oppose an attack by one independent nation on the possession of another."[64] Webster noted, however, that the commissioner should not feel obligated to share these constitutional limitations when discussing the matter with the French.

The most significant U.S. conflict of the latter half of the nineteenth century was the American Civil War. Although Lincoln exercised broad authority as Commander in Chief during the war, he was acting to defend the Union, and many of his actions were approved by Congress, although sometimes after the fact. The war thus did not signal any significant recalibration of authority between Congress and the president over the use of force. In its most important decision during the Civil War, *The Prize Cases,* the Supreme Court upheld the legality of a blockade that Lincoln had imposed on Confederate ports at the outset of the war but also observed that the president "has no power to initiate or declare a war either against a foreign nation or a domestic State."[65] Similarly, at the outset of the war, William Whiting, a lawyer who ended up serving as solicitor for the War Department during the war, published a treatise on war powers that, by 1871, had been republished in forty-three editions. Whiting explained that Congress has the exclusive power under the Constitution to declare war "and to sanction or authorize the commencement of *offensive* war."[66] But no declaration of war is necessary, he noted, "when war is commenced against this country, by aliens or by citizens," and he said that in that situation it was "the duty of the President to call out the army or navy to subdue the enemy, whether foreign or domestic."

The ensuing decades were largely ones of "congressional government,"[67] even in foreign affairs, although presidents continued to authorize small-scale military interventions in Latin America and Asia. A turning point for war powers authority may have been the Spanish-American War at the end of the nineteenth century. Although supported by a congressional declaration of war, the conflict led to a more global U.S. military presence abroad, including in U.S. territorial possessions.[68]

The implications of this global presence quickly became evident in connection with the Boxer Rebellion—a violent uprising in China by a loosely organized group of anti-foreign, anti-Christian nationalists. Some Chinese officials supported the Boxers, and foreign legations in Peking (Beijing), including the U.S. legation, were under siege by the Boxers and the Chinese Imperial Army. There were also Americans barricaded in the city of Tientsin (including a young Herbert Hoover, who was working for a mining consulting firm there). President McKinley responded by sending over 5,000 troops to China as part of a multinational force, without first seeking congressional authorization.[69] The U.S. troops were already in the region (in the Philippines) because of the Spanish-American War.[70] McKinley explained that the U.S. action "involved no war against the Chinese nation" but was limited to "securing wherever possible the safety of American life and property in China."[71]

Although defensive in its aims, the use of force in the Boxer Rebellion was much more extensive, in both size and duration, than earlier protective operations. Nevertheless, there was little objection from Congress. Writing a few years later, however, John Bassett Moore, a prominent international law scholar at Columbia who worked in and out of the government, described the U.S. involvement in the Boxer Rebellion as "perhaps the most remarkable case in which force was used without Congressional authority."[72]

A series of U.S. military interventions in Latin America and the Caribbean followed during the next several decades. For example, Theodore Roosevelt sent the navy to Panama, Taft sent marines to Nicaragua, and Wilson sent troops into Mexico to pursue the Mexican outlaw Pancho Villa after he had conducted raids in New Mexico. One study of this period reports that "between 1890 and 1933, there were forty-eight occasions in which a U.S. President deployed forces to Latin America."[73] This "gunboat diplomacy" was designed to protect U.S. citizens and U.S.-owned companies, keep trade flowing, and collect debts.

Presidents often acted under the theory that these deployments were mere "police" actions designed to restore order. That is how Roosevelt justified what came to be known as the Roosevelt Corollary to the Monroe Doctrine, pursuant to which the United States could intervene in the Western Hemisphere in cases of "chronic wrongdoing, or an impotence which results in a general loosening of the ties of civilized society."[74] Similarly, Taft, writing in the *Yale Law Journal* in 1916, during the period between his presidency and his service on the Supreme Court, distinguished between the use of force against nations that had trouble enforcing their laws and the use of force against other nations. The former, he claimed, could amount to a mere "police duty" rather than a war and thus might not require congressional authorization.[75]

Presidents in this period also often justified their unilateral uses of force on the ground that they were carried out with the consent of the local authorities. The United States had entered into treaties with several Latin American countries, sometimes in the aftermath of prior U.S. uses of force, that granted the United States the right to intervene militarily to defend those countries from external threat or to preserve domestic tranquility.[76] Presidents claimed that these treaties, as part of the supreme law of the land, provided them with additional authority.[77]

In 1912, the State Department distributed a memorandum prepared by its Solicitor, J. Reuben Clark, that set out to justify the "Right to Protect Citizens in Foreign Countries by Landing Forces."[78] Although chiefly focused on the right of nations to engage in such protection under international law, the memorandum included a discussion of the constitutional authority of the president to use military force in these situations without first obtaining congressional authorization. The memorandum argued that acts of protecting U.S. citizens abroad do not constitute "war" under international law and therefore do not implicate Congress's authority to declare war. It also contended that, because international law is part of U.S. law, something that the Supreme Court had remarked in its *Paquete Habana* decision arising out of the Spanish-American War, the president's authority to take care that the laws are faithfully executed includes the authority to take military action when such action is allowed by international law.[79] For this proposition, the memorandum emphasized the Supreme Court's protective power reasoning in *In re Neagle.*

World Wars and Collective Security

Although Congress formally declared war in World War I, President Wilson took unilateral military action against Germany even before Congress's declaration. U.S. merchant vessels were being attacked by German submarines, and Wilson asked Congress for authorization to arm the vessels. The proposed authorization stalled as a result of a filibuster in the Senate, in part because of purported concerns about the propriety of delegating open-ended war authority to the president. Nevertheless, Wilson, decrying a "little group of willful men" in the Senate, simply went ahead and allowed merchant vessels to be outfitted with navy guns (manned by naval officers) and made clear that they could fire on the U-boats.[80] Moreover, during the war, Wilson sent an "expeditionary force" of 20,000 troops into Russia to support the anti-Bolshevik forces, even though Congress's declaration of war did not extend to that conflict.[81]

The end of the war brought new controversy over presidential war power in connection with whether the United States should join the Versailles Treaty, which included a covenant establishing the League of Nations. Article 10 of the covenant provided that "the Members of the League undertake to respect and preserve as against external aggression the territorial integrity and existing political independence of all Members of the League" and that "in case of any such aggression or in case of any threat or danger of such aggression the Council shall advise upon the means by which this obligation shall be fulfilled."

Many senators expressed concern that this article, by potentially imposing an obligation on the United States to use military force in response to aggression when called for by the League, would undermine Congress's power to determine when the United States went to war. To address this concern, a majority of the Senate voted in favor of a reservation (proposed by the leader of the opposition to the league, Senator Henry Cabot Lodge) that disclaimed any obligation to use U.S. armed forces "unless, in any particular case the Congress, which under the Constitution, has the sole power to declare war or authorize the employment of the military or naval forces of the United States in the exercise of full liberty of nation shall by act or joint resolution so provide."[82] This was one of fifteen reservations approved by the Senate. Because some senators were opposed to the treaty even with the inclusion of the reservations and others were supportive of the treaty but opposed to the reservations, the treaty failed to obtain the requisite two-thirds Senate consent.[83] (As discussed in Chapter 4, this development would later be cited in support of a greater reliance on congressional-executive agreements, which require only majority congressional authorization or approval.)

As with World War I, U.S. involvement in World War II was ultimately authorized in a formal declaration of war by Congress, shortly after Japan's attack on Pearl Harbor. But Franklin Roosevelt took a number of unilateral steps before Congress's declaration of war. For example, he entered into an agreement with Great Britain that involved trading Britain fifty old U.S. destroyers in return for some of Britain's overseas bases, and he sent U.S. troops to occupy Greenland and Iceland to protect them against the Nazis, with the consent of the lawful governments there.

The end of World War II, like the end of World War I, saw debates about U.S. participation in a collective security regime. The United Nations Charter prohibits the use of force except in self-defense (individual or collective) or when authorized by the UN Security Council. The Council, in turn, was given the authority to authorize nations to use military force to address threats to, or breaches of, the peace. As a member of the Charter, the United States has promised to "accept and carry out the decisions of the Security Council."

When the United States joined the United Nations, it was assumed that nations would enter into agreements making forces available on a standing basis for use by the Security Council. The UN Participation Act, which Congress enacted the same year that the United States joined the Charter, authorized the president to conclude such an agreement, subject to congressional approval.[84] But Congress accepted that, once such an agreement was approved, the president would not need case-specific congressional authorization for uses of force by these troops. The Senate Foreign Relations Committee justified this anticipated delegation of authority on the ground that "preventive or enforcement action by these forces upon the order of the Security Council would not be an act of war but would be international action for the preservation of the peace."[85] "Consequently," reasoned the committee, "the provisions of the Charter do not affect the exclusive power of Congress to declare war."[86]

In part because of Cold War tensions, however, the contemplated agreements with the United Nations were never concluded. This left the relationship of presidential war powers to the UN Charter system in an uncertain state. Additional uncertainty about the relationship of presidential war powers to treaty obligations arose in connection with the United States' ratification of the North Atlantic Treaty in 1949, which established NATO and imposed on each member a duty, when any member is attacked, to "assist the Party or Parties so attacked by taking forthwith, individually and in concert with the other Parties, such action as it deems necessary, including the use of armed force, to restore and maintain the security of the North Atlantic area." The United States subsequently entered into other collective self-defense treaties, including the Southeast Asia Collective Defense Treaty, which would become important in the Vietnam War. Under these treaties, the obligation of each party to act is subject to its "constitutional processes."

Korea and the Cold War

Uncertainties surrounding the implications of the new UN Charter system for the distribution of war authority in the United States surfaced in 1950, when

North Korean forces crossed the Thirty-Eighth Parallel, a latitude marking that had been adopted as a temporary dividing line between North and South Korea after World War II. The UN Security Council, with the Soviet Union boycotting and thus unavailable to cast a veto, immediately condemned the invasion, and President Truman announced that he had ordered U.S. military forces to give "cover and support" to South Korean troops.[87] Shortly thereafter, the Council recommended that UN members "furnish such assistance to the Republic of Korea as may be necessary to repel the armed attack and to restore international peace and security in the area."[88] Truman responded by directing that U.S. forces be sent to Korea, an action that would eventually lead to the deployment of hundreds of thousands of troops and to tens of thousands of U.S. combat deaths. In doing so, he insisted that the United States was involved in "a UN police action" rather than a war.[89] Although Truman briefed congressional leaders and there was widespread support in Congress for his actions, he did not seek congressional authorization.[90] A lawsuit challenging the legality of the war was dismissed for lack of standing.[91]

In his memoirs, Truman's Secretary of State, Dean Acheson, contended that there was never "any serious doubt—in the sense of nonpolitically inspired doubt"—that the president had the constitutional authority to act unilaterally, and he noted that the administration was concerned that lengthy deliberations in Congress would diminish military morale.[92] He also recalled that Truman did not want to "establish a precedent in derogation of presidential power to send our forces into battle," although others have suggested that Truman was deferring to Acheson's judgment about whether to go to Congress.[93]

The State Department quickly provided legal support for Truman's action, drawing heavily on historical practice.[94] The Department asserted that "the United States has, throughout its history, upon orders of the Commander in Chief to the Armed Forces and without congressional authorization, acted to prevent violent and unlawful acts in other states from depriving the United States and its nationals of the benefits of such peace and security." While acknowledging that in many of these instances the United States was seeking specifically to protect American lives and property, the State Department maintained that in some instances U.S. military forces had been deployed in furtherance of "the broad interests of American foreign policy, and their use could be characterized as participation in international police action." With respect to the situation in Korea, the State Department contended that it was appropriate to use force to support the Security Council's resolutions because "the continued existence of the United Nations as an effective international organization is a paramount United States interest."[95] The next year, the Justice Department's Office of Legal

Counsel (OLC) more expressly suggested that the Security Council resolutions enhanced the president's war authority, contending that these resolutions "furnish a new ground for a decision by the President to use troops abroad."[96]

An especially vocal critic of Truman's actions was Senator Robert Taft, who argued that Truman had "brought about a de facto war . . . without consulting Congress and without congressional approval."[97] Senate majority leader Scott Lucas responded by emphasizing the "traditions and precedents established more than 100 times" by prior presidents in using force. Two notable historians, Henry Commager and Arthur Schlesinger, wrote op-ed pieces disagreeing with Taft, similarly relying on historical practice. Reciting various historical precedents and quoting from John Quincy Adams's eulogy for Madison, Commager argued that Taft's objections "have no support in law or history."[98] Schlesinger noted that "presidents have repeatedly committed American forces abroad without prior Congressional consultation or approval."[99] In language that he would come to regret in the wake of the Vietnam War, Schlesinger went so far as to describe Taft's comments as "demonstrably irresponsible."[100]

Some months after the start of the war, there was a debate in Congress over the president's war powers, prompted in part by the fact that the conflict was not going well and also by Truman's decision to send four divisions of troops to Western Europe on his own authority. The House Foreign Affairs Committee prepared an extensive report on the use of armed forces in foreign countries.[101] The report acknowledged that "on numerous occasions the President has employed landing forces, naval forces on the high seas, and armed guards on national vessels to protect nationals, property, ships, commerce, and the national interest," and it attached a comprehensive list of instances as an appendix to the report. The report also observed, however, that with the exception of the use of troops during the Boxer Rebellion, the number of troops had usually been small and the interventions had been of short duration. The report recited arguments for and against the legality of Truman's actions in Korea but did not take a position.

A joint report of the Senate Foreign Affairs and Armed Services committees was more supportive of what Truman had done.[102] In concluding that he had acted lawfully, it relied heavily on historical practice, noting that "since the Constitution was adopted there have been at least 125 incidents in which the President, without congressional authorization, and in the absence of a declaration of war, has ordered the Armed Forces to take action or maintain positions abroad." The report also argued that the president had the power to use military force to carry out treaty commitments, including the commitment in the UN Charter to support the recommendations of the UN Security Council. In support of this proposition, it cited the U.S. interventions in Latin America in the early twentieth century pursuant to treaties. The debate in Congress ended with a "sense of the Senate" resolution that approved the sending of the four divisions but said that no additional troops should be sent "without further congressional approval."[103]

The Korean War was also the backdrop of the famous *Youngstown* decision, in which the Supreme Court held that President Truman lacked the authority to seize the nation's steel mills to prevent a strike from disrupting production.[104] The Court there did not question the legality of the war but rather simply concluded that Truman's position as Commander in Chief did not give him the authority to take this particular action. The Court observed that "even though 'theater of war' be an expanding concept, we cannot with faithfulness to our constitutional system hold that the Commander in Chief of the Armed Forces has the ultimate power as such to take possession of private property in order to keep labor disputes from stopping production." Justice Jackson did argue in his concurrence, though, that it was troubling to think that a president might be able to act unilaterally in using military force and then use that very action as a justification for enlarging his authority domestically.[105]

Truman's successor, Dwight Eisenhower, was more cautious about presidential war powers, and he sought and obtained congressional authorization for the use of force to protect Taiwan and to address threats in the Middle East.[106] He also made clear when discussing the Taiwan situation, however, that "until Congress can act I would not hesitate, so far as my Constitutional powers extend, to take whatever emergency action might be forced upon us in order to protect the rights and security of the United States."[107] And in 1958, he sent 14,000 troops to Lebanon to shore up its government in response to an insurrection allegedly fomented by the Soviets, without citing the Middle East authorization, instead invoking the Lebanese government's request for the deployment and a purported need to protect Americans living in Lebanon.[108]

In 1962, President Kennedy acted at least somewhat unilaterally in addressing the Cuban Missile Crisis (which involved the Soviet Union's placement of nuclear missiles in Cuba), including by imposing a naval blockade of the island. But his actions were in the context of a rapidly developing emergency that posed a direct threat to U.S. national security, and, although the situation was highly fraught and dangerous, it fortunately did not develop into active hostilities.[109] Moreover, shortly before the crisis, Congress passed a resolution that seemed to support the use of force if necessary.[110]

Vietnam

The dominant U.S. conflict of the 1960s was the Vietnam War. The escalation of U.S. involvement in that conflict was ostensibly authorized by Congress in the 1964 Gulf of Tonkin Resolution. This resolution, passed by Congress with nearly unanimous support in both houses, came in response to alleged attacks by the North Vietnamese forces against U.S. destroyers patrolling in the Gulf of Tonkin. The resolution stated that "Congress approves and supports the determination of the President, as Commander in Chief, to take all necessary measures to repel any armed attack against the forces of the United States and to prevent further aggression."[111] It also provided that "the United States is . . . prepared, as the President determines, to take all necessary steps, including the use of armed force, to assist any member or protocol state of the Southeast Asia Collective Defense Treaty requesting assistance in defense of its freedom." President Johnson described the resolution as being so broad that it was like "grandma's nightshirt" since "it covers everything."[112]

There has long been controversy over whether the Resolution was induced by false or exaggerated accounts of what happened in the Gulf, and historians have tended to conclude that the second of the purported attacks never happened. In addition, there was controversy during the Vietnam War over what precisely the Resolution authorized and whether it constituted an unduly broad delegation of Congress's war authority to the president. A number of lawsuits were brought challenging the legality of the war. But courts dismissed the suits for lack of standing, under the political question doctrine, or based on a determination that, even if congressional authorization were required, the Resolution, along with congressional appropriations legislation and extensions of the military draft, was sufficient to constitute such authorization.[113] The Supreme Court repeatedly declined to review these cases.

In a memorandum assessing the legality of the U.S. military operations in Vietnam, the State Department focused principally on the authority of the United States as a nation under international law, but it also considered the constitutionality of presidential action.[114] The department argued that it has always been understood that the president has defensive war powers and that although the Founders probably only had in mind attacks on the United States, today "an attack on a country far from our shores can impinge directly on our nation's security." The Department also contended, not entirely accurately, that "since the Constitution was adopted there have been at least 125 instances in which the President has ordered the armed forces to take action or maintain positions abroad without obtaining prior congressional authorization, stating with the 'undeclared war' with France (1798–1800)."[115]

In the early 1970s, there were additional controversies over U.S. military actions, as part of the Vietnam War, that took place in Cambodia and Laos. Before being appointed to the Supreme Court, William Rehnquist served as head of OLC. In that capacity, Rehnquist prepared a memorandum discussing the constitutional authority of the president to direct U.S. troops to make incursions into communist sanctuaries in the border area between Vietnam and Cambodia.[116] In terms that were less tendentious than in the earlier State Department memorandum concerning Vietnam, Rehnquist summarized what was accepted and contested with respect to presidential war authority and acknowledged that there were gray areas: "In this area, both Congress and the President have acted in the past. There has been dispute, often bitter, as to how far the President may go alone on his constitutional authority. To date, however, it has always been resolved in the political arena without final constitutional determination by the courts, and without a head-on clash between the Congress and the President."

Rehnquist prepared a longer version of the memorandum a week later that did not include this paragraph.[117] But the longer memorandum did acknowledge that "if the contours of the divided war power contemplated by the framers of the Constitution are to remain, constitutional practice must include executive resort to Congress in order to obtain its sanction for the conduct of hostilities which reach a certain scale." Rehnquist also described the Korean War as the "high water mark of executive action without express congressional approval." But he stressed the importance of historical gloss in this context, observing that "a long continued practice on the part of the Executive, acquiesced in by the Congress, is itself some evidence of the existence of constitutional authority to support such a practice."

War Powers Resolution

In 1973, Congress enacted the War Powers Resolution over President Nixon's veto.[118] The Resolution asserts that "The constitutional powers of the President as Commander-in-Chief to introduce United States armed forces into hostilities, or into situations where imminent involvement in hostilities is clearly indicated by the circumstances, are exercised only pursuant to (1) a declaration of war, (2) specific statutory authorization, or (3) a national emergency created by attack upon the United States, its territories or possessions, or its armed forces." The Resolution also imposes various consulting and reporting requirements relating to the introduction of U.S. forces into situations involving or likely to involve hostilities. Most dramatically, it provides that the president "shall terminate" the use of military force after sixty days if he has not obtained congressional authorization.

President Nixon argued that the Resolution was unconstitutional, and other presidents have sometimes raised questions about the validity of its sixty-day-cutoff provision. Some presidential administrations, however, have appeared to accept the constitutionality of the provision,[119] and there is no instance in which a president has acknowledged acting inconsistently with it. Instead, presidents have concluded military operations before the sixty-day cutoff, interpreted the Resolution as inapplicable to particular operations (for example, because of a purported lack of hostilities), or broadly construed other statutory authorizations that they contend satisfy the Resolution.[120] Moreover, presidents have frequently filed reports with Congress that they describe as "consistent with" the Resolution's reporting requirements.[121]

The Resolution states that it should not "be construed as granting any authority to the President with respect to the introduction of United States Armed Forces into hostilities . . . [that] he would not have had in the absence of this [Resolution]." Nevertheless, the Resolution could be read as acquiescing in, even if not granting, a presidential authority to engage in small-scale conflicts without congressional authorization. The Resolution, after all, assumes that some uses of force will occur without such authorization, and it provides for termination of such use of force only after sixty days. There was also a substantial practice of such presidential uses of force before the enactment of the Resolution. Not surprisingly, executive branch lawyers have made precisely this claim of acquiescence.[122]

Modern Executive Branch Practice and Reasoning

The most significant military conflicts since the enactment of the War Powers Resolution—the two Iraq wars and the conflict in Afghanistan—have been authorized by Congress. But many other uses of force have not been authorized. Some have been small in scope—short-term strikes or discrete rescue operations. But some of them, such as the Reagan administration's invasions of Panama and Grenada, have been much more substantial.

In 1980, in the midst of the Iranian hostage crisis, OLC prepared a memorandum for the Attorney General concerning *Presidential Power to Use the Armed Forces Abroad without Statutory Authorization*.[123] This memorandum, which OLC has since regularly cited and quoted, expressly distanced itself from an originalist approach to war powers. "Early in our constitutional history," the memorandum acknowledged, "it perhaps could have been successfully argued that the Framers intended to confine the President to directing the military forces in wars declared by Congress." But the memorandum expressed the view that "the substantive constitutional limits on the exercise of [the president's inherent powers] are, at any particular time, a function of historical practice and the political relationship between the President and Congress." And it noted that "our history is replete with instances of presidential uses of military force abroad in the absence of prior congressional approval."

Since then, the executive branch has developed a two-part test for determining whether the president needs to obtain congressional authorization, involving an assessment of both the U.S. national interests involved in the operation and the "nature, scope, and duration" of the use of force.[124] Both elements of this test are focused heavily on historical practice. The following examples are illustrative.

In the early 1990s, President George H. W. Bush sent troops to Somalia to help protect UN and other humanitarian relief operations in which the U.S. government personnel and private citizens were participating. OLC concluded that this operation did not require congressional approval, reasoning that "the President's role under our Constitution as Commander in Chief and Chief Executive vests him with the constitutional authority to order United States troops abroad to further national interests such as protecting the lives of Americans overseas."[125] OLC relied heavily on historical practice, starting with Jefferson's actions against the Barbary pirates. "Against the background of this repeated past practice under many Presidents," said OLC, "this Department and this Office have concluded that the President has the power to commit United States troops abroad for the purpose of protecting important national interests." Citing *Durand* and other materials, OLC contended that "at the core of this power is the President's authority to take military action to protect American citizens, property, and interests from foreign threats." Invoking U.S. military actions during the Koszta Affair, the Boxer Rebellion, and other examples, OLC also reasoned that the president's authority extended to protecting non-U.S. citizens as well as citizens: "Past military interventions that extended to the protection of foreign nationals provide precedent for action to protect endangered Somalians and other non–United States citizens." Finally, OLC noted that the UN Security Council had authorized the use of force to protect the humanitarian operations in Somalia, and, citing the Korean War precedent, it reasoned that the president could rely on the UN resolution in concluding that the use of force was in the United States' national interests.

In 2011, after the UN Security Council authorized the use of force, the Obama administration participated with other countries in a campaign of air strikes against Libya in response to the Qadhafi regime's attacks on its own civilians. President Obama acted without congressional authorization, and in fact a resolution that would have authorized the operation was defeated in the House. He explained that he had acted "pursuant to [his] constitutional authority to conduct U.S. foreign relations and as Commander in Chief and Chief Executive."[126] OLC subsequently released an opinion concluding that these strikes did not require congressional authorization.[127] Relying on "the 'historical gloss' placed on the Constitution by two centuries of practice," OLC argued that the large number of prior uses of force without congressional authorization "precludes any suggestion that Congress's authority to declare war covers every military engagement, however limited, that the President initiates." This historical practice "is an important indication of constitutional meaning," claimed OLC, "because it reflects the two political branches' practical understanding, developed since the founding of the Republic, of their respective roles and responsibilities with respect to national defense, and because 'Matters intimately related to foreign policy and national security are rarely proper subjects for judicial intervention.'" OLC then proceeded to reason that the use of force here "was supported by sufficiently important national interests to fall within the President's constitutional power" and that its "nature, scope, and duration" kept it below the threshold that might trigger Congress's power to declare war.[128]

Two years later, as noted at the outset of this chapter, Obama pulled back from using force against Syria. But his successor, President Trump, was more aggressive, ordering air strikes against facilities in Syria in response to that country's use of chemical weapons. OLC reasoned that these actions were constitutional. Again, OLC focused on historical practice, noting that "we have recognized that 'Since judicial precedents are virtually non-existent' in defining the scope of the President's war powers, 'the question is one which of necessity must be decided by historical practice.'" OLC emphasized that "the President's authority in this area has been elucidated by dozens of occasions over the course of 230 years, quite literally running from the halls of Montezuma to the shores of Tripoli and beyond." While accepting that the president must seek congressional authorization to take actions that would bring the United States into a war, OLC reasoned that not all military operations rise to the level of a war for constitutional purposes. In order to constitutionally use military force in the absence of congressional authorization, said OLC, the president must reasonably conclude that the action "serves important national interests" and the "anticipated nature, scope and duration" of the conflict must not rise to the level of a war. Both inquiries, OLC noted, are informed heavily by past practice.[129]

The executive branch's approach to war powers is, in short, based heavily on historical gloss. This is not to suggest that we (or Congress) need to accept OLC's claims about what has been settled by practice. OLC's purported test for when presidents can unilaterally use force is vague and open ended, and it is far from clear that Congress has acquiesced in that test as a general matter. Any argument about what has been settled, moreover, needs to take adequate account of the War Powers Resolution, which (to the extent that it is constitutionally valid) is a binding statute.

Conclusion

Some issues of war powers authority have indisputably been settled by practice. It is settled that the president can act to defend the United States from an armed attack without first obtaining congressional authorization. Presidents have always assumed that they have this authority and have acted accordingly, without disagreement from Congress. In addition, it is settled that congressional authorizations to use military force that do not take the form of a declaration of war are constitutionally sufficient for the United States to engage in even significant and protracted armed conflicts.[130] The United States' first major military conflict against another nation—the Quasi-War with France in the late 1700s—did not involve a declaration of war, and the United States has not issued such a declaration since World War II. Finally, there is a general consensus that presidents have some unilateral constitutional authority to use military force to protect or rescue U.S. citizens abroad, although broad invocations of this authority have sometimes triggered debate. While the War Powers Resolution does not specifically mention this presidential power, some of the key congressional supporters of the Resolution later conceded that such an authority should have been included.[131] Moreover, in the few instances since the Vietnam War in which Congress has imposed funding cutoffs for president-initiated military operations, Congress has included an exception for the protection of U.S. personnel and citizens.[132]

The harder question is whether and to what extent the president has authority to use military force in nondefensive situations without authorization from Congress. Historical practice does not clearly support *unlimited* presidential authority to initiate wars. Some of the most significant U.S. military engagements in recent decades have been authorized by Congress: the two Iraq wars and the war in Afghanistan (and, relatedly, the "war on terror" against al-Qaeda).[133] Before that, Eisenhower sought and obtained advance congressional authorization to use force for Taiwan's protection and in the Middle East, and Johnson obtained authorization during the Vietnam War. Moreover, despite having an incentive to make broad claims of presidential authority, the executive branch has generally avoided claiming that presidents have unlimited authority to start wars. The Korean War might be viewed as precedent for such authority, but it is an outlier in modern practice and can be explained in part by the early uncertainties about how presidential war powers interacted with what was then the new UN Charter collective security framework.

Practice does, however, appear to support the executive branch's claim that limited military engagements that are not expected to be protracted in duration or to involve the commitment of substantial ground troops need not be authorized by Congress. Many of these smaller-scale engagements have been carried out since World War II without congressional authorization, frequently without controversy. The structure of the War Powers Resolution, and the way that it has been applied in practice for the last fifty years, further supports this conclusion: by insisting that the president obtain congressional authorization for uses of force that last more than sixty days, Congress in the Resolution appears to have accepted that it need not authorize short-term engagements. This practice may not be consistent with original constitutional understandings; if not, it is a type of common-law constitutional evolution that has occurred largely outside the courts.[134]

This conclusion is unlikely to be satisfactory to those who think we need greater checks on presidential military actions. Smaller-scale engagements have the potential to develop into larger ones, and, in any event, they can have broader foreign relations repercussions for the United States. Moreover, the line between smaller and larger engagements is far from self-evident (although that is true of many distinctions in the law). In light of what is now longstanding practice, however, and given the understandable reluctance of courts to wade into these issues, more robust checks on the president will likely need to come from Congress.

The historical account in this chapter is contrary to the one that is often presented by scholars who are supportive of congressional control over war making. These scholars suggest that the post–World War II practice is radically different from what came before. According to this narrative, Truman's commitment of troops to the Korean War in 1950 without congressional authorization marks a sharp break from earlier understandings of presidential war powers.[135] As we have seen, however, this account gets it wrong in both historical directions.

Looking backward, the expansionist dynamics of presidential war authority can be traced to events long before the Korean War, and defenders of Truman's actions in Korea relied on the past practice. Looking forward after 1950, the Korean War seems unusual, not the beginning of a transformation in U.S. practice. If there was a turning point in presidential war powers, it was more likely the period following the Spanish-American War, a period that began fifty years before the war in Korea. Even the exercises of war authority in that period, however, built on prior customary practices and understandings. The model of constitutional change here, as in the other examples covered in this book, is much more one of accretion rather than one centered on a particular constitutional moment.[136]

Finally, the historical practice relating to U.S. war making suggests the need for a dose of realism in debates about presidential war authority. As illustrated throughout this chapter, the president's other foreign relations powers mean that a requirement of congressional authorization for offensive hostilities may be thin protection against president-initiated wars. Imagine, for example, if a president announced that they were recognizing Taiwan as the government of China. Such an action easily could produce a war, either forcing Congress's hand or triggering the president's acknowledged defensive war powers. Yet there seems to be general acceptance that such an action would be constitutional. Or imagine, for example, if a president stationed a large number of U.S. troops in a country facing a potential invasion; if the invasion occurred, the president's defensive war powers would be engaged by the attack on U.S. troops. As these and many other scenarios indicate, there is a certain artificiality to modern war powers scholarship, which has tended to focus almost exclusively on the formal legal requirements for presidential uses of force.

7

CONGRESS'S GLOSS-BASED AUTHORITY

AFTER THE SEPTEMBER 11, 2001, TERRORIST ATTACKS, PRESIDENT George W. Bush ordered that "military commissions" be created to try noncitizens suspected of being members of the al-Qaeda terrorist organization or otherwise being involved in acts of terrorism.[1] There was substantial debate over whether Bush had the legal authority to create the commissions. In arguing that he had this authority, executive branch lawyers emphasized historical practice, observing that "military commissions have been convened by the President in numerous conflicts since the founding and have often been used during wartime without congressional authorization."[2] This historical practice, they said, "strongly (if not conclusively) confirms the existence of that war power."[3]

In *Hamdan v. Rumsfeld,* the Supreme Court decided that it need not resolve whether the president had the constitutional authority to create military commissions.[4] This was because, the Court found, Congress had placed limitations on the creation of such commissions, which the Bush administration had failed to follow. In particular, the Court found that in the Uniform Code of Military Justice (which regulates the trial of U.S. service members), Congress had directed that military commissions should use the same procedures as are used for courts-martial "insofar as practicable,"[5] and further found that Bush had not done so. Citing Justice Jackson's framework from *Youngstown,* the Court concluded: "Whether or not the President has independent power, absent congressional authorization, to convene military commissions, he may not disregard limitations that Congress has, in proper exercise of its own war powers, placed on his powers."[6]

The majority in *Hamdan* did not explain why it thought that Congress was acting "in proper exercise of its own war powers" in regulating the president's treatment of enemy combatants. But the majority appeared to credit the fact that Congress had long referred to military commissions in its regulations of the military.[7] In a concurrence, Justice Kennedy made this historical practice point more directly, noting that "in this case, as the Court observes, the President has acted in a field with a history of congressional participation and regulation." In other words, in an area in which both Congress and the president could claim historically based authority, Congress prevailed in the event of a conflict. Congress responded to this decision by enacting (with presidential support) a statute that extensively regulated both the procedures to be used in the commissions and the crimes that could be tried there.[8]

This chapter describes examples of congressional (and senatorial) powers relating to foreign affairs that have potentially been enhanced by historical gloss. By necessity, the examples in this chapter are highly selective, provided as illustrations rather than as anything like a comprehensive account of Congress's authority. Additional examples of congressional authority relating to foreign affairs can be found in other chapters of this book.

The Constitutional Text

As noted in Chapter 2, the Constitution conveys an array of foreign relations–related powers to Congress. These include the power to regulate commerce with foreign nations; to punish piracies and offenses against the law of nations; to declare war, grant letters of marque and reprisal, and regulate captures on land and water; to raise and support the army and navy; and to make rules for the armed forces. Some of Congress's general powers, such as over appropriations, also give it significant ability to regulate foreign affairs. The president is dependent on congressional appropriations to carry out foreign affairs activities, and, because of that, Congress can often induce the president to accept potentially objectionable provisions by including them in appropriations legislation. In addition, Congress has the authority to enact laws that are "necessary and proper" for carrying into execution not only its own powers but also those of the other parts of the government, including the president's foreign affairs powers.

Congress's long list of powers stands in sharp contrast with the sparse textual grants of authority to the president, some of which, like the treaty power, are divided with the Senate. Congress has so many plausible textual hooks for the exercise of authority that it probably has less need for historical gloss than does the president. This difference between the two branches became evident early in U.S. history. As discussed in earlier chapters, when George Washington issued a Neutrality Proclamation in 1793 to keep the United States out of a European war, there was significant debate (including between Alexander Hamilton and James Madison) over the president's authority to take that action, and especially his authority to criminalize breaches of the proclamation.[9] But when Congress enacted a neutrality statute the next year, there was no question about its authority to do so: Congress could rely on, among other things, its express power to define and punish offenses against the law of nations (in that case, the law of nations concerning neutrality).[10] In fact, Congress's authority over foreign affairs is sufficiently wide-ranging that one of the most significant things it does is to *delegate* foreign affairs authority to the executive branch, as discussed in the next chapter.

Another difference between congressional and presidential exercises of foreign affairs powers is that congressional exercises are more likely to be reviewed by the courts. This is because Congress, by enacting laws, can (and often does) operate directly on private interests in a way that allows for standing to sue. As discussed in Chapter 1, gloss is less likely to flourish amid conditions of frequent judicial review. This is not to suggest that congressional powers have not evolved over time. They clearly have (think of the expansion of Congress's authority to regulate commerce, for example), but often that has been due at least as much to judicial decisions as to an accretion of historical practice.

That said, as *Hamdan* illustrates, gloss is potentially relevant to some aspects of congressional (and senatorial) authority, especially in questions concerning the relationship between congressional and presidential authority. In particular, longstanding congressional practice can defeat claims of exclusive presidential authority, and when it does, Congress takes precedence under Justice Jackson's canonical framework from *Youngstown*. While gloss is most relevant to presidential power in the second "zone of twilight" category from that framework, it is most relevant to congressional power in the third, "lowest ebb" category from the framework.

The Senate's Conditional Consent Power

The Constitution provides that, in order to conclude treaties, presidents must obtain the advice and consent of two-thirds of the senators present. In part as a response to not being consulted during the treaty negotiation process, the Senate has long had a practice of sometimes conditioning its consent to treaties.[11] It first did so in 1795, in connection with its consideration of the controversial Jay Treaty, which aimed to resolve compensation, trade, and boundary disputes between the United States and Great Britain. The Senate conditioned its advice and consent to the treaty on the suspension of a provision allowing Britain to restrict U.S. trade in the West Indies.[12] President Washington accepted the condition, and Britain agreed to the treaty as modified.[13]

In a world of monarchs, such conditional consent was a novelty in international practice, and U.S. negotiators had to explain to other countries that it arose from the Constitution's division of the treaty power between the president and Senate.[14] Some years after the conclusion of the Jay Treaty, the British foreign minister criticized the U.S. practice as "new, unauthorized and not to be sanctioned."[15] Eventually, though, conditional consent became a common feature of treaty relations. For bilateral treaties, it is understood that the other party must agree to the conditions, and some treaties have failed because of a lack of agreement about the U.S. conditions.[16]

The Senate has used a variety of labels for its conditions, including "amendment," "reservation," "proviso," "understanding," and "declaration."[17] In general, the terms "amendment" and "reservation" have been used for conditions that alter the U.S. obligations under the treaty, and other labels are used for conditions that relate to how the United States interprets or will implement the treaty.[18] Whatever the label, it is understood that the conditions are binding on the president and that the president cannot ratify a treaty without accepting them.[19] On a few occasions, presidents have deemed the proposed conditions to be unacceptable and have declined to move forward on a treaty.[20]

A 1996 study reported that, since the Founding, approximately 15 percent of the treaties approved by the Senate had been subject to conditional consent.[21] In recent decades, the Senate has been especially likely to attach conditions to important multilateral agreements, such as those governing human rights, sometimes insisting on a broad package of "reservations, understandings, and declarations," or "RUDs." As discussed in Chapter 4, presidential use of the Article II treaty process has been declining, but that is not because of senatorial conditions; rather, it is because it has become too difficult to obtain the requisite two-thirds senatorial consent even *with* conditions.

Although well established, the Senate's conditional consent authority is not obvious from the constitutional text.[22] One might view the Senate's consent role in the treaty process as analogous to that of the president when deciding whether to sign legislation passed by Congress—that is, as simply determining whether to approve it as a package. But historical practice is viewed by most observers as having settled the matter.[23] This is true for a number of reasons: the practice is longstanding, dating almost to the beginning of the Republic; the executive branch has not contested the Senate's authority to impose conditions, and in fact the executive branch often suggests conditions for the Senate to consider; and, even if the practice is not clearly indicated by the constitutional text, it is not sharply at odds with it.

Some aspects of the Senate's conditional consent practice, it should be noted, are of modern vintage. In particular, the Senate now sometimes includes a declaration with its advice and consent stating that the terms of a treaty are "not self-executing," something that has been construed by courts to mean that the treaty cannot be applied domestically unless and until it has been implemented by Congress. While in the nineteenth century the Senate had sometimes insisted that treaties not take effect until Congress passed implementing legislation, non-self-execution declarations are different: they allow the treaty to become operative, but they disallow domestic judicial enforcement.[24] Because of this effect, some commentators have suggested that these declarations improperly aim to legislate the domestic effect of treaties, which, they maintain, should be governed solely by the Supremacy Clause and federal statutes.[25] But these non-self-execution declarations have now been around for decades and have not produced interbranch disagreement. In fact, the executive branch itself often suggests these declarations when submitting treaties to the Senate.[26] The Supreme Court has also seemed to accept them,[27] and the lower courts have consistently given them effect.[28]

The Content of Passports

As discussed in Chapter 3, the Supreme Court invalidated a statutory provision relating to passports in a 2015 decision, *Zivotofsky v. Kerry*.[29] In that case, Congress had mandated that the Secretary of State record Israel as the place of birth for children born in Jerusalem to U.S. citizen parents if the child or their parents requested that designation. President Obama (like his predecessor, President Bush) had directed the Secretary of State not to comply with this statute, and the Supreme Court sided with the president, holding that the statute invaded his exclusive authority over the recognition of foreign governments.

One of the issues lurking in the background of the *Zivotofsky* case concerned Congress's authority to enact the passport provision in the first place. The Constitution gives Congress the power to regulate the process of naturalization, but passports are not directly related to that process. Congress also has the authority to regulate foreign commerce, but it is not clear to what extent that authority gives Congress the ability to regulate the content of passports. Finally, as discussed above, Congress has authority to enact laws necessary and proper for effectuating other governmental powers, but how that authority intersects with the executive branch's authority over passports—especially when the two branches are in conflict—is uncertain. If Congress lacked constitutional authority to issue the statutory mandate in question, it would not matter whether the mandate invaded the president's recognition power. The statute would be invalid because of a lack of a basis for it in Article I of the Constitution, regardless of whether it violated Article II.

Before the Court issued its decision, a number of commentators made precisely this lack-of-congressional-power argument.[30] Ultimately, however, only

Justice Thomas seemed persuaded by it. In his concurrence in the judgment, Thomas noted that "the Constitution contains no Passport Clause, nor does it explicitly vest Congress with 'plenary authority over passports.'"[31] He then proceeded to explain why he thought that the passport law in question did not fall within Congress's authority to regulate naturalization, its authority over commerce, or its Necessary and Proper Clause authority.

The Court majority, by contrast, said that it did "not question the power of Congress to enact passport legislation of wide scope," a proposition that it said was "consistent with the extensive lawmaking power the Constitution vests in Congress over the Nation's foreign affairs." Justice Scalia, in a dissent joined by Chief Justice Roberts and Justice Alito, offered a more direct response to Thomas. Among other things, Scalia recounted the long history of congressional regulation of passports. From this, Scalia concluded: "History and precedent thus refute any suggestion that the Constitution disables Congress from regulating the President's issuance and formulation of passports."[32] The Senate had filed a brief in the case similarly emphasizing the long history of congressional passport regulation.[33] Citing the Court's *Noel Canning* decision (in which the Court, as discussed in Chapter 2, relied heavily on historical practice in discerning the scope of the president's recess appointments power), the brief argued that "this longstanding, unchallenged legislative direction of the Executive affirms Congress' plenary authority to regulate issuance of passports."

The relevant history of congressional passport regulation, which Scalia and the Senate adverted to, is as follows: Except during wartime, the United States did not originally require its citizens to have passports to exit and reenter the country, although passports could be useful for traveling to other countries.[34] A U.S. passport, as the Supreme Court explained, was "addressed to foreign powers, purporting only to be a request that the bearer of it may pass safely and freely, and is to be considered rather in the character of a political document by which the bearer is recognized in foreign countries as an American citizen, and which, by usage and the law of nations, is received as evidence of the fact."[35] Before the mid-nineteenth century, some states, cities, and even notaries public issued passports.

At the federal level, the issuance of passports was initially handled solely by the executive branch. In essence, it was viewed as a form of diplomatic speech by which the government vouched for its citizens. But Congress sometimes addressed issues relating to passports. For example, an 1803 statute prohibited the State Department from knowingly issuing passports to aliens,[36] and an 1815 statute (enacted near the end of the War of 1812) prohibited travel to or from enemy territory "without a passport first obtained from the Secretary of State, the Secretary of War, or other officer . . . authorized by the President of the United States, to grant the same."[37] But otherwise the federal government's issuance and denial of passports was largely subject to the discretion of the executive branch.[38]

This changed in 1856. That year, Congress made the issuance of passports solely a federal function and for the first time purported to authorize the executive branch to issue passports, stating: "The Secretary of State shall be authorized to grant and issue passports, and cause passports to be granted, issued, and verified in foreign countries by such diplomatic or consular officers of the United States, and under such rules as the President shall designate and prescribe for and on behalf of the United States."[39] Subsequent versions of the statute have had similarly worded grants of authority.

Despite granting passport control to the executive branch, Congress has over the years regulated many issues relating to passports. It has imposed limitations on who may be issued passports, disallowing them, for example, to people convicted of certain criminal offenses.[40] It has regulated the fees that the State Department can charge for issuing passports, the duration during which passports remain valid, and even the type of paper to be used for them. In addition, Congress has imposed criminal penalties for making false statements in connection with obtaining passports, for misusing passports, and for counterfeiting and forging passports. Perhaps of most relevance to the issue in *Zivotofsky*, Congress since 1994 has allowed U.S. citizens born in Taiwan the option of having Taiwan rather than China recorded as their place of birth in their passports.[41] The executive branch, for its part, has complied with this statutory requirement, despite its recognition of the People's Republic of China "as the sole legal government of China."[42]

There was thus substantial historical practice that Congress could draw upon in *Zivotofsky* to support its authority to regulate passports. It is also worth keeping in mind that, if Congress had been found to lack the authority to address the issue in that case (as Justice Thomas had argued), the next question would have been where the executive branch was getting the authority to regulate it. To answer that question, Justice Thomas resorted to the Article II Vesting Clause. As discussed in Chapter 2, however, that is a controversial source of executive foreign affairs authority. The majority in *Zivotofsky* declined to address the Vesting Clause issue, and Scalia (along with Roberts and Alito) criticized Thomas's "assertion of broad, unenumerated 'residual powers' in the President."[43] A better answer to the executive power question is one based on historical gloss, given that the executive branch had regulated passports without congressional authorization up until 1856. But if relying on historical gloss is appropriate for discerning the scope of executive authority over passports, it should also be appropriate for discerning the scope of congressional authority.[44]

Regulating Diplomacy

The Justice Department's Office of Legal Counsel (OLC) has asserted that it is "well settled that the Constitution vests the President with the exclusive authority to conduct the Nation's diplomatic relations with other States."[45] According to OLC, this means, for example, that "Congress's power to legislate in the foreign affairs area does not include the authority to attempt to dictate the modes and means by which the President engages in international diplomacy with foreign countries and through international fora."[46] From this purported exclusive authority over diplomacy, OLC has claimed other exclusive presidential powers, such as over the termination of treaties.[47] The *Zivotofsky* decision, which held that the president has exclusive authority over the recognition of foreign governments and their territories (in part because of historical practice), is viewed by OLC as having bolstered such claims.

Historical practice suggests, however, that OLC's claims about an exclusive presidential power over diplomacy require substantial qualification.[48] As an initial matter, there is little dispute that Congress can enact a wide variety of laws that affect U.S. diplomatic relations.[49] Congress can, for example, mandate economic sanctions against a regime over the objections of a president—as it did against Russia in 2017 in response to Russia's interference in the 2016 presidential election, despite objections from President Trump.[50] Congress can strip away a regime's sovereign immunity from suit, as it effectively did, over President Obama's objection, with respect to Saudi Arabia in litigation concerning its alleged involvement in the September 11 terrorist attacks.[51] It can use foreign aid allocations to promote its foreign policy goals, sometimes in ways inconsistent with presidential preferences.[52] It can decline to give its consent to treaties or other agreements, or it can override their domestic effect, regardless of how important they are to the president's foreign policy agenda. For example, the Senate dealt a major blow to President Clinton's foreign policy when it declined to approve the Comprehensive Nuclear Test Ban Treaty in 1999.[53] Congress can also restrict U.S. cooperation with an international organization, as it has done with respect to the International Criminal Court.[54] It is also assumed that Congress can override the "act of state doctrine"—pursuant to which U.S. courts normally presume the validity of foreign government acts—even though the doctrine is designed in part to facilitate executive management of foreign affairs.[55] These and countless other congressional actions substantially affect diplomacy.

In addition, from the beginning of the nation, Congress has regulated the chief diplomatic arm of the executive branch—the Department of State.[56] It established the Department in 1789 and assigned it various duties, subject to the direction of the president.[57] In addition to regulating the department's budget and facilities and the salaries of its diplomatic personnel, Congress has often made adjustments to the department's structure—creating and abolishing offices within the department and creating new classifications of diplomatic personnel. To take a few recent examples, by statutory directive there is now in the Department an Office of International Religious Freedom, a Coordinator for International Terrorism, a Coordinator of United States Government Activities to Combat HIV/AIDS, and an Office of Sanctions Coordination.[58] These structures inevitably affect U.S. diplomacy. Congress has also long required the State Department to carry out specific fact-finding and reporting duties relating to foreign affairs, duties that also have diplomatic effects. Today, these duties include the publication and reporting to Congress of all binding executive agreements and some nonbinding ones,[59] the transmission to Congress of country reports relating to terrorism,[60] and the publication of country reports on human rights practices.[61]

The Constitution also gives the Senate a direct check on the president's conduct of diplomacy, in that it requires the president to obtain the Senate's advice and consent for diplomatic appointments. Presidents have sometimes bypassed this check through the use of ad hoc diplomats for particular missions, but Congress recently imposed constraints on their use.[62] Moreover, since the 1920s, Congress has comprehensively regulated the qualifications for joining the Foreign Service, which is the diplomatic staff of the executive branch.[63] Congress has also at times created high-level diplomatic offices, including a number of ambassadorships in the early twentieth century and a number of offices for ambassadors at large in recent decades.[64]

Congress also often requires the executive branch to certify international facts, including facts about other countries, as a condition of taking foreign relations actions, and these certifications are often related to U.S. diplomacy. Title III of the 1996 Helms Burton Act, for example, authorizes lawsuits against any person trading in property confiscated by Cuba, a measure that has generated international controversy. The law allows presidents to suspend this allowance for six months at a time, but to do so presidents must certify that the suspension "is necessary to the national interests of the United States and will expedite a transition to democracy in Cuba."[65] Also in 1996, Congress directed that sanctions against Burma remain in place "until such time as the President determines and certifies to Congress that Burma has made measurable and substantial progress in improving human rights practices and implementing democratic government."[66] In addition, Congress has delegated authority to the executive branch to designate countries as supporters of terrorism, but it has conditioned the executive's ability to rescind such designations upon its certification of particular findings.[67] The Iran Nuclear Agreement Review Act, passed in 2015 when President Obama was concluding a deal with Iran to halt its nuclear weapons program in return for suspension of U.S. sanctions, required presidents to certify every ninety days that Iran was in compliance with the deal and that the suspension of U.S. sanctions continued to be "appropriate and proportionate" in light of Iran's actions and "vital" to American national security.[68] A 2016 statute allows presidents to suspend sanctions against North Korea, but only if they certify to congressional committees that North Korea is making progress in a number of specified areas.[69] There are many other examples of these sorts of certification requirements.[70]

A recent statute in this area that has prompted constitutional disagreement is the Global Magnitsky Human Rights Accountability Act, which Congress enacted in 2016.[71] The Act authorizes the president to impose sanctions against foreign persons for various human rights abuses or involvement in corruption, and it says that if the president receives a request from congressional leadership to investigate whether to impose sanctions against particular persons, the president must make a sanctions determination and report back to Congress within 120 days.[72] When signing the Act into law, President Obama stated, "Consistent with the constitutional separation of powers, which limit the Congress's ability to dictate how the executive branch executes the law, I will maintain my discretion to decline to act on such requests when appropriate."[73] The Trump administration similarly maintained that, "consistent with the previous administration's position and the constitutional separation of powers, the President maintains his discretion to decline to act on congressional committee requests when appropriate." Nevertheless, the executive branch has imposed sanctions under the act, including in response to congressional pressures—for example, against Saudi officials in response to the 2018 killing of journalist Jamal Khashoggi.[74]

In addition to these various statutes, Congress also sometimes engages directly in diplomatic activities. While formal communications between the United States and other nations have long been channeled through the executive branch, Congress routinely hosts foreign officials, its members frequently travel abroad to investigate conditions and interact with foreign leaders about policy issues, and it often expresses views—in both statutes and nonbinding resolutions—about the behavior of other countries and U.S. relations with those countries. In 2022, for example, Speaker of the House Nancy Pelosi traveled to Taiwan to meet with its leadership, a trip that was discouraged by the Biden administration.[75] Years earlier, Pelosi had traveled to Syria to meet with Syrian president Bashar al-Assad, to the dismay of the Bush administration.[76] During the Obama administration, House Speaker John Boehner twice invited Israeli president Benjamin Netanyahu to address Congress while Netanyahu was in the midst of policy disputes with the administration.[77]

Also during the Obama administration, when the administration was seeking to conclude an agreement with Iran that would eliminate U.S. sanctions in return for Iran's agreement to limit its nuclear weapons program, Senator Tom Cotton and forty-six other senators sent an "open letter" to Iran stating that they would "consider any agreement regarding your nuclear-weapons program that is not approved by the Congress as nothing more than an executive agreement . . . [that] the next president could revoke . . . with the stroke of a pen."[78] Such a communication was unusual and constituted a breach of political norms, but it was not entirely unprecedented. In 1984, ten Democratic members of Congress sent a letter to Nicaragua's then coordinator of the Junta of National Reconstruction—who later became the president of Nicaragua—urging him to ensure free and open elections.[79] The letter explained that the signatories opposed the Reagan administration's support of "military action directed against the people or government of Nicaragua" and suggested that if the country held free and open elections, "those responsible for supporting violence against your government . . . would have far greater difficulty winning support for their policies."

As these examples illustrate, and as Professor Ryan Scoville has further documented, Congress and its members have long engaged in a variety of actions that can be described as "legislative diplomacy."[80] Scoville concludes that, "due to the frequent, widespread, and longstanding nature of the practice and executive acquiescence, [legislative] communications that do not intrude on Article II power are likely entitled to the status of constitutional custom under a converted Frankfurter analysis."[81] In other words, these diplomatic activities are supported by historical gloss.[82]

Consider also U.S. participation in international organizations, which is a form of diplomacy. The United States' participation in the institutions is typically structured by a mix of international agreements and statutory law. For example, although the United States joined the United Nations through a treaty, Congress, in the UN Participation Act, directed how the president is to staff U.S. representation in the organization, while specifying that the U.S. representatives shall "act in accordance with the instructions of the President transmitted by the Secretary of State unless other means of transmission is directed by the President."[83] Moreover, even the underlying treaty establishing the United Nations, which required senatorial approval, has been found to limit executive power. The Supreme Court concluded in *Medellin v. Texas* that, by agreeing to a treaty that implicitly made decisions of the International Court of Justice (the central adjudicatory institution of the United Nations) non-self-executing in the United States, the Senate had implicitly disallowed presidents from giving preemptive legal effect to such decisions.[84]

The United States has joined other international organizations, like the World Bank, the International Monetary Fund, UNESCO, the World Health Organization, and the World Trade Organization, pursuant to statutory provisions—that is, it has joined these organizations through congressional-executive agreements rather than Article II treaties. When approving membership in these organizations, Congress has sometimes imposed limitations: for example, the statute governing U.S. involvement in the World Health Organization indicates that the United States must give one year's notice before withdrawing from the Organization—a limitation that the Trump administration appeared to follow when it announced its intent to withdraw in 2020.[85] As a practical matter, Congress is also often able to use its power over appropriations to influence how the executive branch engages with international institutions. In the 1990s, for example, Congress refused to fund U.S. dues to the United Nations, a move that prompted the executive branch to push for UN reforms in order to satisfy Congress.[86]

In a 2013 study of congressional influence on U.S. participation in the World Bank, Professor Kristina Daugirdas found that Congress's funding authority gave it powerful leverage. She observed that "over the past forty years, Congress has undertaken persistent and often successful efforts to shape day-to-day U.S. participation in the [World] Bank, a key international organization," and that, despite sometimes objecting to this practice on constitutional grounds, "the executive branch consistently implemented at least the letter of Congress's voting and negotiation instructions."[87] Sometimes Congress just flat out tells the executive branch what position it thinks should be taken in an international organization. As Daugirdas notes, this has happened numerous times with respect to the World Bank, and—at least before the late 1980s—without constitutional objection from the executive branch. For example, a 1974 statute directed the executive to "vote against any loan or other utilization of the funds of the Association for the benefit of any country which develops any nuclear explosive device, unless the country is or becomes a State Party to the Treaty on the Non-Proliferation of Nuclear Weapons,"[88] and the executive did so until the law was repealed several years later.

To take a non–World Bank example, the 1996 Helms Burton Act (referred to above) said that "the President should instruct the United States Permanent

Representative to the Organization of American States to oppose and vote against any termination of the suspension of the Cuban Government from participation in the Organization until the President determines . . . that a democratically elected government in Cuba is in power."[89] When signing the Act, President Clinton issued a statement saying that he would interpret certain identified provisions "as not derogating from the President's authority to conduct foreign policy," but he did not mention this provision (probably because it said "should" rather than "shall").[90]

In recent decades, it has become much more likely that the executive branch will raise constitutional objections against provisions like these. In a 2009 appropriations act, Congress attempted to stop the use of funds to pay for any U.S. delegation "to any specialized agency, body, or commission of the United Nations if such commission is chaired or presided over by a country, the government of which [has been determined to] support[] international terrorism."[91] President Obama signed the act into law but said in a signing statement that some provisions in it "would unduly interfere with my constitutional authority in the area of foreign affairs."[92] OLC subsequently released an opinion reasoning that the restriction quoted above was unconstitutional and thus could be disregarded by the president.[93]

Objections like these show that congressional authority in this domain is contested. Nevertheless, the extensive legislative practice makes it harder—at least from the perspective of historical gloss—for the executive branch to claim that Congress is powerless to act in the realm of diplomacy. As Professor Jean Galbraith has pointed out, in its opinions OLC normally places a lot of emphasis on historical practice, but this is less true of its opinions concerning executive power over diplomacy, presumably because the practice is less favorable to the executive branch in this domain.[94] To its credit, OLC in 2022 acknowledged (citing Galbraith's article) that "Congress has enacted many statutes purporting to direct the conduct of Executive Branch diplomatic engagements, often without Executive Branch objection," although OLC still insisted that "the President's authority to determine the form and manner of diplomacy is indefeasible by statute."[95] Importantly, Congress appears not to have been deterred by the executive branch's constitutional claims, so it is unlikely that the executive can claim congressional acquiescence in its positions.[96]

Even with respect to the actual conduct of international negotiations, which is indisputably an executive prerogative (in part because of historical practice),[97] the presidential monopoly has been less complete than executive branch lawyers have sometimes suggested. In recent decades, these lawyers have claimed that the president has exclusive control over "the time, scope, and objectives" of international negotiations. But, in fact, Congress has often directed the executive branch to negotiate on specific objectives, frequently without triggering controversy.[98] To take one of countless examples, Congress in 1996 stated that "the President shall seek to develop, in coordination with . . . other countries . . . a comprehensive, multilateral strategy to bring democracy to . . . Burma,"[99] and the Supreme Court cited this directive as one of the justifications for finding that Congress had preempted state laws that might undercut the president's efforts.[100] And, as for timing, Congress has sometimes imposed waiting periods before any resulting agreement can take effect, to give Congress time to review it. An especially noteworthy example of such a "report-and-wait" provision was the Iran Nuclear Agreement Review Act of 2015, pursuant to which Congress mandated that the deal reached by the Obama administration with Iran concerning the freezing of Iran's nuclear weapons program would not take effect for sixty days while Congress reviewed it and considered whether to block it by statute.[101] Obama signed the Act into law and complied with the waiting period.[102]

Regulating War

The Constitution makes the president the Commander in Chief of the armed forces. As Justice Jackson noted in his concurrence in *Youngstown*, the Commander in Chief Clause "undoubtedly puts the Nation's armed forces under presidential command."[103] As a result, there are likely constitutional limits on the extent to which Congress can interfere with that command.[104] In 1996, when Congress was considering a bill that would have disallowed the Department of Defense from using funds to place the armed forces "under United Nations operational or tactical control," OLC concluded, not implausibly, that the restriction would violate the president's Commander in Chief authority, reasoning that "the Commander-in-Chief Clause commits to the President alone the power to select the particular personnel who are to exercise tactical and operational control over U.S. forces."[105]

Nevertheless, Congress has an array of constitutional powers relating to war, and it has often used those powers to regulate how the president conducts military campaigns. An early example arose out of the Quasi-War that the United States fought against France in the late 1700s. As discussed in Chapter 6, Congress authorized that war through a series of statutes. In one of these statutes, Congress, attempting to stop U.S. trade with the enemy, authorized the navy to seize U.S. vessels "if upon examination it should appear that such ship or vessel is bound or sailing *to* any or place within the territory of the French Republic or her dependencies."[106] However, the Adams administration instructed U.S. forces to also seize U.S. vessels coming *from* French ports. Consistent with that instruction, a navy captain seized a vessel coming from the French port of Jeremie (in present-day Haiti), believing it to be a U.S. vessel. The vessel turned out to be Dutch, and a court restored possession of the vessel to its owners. The question before the Supreme Court was whether the captain was liable for damages, which turned on whether he had probable cause to seize the vessel. The Supreme Court held, in *Little v. Barreme,* that the captain could not have had probable cause because, even if he reasonably thought the vessel was American, there was statutory authority only to seize vessels sailing to French ports.[107] Writing for the Court, Chief Justice Marshall observed that the president might have had broader authority to order the seizure of U.S. vessels trading with the enemy *if there had been no statute on point.* But, he reasoned, once Congress regulated the issue, its enactment became controlling.[108]

Limitations like these have been especially relevant when Congress has, as in the Quasi-War, authorized limited military engagements. When Congress has formally declared war, it has broadly delegated to the president the authority to use the armed forces as the president sees fit. Even in declared wars, however, there have sometimes been questions about what is encompassed within Congress's delegation. In the War of 1812, for example, Congress had formally declared war, and it had broadly authorized the president to use "the whole land and naval forces" against the British and to "issue to private armed vessels of the United States commissions or letters of marque and general reprisal, in such form as he shall think proper . . . against the vessels, goods, and effects of the government of the said United Kingdom of Great Britain and Ireland, and the subjects thereof." But Congress did not specifically delegate authority to seize private British property in the United States. Before the war, Congress had enacted a general statute governing the treatment of enemy aliens, but that statute did not provide for seizure of their property. When the Madison administration seized timber owned by a British citizen, the Supreme Court held in *Brown v. United States* that it had acted without authority.[109] The Court reasoned that seizing enemy property in the United States requires legislative authorization, and it declined to construe the declaration of war as providing it, in part because Congress has the power to regulate captures of property and also because Congress had previously regulated the treatment of enemy aliens without providing for property seizure. "The act concerning alien enemies," the Court said, "affords a strong implication that [the president] did not possess those powers by virtue of the declaration of war."[110] It seems likely that courts today would construe a declaration of war, or a broad use-of-force delegation, more generously in favor of the president.[111] The key point, however, is that even during a war it was accepted that Congress's enactments were controlling.

Congressional limitations on presidential uses of force have been ubiquitous throughout American history, especially outside the context of declared wars. Congress's first neutrality statute in 1794, for example, authorized the president to use the military to help enforce the statute, but only "as shall be necessary to compel any foreign ship or vessel to depart the United States, in all cases in which, by the laws of nations or the treaties of the United States, they ought not to remain within the United States."[112] An early statute authorizing the president to call out the militia to address domestic disturbances limited the duration during which the forces could be used to no more than thirty days after the start of the next congressional session.[113] In a study of congressional authorizations of force made during the nineteenth and early twentieth centuries outside the context of declared wars, Professor Jack Goldsmith and I found that they commonly contained limitations relating to one or more of the following: "(1) the authorized military resources; (2) the authorized methods of force; (3) the authorized targets; (4) the purpose of the use of force; and (5) the timing and procedural restrictions on the use of force."[114]

None of this is to suggest, of course, that presidents have always perfectly complied with statutory restrictions. Among other things, some presidents have resorted to creative statutory interpretation to avoid congressional mandates that they have found to be too constraining. As early as the Washington administration, for example, presidents have sometimes loosely interpreted appropriations restrictions on military spending.[115] In the late 1930s and early 1940s, the Franklin Roosevelt administration interpreted its way around neutrality statutes that it found to be too constraining in its efforts to help the British in World War II.[116] But in these and similar instances, presidents did not suggest that the laws were unconstitutional, and in many instances, they have simply complied with restrictions, however grudgingly.

In addition to regulating war, Congress has also been involved at times in ending it. In part because of longstanding practice, it was once thought that the only way the United States could permanently end a state of war was through a peace treaty.[117] That gave the Senate, but not the House of Representatives, a role in ending U.S. wars. This was how the United States ended the Quasi-War against France, the Barbary Wars of the early 1800s, the War of 1812, the Mexican-American War of the 1840s, and the Spanish-American War of the late 1800s.[118] Before the conclusion of these treaties, presidents sometimes entered into armistice agreements on their own authority, which ended the fighting but not the formal state of war.

After fighting had ceased in World War I and the Senate had failed to approve the Versailles Treaty, however, the question arose whether Congress could simply declare the war over. After substantial debate, Congress passed a law purporting to do just that, but President Wilson vetoed the measure on the ground that he first wanted to extract concessions from Germany. Congress tried again during the next congressional session, and the new president, Warren Harding, signed the measure into law.[119] Something similar happened after active fighting had ceased in World War II. The United States entered into a peace treaty with most of the Axis powers but never entered into one with Germany. Instead, Congress simply declared the state of war with Germany to be over in 1951.[120]

Congressional authority to end wars is even more apparent in modern conflicts, which do not involve formal declarations of war. As recounted in Chapter 6, when presidents do not act unilaterally today, they act pursuant to statutory authorizations of force. Congress can, of course, terminate these statutory authorizations. In 1971, for example, Congress repealed the Gulf of Tonkin Resolution that had provided statutory authorization for the Vietnam War.[121] That same year, it disallowed the use of funds to finance the introduction of ground troops into Cambodia.[122] Eventually, in 1973, Congress prohibited the use of funds for "combat in or over or from off the shores of North Vietnam, South Vietnam, Laos or Cambodia."[123]

When U.S. troops suffered casualties in Lebanon in 1982, Congress pressured President Reagan into agreeing by statute to a 180-day deadline on the military mission.[124] Similarly, after U.S. troops suffered casualties in Somalia in 1993, Congress enacted a funding cutoff for operations that would take effect after a specified date.[125] In 2019, Congress voted to approve a bill that would have directed the president to remove U.S. troops from Yemen within thirty days,[126] but President Trump vetoed the bill, describing it as "an unnecessary, dangerous attempt to weaken my constitutional authorities."[127]

Although more controversial, the 1973 War Powers Resolution is also an important part of the legislative practice.[128] As discussed in Chapter 6, this statute, enacted over President Nixon's veto, provides that the president must terminate the use of the armed forces after sixty days unless Congress authorizes their use.[129] Some presidents (including Nixon) have contended that this sixty-day-cutoff provision is an unconstitutional interference with the Commander in Chief power, but other administrations have appeared to accept the constitutionality of the provision.

It is noteworthy that presidents have never openly acknowledged violating the Resolution's sixty-day-cutoff provision. To be sure, they have often used force without seeking congressional authorization, but many of these operations have been concluded before sixty days have elapsed—sometimes apparently to avoid a conflict with the statute.[130] In other situations, presidents argue either that they have statutory authorization or that they are not violating the terms of the resolution.[131] The statutory arguments are not always persuasive, but the main point is that the executive branch does not simply disregard the statute. If nothing else, the existence of this statute, even when its constitutionality is contested, undercuts practice-based claims of executive exclusivity since Congress has not ceded the field to the executive.

Treatment of Prisoners of War

Congress (and the Senate through treaties) has also regulated the detention and treatment of prisoners of war, even though this issue also falls within the president's Commander in Chief authority. Throughout U.S. history, presidents have ordered the detention of captured enemy forces, without constitutional controversy. And, as noted in Chapter 4, one of the earliest sole executive agreements was an agreement that President Madison made with Great Britain concerning the treatment and exchange of prisoners during the War of 1812. During the "war on terror," OLC argued not only that presidents had this authority but that *Congress could not regulate it.* In contending that a general statute limiting detention of U.S. citizens was inapplicable to the war on terror, for example, OLC argued that if the statute were applicable, it would be unconstitutional.[132] In another memo, OLC argued that Congress could not regulate the manner in which the executive branch interrogated wartime prisoners.[133]

These claims of exclusive Commander in Chief authority over the detention and treatment of prisoners are belied by historical practice. As an initial matter, Congress has from the earliest days regulated the conduct of the U.S. military, as the Constitution expressly empowers it to do. During the Revolutionary War, U.S. forces operated under Articles of War enacted by the Continental Congress, and, after the adoption of the Constitution, Congress directed the continued application of these Articles.[134] Congress periodically amended and updated the Articles, which were the precursor to the modern Uniform Code of Military Justice. Although both the Articles of War and the Uniform Code of Military Justice have extensively governed the conduct of the military, including during battle, they have not for the most part addressed the treatment of prisoners. During the nineteenth century, this issue was primarily addressed by the military itself, as informed by its understandings of the laws of war. For example, during the Civil War, the Army adopted the Lieber Code, an extensive set of provisions governing conduct during wartime, including provisions disallowing the mistreatment of prisoners of war—a code that had a significant effect on the development of international law on the topic.[135]

At times in the nineteenth century, however, Congress did touch on issues relating to the treatment of prisoners of war. During the Quasi-War, Congress enacted two provisions relating to prisoners of war, one concerning their exchange and the other authorizing retaliation against them.[136] At the outset of the War of 1812, Congress passed an "Act for the Safe Keeping and Accommodation of Prisoners of War," stating that "the President of the United States be, and he is hereby authorized to make such regulations and arrangements for the safe keeping, support and exchange of prisoners of war as he may deem expedient, until the same shall be otherwise provided for by law," and providing appropriations for these actions.[137] The next year, Congress authorized the president to retaliate against British violations of the laws of war carried out against U.S. soldiers.[138]

Starting in the early twentieth century, the United States began joining treaties regulating the conduct of war, including the detention and treatment of prisoners of war. The 1899 and 1907 Hague Conventions (which the United States ratified in 1902 and 1909, respectively) mandate that prisoners of war be treated humanely and that, absent a special agreement among the belligerents, they be given the same lodging, food, and clothing as the troops of the government that captures them. The Third Geneva Convention of 1949 (which the United States ratified in 1955) contains a more expansive set of protections—stating, for example, that prisoners "must at all times be protected, particularly against acts of violence or intimidation and against insults and public curiosity," and that "no physical or mental torture, nor any other form of coercion, may be inflicted on prisoners of war to secure from them information of any kind whatever." These treaties, regardless of whether they are judicially enforceable, are part of the laws of the land under the Supremacy Clause, and the U.S. military has long incorporated them into its regulations and field manuals.[139] Noncompliance with military regulations can in turn lead to court-martial under the Uniform Code of Military Justice. In 1996, Congress went further and incorporated aspects of these treaties into federal criminal law, in the War Crimes Act.[140] As amended, the Act criminalizes "grave breaches" of the Conventions, and it expressly applies to members of the U.S. Armed Forces. President Clinton raised no constitutional objection to the Act and in fact said that he was "committed to working with the Congress to expand the scope of this legislation."[141]

During the war on terror, there was dispute about whether and to what extent the Geneva Conventions applied given the unconventional nature of the conflict, but the Supreme Court in the *Hamdan* decision concluded that at least "Common Article 3" of the Conventions governed.[142] That provision, among other things, prohibits the "cruel treatment and torture" and "humiliating and degrading treatment" of detainees. Moreover, even before *Hamdan,* Congress had responded to revelations of prisoner abuse at the Abu Ghraib facility in Iraq by enacting the Detainee Treatment Act.[143] This Act prohibits the "cruel, inhuman, or degrading treatment or punishment" of anyone in U.S. custody and also states that no person within the custody of the Department of Defense shall "be subject to any treatment or technique of interrogation not authorized by and listed in the United States Army Field Manual on Intelligence Interrogation." President George W. Bush issued a statement when signing this statute saying (vaguely) that the executive branch would construe it "in a manner consistent with the constitutional authority of the President to supervise the unitary executive branch and as Commander in Chief and consistent with the constitutional limits on the judicial power." Subsequent news reports indicated, however, that the administration had changed its practices in response to the statute.[144]

Also before *Hamdan,* Congress had criminalized acts of torture, as part of its implementation of the Convention against Torture and Other Cruel, Inhuman or Degrading Treatment or Punishment. The criminal statute, by its terms, applies to any U.S. national (and anyone found in the United States) who commits torture under color of law outside the United States, and it contains no exception for conduct during a military conflict.[145] Moreover, the executive branch has not disputed that this statute applies in that context.[146] Finally, as noted at the outset of this chapter, the Supreme Court concluded in *Hamdan* that Congress, in the Uniform Code of Military Justice, had validly placed limitations on the use of military commissions to try enemy combatants. Since that decision, Congress has enacted two comprehensive military commission statutes for trying the war on terror detainees at Guantanamo.[147] There has been no dispute about Congress's constitutional authority to enact these statutes.

To its credit, OLC has retracted some of its early war on terror claims concerning exclusive executive authority over detainees. First, in 2004, it withdrew and replaced its August 2002 memorandum concerning the interrogation of detainees and explained that, because "the discussion in that memorandum concerning the President's Commander-in-Chief power and the potential defenses to liability was—and remains—unnecessary, it has been eliminated from the analysis that follows."[148] And then in 2009, after President Obama took office, OLC conducted a review of its war on terror memos and said that "the assertion in these opinions that Congress has no authority under the Constitution to address these matters by statute does not reflect the current views of OLC and has been overtaken by subsequent decisions of the Supreme Court and by legislation passed by Congress and supported by the President."[149]

The issue of congressional regulation of wartime detainees surfaced again when, starting in 2011, Congress began placing restrictions on the transfer of detainees out of the Guantanamo Bay detention facility.[150] First, it completely prohibited the use of funds to transfer any of the Guantanamo detainees to the United States. Second, for transfers to other countries, it required that presidents give thirty days' notice to Congress before the transfer and certify that the receiving country had taken the steps "necessary to ensure that the individual cannot engage or re-engage in any terrorist activity." When signing this legislation, President Obama said that the restriction on transferring detainees to the United States "intrudes upon critical executive branch authority to determine when and where to prosecute Guantanamo detainees" and that the notice provision for foreign transfers "would, under certain circumstances, violate constitutional separation of powers principles."[151]

Despite his signing statement, Obama complied with the restriction concerning the transfer of detainees to the United States.[152] But he appeared to violate the notice provision for foreign transfers when he transferred five detainees to Afghanistan as part of a prisoner exchange in May 2014. The Government Accountability Office, which is an investigatory arm of Congress, concluded that the transfer violated the statute but, per its usual practice, took no position on the statute's constitutionality.[153] Other than in this instance, presidents have complied with the statute when transferring detainees to other countries.

Conclusion

A common complaint about giving weight to historical practice when interpreting the separation of powers is that it unduly favors the expansion of executive authority. The executive branch, it is argued, can take actions more easily than can Congress, and Congress is left having to react, which it has trouble doing because of collective action and partisan limitations. While there is truth to this account, it is only a partial story. Congress has an extensive array of textual sources of authority in the Constitution that are unavailable to the executive branch, and its control over appropriations gives it particular leverage in interbranch disputes. When those constitutional authorities are combined with the historical gloss that comes from legislative practice, Congress looks more formidable than it is sometimes described, especially in its ability to defeat claims of exclusive executive power.

The executive branch is aware of the potential importance of gloss in bolstering congressional authority, which is one reason that in recent decades it has often issued signing statements suggesting that legislative provisions are unconstitutionally intruding on its authority.[154] Even when subject to these statements, however, legislative enactments are relevant to Congress's gloss-based authority. At a minimum, these enactments show that claims of exclusive executive authority for these issues are contested, thus undercutting any gloss-based claims that the executive may make in support of such authority. Understood in this light, historical gloss promotes rather than undermines checks and balances.

The legislative practices described in this chapter, it should be emphasized, are just the tip of the iceberg of vast congressional regulation of foreign affairs, across almost every issue area. As will become evident in the next chapter, when Congress regulates, it often delegates broad authority to the executive branch. But the very act of delegating is implicitly a claim by Congress that it has authority over the subject, and Congress can and sometimes does place meaningful limitations on its delegations. Courts, moreover, generally assume that presidents are bound by the statutes. Decisions that, like *Zivotofsky*, uphold presidential disregard of a statute are very rare; in fact, *Zivotofsky* was the first and only Supreme Court decision ever to allow a president to disregard a statutory foreign affairs directive. Despite the frequent claims of an imperial presidency, Congress can often have the last word in foreign affairs.

8

DELEGATIONS OF AUTHORITY

THE BLOODIEST INTERSTATE CONFLICT IN SOUTH AMERICA DURING THE twentieth century was the 1932–1935 Chaco War between Bolivia and Paraguay, so named because it involved a dispute over the Gran Chaco region, which was thought (falsely) to be rich in oil deposits. It was also the first officially declared war since the issuance of the Kellogg-Briand Pact in 1928, in which the signatories (which by the time of the Chaco War included Paraguay but not Bolivia) had renounced war as an instrument of foreign policy. At the request of President Franklin Roosevelt, Congress passed a joint resolution in 1934 stating that it would be a crime to sell arms or munitions from the United States to the participants in the Chaco War "if the President finds that the prohibition of the sale of arms and munitions . . . may contribute to the reestablishment of peace between those countries."[1] Once triggered, the criminal prohibition would apply "except under such limitations and exceptions as the President prescribes" and would last "until otherwise ordered by the President or by Congress." That same day, Roosevelt issued a proclamation making the requisite finding.[2]

The Justice Department subsequently obtained an indictment against the Curtiss-Wright Export Corporation and its officers for shipping aircraft machine guns to Bolivia. The case made its way to the Supreme Court, and the central question was whether it was constitutionally permissible for Congress to have delegated authority to the president to put into effect the criminal prohibition. The case arose at a time in which the Supreme Court enforced a "nondelegation doctrine," pursuant to which Congress was limited in its ability to delegate to the executive branch discretion in carrying out statutory mandates. The lower court held that the doctrine applied in this context, and it found that the joint resolution constituted an unconstitutional delegation.[3] But the Supreme Court reversed. In an opinion written by Justice Sutherland, the Court held that the nondelegation doctrine did not apply as strictly to foreign affairs statutes. Among other things, the Court emphasized a longstanding practice of broad congressional delegations of foreign affairs authority to the president, something that the Court said "goes a long way in the direction of proving the presence of unassailable ground for the constitutionality of the practice, to be found in the origin and history of the power involved, or in its nature, or in both combined." In other words, the Court relied on historical gloss.[4]

This chapter recounts some of the relevant legislative practice involving delegations of foreign affairs authority, both before and after *Curtiss-Wright*. Because statutory delegations are endemic across wide swaths of American law, including most areas of foreign relations law, the examples are necessarily selective. But they should be sufficient to show that nondelegation concerns have not played much of a constraining role in the foreign affairs area. The chapter concludes with reflections about the implications of this practice.

Statutory Delegations and Foreign Affairs

Article I of the Constitution vests "all legislative Powers granted herein" in Congress. It has been argued at times that Congress cannot delegate these legislative powers to other actors. It is not entirely clear what it would mean for Congress to do so. A narrow view of legislating is that it simply means enacting a law through the process specified in Article I of the Constitution (i.e., majority votes in both chambers and presentment to the president for signature or supermajority votes in both chambers to override a presidential veto). If that is all that it means, then a properly enacted law never delegates legislative power, regardless of how much authority the law assigns to other actors.[5]

A broader view is that the power to legislate involves the power to make certain policy choices. Under that view, Congress can delegate to the executive branch the task of implementing and enforcing policy choices that Congress has made, perhaps even contingent on the executive branch's factual assessments, but it cannot delegate the responsibility for developing the policy in the first instance. It is not clear how feasible it is for courts to draw this sort of policymaking-versus-implementation distinction.[6] Nor is it clear that doing so would be good for governance: modern conditions are sufficiently complex that Congress, by necessity, must delegate vast amounts of responsibility to the executive branch, and judicially imposed limitations might make it unduly difficult for the government to act effectively.[7]

The practical need for broad delegations is not a new phenomenon. A constitutional law scholar observed in 1910: "During recent years, with the increase of governmental functions, both in number and complexity, and especially with the extension of the law's control over matters of industrial and technical interest, the delegation to administrative agents and in particular to boards or commissions, of wide spheres of discretionary duties, has become a necessity."[8] The Supreme Court nevertheless applied a "nondelegation doctrine" in the mid-1930s as a basis for invalidating two pieces of New Deal legislation.[9] The Court did not dispute that Congress can "leav[e] to selected instrumentalities the making of subordinate rules within prescribed limits and the determination of facts to which the policy as declared by the Legislature is to apply."[10] But in these cases the Court concluded that Congress had failed to declare the relevant policy and instead had improperly left that determination to the executive branch.

Since those two New Deal decisions, however, the Court has not enforced the nondelegation doctrine with any rigor. Nominally, the Court has insisted that the legislature "lay down by legislative act an intelligible principle to which the person or body authorized to [act] is directed to conform."[11] But in practice it has deferred to Congress's judgments about the proper breadth of the delegations, and it has not invalidated a single statute under the nondelegation doctrine since 1935. It has also made clear that the "outer limits" of its nondelegation decisions allow Congress to confer substantial discretion on the executive branch.[12]

This could change. In recent years, a number of justices have expressed interest in reinvigorating the nondelegation doctrine.[13] As a possible step in that direction, the Court has applied a "major questions doctrine," pursuant to which administrative agencies must have "clear congressional authorization" before being allowed to make certain significant policy decisions.[14] Some justices who seek to revive the nondelegation doctrine, however, appear willing to allow for broader delegations in foreign affairs, consistent with the holding in *Curtiss-Wright*.[15] Meanwhile, there has been robust academic debate about whether an originalist approach to constitutional interpretation provides support for a nondelegation doctrine, whether in domestic or foreign affairs.[16]

In *Curtiss-Wright*, the Court reviewed what it described as an "unbroken legislative practice which has prevailed almost from the inception of the national government to the present day." In describing this practice, it began with a 1794 embargo statute, discussed below.

Embargoes, Tariffs, and Other Trade Restrictions

From early in U.S. history, statutes gave presidents discretionary authority with respect to embargoes, tariffs, and other trade restrictions. Some of these delegations were conditioned on factual assessments by the president, but others were conditioned merely on the president's policy or predictive judgments. In 1794, for example, Congress authorized the president to impose "an embargo on ships and vessels" while Congress was out of session "whenever, in his opinion, the public safety shall so require" and "under such regulations as the circumstances . . . may require."[17] Despite its breadth, there is no record of any constitutional objection to this delegation.[18] A 1799 statute suspending trade with France authorized the president, "if he shall deem it expedient and consistent with the interest of the United States," to stop the suspension "whenever, in his opinion the interest of the United States shall require."[19] Again, the delegation did not appear to trigger constitutional concerns. Some members of Congress did object on nondelegation grounds to an 1808 law that allowed the president to suspend an embargo whenever he concluded that the actions of warring European powers "rendered . . . the United States sufficiently safe,"[20] but they were in the minority.

The Supreme Court did not disapprove any of these delegations. An 1810 statute authorized the president to exempt Great Britain and France from the revival of a trade embargo if he determined that they were respecting the neutral commerce of the United States.[21] After the president exempted France but not Great Britain and goods shipped from Great Britain were seized, the statute was challenged on nondelegation grounds, in *Cargo of the Brig Aurora v. United States*.[22] The challenger argued that the statute should not be construed as allowing the president to revive the prior embargo statute, because "Congress could not transfer the legislative power to the President." The government responded that Congress "did not transfer any power of legislation to the President" but rather "only prescribed the evidence which should be admitted of a fact, upon which the law should go into effect." The Supreme Court did not address the nondelegation issue directly, but it upheld the statute, noting that "we can see no sufficient reason why the legislature should not exercise its discretion in reviving the [embargo law], either expressly or conditionally, as their judgment should direct." This decision was cited by early commentators for the proposition that Congress has substantial ability to delegate authority to the president.[23]

Congress similarly delegated authority to the president to impose or repeal tariffs and duties on imports. An 1815 statute, for example, allowed for a repeal of duties on goods imported into the United States "whenever the President . . . shall be satisfied that the discriminating or countervailing duties of such foreign nation, so far as they operate to the disadvantage of the United States, have been abolished."[24] Many similar delegations were made throughout the nineteenth century.

The delegation in the McKinley Tariff Act of 1890 was broader. It authorized the president to impose duties on imports "for such time as he may deem just" whenever, in his judgment, the duties imposed by the importing country were "reciprocally unequal or unreasonable."[25] As noted in Chapter 4, in addition to relying on this statute to make tariff adjustments, presidents treated it as a source of authority for concluding agreements with other nations. The Supreme Court rejected a nondelegation challenge to the statute in *Field v. Clark.*[26] The challengers argued that the statute was "unconstitutional, as delegating to [the president] both legislative and treaty-making powers." In addressing this claim, the Court extensively reviewed the historical practice of congressional delegations, starting with the 1794 embargo statute discussed above, and it concluded that the statute before it "has the sanction of many precedents in legislation." Even if *Brig Aurora* had never been decided, said the Court, "the practical construction of the Constitution, as given by so many acts of Congress and embracing almost the entire period of our national existence, should not be overruled unless upon a conviction that such legislation was clearly incompatible with the supreme law of the land." In other words, as it did more than forty years later in *Curtiss-Wright,* the Court placed substantial weight on historical gloss.

The Court in *Field* did not, it should be emphasized, deny that there were limits on the extent to which Congress could delegate authority. Indeed, it said that a nondelegation limitation is "universally recognized as vital to the integrity and maintenance of the system of government ordained by the constitution." The Court simply concluded, in part on the basis of historical practice, that the 1890 statute "does not in any real sense invest the President with the power of legislation." Two justices dissented on this point, contending that the statute gave the president too much discretion.

Later statutes, such as the Dingley Tariff Act of 1897, expressly delegated to the president agreement-making authority relating to tariffs.[27] Another statute enacted that year authorized the Secretary of the Treasury, upon recommendation of a board of experts, to "establish uniform standards of purity, quality, and fitness for consumption of all kinds of teas imported into the United States."[28] The Supreme Court upheld this delegation in a 1904 decision, *Buttfield v. Stranahan,* reasoning that Congress had "fixed a primary standard" and committed to the Secretary of the Treasury "the mere executive duty to effectuate the legislative policy declared in the statute."[29]

By the 1930s, Congress was delegating even more general authority to the executive branch to negotiate trade-related executive agreements. For example, in the 1934 Reciprocal Trade Agreements Act, Congress provided that "the President, whenever he finds as a fact that any existing duties or other import restrictions of the United States or any foreign country are unduly burdening and restricting the foreign trade of the United States . . . is authorized from time to time—to enter into foreign trade agreements with foreign governments and instrumentalities thereof."[30] The Act provided that the delegated authority would sunset every three years, but Congress extended it numerous times. This statute was part of a more general shift in the early twentieth century toward executive control over U.S. trade policy.[31]

Congress also delegated other trade-related authority in this period. For example, the Tariff Act of 1922 included a "flexible tariff" provision that allowed the president, with the advice of the U.S. Tariff Commission, to change tariff rates by as much as 50 percent to account for differentials in foreign and domestic production costs. The Supreme Court approved this delegation in *J. W. Hampton Jr. & Co. v. United States*.[32] In doing so, it announced the now-canonical "intelligible principle" test, stating: "If Congress shall lay down by legislative act an intelligible principle to which the person or body authorized to fix such rates is directed to conform, such legislative action is not a forbidden delegation of legislative power."

Congress conferred additional trade-related authority on the president in the Trade Expansion Act of 1962. This statute allowed the president to reduce tariffs across entire categories of products, rather than on an item-by-item basis, as the Reciprocal Trade Agreements Act had required. At the same time, Congress created a Special Trade Representative agency within the executive branch, hoping to reduce the influence of general foreign policy considerations, as opposed to domestic economic policy concerns, on U.S. trade policy. Although Congress in this legislation did not delegate authority to negotiate nontariff barriers, the Johnson administration exercised such authority anyway, contending that these agreements could be concluded as sole executive agreements—a move that not surprisingly created friction with Congress. But, in 1974, Congress delegated authority to negotiate on nontariff barriers as well. It also agreed to approve such agreements through a fast-track congressional process.

The 1962 Act, as amended in 1974, also includes broad authority to regulate trade in order to promote U.S. national security. Section 232 provides that if the Secretary of Commerce finds that an "article is being imported into the United States in such quantities or under such circumstances as to threaten to impair the national security," the president is authorized to "take such action, and for such time, as he deems necessary to adjust the imports of [the] article and its derivatives so that . . . imports [of the article] will not threaten to impair the national security."[33] In a 1976 decision, the Supreme Court dismissed nondelegation concerns with respect to this statute, insisting that it easily meets the intelligible principle test.[34] President Trump controversially used Section 232 to impose high tariffs on aluminum and steel imports, and, on the basis of precedent, the lower courts rejected nondelegation challenges to his actions.[35]

Emergency Power and Defense

The Constitution does not confer a general emergency power, but it does confer a variety of powers that are relevant in emergencies. Congress is given the authority to, among other things, regulate commerce, create and maintain the armed forces, and declare war—powers that are all potentially relevant in an emergency. It also has the authority to "provide for calling forth the militia to execute the laws of the union, suppress insurrections and repel invasions." As for presidents, they have the status of Commander in Chief, which, as discussed in Chapter 6, has long been assumed to include the authority to defend the United States from an attack. The president is also directed by the Constitution to take care that the laws are faithfully executed, which may carry some authority to take actions during emergencies.

Congress has long delegated a variety of powers to the president relating to emergencies and defense. For example, since the early days of the nation, it has given the president broad discretion over calling forth the militia.[36] Responding to hostilities between Native Americans and western settlers, Congress in 1790 authorized the president "to call into service from time to time, such part of the militia of the states . . . as he may judge necessary for the purpose" of protecting the inhabitants of the frontiers.[37] A 1795 statute provided that "whenever the United States shall be invaded or be in imminent danger of invasion from any foreign nation or Indian tribe, it shall be lawful for the President of the United States to call forth such number of the militia of the state or states most convenient to the place of danger or scene of action as he may judge necessary to repel such invasion."[38] The Supreme Court upheld this delegation and noted, in an opinion by Justice Story, that the justices "are all of opinion that the authority to decide whether the exigency has arisen belongs exclusively to the President, and that his decision is conclusive upon all other persons."[39]

Congress also early on gave presidents authority over whether to raise additional troops or build more ships. A 1791 law authorized the president to raise 2,000 soldiers for the protection of the frontier "if the President should be of opinion, that it will be conducive to the public service."[40] In 1792, Congress provided for three additional regiments to protect the frontier but said that it was "lawful for the President of the United States, to forbear to raise, or to discharge, after they shall be raised, the whole or any part of the said three additional regiments, in case events shall in his judgment, render his doing so consistent with the public safety."[41]

Delegation concerns were sometimes raised about these measures. In 1794, Congress rejected a proposal to authorize the president to raise up to 10,000 troops, after James Madison and others objected that it would effectively transfer to the president Congress's power to raise armies.[42] But just a few days later, Congress authorized the president, while it was out of session, to commission up to ten galleys "if the same shall appear to him necessary for the protection of the United States."[43]

In 1797, a proposal was made in the House of Representatives to authorize the president to build more naval ships "whenever, in his opinion, the circumstances of the country shall require."[44] An objection was raised that such a measure would improperly delegate Congress's authority over the military to the president. The House member who had suggested the measure replied that he saw no constitutional problem with Congress empowering the president to act on its behalf, especially when Congress was out of session, and he cited various precedents, including the 1794 embargo statute. The House passed the measure after making clear that it applied only when Congress was out of session and only if the president determined that the vessels were needed for the defense of the seacoast.

In 1798, on the eve of war with France, Congress made an array of delegations, most of which passed without controversy.[45] One proposed delegation, however, prompted significant debate. A bill that was approved by the Senate would have given the president the authority to raise a provisional army of 20,000 troops "whenever he shall judge the public safety shall require the measure."[46] In addition to making policy objections, a number of representatives in the House objected to the bill on the ground that it unconstitutionally delegated Congress's authority to raise the troops.[47] One of the leading opponents, Representative Gallatin, contended that "if Congress were once to admit the principle that they have a right to vest in the President powers placed in their hands by the Constitution, that instrument would become a piece of blank paper."[48] Supporters of the bill responded by, among other things, invoking legislative precedent in which Congress had previously delegated broad discretion to the president.[49] Representative Pinckney expressed the view, for example, that "where a thing has frequently been done in one way, and no objections raised to that course, it was reasonable to suppose that course was not unconstitutional."[50]

Some opponents of the troops bill questioned the extent to which the precedent was on point, arguing, for example, that the delegation here was more substantial than in past instances.[51] Others argued that, even if on point, the precedent could not legitimize what they viewed as an unconstitutional action.[52] Gallatin also raised a slippery slope argument, expressing concern that if the precedent were "to induce Congress to pass this bill, would not it be brought as a precedent to induce future Legislatures to make further and still more dangerous transfers of power?"[53] In response to these arguments, Representative Dayton expressed surprise that a nondelegation argument "was now, for the first time, made by the enlightened members of the 5th Congress, although not a session had passed since 1791, in which the same had not been acted upon and sanctioned."[54]

The troops bill was narrowed before it was passed, although not sufficiently to assuage the concerns of Gallatin and others who ultimately voted against it. The revised bill limited the president's authority to raise a provisional army to situations involving a declared war, an actual invasion, or an "imminent danger of such invasion discovered in his opinion to exist," and only when Congress was in recess.[55] Gallatin argued that the third contingency in the revised bill was "liable to the same Constitutional objection to which the original bill was liable, as it left it to the opinion of the President to decide the proper time of raising an army,"[56] but he was in the minority.

Congress continued to delegate broad defense and emergency authority to the president. The 1807 Insurrection Act supplemented the president's authority under the 1795 Militia Act by allowing him to call out the regular armed forces, whenever it was appropriate to call out the militia, "for the purpose of suppressing such insurrection, or of causing the laws to be duly executed," "as shall be judged necessary."[57] An 1861 statute passed at the outset of the Civil War delegated even broader authority, to be exercised by the president "as he may deem necessary."[58] The modern version of these statutory provisions states that "whenever the President considers that unlawful obstructions, combinations, or assemblages, or rebellion against the authority of the United States, make it impracticable to enforce the laws of the United States in any State by the ordinary course of judicial proceedings, he may call into Federal service such of the militia of any State, and use such of the armed forces, as he considers necessary to enforce those laws or to suppress the rebellion."[59]

Congress has at times also delegated to the president the authority to suspend the writ of habeas corpus. The Constitution provides that the privilege of seeking habeas corpus (that is, judicial review of the legality of the government's detention of an individual) cannot be suspended except "when in Cases of Rebellion or Invasion the public Safety may require it." Because this clause is contained in Article I, which sets forth Congress's powers, it has generally been assumed that only Congress has the authority to suspend the writ. Controversially, President Lincoln acted on his own authority to suspend the writ during the Civil War.[60] Eventually, in 1863, Congress authorized the president to suspend the writ "whenever, in his judgment, the public safety may require it."[61]

Since the Civil War, Congress has delegated suspension authority to the president seven times, each time letting the president decide whether suspension was warranted under the circumstances.[62] On the basis of this authority, presidents have acted to suspend habeas corpus in three situations since the Civil War: in 1871, during Reconstruction, when a number of South Carolina counties were overrun by the Ku Klux Klan; in the Philippines during a 1905 insurrection while the United States was occupying the territory; and in Hawaii in 1941 after the bombing of Pearl Harbor. Notably, Congress did not act to suspend the writ (or authorize suspension of the writ) after the September 11, 2001, terrorist attacks. Congress did attempt to prevent federal court review of the U.S. government's detention of alleged terrorists at the Guantanamo Bay detention facility in Cuba, but the Supreme Court held that this effort improperly violated the habeas rights of the detainees, given that there had been no suspension of the writ.[63]

Congress has also delegated to the president more general emergency powers relating to both domestic and foreign affairs. These delegations include the authority to impose a variety of economic sanctions on other nations and their citizens. In 1917, after the United States had declared war against Germany, Congress passed the Trading with the Enemy Act (TWEA).[64] As originally enacted, the statute gave the president broad authority to regulate trade and financial transactions with individuals and entities connected with countries with which the United States was at war. The Act was expanded during the 1930s to operate not only during time of war but also "during any other period of national emergency declared by the President."[65]

Concerned about potential abuses of emergency authority by the president, Congress in 1976 enacted the National Emergencies Act (NEA), which imposed a variety of procedural limitations on the use of emergency authority.[66] Among other things, the NEA directs that national emergencies are to end after a year unless the president publishes a notice of renewal in the *Federal Register*. It also states that Congress is to meet every six months to consider whether to end a national emergency by joint resolution, although Congress has almost never done so.[67]

Presidents have frequently used the NEA provision allowing for renewal of emergencies. As of the fall of 2023, there were over forty national emergencies in effect, the earliest of which dated to 1979 (during the Iranian hostage crisis). It would take a statutory override to terminate such an emergency against the wishes of a president, which might require overriding a presidential veto. The original NEA authorized termination through a "concurrent resolution," which does not require presidential approval. However, in response to the Supreme Court's decision in *INS v. Chadha,* discussed below, Congress amended the NEA in 1985 to require the enactment of a joint resolution (the equivalent of a statute).

Many of the existing national emergencies were declared under the authority granted in a 1977 statute, the International Emergency Economic Powers Act (IEEPA).[68] While limiting the president's TWEA authority to wartime, IEEPA confers on the president broad powers to regulate foreign-owned property and international commercial transactions upon a declaration of emergency.[69] Presidents are authorized to declare such an emergency upon a finding of "any unusual and extraordinary threat, which has its source in whole or substantial part outside the United States, to the national security, foreign policy, or economy of the United States."[70] IEEPA has been used to address a broad range of issues, including international terrorism, the proliferation of weapons of mass destruction, foreign election interference, and the promotion of human rights and democracy.[71] Lower courts have consistently rejected nondelegation challenges to IEEPA, even though the violation of regulations issued under the statute can carry criminal penalties.[72]

The president has also been granted significant discretion under the Arms Export Control Act. The Act authorizes the president, "in furtherance of world peace and the security and foreign policy of the United States . . . to control the import and export of defense articles and services" and to "designate those items which will be considered as defense articles and defense services," and it directs the president to take various considerations into account in deciding whether to issue export licenses.[73] As with IEEPA, lower courts have rejected nondelegation challenges to the Act, concluding that it satisfies the intelligible principle standard.[74]

Another emergency-related statute is the Defense Production Act of 1950, which was enacted during the Korean War.[75] This statute allows the president to, among other things, contract with and incentivize U.S. manufacturers to expand and redirect their production to support national defense and responses to emergencies, and both President Trump and President Biden invoked it in response to the COVID-19 pandemic. Most of the provisions in the Act must be periodically renewed by Congress, which it has done over fifty times.

Exclusion of Aliens and Passport Control

Congress has also at times delegated to the president broad authority to exclude aliens from the United States. The Alien Friends Act of 1798 (one of the statutes that made up the infamous Alien and Sedition Acts) authorized "the President of the United States . . . to order all such aliens as he shall judge dangerous to the peace and safety of the United States" to depart the country.[76] Nondelegation concerns (as well as constitutional rights objections) were expressed in connection with this legislation,[77] but the legislation was adopted anyway. The legislation expired two years later and was not renewed. Another statute that was part of the Alien and Sedition Acts was the Alien Enemies Act, which delegated broad authority to the president during wartime to detain and remove aliens who are from enemy countries,[78] and this delegation remains in effect today.[79]

After this period, Congress was relatively inactive on immigration issues throughout the nineteenth century, leaving the area to be addressed through state legislation and treaty making.[80] That changed by the late nineteenth century—when Congress began, for example, barring Chinese laborers.[81]

Legislation enacted during World War I gave the president the authority to exclude aliens during times of war.[82] In 1941, on the eve of U.S. entry into World War II, Congress expanded this delegation to allow the president to "impose additional restrictions and prohibitions on the entry into and departure of persons from the United States during the national emergency proclaimed May 27, 1941."[83] Pursuant to this statute, President Roosevelt issued a proclamation that provided that "no alien should be permitted to enter the United States if it were found that such entry would be prejudicial to the interest of the United States." The Supreme Court rejected a nondelegation challenge to the statute in a 1950 decision, *Knauff v. Shaughnessy.*[84] The Court reasoned that the right to exclude aliens "stems not alone from legislative power but is inherent in the executive power to control the foreign affairs of the nation." As a result, said the Court, "when Congress prescribes a procedure concerning the admissibility of aliens, it is not dealing alone with a legislative power" but rather "is implementing an inherent executive power."

The modern exclusion legislation, which dates to 1952, is even broader, giving presidents the authority to restrict the entry of aliens whenever they find that their entry "would be detrimental to the interests of the United States."[85] Based on that authority, President Trump temporarily excluded aliens from eight countries, contending that their systems for managing and sharing information about their nationals were inadequate.[86] The Supreme Court upheld the exclusion, in *Trump v. Hawaii,* noting that the statute "exudes deference to the President in every clause" and concluding that Trump's order "is well within this comprehensive delegation."[87] In response to the plaintiffs' argument that the delegation should be construed in light of past executive branch practice, the Court said that even if this were so, that history did not clearly show limitations on the use "of a statute that grants the President sweeping authority to decide whether to suspend entry, whose entry to suspend, and for how long." The dissenters challenged the ban on constitutional grounds relating to religious discrimination, but they did not contend that the underlying statute violated the nondelegation doctrine.[88]

Since the mid-nineteenth century, Congress has also delegated extensive authority to the president over the issuance of passports to U.S. citizens. As discussed in Chapter 7, the issuance of passports was initially handled by the executive branch, without any specific delegation of authority from Congress. In part, this was because passports did not play a significant role in international travel at that time. In 1856, however, Congress made the issuance of passports solely a federal function and for the first time purported to authorize the executive branch to issue passports, "under such rules as the President shall designate and prescribe for and on behalf of the United States."[89] Subsequent versions of the statute have had similarly worded grants of authority.

Starting in 1952, authority over passports became more closely connected with issues of individual liberty because they became mandatory for U.S. citizens leaving the country.[90] In light of this change, restrictions on passports might infringe on a U.S. citizen's right to travel. In several decisions, the Supreme Court considered the scope of the executive branch's authority concerning passports in light of this potential impact on individual liberty. Although the passport statute allows the State Department to issue passports "under such rules as the President shall designate," the Court looked to historical practice to discern limitations in the scope of the delegation. Because of the limiting effect of such practice, as well as the need for flexibility in foreign affairs, the Court did not perceive there to be a serious nondelegation problem, despite the statute's broad language.

The first decision in this line of cases is *Kent v. Dulles,* a 1958 decision in which the Court invalidated State Department regulations that had required the denial of passports to members of the Communist Party.[91] In discerning the scope of authority that Congress had delegated to the executive branch under the then-operative 1926 version of the passport statute, the Court relied heavily on historical practice. The Court noted that, before the enactment of the statute, the executive branch had generally denied passports only for reasons relating to the citizenship or allegiance of the applicant or for fraud or violation of U.S. laws. As a result, said the Court, only those grounds "could fairly be argued were adopted by Congress in light of prior administrative practice."

In the next decision, *Zemel v. Rusk,* the Court held in 1965 that the executive branch could refuse to allow U.S. passports to be used for entering Cuba.[92] In concluding that the 1926 passport statute conveyed this authority, the Court cited a record of executive branch imposition of both peacetime and wartime area restrictions during the decade prior to enactment of the 1926 statute, as well as "the State Department's continued imposition of area restrictions during both times of war and periods of peace since 1926." Unlike in *Kent v. Dulles,* said the Court, here there was "an administrative practice sufficiently substantial and consistent to warrant the conclusion that Congress had implicitly approved it." Finally, citing *Curtiss-Wright* and noting that in foreign affairs Congress "must of necessity paint with a brush broader than that it customarily wields in domestic areas," the Court rejected a nondelegation challenge to the statute. While emphasizing that "this does not mean that, simply because a statute deals with foreign relations, it can grant the Executive totally unrestricted freedom of choice," the Court said that the 1926 statute "contains no such grant."

In the final passport decision, *Haig v. Agee*, the Court held in 1981 that the passport statute authorized the Secretary of State to revoke a passport if the passport holder's activities abroad were determined likely to cause serious damage to U.S. national security or foreign policy.[93] (In that case, the passport holder, a former Central Intelligence Agency employee, was seeking to expose CIA agents in other countries.) Again, the Court looked to historical practice, noting that both before and after the enactment of the 1926 statute, the executive branch had asserted authority to withhold passports on this basis. Judicial deference to such consistent administrative practice is especially warranted, the Court reasoned, "in the areas of foreign policy and national security, where congressional silence is not to be equated with congressional disapproval."[94]

Thus, notwithstanding the individual liberty issues at stake, the Court allowed Congress in these cases to delegate broad discretion to the executive branch, at least in areas in which the executive branch had previously exercised discretion. Moreover, even in the most restrictive of these decisions, *Kent v. Dulles*, the Court made clear that it would be even more generous when interpreting a delegation "dealing with political questions entrusted to the Chief Executive by the Constitution" rather than questions implicating individual liberty.[95]

Using Military Force

Congress has often delegated authority to the president to use military force. The Constitution assigns to Congress the power to declare war, and throughout U.S. history Congress has issued eleven declarations of war, in connection with five military conflicts. The last such declaration was against Romania in 1942, in connection with World War II.[96] Each of the eleven declarations has included an authorization of force that has left it to the president to decide how best to use U.S. forces to bring the conflict to a successful resolution.[97] These authorizations do not involve delegations of Congress's formal authority to declare war, since Congress is itself issuing the declaration. But they do purport to be broad delegations of use-of-force authority in the context of a declared war. It might be argued that these delegations are superfluous: perhaps the declaration of war triggers broad authority in the Commander in Chief to use the armed forces as he or she sees fit. But it is noteworthy that Congress's consistent practice has been to include these authorizations in addition to declaring war and that the authorizations purport to grant the president broad discretion.

In addition to its five declared wars, the United States has been involved in hundreds of other military conflicts and engagements, of varying scope and duration. As discussed in Chapter 6, in many of these instances presidential uses of force have not been specifically authorized by Congress. When Congress has authorized the use of force outside the context of declared wars, it has often conveyed substantial discretion to the president, especially in the post–World War II era.[98]

The United States' first war against a foreign power was the Quasi-War against France at the end of the 1700s, which was a response to French seizures of U.S. merchant vessels throughout the Atlantic and Caribbean. Congress never formally declared war on France, but it did authorize a variety of war-related actions.[99] For example, it authorized the president "to subdue, seize and take any armed French vessel, which shall be found within the jurisdictional limits of the United States, or elsewhere, on the high seas."[100] In part because of the need to address issues arising in connection with the seizure of prize vessels (that is, vessels captured because they belonged to the enemy or were engaged in unlawful trade with the enemy), the Supreme Court was more active in addressing war powers questions in the early years of U.S. history than in the modern era. In connection with the Quasi-War, the Court held that Congress need not formally declare war to authorize hostilities and that the navy was required to comply with restrictions that Congress had placed on its authorizations.[101]

Congress subsequently gave presidents broad authority to address threats posed by the Barbary pirates operating off the coast of North Africa. In an 1802 statute, Congress authorized the president to seize vessels belonging to the bey of Tripoli and his subjects "and also to cause to be done all such other acts of precaution or hostility as the state of war will justify, *and may, in his opinion, require.*"[102] Congress issued a similarly worded authorization in 1815 with respect to Algiers.[103] In both situations, Congress was effectively authorizing war in response to hostile actions against U.S. interests, and, as in situations in which it has formally declared war, it left the details of the prosecution of the war to the president, as Commander in Chief.

In 1839, in response to a dispute with Great Britain over the northeast boundary between the United States and Canada, Congress authorized President Van Buren "to resist any attempt on the part of Great Britain, to enforce, by arms, her claim to exclusive jurisdiction over that part of the State of Maine which is in dispute," by "employ[ing] the naval and military forces of the United States and such portions of the militia as he may deem advisable to call into service."[104] In 1858, in response to an attack by Paraguay on a U.S. ship, the *Water Witch,* Congress authorized President Buchanan to "adopt such measures and use such force" as needed to induce Paraguay to give "just satisfaction" for the attack.[105] Some House members raised delegation concerns about that legislation, but they were outvoted.[106] Buchanan then sent a squadron of ships to Paraguay, which was enough to convince that country to sign a treaty with the United States and agree to pay damages.

In some instances in the nineteenth century, Congress rejected presidential requests for use-of-force authorizations at least in part out of a concern that the requested authorizations would constitute improper delegations of war authority to the president. In 1834, President Jackson asked Congress for authority to exact reprisals from French shipping to satisfy a French debt (arising from harm to American shipping during the Napoleonic wars) if France did not appropriate the funds. In a lengthy report, the Senate Foreign Relations Committee, through its chairman, Henry Clay, explained why it thought that a threat of force was not a good approach at that point.[107] But it also stated that it did not think it was proper for Congress to delegate its authority to issue what would in effect be letters of marque and reprisal. Rather, said the committee, "Congress ought to retain to itself the right of judging of the expediency of granting them, under all the circumstances existing at the time when they are proposed to be actually issued." Following the Committee's recommendation, the Senate unanimously rejected Jackson's request. In the 1850s, President Buchanan made numerous requests for contingent legislation permitting him to intervene militarily in Mexico and Central America to protect U.S. citizens and their property, all of which were rejected.[108] Some of the opposition to these requests reflected delegation concerns. For example, Senator Seward (who would go on to serve as President Lincoln's Secretary of State) objected that nothing would "be more strange and preposterous than the idea of the President of the United States making hypothetical wars, conditional wars, without any designation of the nation against which war is to be declared."[109]

At the outset of the Civil War, President Lincoln took a variety of unilateral actions to prosecute the war, and Congress approved these actions after the fact. In a closely divided decision, the Supreme Court held in the *Prize Cases* that Lincoln had acted constitutionally in imposing a naval blockade of Southern ports.[110] The Court reasoned that this action fell within Lincoln's authority as Commander in Chief to defend the United States and that if congressional authorization had been needed, the problem was cured by Congress's ratification of Lincoln's actions. It also noted that under the militia statutes Lincoln had preexisting authority to call out the armed forces to suppress insurrection.

The United States eventually became involved in several more declared wars—the Spanish-American War, World War I, and World War II—all of which involved open-ended delegations of use-of-force authority to the Commander in Chief.[111] Outside the context of declared wars and the Civil War, the delegations in the nineteenth and early twentieth centuries tended to be focused on a particular enemy and point in time, and often on a particular goal.[112] Increasingly, though, presidents initiated military conflicts, especially in Latin America, that were not even authorized by Congress. The post–World War II practice similarly is characterized by frequent unilateral uses of force by presidents, along with occasional congressional authorizations. Some of the authorizations, it should be noted, have been very open ended.

In 1955, in response to a request from President Eisenhower, Congress authorized the president to employ armed forces "as he deems necessary" to protect Formosa and the Pescadores against an armed attack and to take "such other measures as he judges to be required or appropriate in assuring the defense of Formosa and the Pescadores."[113] The resolution stated that it would expire when the president determined and reported to Congress that the "peace and security of the area is reasonably assured." Congress repealed the resolution in 1974.

In 1957, Congress passed a joint resolution providing that "if the President determines the necessity thereof, the United States is prepared to use armed forces to assist" any Middle Eastern nation or group of nations "against armed aggression from any country controlled by international communism."[114] It further stated that the resolution would expire "when the President shall determine that the peace and security of the nations in the general area of the Middle East are reasonably assured by international conditions created by action of the United Nations or otherwise except that it may be terminated earlier by a concurrent resolution of the two Houses of Congress." Some nondelegation concerns were raised during the congressional debates over the resolution,[115] but it passed anyway, and it remains in effect today.

The Gulf of Tonkin Resolution, which authorized the use of force in Vietnam, stated that "Congress approves and supports the determination of the President, as Commander in Chief, to take all necessary measures to repel any armed attack against the forces of the United States *and to prevent further aggression*."[116] Congress repealed the Resolution in 1971. Some commentators argued that the Gulf of Tonkin Resolution was so open ended that it violated the nondelegation doctrine.[117] William Rehnquist, when he was working in the Justice Department, responded to this argument by invoking *Curtiss-Wright* for the proposition that "the principle of unlawful delegation of powers does not apply in the field of external affairs."[118] Writing later, Professor John Hart Ely added that the nondelegation doctrine was not much of a constraint even in domestic affairs and that, in any event, the Gulf of Tonkin Resolution was functionally equivalent to a declaration of war against North Vietnam, something that can convey substantial discretion to the Commander in Chief.[119]

Congress's authorizations of force for both of the Iraq wars—in 1991 and in 2002—conferred substantial discretion on the president. The 1991 statute, passed after Iraq had invaded Kuwait, authorized the president to use force to implement UN Security Council resolutions demanding that Iraq withdraw.[120] The 2002 authorization for the use of force against Iraq, issued after the Saddam Hussein government had failed to cooperate with UN weapons inspectors, states that "the President is authorized to use the Armed Forces of the United States *as he determines to be necessary and appropriate* in order to—(1) defend the national security of the United States against the continuing threat posed by Iraq; and (2) enforce all relevant United Nations Security Council resolutions regarding Iraq."[121] This statute remains in effect (although there has been recent talk of repealing it), and presidents have continued to rely on it for military actions in Iraq that are quite remote from the conditions that existed in 2002.

Another broad modern use-of-force authorization is the 2001 resolution that authorized the post–September 11 "war on terror." It states that the president "is authorized to use all necessary and appropriate force against those nations, organizations, or persons *he determines* planned, authorized, committed, or aided the terrorist attacks that occurred on September 11, 2001, or harbored such organizations or persons, in order to prevent any future acts of international terrorism against the United States by such nations, organizations or persons."[122] More than twenty years later, this statute continues to serve as the primary statutory authorization for the war on terror.

When considering the breadth of these authorizations, it is worth remembering that the United States no longer issues declarations of war. For conflicts that rise to the level of what might in the past have involved a declaration of war, it is perhaps not surprising that the authorization of force resembles what would have been issued in a declared war. That said, some of the authorizations, like the Middle East resolution, have gone even beyond the authorizations in declared wars in delegating use-of-force discretion to the president into the future, outside the context of a particular conflict. Other authorizations, like the one in 2001, have developed into such a future-oriented delegation, in part because of the lack of any sunset clause in the legislation.[123] A complication with the 2001 authorization, however, is that when presidents act under that statute, they are also purporting to defend the United States from threats, and, as discussed in Chapter 6, it is widely agreed that presidents have some unilateral defensive authority.[124]

Concerns about delegating to the president the decision whether to go to war have surfaced in debates over whether treaties can authorize future presidential uses of force. One objection to the League of Nations Covenant, which was part of the Versailles Treaty, was that in giving the league the authority to decide how to respond to acts of aggression, the United States might be binding itself to that body's determinations about whether to use force. To address this concern, one of the reservations proposed in the Senate would have made clear that the United States would not become involved in uses of force under the covenant "unless in any particular case the Congress which under the Constitution has the sole power to declare war or authorize the employment of the military or naval forces of the United States shall in the exercise of full liberty of action by act or joint resolution so provide."[125] Years later, however, when implementing the UN Charter, Congress was amenable to the president making an agreement with the United Nations, subject to Congress's approval, that would allow U.S. forces to be used in support of UN operations without the need for congressional authorization each time.[126] The Senate Foreign Relations Committee justified this anticipated delegation of authority on the ground that "preventive or enforcement action by these forces upon the order of the Security Council would not be an act of war but would be international action for the preservation of the peace."[127] It also noted that "there exist several well-recognized and long-standing precedents for the delegation to the President of powers of this general nature." But, because of Cold War tensions, an agreement was never concluded.

Defenders of President Truman's actions in the Korean War, which was never specifically authorized by Congress, argued that, despite the lack of a congressionally approved agreement with the UN, the charter gave Truman authority to use force.[128] The North Atlantic Treaty, approved by the Senate in 1949, states that if any party is attacked, the other parties shall assist the attacked party by taking "such action as it deems necessary, including the use of armed force, to restore and maintain the security of the North Atlantic area." But the treaty also says that the obligations under the treaty are to be carried out by the parties "in accordance with their respective constitutional processes," which can be read as not displacing Congress's war authority. Other collective self-defense treaties have a similar provision.[129] In any event, since the Korean War, presidents have not expressly claimed that treaties can provide an alternative to congressional authorizations of force for purposes of domestic war powers authority.

In sum, throughout American history Congress has made delegations of use-of-force authority of varying breadth, usually depending on perceived functional needs. Members of Congress have sometimes raised nondelegation concerns about the broad delegations, but often to little effect, and it is difficult to disentangle their constitutional nondelegation concerns from policy-based objections. Delegations outside the context of declared wars have been broader since the 1950s, with little nondelegation controversy.

Delegation and Independent Powers

One reason that the Supreme Court has suggested that nondelegation concerns are weaker in the area of foreign affairs is that the president has independent constitutional authority in this area. If so, then the delegation can in effect be combined with the president's own authority, and there is less concern that the president is acting in place of Congress. A different way of framing this point is to say that in areas of independent presidential authority, the actions that a president takes are not as legislative in character, so there is less of an issue of Congress transferring legislative authority. A more subtle form of the argument would be that in some subject areas the precise distribution of authority over an issue between Congress and the executive branch is unclear. In those instances, underenforcement of nondelegation constraints allows courts, and the political branches themselves, to avoid having to resolve the precise distribution.

The Supreme Court invoked the independent powers idea in *Curtiss-Wright,* noting that it was "dealing not alone with an authority vested in the President by an exertion of legislative power, but with such an authority plus the very delicate, plenary and exclusive power of the President as the sole organ of the federal government in the field of international relations—a power which does not require as a basis for its exercise an act of Congress."[130] Justice Jackson's framework from the *Youngstown* steel seizure case similarly reflects this idea: the highest category of presidential power under the framework is for situations in which the president acts pursuant to a statutory delegation, because his power in that situation "includes all that he possesses in his own right plus all that Congress can delegate."[131] For that proposition, Jackson cited back to *Curtiss-Wright.*

A more recent decision relying on this independent powers point is *Loving v. United States.*[132] In that case, the Court upheld a broad delegation to the president of authority to prescribe the aggravating factors to be considered in death penalty cases tried before military courts-martial. In doing so, the Court emphasized that the delegation was "to the President in his role as Commander in Chief." As a result, said the Court, "the delegated duty . . . is interlinked with duties already assigned to the President by express terms of the Constitution, and the same limitations on delegation do not apply 'where the entity exercising the delegated authority itself possesses independent authority over the subject matter.'"[133]

The independent powers idea may also help explain a number of the other examples in this chapter, such as delegations relating to the exclusion of aliens, the issuance of passports, defensive uses of force, and uses of force in declared wars. In all of those areas, the president likely has some independent executive authority (some of which may be based on historical practice). This will not always be the case, however. Consider, for example, the regulation of trade and tariffs. Given the Constitution's assignment to Congress of the authority to regulate foreign commerce, it is not clear to what extent the president has independent authority to bring to the table. Yet, as we have seen, there is a long history of broad delegations of authority to the president in this area. Relatedly, as we saw in Chapter 4, Congress often has delegated broad authority to the president to conclude executive agreements, and many of those ex ante congressional-executive agreements address topics that seem to fall entirely within Congress's authority (such as trade, investment, education, and environmental protection, just to name a few subjects).[134]

Historical gloss is relevant here, although the picture is more complicated than what was described by the Court in *Curtiss-Wright*. As the examples in this chapter make clear, historical practice suggests that Congress has broad leeway to delegate foreign affairs authority to the president. Broad delegations of discretionary foreign affairs authority date back to near the Founding.[135] In the nineteenth century, proposed delegations were sometimes rejected or modified in the face of nondelegation concerns, especially with respect to uses of force, but overall it is difficult to find any consistent and meaningful nondelegation constraints even during that period. This is true even though participants in congressional debates (and the Supreme Court) accepted that, in theory, there were nondelegation limits. As the examples in this chapter show, Congress often perceives the need for executive branch discretion in carrying out foreign affairs directives. And the Supreme Court has generally accepted Congress's assessment.

What this study cannot resolve is whether or to what extent the history supports *differential* treatment of foreign and domestic affairs with respect to the nondelegation doctrine, as the Court in *Curtiss-Wright* contended. The claim of such differential treatment was not prominently made early in U.S. history.[136] If anything, some foreign affairs delegations, especially those relating to raising troops and deciding whether to initiate hostilities, were thought to raise particular nondelegation worries.[137] Instead of referring generally to "foreign affairs" as an exception to the nondelegation doctrine, it probably makes more sense to focus on the scope of independent presidential authority *in particular areas*, something that is likely to be heavily informed by practice. In general, presidents have more independent authority to act in foreign affairs than in domestic affairs, but the inquiry would need to be issue specific.[138]

At the time that this book was written, the Supreme Court had not revived a strict nondelegation doctrine even in the domestic realm. Instead, it has sometimes used tools of statutory construction to narrowly construe statutes that are perceived to raise nondelegation concerns.[139] Most dramatically, it has said that, because of "both separation of powers principles and a practical understanding of legislative intent," there must be clear congressional authorization before an administrative agency will be allowed to decide certain major policy questions.[140]

To the extent that this "major questions doctrine" is an attempt to avoid constitutional concerns relating to delegations, many foreign affairs delegations are unlikely to be perceived to raise such concerns, in part because of the historical gloss already discussed. If the doctrine is an effort to assess likely congressional intent, the Supreme Court has long said that Congress perceives a need for broad executive branch discretion in carrying out foreign affairs directives, which would suggest that the major questions doctrine will not typically be an issue for foreign affairs delegations.[141] That said, there is not always a clear line between foreign and domestic affairs. For areas in which the lines are blurred, it is more difficult to justify differential treatment of the two domains, even for purposes of statutory interpretation.[142] Such differential treatment, to be justified, may itself depend on historical practice: As the Supreme Court has emphasized in a number of decisions, when Congress has enacted delegations against the backdrop of a history of unilateral executive branch action, it can be seen as accepting the breadth of discretion embodied in that practice.[143] In general, there is likely to be more such practice in the area of foreign affairs.

Conclusion

Edward Corwin famously described the Constitution as "an invitation to struggle for the privilege of directing American foreign policy."[144] But this description is misleading. In the event of a struggle, Congress can generally prevail. But Congress often does not struggle. In fact, as this chapter has shown, there is a long-standing and bipartisan practice of broad congressional delegations of foreign affairs authority to the executive branch, even in areas in which the president lacks independent authority to act. Given that the nondelegation doctrine is at most a structural inference rather than something mandated by specific constitutional text, the arguments for crediting historical gloss are especially strong in this context. Perceiving this, the courts and the political branches have given significant weight to the legislative practice in deliberating over whether and to what extent the Constitution limits delegations. While the participants in these deliberations have often accepted that there are nondelegation limits as a matter of principle, in practice they have treated these limits as imposing few constraints, especially constraints that would be judicially enforceable. On this issue, *Curtiss-Wright* was right.

Of course, broad foreign affairs delegations may not always be desirable as a matter of policy. Instead of reflecting a sensible reliance on executive expertise, some of the delegations may stem from a congressional desire to avoid accountability, partisan calculations, or interest group influence.[145] If there were sufficient institutional will (a big if), it would likely be useful for Congress to include more sunset provisions in its delegations, to ensure that there continues to be legislative support as conditions—and executive branch uses of the delegation—change. It might also make sense for Congress to impose more process requirements for the exercise of delegated authority, such as "review and wait" provisions, and perhaps even provisions about how decisions to implement delegated authority are to be made within the executive branch.[146] The Administrative Procedure Act imposes important process checks on the exercise of delegated authority by administrative agencies, but the act is often inapplicable in the foreign affairs area; perhaps its coverage should be expanded.[147] The key point is that, at least from the perspective of historical practice, these are issues for Congress, rather than the courts, to address.[148]

CONCLUSION

AS THIS BOOK HAS SHOWN, MUCH OF THE U.S. CONSTITUTIONAL LAW of foreign affairs has been worked out through historical governmental practice. The text of the Constitution is unclear about many issues of foreign affairs authority, especially with respect to issues of executive power. Even when the text is clear about foreign affairs authority, it speaks to conditions that are markedly different from those today. Over the course of U.S. history, Congress and the executive branch have determined the details of institutional authority in this area, often in ways that have helped the United States better respond to changes in the world. Sometimes the political branches developed the law in this area through mutual understandings and cooperation, and at other times they did so through conflict. The courts, meanwhile, have largely deferred to these arrangements unless they have violated individual rights.

Consider for a moment the changes to the country, and to the world, since the United States first adopted its Constitution. At the Founding, the United States consisted of thirteen former colonies hugging the eastern seacoast, and it was a minor player in world politics. It is now a superpower that extends from the Atlantic to the Pacific Oceans and to Alaska and Hawaii. Transportation at the Founding consisted of horse-drawn buggies and slow-moving sailing ships; today it includes cars and jet planes. Long-distance communication at the Founding was accomplished by the delivery of handwritten letters, which often took weeks if not longer to arrive. Today we have instantaneous communication through cell phones, emails, text messages, and the like. The United States at the Founding had a standing army of about 700 men and no navy; it now has a standing military of well over a million men and women in the army, navy, air force, marines, and even space force, with hundreds of military bases around the world. According to the first census (in 1790), the U.S. population was under four million; today it is over 330 million. Adjusting for inflation, the gross domestic product in 1790 was about $5 billion; today it is over $20 *trillion.* The

United States initially fought wars with muskets and cannons; it now uses drones, cruise missiles, tanks, and fighter jets, and it has the capacity to use nuclear weapons.

As for the rest of the world, at the Founding it was thought that there were only a handful of "civilized states" with which a country like the United States might have formal diplomatic relations; now there are over 190 recognized nations, and the United States has embassies in over 160 of them. Today, threats to the United States arise less from the danger of an invasion than from the possibility of terrorist attacks, nuclear proliferation, cyber warfare, and global pandemics. International law, meanwhile, has changed dramatically, banning war as an instrument of foreign policy, regulating the protection of human rights, and seeking to protect the global environment, to name just a few of the many developments. At the Founding, the United States was a party to only seven treaties with foreign nations; today it is a party to thousands, many of which have been concluded as executive agreements. Some of these modern treaties, moreover, are multilateral agreements that resemble legislative codes and establish complex international institutions. In 1790, the U.S. State Department consisted of Thomas Jefferson and a few staff members; today, its workforce includes some 13,000 members of the Foreign Service, 11,000 civil service employees, and 45,000 locally employed staff at more than 270 diplomatic missions around the world.

Despite these changes, in the Constitution's more than 230 years of history, there has not been a single amendment to its text relating to the foreign affairs powers of the government. Textually speaking, the United States conducts international relations with a horse-and-buggy Constitution. Fortunately, the text is not the only—or, in many cases, even the most important—element of our constitutional law of foreign relations. As this book has shown, throughout U.S. history, participants in constitutional interpretation and debates concerning foreign affairs authority have often reasoned from historical practice rather than from the text or original understandings. This is not a mere coincidence. The text of the Constitution provides insufficient guidance even for the issues that the country had to face in the late 1700s, let alone the issues of the twenty-first century, and gloss provides a practical way of addressing its gaps and ambiguities. At least in foreign affairs, the United States has a gloss-based Constitution.

The examples in the book illustrate different ways that gloss can relate to the constitutional text. Sometimes gloss resolves potential ambiguities, such as whether the president can speak for the country on issues of recognition (Chapter 3) or whether the Constitution allows Congress to delegate broad discretion to the president over foreign affairs (Chapter 8). Sometimes gloss fills in gaps, such as for treaty termination (Chapter 5), defensive uses of force not involving U.S. declarations of war (Chapter 6), and certain congressional powers that are not specifically listed in Article I (Chapter 7). Sometimes gloss largely supersedes (or at least overshadows) the text, as with the loss of a formal "advice" role for the Senate in connection with treaties and, more dramatically, the rise of executive agreements (Chapter 4).

The precise contours of this gloss-based constitutional law are sometimes uncertain, but that is not necessarily a drawback for a legal regime that is administered primarily by political actors rather than by the courts. Even when its implications are clear, the gloss-based Constitution will not irrevocably settle an issue: the details of this constitutional law have changed before, and they could change again. But this flexibility is one of gloss's strengths: it allows for common-law-style development and thus provides needed play in the joints of an old and difficult-to-amend Constitution.

Readers may wonder whether the governmental practices described in this book should count as evidence of our constitutional law, as opposed to being reflections of "mere politics." Perhaps consistency between institutional behavior and the practice-based norms described herein is simply the result of political and policy considerations rather than understandings about our constitutional law. If so, it might be argued that they should not be given weight in constitutional interpretation.

The governmental practices described in this book do emanate from politics. But that does not distinguish gloss from other aspects of constitutional law. Even materials that are widely accepted as legal in nature rest on political foundations. Consider, for example, why Supreme Court decisions are generally considered authoritative. It is not an answer to say that "the law makes it so." What law? Rather, the answer lies in our practices and understandings.[1] The same can be said about the text of the Constitution. Why is it binding today? Again, it is no answer to say that the law requires this, because it is not clear what that law is outside of the text. As a result, the fact that the historical practices recounted in this book arise from politics does not show that they are themselves mere politics.

Moreover, under prominent jurisprudential accounts most famously associated with H. L. A. Hart, what is "law" is determined by how the participants in the system understand the relevant "rules of recognition." As this book has shown, gloss is considered by the participants in our system as relevant to constitutional interpretation, and this has been true since the Founding era. These participants frequently give it weight in their legal analysis. Moreover, government lawyers are heavily involved in assessing and relying on gloss in their constitutional interpretation and argumentation. Courts, too, look to it when addressing these issues. The fact that institutional actors reason in this way is evidence that there is something important about doing so, as opposed to appealing merely to political and functional arguments.[2]

Historical gloss often supports claims of executive power, so it is no surprise that it is popular with executive branch lawyers. But it is popular with Congress too; it was a central focus of discussion in many of the congressional debates recounted in this book. Congress, no less than the president, seeks practical and principled constructions of the Constitution that are informed by the lessons of the past. Indeed, given the frequent claims of an imperial presidency, it is easy to forget that Congress regulates today across a vast spectrum of foreign affairs topics, and its ability to do so is informed by practice. In many instances, to be sure, Congress chooses to delegate discretionary authority to the executive branch, but what is delegated can be withdrawn or cabined.

None of this is to suggest, of course, that our system of checks and balances is working well. In *The Federalist Papers,* James Madison suggested that the government's "constituent parts" would, "by their mutual relations, be the means of keeping each other in their proper places."[3] In practice, though, the protection of legislative prerogatives often depends on partisan politics rather than institutional interests.[4] But even our partisan-laden system can and sometimes does produce needed separation of powers reforms. There was a spate of such reforms, for example, near the end of the Vietnam War. As I was working on this book, Congress enacted its most sweeping transparency reforms relating to executive agreements in the past fifty years.[5] Far from impeding such efforts, the historical gloss approach to constitutional interpretation invites them.

International law plays a somewhat surprising role in this book. Many scholars who favor a broader role for international law in the U.S. legal system are also skeptical of executive authority. For the examples in this book, though, international law has been more of an enabler of such authority than a constraint. International law is structured in a way that tends to favor executive control over foreign relations, and it also provides presidents with an alternate frame from which to justify their actions when the domestic law arguments are weak or uncertain. Those who study the separation of powers should be more attentive to this dynamic.

It is hard to imagine what our constitutional law would look like without gloss, were that even possible. In the foreign affairs area, if presidents had not developed gloss-based authority, perhaps they would terminate fewer treaties and engage in fewer military actions. And perhaps that would be good, although it is worth noting that, since the Korean War, the two U.S. wars that are generally viewed as the most problematic in terms of their foreign policy justifications and their costs to the United States—the Vietnam War and the 2003 Iraq War—were both authorized by Congress.[6] But it might also mean that presidents would make many fewer international agreements, including important agreements facilitating trade and establishing international institutions, and that U.S. uses of force in the service of international peace and security, including humanitarian intervention, would be less likely. The fact that it is difficult even for informed experts to have confident judgments about such matters is a reason for courts to be cautious about upsetting settled practices.

In any event, it is a fanciful scenario. Think, for example, about the role of a lawyer in the executive branch today asked whether the president has the constitutional authority to take a particular action—for example, to make an important agreement without seeking the Senate's advice and consent. No responsible lawyer would focus their answer primarily on the constitutional Founding. They would instead look to what presidents have done before, how the Senate has responded, how the full Congress has viewed the question, and the like. Although perhaps less obvious, that is also how a responsible lawyer serving the Senate Foreign Relations Committee would likely address the question. In the absence of judicial precedent, these and other actors would look to the nonjudicial precedent that has been developed through the actions and interactions of the political branches. It has been this way from the very beginning.

Notes

Introduction

1. Harry S. Truman, Radio and Television Address (Apr. 8, 1952). See also Harry S. Truman, Executive Order 10340—Directing the Secretary of Commerce to Take Possession of and Operate the Plants and Facilities of Certain Steel Companies (Apr. 8, 1952).

2. Youngstown Sheet & Tube Co. v. Sawyer, 343 U.S. 579, 585 (1952).

3. See id. at 593 (Frankfurter, J., concurring).

4. See id. at 634 (Jackson, J., concurring). The Supreme Court has invoked this three-tiered framework in a number of subsequent separation of powers cases relating to foreign affairs. See Zivotofsky v. Kerry, 576 U.S. 1, 10 (2015); Medellin v. Texas, 552 U.S. 491, 524 (2008); Hamdan v. Rumsfeld, 548 U.S. 557, 593 n.23 (2006); Dames & Moore v. Regan, 453 U.S. 654, 661–62 (1981).

5. Compare, for example, Dames & Moore, 453 U.S. at 686 (finding implied congressional support for a presidential resolution of the Iranian hostage crisis on the basis of "the history of [congressional] acquiescence in executive claims settlement"), with Medellin, 552 U.S. at 532 (finding no congressional acquiescence in presidential preemption of state law to implement an international court judgment, in part because of the lack of similar past actions).

6. 343 U.S. at 637 (Jackson, J., concurring).

7. See, e.g., Zivotofsky, 576 U.S. at 23 (considering the "weight of historical evidence" in determining whether the president's power over recognition can be limited by Congress).

8. William Howard Taft, Our Chief Magistrate and His Powers 2 (1916).

9. See generally Arthur Schlesinger Jr., The Imperial Presidency (1973) (2004 ed.).

10. 343 U.S. at 637–38.

11. See Curtis A. Bradley & Eric A. Posner, Presidential Signing Statements and Executive Power, 23 Const. Comm. 307, 340 (2006).

12. See Philip Bobbitt, Constitutional Interpretation 12–13 (1991).

13. See, e.g., Larry D. Kramer, The People Themselves (2004); Keith E. Whittington, Constitutional Construction (1999); Mark Tushnet, Taking the Constitution Away from the Courts (1999); Ernest A. Young, Constitutionalism Outside the Courts, in The Oxford Handbook of the U.S. Constitution (Mark Tushnet, Sanford Levinson, and Mark A. Graber eds., 2015).

14. See, e.g., William Baude, Is Originalism Our Law?, 115 Colum. L. Rev. 2349 (2015); Charles L. Barzun, The Positive U-Turn, 69 Stan. L. Rev. 1323 (2017).

15. See Louis Henkin, Foreign Affairs and the United States Constitution 3 (2d ed. 1996) ("Students of constitutional law have long been students only of the cases of the Supreme Court, and constitutional issues of foreign affairs rarely come to court.").

16. For accounts of the drafting of the Constitution, see, e.g., Richard Beeman, Plain, Honest Men: The Making of the American Constitution (2009); Catherine Drinker Bowen, Miracle at Philadelphia: The Story of the Constitutional Convention, May to September 1787 (1986); Michael J. Klarman, The Framers' Coup: The Making of the United States Constitution (2018); David O. Stewart, The Summer of 1787: The Men Who Invented the Constitution (2007).

17. See, e.g., Deborah N. Pearlstein, Ratcheting Back: International Law as a Constraint on Executive Power, 26 Const. Comm. 523 (2010); Jules Lobel, The Limits of Constitutional Power: Conflicts between Foreign Policy and International Law, 71 Va. L. Rev. 1071 (1985). See also Eyal Benvenisti, Reclaiming Democracy: The Strategic Uses of Foreign and International Law by National Courts, 102 Am. J. Int'l L. 241 (2008).

18. See also Jean Galbraith, International Law and the Domestic Separation of Powers, 99 Va. L. Rev. 987 (2013) (discussing the interactive relationship between international law and the separation of powers); Rebecca Ingber, International Law Constraints as Executive Power, 57 Harv. Int'l L.J. 49, 55 (2016) (examining "the invocation of international law—even of international law limits—not as a constraining force within the domestic legal system, but as an enabling one"). Cf. Curtis A. Bradley & Jack L. Goldsmith, Presidential Control over International Law, 131 Harv. L. Rev. 1201, 1204 (2018) (documenting "a long accretion of presidential control over international law since the constitutional Founding").

19. The *Digests* are not neutral in that they reflect a U.S. perspective on issues of international law, but they contain comprehensive accounts of executive branch and congressional practice and tend to avoid making claims about the constitutional implications of the materials.

1. Historical Gloss and Constitutional Interpretation

1. U.S. Const. art. II, § 2.

2. Transcript, Oral Argument in National Labor Relations Board v. Noel Canning, at 6 (Jan. 13, 2014).

3. Id. at 8. When Justice Alito asked the lawyer for Noel Canning the same question, the lawyer said that in such a situation "the language has to govern." Id. at 42. Justice Kagan, however, questioned his answer, and Justice Breyer pointed out that both the Due Process Clause and the Commerce Clause had acquired meanings different from what the language of those clauses might suggest.

4. NLRB v. Noel Canning, 573 U.S. 513, 538 (2014).

5. The majority in *Noel Canning,* despite agreeing with the executive branch on the two principal constitutional questions, concluded that the particular Senate break in this case was too short to qualify as a recess and thus held that Obama's appointments were invalid. Scalia's opinion was therefore a concurrence rather than a dissent because he, too, concluded that the appointments were invalid.

6. A number of my law review articles discussing the concept of historical gloss were cowritten, some with Trevor Morrison and others with Neil Siegel, and this chapter reflects many of their ideas as well as my own.

7. For this reason, it is hazardous to analogize gloss to types of custom that do operate as freestanding law, such as customary international law. For commentators who have made that analogy, see, e.g., Michael J. Glennon, The Use of Custom in Resolving Separation of Powers Disputes, 64 B.U. L. Rev. 109, 134 (1984); Shalev Roisman, Constitutional Acquiescence, 84 Geo. Wash. L. Rev. 668, 675 (2016).

8. See Curtis A. Bradley, Doing Gloss, 84 U. Chi. L. Rev. 59 (2017) (using somewhat different labels); Curtis A. Bradley & Neil S. Siegel, Historical Gloss, Madisonian Liquidation, and the Originalism Debate, 106 Va. L. Rev. 1, 23–26 (2020) (same).

9. See Edmund Burke, Reflections on the Revolution in France 76 (1790) (J. G. A. Pocock ed., 1987).

10. See, e.g., Noel Canning, 573 U.S. at 549 (noting that the Court was concerned about "upset[ting] the compromises and working arrangements that the elected branches of Government themselves have reached," as well as about "seriously shrink[ing] the authority that Presidents have believed existed and have exercised for so long"); United States v. Midwest Oil Co., 236 U.S. 459, 472–73 (1915) (noting that "officers, law-makers and citizens naturally adjust themselves to any long-continued action of the Executive Department—on the presumption that unauthorized acts would not have been allowed to be so often repeated as to crystallize into a regular practice").

11. See, e.g., Mitchell Pearsall Reich, Incomplete Designs, 94 Tex. L. Rev. 807, 831 (2016).

12. See, e.g., Medellin v. Texas, 552 U.S. 491, 532 (2008) ("The Government has not identified a single instance in which the President has attempted (or Congress has acquiesced in) a Presidential directive issued to state courts, much less one that reaches deep into the heart of the State's police powers and compels state courts to reopen final criminal judgments and set aside neutrally applicable state laws.").

13. See, e.g., Rucho v. Common Cause, 139 S. Ct. 2484 (2019) (relying on this justification in concluding that a constitutional challenge to partisan gerrymandering of electoral districts presented a political question); Nixon v. United States, 506 U.S. 224, 230 (1993) (relying in part on this justification in declining to adjudicate a challenge to an impeachment procedure used by the Senate).

14. See also, e.g., Peter M. Shane, Democracy's Chief Executive: Interpreting the Constitution and Defining the Future of the Presidency 181 (2022) ("Though some justices may occasionally appear willing to upset long-established interbranch modes of operation, the prospect is understandably uncomfortable for unelected jurists surveying the handiwork of the elected branches.").

15. See, e.g., Richard Albert, The World's Most Difficult Constitution to Amend?, 110 Calif. L. Rev. 2005, 2007 (2022) (noting that it is "virtually impossible today for any constitutional amendment proposal to be ratified"); David A. Strauss, The Irrelevance of Constitutional Amendments, 114 Harv. L. Rev. 1457, 1458 (2001) ("Through most of our history, the amendment process has not been an important means of constitutional change.").

16. Jonathan Gienapp, The Second Creation: Fixing the American Constitution in the Founding Era 28 (2018).

17. See also, e.g., Edward S. Corwin, The Constitution and World Organization 41 (1944) ("The most beneficial type of constitutional change is that which issues gradually from, and so has been thoroughly tested by, successful practice."); 1 Joseph Story, Commentaries on the Constitution of the United States § 408, at 392 (1833) ("The most unexceptionable source of

collateral interpretation is from the practical exposition of the government itself in its various departments upon particular questions discussed, and settled upon their own single merits.").

18. See generally H. L. A. Hart, The Concept of Law 94–99 (2d ed. 1994) (discussing secondary "rules of recognition").

19. Cf. Henry Paul Monaghan, Supremacy Clause Textualism, 110 Colum. L. Rev. 731, 790 (2010) ("Any acceptable theory of constitutional adjudication should . . . have two qualities: (1) It must be normatively acceptable and (2) It must be able to account for most (though not necessarily every last bit) of the current constitutional order."). To be clear, a mere descriptive account of the law cannot by itself provide a normative justification for accepting or following that law. See J. Joel Alicea, Practice-Based Constitutional Theories, 133 Yale L.J. 568 (2023); Richard H. Fallon Jr., How to Choose a Constitutional Theory, 87 Calif. L. Rev. 535, 545 (1999).

20. See generally Curtis A. Bradley & Trevor W. Morrison, Historical Gloss and the Separation of Powers, 126 Harv. L. Rev. 411 (2012).

21. 17 U.S. (4 Wheat.) 316 (1819).

22. Id. at 401. But cf. 22 Annals of Cong. 643 (1811) (Rep. Porter) (criticizing, in a debate over the constitutionality of the national bank, the idea of "prescriptive Constitutional rights" emanating from customary practice).

23. See Aziz Z. Huq, The Negotiated Structural Constitution, 114 Colum. L. Rev. 1595, 1602 (2014) ("Sifting good from bad intermural arrangements [between government institutions] should be the task of elected actors and their publics, not the responsibility of federal courts."). See also Samuel Issacharoff & Trevor Morrison, Constitution by Convention, 108 Calif. L. Rev. 1913, 1917 (2020) ("In a constitutional order responsible for governing an immense and complicated polity, the need to find workable solutions to everyday problems of government is bound to find its way into the law over time.").

24. See generally Richard H. Fallon Jr., The Many and Varied Roles of History in Constitutional Adjudication, 90 Notre Dame L. Rev. 1753 (2015); Jack M. Balkin, The New Originalism and the Uses of History, 82 Fordham L. Rev. 641 (2013).

25. See, e.g., Marc O. DeGirolami, The Traditions of American Constitutional Law, 95 Notre Dame L. Rev. 1123 (2020); Sherif Girgis, Living Traditionalism, 98 N.Y.U. L. Rev. 1477 (2023). See also Rebecca L. Brown, Tradition and Insight, 103 Yale L.J. 177 (1993).

26. See, e.g., Henry P. Monaghan, Presidential War-Making, 50 B.U. L. Rev. 19, 31 (1970); Cass R. Sunstein, Burkean Minimalism, 105 Mich. L. Rev. 353, 400 (2006). But cf. Matthew B. Lawrence, Subordination and Separation of Powers, 131 Yale L.J. 78 (2021) (arguing that separation of powers issues can sometimes affect marginalized groups).

27. See, e.g., Aziz Z. Huq, Fourth Amendment Gloss, 113 Nw. U. L. Rev. 701 (2019) (arguing that those reasons do not support reliance on gloss in the Fourth Amendment context).

28. See Youngstown Sheet & Tube Co. v. Sawyer, 343 U.S. 579, 593 (1952) (Frankfurter, J., concurring).

29. 236 U.S. 459 (1915).

30. Ex parte Grossman, 267 U.S. 87, 118–19 (1925).

31. The Pocket Veto Case, 279 U.S. 655, 689 (1929). See also Myers v. United States, 272 U.S. 52, 283 (1926) (Brandeis, J., dissenting) ("A persistent legislative practice which involves a delimitation of the respective powers of Congress and the President, and which has been so established and maintained, should be deemed tantamount to judicial construction, in the absence of any decision by any court to the contrary.").

32. 143 U.S. 649, 690 (1892).

33. 299 U.S. 304, 329 (1936).

34. 453 U.S. 654 (1981).

35. 488 U.S. 361 (1989).

36. 576 U.S. 1 (2015).

37. 462 U.S. 919 (1983).

38. See id. at 942 n.13. For another decision giving little weight to historical practice, in construing the scope of Congress's authority to exclude elected members from taking their seats, see Powell v. McCormack, 395 U.S. 486, 546–47 (1969).

39. Nonoriginalist approaches are sometimes labeled "living constitutionalism" because they allow for constitutional evolution even without changes to the text. I find that term to be unhelpful, both because it obscures the differences among the approaches and because it relies on a potentially misleading analogy to living organisms.

40. See, e.g., Lawrence B. Solum, The Fixation Thesis: The Role of Historical Fact in Original Meaning, 91 Notre Dame L. Rev. 1, 6–7 (2015); see also Keith E. Whittington, The New Originalism, 2 Geo. J.L. & Pub. Pol'y 599, 599 (2004) ("Originalism regards the discoverable meaning of the Constitution at the time of its initial adoption as authoritative for purposes of constitutional interpretation in the present.").

41. See, e.g., Saikrishna Bangalore Prakash, Against Constitution by Convention, 108 Calif. L. Rev. 1975, 1979 (2020); Michael B. Rappaport, The Original Meaning of the Recess Appointments Clause, 52 UCLA L. Rev. 1487, 1537 (2005).

42. Keith E. Whittington, Constructing a New American Constitution, 27 Const. Comm. 119, 120–21 (2019); see also Keith E. Whittington, Constitutional Construction: Divided Powers and Constitutional Meaning (1999). For additional discussion of constitutional construction and its relationship to "new originalism," see Lawrence B. Solum, Originalism and Constitutional Construction, 83 Fordham L. Rev. 453 (2013).

43. See Jack M. Balkin, Framework Originalism and the Living Constitution, 103 Nw. U. L. Rev. 549, 550 (2009); Balkin, supra note 24; see also Jack M. Balkin, Living Originalism (2011).

44. For example, Justice Scalia accepted the idea of stare decisis—that is, deference to judicial precedent—although he made clear that "stare decisis is not *part of* my originalist philosophy; it is a pragmatic *exception* to it." Antonin Scalia, A Matter of Interpretation 140 (Amy Gutmann ed., 1997) (emphasis in original). For additional discussion of the compatibility of originalism with deference to judicial precedent, see, e.g., John O. McGinnis & Michael B. Rappaport, Reconciling Originalism and Precedent, 103 Nw. U. L. Rev. 803 (2009); Randy E. Barnett, Trumping Precedent with Original Meaning: Not as Radical as It Sounds, 22 Const. Comment. 257 (2005).

45. See Michael J. Gerhardt, Non-Judicial Precedent, 61 Vand. L. Rev 713, 764–76 (2008); Trevor W. Morrison, Stare Decisis in the Office of Legal Counsel, 110 Colum. L. Rev. 1448 (2010). See also Peter J. Spiro, Treaties, Executive Agreements, and Constitutional Method, 79 Tex. L. Rev. 961, 964 (2001) ("The ongoing interplay among the branches gives rise to an accreted refinement of norms, in much the same way as judicial decisions do in other areas of the law.").

46. See, e.g., Stephen M. Griffin, Pluralism in Constitutional Interpretation, 72 Tex. L. Rev. 1753 (1994).

47. See generally David A. Strauss, Common Law Constitutional Interpretation, 63 U. Chi. L. Rev. 877 (1996).

48. Id. at 892.

49. See id. at 905; Ernest Young, Rediscovering Conservatism: Burkean Political Theory and Constitutional Interpretation, 72 N.C. L. Rev. 619, 664 (1994).

50. See, e.g., Larry D. Kramer, The People Themselves (2004); Mark Tushnet, Taking the Constitution Away from the Courts (1999).

51. See, e.g., Robert Post & Reva Siegel, Popular Constitutionalism, Departmentalism, and Judicial Supremacy, 92 Cal. L. Rev. 1027 (2004); Tom Donnelly, Popular Constitutional Argument, 73 Vand. L. Rev. 73 (2022).

52. See, e.g., Stephen M. Griffin, American Constitutionalism 45 (1996); Whittington, Constitutional Construction, supra note 42, at 209–14.

53. See Bruce Ackerman, We the People: Foundations 22 (1991); Eric A. Posner & Adrian Vermeule, Constitutional Showdowns, 156 U. Pa. L. Rev. 991, 997–98 (2008).

54. See William Baude, Constitutional Liquidation, 71 Stan. L. Rev. 1 (2019); Caleb Nelson, Originalism and Interpretive Conventions, 70 U. Chi. L. Rev. 519 (2003).

55. See, e.g., Federalist No. 37 (James Madison), in The Federalist Papers 225 (Clinton Rossiter ed., 1961) (stating that the meaning of the Constitution, like that of all laws, would be "liquidated and ascertained by a series of particular discussions and adjudications").

56. See, e.g., Myers v. United States, 272 U.S. 52, 175 (1926); J. W. Hampton Jr. & Co. v. United States, 276 U.S. 394, 412 (1928); McGrain v. Daugherty, 273 U.S. 135, 174 (1927); Stuart v. Laird, 5 U.S. (1 Cranch) 299, 309 (1803).

57. 573 U.S. at 525.

58. See Bradley & Siegel, supra note 8, at 39–59.

59. See Nelson, supra note 54, at 547.

60. 573 U.S. at 525.

61. See Baude, supra note 54.

62. See Curtis A. Bradley & Neil S. Siegel, Constructed Constraint and the Constitutional Text, 64 Duke L.J. 1213, 1231 (2015). For this reason, interpreters tend to be more comfortable with the idea of practice-based changes in *how the Constitution is interpreted* than with the idea of practice-based *amendments* to the Constitution, even though the result may be the same.

63. See Daryl J. Levinson, Parchment and Politics: The Positive Puzzle of Constitutional Commitment, 124 Harv. L. Rev. 657, 709 (2011); John O. McGinnis, Constitutional Review by the Executive in Foreign Affairs and War Powers: A Consequence of Rational Choice in the Separation of Powers, Law & Contemp. Probs., Autumn 1993, at 293, 300–301.

64. Cf. William Howard Taft, Our Chief Magistrate and His Powers 135 (1916) ("Executive power is sometimes created by custom, and so strong is the influence of custom that it seems almost to amend the Constitution.").

65. See Glennon, supra note 7, at 146 ("Constitutional facts have seldom been legitimized by the Court, in part because they are usually taken as beyond challenge by both branches. . . . The power of the president to recognize foreign governments, tracing to Washington's reception of Citizen Genet, is properly regarded as a constitutional fact.").

66. Cf. Henry P. Monaghan, The Protective Power of the Presidency, 93 Colum. L. Rev. 1, 15 n.64 (1993) (noting that the acceptance of a presidential recognition power was "by no means inevitable").

The constitutional text also likely has another effect, which is to induce interpreters to connect their gloss-based arguments to textual and structural interpretations rather than to make freestanding claims of constitutional custom. See Michael C. Dorf, How the Written Constitution Crowds Out the Extraconstitutional Rule of Recognition, in The Rule of Recognition and the U.S. Constitution (Matthew D. Adler & Kenneth Einar Himma eds., 2009).

67. See Jean Galbraith, Prospective Advice and Consent, 37 Yale J. Int'l L. 247, 258–60 (2012); see also Curtis A. Bradley & Martin S. Flaherty, Executive Power Essentialism and Foreign Affairs, 102 Mich. L. Rev. 545, 626 (2004) ("This deviation from original understanding became common practice and remains the practice today.").

68. See Alison L. LaCroix, Historical Gloss: A Primer, 126 Harv. L. Rev. F. 75, 81 (2013).

69. Compare 462 U.S. 919, 945 (1983) ("Explicit and unambiguous provisions of the Constitution prescribe and define the respective functions of the Congress and of the Executive in the legislative process."), with id. at 976 (White, J., dissenting) ("If the legislative veto were as plainly unconstitutional as the Court strives to suggest, its broad ruling today would be more comprehensible. But, the constitutionality of the legislative veto is anything but clear-cut.").

70. See, e.g., Baker v. Carr, 369 U.S. 186, 267 (1962) (Frankfurter, J., dissenting) ("The Court's authority—possessed of neither the purse nor the sword—ultimately rests on sustained public confidence in its moral sanction. Such feeling must be nourished by the Court's complete detachment, in fact and in appearance, from political entanglements and by abstention from injecting itself into the clash of political forces in political settlements."); Coleman v. Miller, 307 U.S. 433, 463–64 (1939) (Frankfurter, J.) ("The scope and consequences of our doctrine of judicial review over executive and legislative action should make us observe fastidiously the bounds of the litigious process within which we are confined."). See also Brad Snyder, Democratic Justice: Felix Frankfurter, the Supreme Court, and the Making of the Liberal Establishment (2022) (describing Frankfurter's longstanding skepticism of broad judicial review).

71. See generally Cass R. Sunstein, One Case at a Time: Judicial Minimalism on the Supreme Court (2001).

72. See Girgis, supra note 25.

73. See, e.g., H. Jefferson Powell, The President's Authority over Foreign Affairs: An Executive Branch Perspective, 67 Geo. Wash. L. Rev. 527, 539–40 (1999).

74. For this reason, gloss is distinguishable from what are sometimes called "constitutional conventions"—that is, non-legally-binding norms of good government behavior. Gloss can inform binding constitutional law, whereas conventions traditionally have not been viewed as having that effect. See Curtis A. Bradley & Neil S. Siegel, Historical Gloss, Constitutional Conventions, and the Judicial Separation of Powers, 105 Georgetown L.J. 255, 267–68 (2017). See also James Durling & E. Garrett West, Appointments Without Law, 105 Va. L. Rev. 1281, 1345–46 (2019) (noting that, "while gloss and liquidation create legally binding obligations, conventions constitute non-legal obligations"). Cf. Daphna Renan, Presidential Norms and Article II, 113 Harv. L. Rev. 2187, 2243 (2018) ("Structural norms . . . are reinforced through a variety of mechanisms (such as administrative procedures or congressional oversight) that are not amenable to neat categorization as legal or nonlegal.").

75. 573 U.S. at 549.

76. See, e.g., Martin S. Flaherty, Post-Originalism, 68 U. Chi. L. Rev. 1089, 1105 (2001) (reviewing David P. Currie, The Constitution in Congress: The Jeffersonians, 1801–29 (2000)) ("As a theoretical matter, custom has its own problems. Not least among these are the questions of what counts as the relevant custom, at what level of generality, and for how long.").

77. See Stephen M. Griffin, Against Historical Practice: Facing Up to the Challenge of Informal Constitutional Change, 35 Const. Comm. 79, 87 (2020).

78. Although less relevant to this book, the House and Senate have also compiled extensive collections of precedent relating to the procedures to be followed in those chambers. See, e.g., Precedents of the U.S. House of Representatives (2017 Series); Riddick's Senate Procedure: Precedents and Practices (rev. 1992).

79. Such reglossing need not favor the executive branch. See, e.g., Shane, supra note 14, at 182 ("Congress . . . should have room under the Constitution to cut back on a prior pattern of acquiescence in executive power and to begin to insist on a reinvigorated legislative role.").

80. See, e.g., Glennon, supra note 7, at 134; Harold Hongju Koh, Focus: Foreign Affairs under the United States Constitution, 13 Yale J. Int'l L. 1, 3 n.7 (1988); Peter J. Spiro, War Powers and the Sirens of Formalism, 68 N.Y.U. L. Rev. 1338, 1356 (1993) (reviewing John Hart Ely, War and Responsibility (1993)); Jane C. Stromseth, Understanding Constitutional War Powers Today: Why Methodology Matters, 106 Yale L.J. 845, 880 (1996) (reviewing Louis Fisher, Presidential War Power (1995)).

81. See, e.g., Dames & Moore v. Regan, 453 U.S. 654, 680, 686 (1981) ("Crucial to our decision today is the conclusion that Congress has implicitly approved the practice of claim settlement by executive agreement.").

82. See, e.g., Noel Canning, 573 U.S. at 526 ("We have not previously interpreted the [Recess Appointments] Clause, and, when doing so for the first time in more than 200 years, we must hesitate to upset the compromises and working arrangements that the elected branches of Government themselves have reached.").

83. See, e.g., Midwest Oil, 236 U.S. at 472–73 ("Both officers, lawmakers and citizens naturally adjust themselves to any long-continued action of the Executive Department—on the presumption that unauthorized acts would not have been allowed to be so often repeated as to crystallize into a regular practice.").

84. See, e.g., Roisman, supra note 7.

85. See also Ernest A. Young, Our Prescriptive Judicial Power: Constitutive and Entrenchment Effects of Historical Practice in Federal Courts Law, 58 Wm. & Mary L. Rev. 535, 557–58 (2016) (contending that Burkean justifications for crediting historical practice do not require a showing of institutional acquiescence).

86. See, e.g., Saikrishna Bangalore Prakash, The Living Presidency 129 (2020) (expressing concern that practice may operate as "a one-way ratchet" in favor of presidential authority); Griffin, supra note 77, at 88 ("Somehow, the use of practice has morphed into a one-way rachet that favors continual increases in executive power.").

87. See Terry M. Moe & William G. Howell, The Presidential Power of Unilateral Action, 15 J. Law, Econ. & Org. 132 (1999) (describing a variety of ways that presidents can take actions that have legal effect without the participation of Congress); see also Bradley & Morrison, supra note 20, at 441–44.

88. 573 U.S. at 593.

89. 343 U.S. at 654.

90. For an extensive argument about why this is a positive development, see Oona A. Hathaway, Treaties' End: The Past, Present, and Future of International Lawmaking in the United States, 117 Yale L.J. 1236 (2009).

91. See, e.g., Prakash, supra note 86, at 9. See also Noel Canning, 573 U.S. at 570 (Scalia, J., concurring in the judgment).

92. See Curtis A. Bradley & Neil S. Siegel, After Recess: Historical Practice, Textual Ambiguity, and Constitutional Adverse Possession, 2014 Sup. Ct. Rev. 1, 52–55.

93. See, e.g., Hamdan v. Rumsfeld, 548 U.S. 557, 593 n.23 (2006) ("Whether or not the President has independent power, absent congressional authorization, to convene military commissions, he may not disregard limitations that Congress has, in proper exercise of its own war powers, placed on his powers."). Cf. Zivotofsky v. Kerry, 576 U.S. 1, 63–64 (Roberts, C.J., dissenting) ("We have held that congressional acquiescence is only 'pertinent' when the President acts in the absence of express congressional authorization, not when he asserts power to disregard a statute, as the Executive does here.").

94. For discussion of congressional soft law, see Josh Chafetz, Congress's Constitution, 160 U. Pa. L. Rev. 715 (2012); Jacob E. Gersen & Eric A. Posner, Soft Law: Lessons from Congressional Practice, 61 Stan. L. Rev. 573 (2008).

95. 573 U.S. at 531 (emphasis added).

96. See Bradley & Morrison, supra note 20, at 542–54.

97. Even aside from the role of historical gloss, it is a mistake to consider only legislative enactments when thinking about the degree of congressional influence. Congress exercises influence in a host of ways—including through oversight hearings, express or implicit threats of funding reductions, and interactions between congressional and executive staff members—that are not captured simply by looking at statutes.

2. The Laconic Foreign Affairs Constitution

1. The Continental Congress, which was the governing body for the United States before the Constitution, did establish an appellate tribunal to review prize decisions from the state courts, which operated from 1780–1787. See Henry J. Bourguignon, The First Federal Court (1977). The Continental Congress also had a "president," but this was a largely ceremonial position.

2. Federalist No. 15 (Hamilton), in The Federalist Papers 107 (Clinton Rossiter ed., 1961).

3. See, e.g., Frederick W. Marks, Independence on Trial: Foreign Affairs and the Making of the Constitution (1973); Bradford Perkins, The Creation of a Republican Empire, 1776–1865, in 1 Cambridge History of American Foreign Relations, at 58 (1993); Jack N. Rakove, Making Foreign Policy: The View from 1787, in Foreign Policy and the Constitution (Robert A. Goldwin & Robert A. Licht eds., 1990).

4. The Federalist Papers, No. 70 (Hamilton), supra note 2, at 427. See also Federalist No. 1 (Hamilton), supra, at 35 (contending that "the vigor of government is essential to the security of liberty"); Federalist No. 5 (Jay), supra, at 50 (noting that "weakness and divisions at home would invite dangers from abroad"). The Founders were also concerned about potential abuses of authority by the legislature, which could be checked by a strong executive. See, e.g., Federalist No. 48 (Madison), supra, at 309–10.

5. McCulloch v. Maryland, 17 U.S. (4 Wheat.) 316, 423 (1819). See also, e.g., United States v. Comstock, 560 U.S. 126, 134 (2010) (requiring only that the legislation be "rationally related to the implementation of a constitutionally enumerated power").

6. See U.S. Const. art. IV, § 3, cl. 2.

7. The Federalist Papers, No. 69 (Hamilton), supra note 2, at 418. For an argument that the Commander in Chief Clause had a narrow original meaning, see Saikrishna B. Prakash, Deciphering the Commander-in-Chief Clause, 133 Yale L.J. 1 (2023).

8. Youngstown Sheet & Tube Co. v. Sawyer, 343 U.S. 579, 641 (1952).

9. See, e.g., Jack Goldsmith & John F. Manning, The President's Completion Power, 115 Yale L.J. 2280 (2006); Edward T. Swaine, Taking Care of Treaties, 108 Colum. L. Rev. 331 (2008). The dissent in *Youngstown* reflects a broad view of this presidential power. See 343 U.S. 579, 667 (1952) (Vinson, C.J., dissenting).

10. 135 U.S. 1, 64 (1890). See also Henry P. Monaghan, The Protective Power of the Presidency, 93 Colum. L. Rev. 1, 11 (1993) ("The constitutional conception of a Chief Executive authorized to enforce the laws includes a general authority to protect and defend the personnel, property, and instrumentalities of the United States from harm."). For background on *Neagle*, see John Harrison, The Story of In re Neagle: Sex, Money, Politics, Perjury, Homicide, Federalism, and Executive Power, in Presidential Power Stories 133 (Christopher H. Schroeder & Curtis A. Bradley eds., 2009).

11. See Medellin v. Texas, 552 U.S. 491, 532 (2008) ("This authority allows the President to execute the laws, not make them."); Youngstown, 343 U.S. at 587 ("The President's power to see that the laws are faithfully executed refutes the idea that he is to be a lawmaker.").

12. See, e.g., Michael W. McConnell, The President Who Would Not Be King: Executive Power under the Constitution 235–62 (2020); Saikrishna B. Prakash & Michael D. Ramsey, The Executive Power over Foreign Affairs, 111 Yale L.J. 231 (2001).

13. See, e.g., Curtis A. Bradley & Martin S. Flaherty, Executive Power Essentialism and Foreign Affairs, 102 Mich. L. Rev. 545 (2004); Julian Davis Mortenson, Article II Vests the Executive Power, Not the Royal Prerogative, 119 Colum. L. Rev. 1169 (2019). Cf. Ilan Wurman, In Search of Prerogative, 70 Duke L.J. 93 (2020) (concluding that the Article II vesting clause conveys only a power to execute the laws but advancing a thick understanding of that power). Even if the Article II vesting clause is not a source of substantive authority, it might provide a basis for presidential control over the executive branch. See, e.g., Myers v. United States, 272 U.S. 52 (1926).

14. Daniel Webster, the famous early nineteenth-century lawyer and statesman, observed that "executive power is not a thing so well known, and so accurately defined, as that the written constitution of a limited government can be supposed to have conferred it in the lump." Daniel Webster, Speech on the Appointing and Removing Power Delivered in the Senate (Feb. 16, 1835), in 4 The Works of Daniel Webster 179, 186 (1851). See also The Federalist Papers, No. 37 (Madison), supra note 2 ("Experience has instructed us that no skill in the science of government has yet been able to discriminate and define, with sufficient certainty, its three great provinces the legislative, executive, and judiciary."); 3 Joseph Story, Commentaries on the Constitution of the United States 277 (1833) ("What is the best constitution for the executive department, and what are the powers, with which it should be entrusted, are problems among the most important, and probably the most difficult to be satisfactorily solved, of all, which are involved in the theory of free government.").

15. 343 U.S. 579, 640–41 (1952).

16. 576 U.S. 1, 14, 20 (2015).

17. See Louis Henkin, Foreign Affairs and the United States Constitution 15 (2d ed. 1996) (describing a variety of "missing" foreign affairs powers that "have always been exercised"); Harold Hongju Koh, The National Security Constitution: Sharing Power after the Iran-Contra Affair 67 (1990) ("One cannot read the Constitution without being struck by its astonishing brevity regarding the allocation of foreign affairs authority among the branches.").

18. It might be that some of these matters could be addressed by Congress through its authority to "make all Laws which shall be necessary and proper for carrying into Execution" both its powers and "all other Powers vested by this Constitution in the Government of the United States, or in any Department or Officer thereof." U.S. Const. art. I, § 8. But there is substantial debate about the scope of that power and its relationship to other constitutional powers. Moreover, as will be seen, it is generally accepted that the president has independent authority over some of these matters and thus can act even when Congress has not exercised its Necessary and Proper Clause authority.

19. See Koh, supra note 17, at 67 (noting that the text of the Constitution "frequently . . . grants clearly related powers to separate institutions, without ever specifying the relationship between those powers").

20. Edward S. Corwin, The President: Office and Powers, 1787–1957, at 171 (4th rev. ed. 1957).

21. See Martin S. Flaherty, The Story of the Neutrality Controversy: Struggling over Presidential Power outside the Courts, in Presidential Power Stories (Christopher H. Schroeder & Curtis A. Bradley eds., 2009).

22. George Washington, Proclamation (Apr. 22, 1793). See generally Stanley Elkins & Eric McKitrick, The Age of Federalism: The Early American Republic, 1788–1800, at 337–38 (1993).

23. Alexander Hamilton, Pacificus No. 1 (June 29, 1793), in 15 The Papers of Alexander Hamilton 38 (Harold C. Syrett ed. 1969).

24. In his earlier accounts of presidential power in *The Federalist Papers,* Hamilton did not seem to view the Vesting Clause as a source of authority. See, e.g., The Federalist Papers, No. 77 (Hamilton), supra note 2 (proceeding to discuss "the only remaining" powers of the president, all of which are enumerated).

25. See also David P. Currie, The Constitution in Congress: The Federalist Period, 1789–1801, at 177 (1997) (noting that "the validity of the neutrality proclamation does not stand or fall with Hamilton's all-encompassing approach to the vesting clause"); Robert J. Reinstein, Executive Power and the Law of Nations in the Washington Administration, 46 U. Rich. L. Rev. 373 (2012) (concluding that the most plausible source of authority for the proclamation was the president's duty to implement the law of nations under the Take Care Clause).

26. Madison had been urged by his friend Thomas Jefferson to respond to Hamilton. "Nobody answers him," said Jefferson, "& his doctrine will therefore be taken for confessed. For god's sake, my dear Sir, take up your pen, select the most striking heresies, and cut him to pieces in the face of the public." Letter from Thomas Jefferson to James Madison (July 7, 1793), in 26 The Papers of Thomas Jefferson 444 (John Catanzariti ed., 1995).

27. Madison's argument that a presidential power to declare neutrality is inconsistent with the Constitution's assignment of the power to declare war to Congress is not compelling. See, e.g., David P. Currie, The Constitution in Congress: The Jeffersonians, 1801–1829, at 208 (2001) ("The reason for giving Congress power to declare war was to keep the country out of hostilities without popular approval. Washington's action was fully in accord with this principle, for its thrust was to prevent an undeclared war.").

28. 1 Stat. 381 (June 6, 1794). In his address to Congress, Washington said that "it will probably be found expedient to extend the legal code and the jurisdiction of the courts of the United States to many cases which, though dependent on principles already recognized, demand some further provisions." George Washington, Fifth Annual Address to Congress (Dec. 3, 1793). A version of this neutrality statute still exists, and there were questions during 2022–2023 about

whether it might be implicated by the participation of U.S. citizens in the conflict between Russia and Ukraine. See Dakota S. Rudesill, American Fighters, Ukraine, and the Neutrality Act: The Law and the Urgent Need for Clarity, Just Security (Mar. 15, 2022).

29. There have since been other presidential proclamations of neutrality. See, e.g., Martin Van Buren, Proclamation, Neutrality with Respect to Canadian Affairs (Jan. 5, 1838); Woodrow Wilson, Proclamation of Neutrality (Aug. 18, 1914); Franklin Roosevelt, Proclaiming the Neutrality of the United States in the War between Germany and France; and the United Kingdom, India, Australia, and New Zealand (Sept. 5, 1939).

30. My own view is that, although Hamilton's Vesting Clause argument was unpersuasive, he nevertheless had the stronger side of the debate. By necessity, presidents carrying out their duties must interpret the international law obligations of the United States, including obligations relating to neutrality, and Washington did not purport to be displacing Congress's authority to act. See also Bradley & Flaherty, supra note 13, at 682 (noting that "Hamilton was defending only the limited argument that the President had the power to declare the default position of the United States under international law in the absence of congressional or judicial action").

31. 299 U.S. 304 (1936).

32. See George Sutherland, The International and External Powers of the National Government, 191 N. Am. L. Rev. 373 (1910); George Sutherland, Constitutional Power and World Affairs (1919).

33. David M. Levitan, The Foreign Relations Power: An Analysis of Mr. Justice Sutherland's Theory, 55 Yale L.J. 467, 476 (1946). The following year, Sutherland wrote the opinion for the Court in United States v. Belmont, 301 U.S. 324, 331 (1937), holding that an executive agreement that settled claims with the Soviet Union preempted contrary state law. "Plainly," said the Court, "the external powers of the United States are to be exercised without regard to state laws or policies." This decision is discussed in Chapter 4.

34. See, e.g., Charles A. Lofgren, United States v. Curtiss-Wright Export Corporation: An Historical Reassessment, 83 Yale L.J. 1 (1973); Michael J. Glennon, Two Views of Presidential Foreign Affairs Power: Little v. Barreme or Curtiss-Wright?, 13 Yale J. Int'l L. 5 (1988); Michael D. Ramsey, The Myth of Extraconstitutional Foreign Affairs Power, 42 Wm. & Mary L. Rev. 379 (2000). See also Sarah H. Cleveland, Powers Inherent in Sovereignty: Indians, Aliens, Territories, and the Nineteenth-Century Origins of Plenary Power over Foreign Affairs, 81 Tex. L. Rev. 1 (2002). For additional discussion of Sutherland's distinction between domestic and foreign affairs, see G. Edward White, The Transformation of the Constitutional Regime of Foreign Relations, 85 Va. L. Rev. 1, 47–62 (1999). For discussion of the internal deliberations on the Court and the potential influence of Chief Justice Hughes on some of the executive power reasoning in the opinion, see Edward A. Purcell Jr., Understanding Curtiss-Wright, 31 Law & Hist. Rev. 653 (2013).

35. Henkin, supra note 17, at 20; see also Fong Yue Ting v. United States, 149 U.S. 698, 737 (1893) (Brewer, J., dissenting) ("This doctrine of powers inherent in sovereignty is one both indefinite and dangerous. Where are the limits to such powers to be found, and by whom are they to be pronounced?").

36. See, e.g., McCulloch v. Maryland, 17 U.S. (4 Wheat.) 316, 405 (1819) ("This government is acknowledged by all to be one of enumerated powers."); United States v. Morrison, 529 U.S. 598, 607 (2000) ("Every law enacted by Congress must be based on one or more of its powers

enumerated in the Constitution."); Murphy v. National Collegiate Athletic Association, 138 S. Ct. 1461, 1476 (2018) ("The Constitution confers on Congress not plenary legislative power but only certain enumerated powers."). See also U.S. Const. Amendment X ("The powers not delegated to the United States by the Constitution, nor prohibited by it to the States, are reserved to the States respectively, or to the people."); Federalist No. 45 (James Madison), in The Federalist Papers 292 (Clinton Rossiter ed., 1961) ("The powers delegated by the proposed Constitution to the federal government, are few and defined. Those which are to remain in the State governments are numerous and indefinite.").

37. See also Reid v. Covert, 354 U.S. 1, 5–6 (1956) (plurality opinion) ("The United States is entirely a creature of the Constitution. Its power and authority have no other source. It can only act in accordance with all the limitations imposed by the Constitution.").

38. 343 U.S. 579, 635 n.2 (1952) (Jackson, J., concurring).

39. See U.S. Const. art. I, § 8, cl. 4.

40. Before that time, states often regulated immigration matters. See Gerald L. Neuman, The Lost Century of American Immigration Law (1776–1875), 93 Colum. L. Rev. 1833 (1993).

41. See, e.g., The Head Money Cases, 112 U.S. 580, 600 (1884).

42. Nishimura Ekiu v. United States, 142 U.S. 651, 659 (1892). See also The Chinese Exclusion Case, 130 U.S. 581, 603–4 (1889) ("The United States, in their relation to foreign countries and their subjects or citizens are one nation, invested with powers, which belong to independent nations, the exercise of which can be invoked for the maintenance of its absolute independence and security throughout its entire territory."). The Court also relied on historical practice. See, e.g., id. at 606–7 ("The power of the government to exclude foreigners from the country whenever in its judgment the public interests require such exclusion has been asserted in repeated instances, and never denied by the executive or legislative departments."). For additional discussion of the uncertain constitutional basis for immigration law, see Nikolas Bowie & Norah Rast, The Imaginary Immigration Clause, 120 Mich. L. Rev. 1419 (2022). Somewhat relatedly, sovereignty may be part of the justification for the national government's authority to regulate passports. See Calvin H. Johnson, The Dubious Enumerated Power Doctrine, 22 Const. Comment. 25, 39–42 (2005).

43. 252 U.S. 416 (1920). This interpretation of the Necessary and Proper Clause as applied to treaties is supported by historical practice. See Jean Galbraith, Congress's Treaty-Implementing Power in Historical Practice, 56 Wm. & Mary L. Rev. 69 (2014).

44. 252 U.S. at 433.

45. See, e.g., Champion v. Ames, 188 U.S. 321, 373 (1903) (reasoning that the foreign commerce power "clothed Congress with that power over international commerce, pertaining to a sovereign nation in its intercourse with foreign nations").

46. Letter from Thomas Jefferson to John Dickinson (Aug. 9, 1803). See also Letter from Thomas Jefferson to John Breckinridge (Aug. 12, 1803) ("The Constitution has made no provision for our holding foreign territory, still less for incorporating foreign nations into our Union.").

47. Letter from Albert Gallatin to Thomas Jefferson (Jan. 13, 1803); see also Gary Lawson & Guy Seidman, The Constitution of Empire: Territorial Expansion and American Legal History 22 (2004) ("Several members of Congress, in discussing ratification and implementation of the treaty for the acquisition of Louisiana, maintained that acquisition of territory is a necessary incident of sovereignty and therefore requires no specific constitutional authorization."). For additional discussion, see Currie, supra note 27, at 95–107; Eberhard P. Deutsch,

The Constitutional Controversy over the Louisiana Purchase, 53 A.B.A. J. 50 (1967); see also 3 Joseph Story, Commentaries on the Constitution of the United States § 1282 (1833) ("As an incidental power, the constitutional right of the United States to acquire territory would seem so naturally to flow from the sovereignty confided to it, as not to admit of very serious question."). My own view is that, even from an originalist perspective, the purchase was constitutional without the need to appeal to general notions of sovereignty. It was reasonable to construe the treaty power as encompassing the sorts of things that nations made treaties about at the Founding, which included the acquisition of territory, and it was not too much of a stretch to construe Congress's authority over territory in Article IV as including the authority to incorporate new territory into the Union.

48. American Insurance Co. v. Canter, 26 U.S. (1 Pet.) 511, 542 (1828).

49. See, e.g., Jones v. United States, 137 U.S. 202, 212 (1890) ("By the law of nations . . . dominion of new territory may be acquired by discovery and occupation as well as by cession or conquest, and when citizens or subjects of one nation, in its name and by its authority or with its assent, take and hold actual, continuous, and useful possession . . . of territory unoccupied by any other government or its citizens, the nation to which they belong may exercise such jurisdiction and for such period as it sees fit over territory so acquired."); Dorr v. United States, 195 U.S. 138, 140 (1904) ("It is equally well settled that the United States may acquire territory in the exercise of the treatymaking power by direct cession as the result of war, and in making effectual the terms of peace, and for that purpose has the powers of other sovereign nations.").

50. See, e.g., United States v. Lara, 541 U.S. 193, 201 (2004) (citing *Curtiss-Wright*); United States v. Kagama, 118 U.S. 375, 380 (1886). But cf. Haaland v. Brackeen, 143 S. Ct. 1609, 1660 (2023) ("Like the rest of its legislative powers, Congress's authority to regulate Indians must derive from the Constitution, not the atmosphere."). See also Gregory Ablavsky, Beyond the Indian Commerce Clause, 124 Yale L.J. 1012 (2015); Nell Jessup Newton, Federal Power over Indians: Its Sources, Scope, and Limitations, 132 U. Pa. L. Rev. 195 (1984).

51. United States v. Western Union Tel., 272 F. 311, 313 (S.D.N.Y. 1921) (Augustus Hand). See also, e.g., Henkin, supra note 17, at 70–72 (describing various ways that a sovereignty-based foreign affairs power can be exercised by Congress); Youngstown, 343 U.S. at 604 (Frankfurter, J., concurring) (noting that "the fact that power exists in the Government does not vest it in the President"); United States v. Western Union Tel., 272 F. 311, 313 (S.D.N.Y. 1921) (Augustus Hand) (observing that, even if "the United States . . . must be deemed to have all customary national powers . . . it does not follow that the Executive has the necessary authority"). Sovereignty considerations might, however, inform the scope of the powers enumerated in the Constitution, and the enumeration might itself identify which institution has the authority. Cf. In re Debs, 158 U.S. 564, 578 (1885) (noting that, "while the [federal government] is properly styled a government of enumerated powers, *yet within the limits of such enumeration*, it has all the attributes of sovereignty") (emphasis added).

52. 299 U.S. at 319.

53. For accounts of the historical and legal context, see Michael P. Van Alstine, Taking Care of John Marshall's Political Ghost, 53 St. Louis L.J. 93 (2008); Larry D. Cress, The Jonathan Robbins Incident: Extradition and the Separation of Powers in the Adams Administration, 111 Essex Inst. Hist. Collections 99 (1975); H. Jefferson Powell, The Founders and the President's Authority over Foreign Affairs, 40 Wm. & Mary L. Rev. 1471, 1511–28 (1999); Ruth Wedgwood, The Revolutionary Martyrdom of Jonathan Robbins, 100 Yale L.J. 229 (1990).

54. See United States v. Robins [*sic*], 27 Fed. Cas. 825, 832 (1799) (Case No. 16,175).

55. 10 Annals of Cong. 533 (resolution by Rep. Livingston on Feb. 20, 1800).

56. 10 Annals of Cong. 613 (1800).

57. See, e.g., Henkin, supra note 17, at 42 ("That the President is the sole organ of official communication by and to the United States has not been questioned and has not been a source of significant controversy."); Corwin, supra note 20, at 184 ("There is no more securely established principle of constitutional practice than the exclusive right of the President to be the nation's intermediary in its dealings with other nations."). See also United States v. Curtiss-Wright Export Corp., 299 U.S. 304, 319 (1936) (noting that "the President alone has the power to speak or listen as a representative of the nation"); United States v. Louisiana, 363 U.S. 1, 35 (1960) ("The President . . . is the constitutional representative of the United States in its dealings with foreign nations.").

58. See Letter from Thomas Jefferson to the French Minister (Nov. 22, 1793) (explaining that the president was "the only channel of communication between this country and foreign nations" and that "it is from him alone that foreign nations or their agents are to learn what is or has been the will of the nation").

59. 10 Annals of Cong. 614 (1800). That said, Marshall clearly viewed the president as more than a mere spokesperson. See, e.g., id. (stating that the president "possesses the whole Executive power" and "holds and directs the force of the nation").

60. Koh, supra note 17, at 94.

61. See generally Curtis A. Bradley, Introduction: The Irrepressible Functionalism in U.S. Foreign Relations Law, in 1 Foreign Relations Law (Curtis A. Bradley ed., 2019). See also, e.g., Zivotofsky v. Kerry, 576 U.S. 1, 14 (2015) (relying in part on "functional considerations" in concluding that the president's authority over recognition was exclusive).

62. For example, the Alien Tort Statute gives the federal courts jurisdiction to hear suits brought by aliens for torts in violation of international law. See 28 U.S.C. § 1350. When interpreting this statute, the Supreme Court has applied a strict presumption against extraterritoriality, in part to avoid the "danger of unwarranted judicial interference in the conduct of foreign policy." Kiobel v. Royal Dutch Petroleum Co., 569 U.S. 108, 116 (2013). To take another example, the Supreme Court has described the act of state doctrine, pursuant to which U.S. courts will presume the validity of foreign government acts taken within their territory, as "express[ing] the strong sense of the Judicial Branch that its engagement in the task of passing on the validity of foreign acts of state may hinder, rather than further, this country's pursuit of goals both for itself and for the community of nations as a whole in the international sphere." Banco Nacional de Cuba v. Sabbatino, 376 U.S. 398, 423 (1964).

63. Haig v. Agee, 453 U.S. 280, 292 (1981). For a more recent endorsement of this statement, see Egbert v. Boule, 142 S. Ct. 1793, 1804–5 (2022).

64. See, e.g., TransUnion LLC v. Ramirez, 141 S. Ct. 2190, 2203 (2022); Lujan v. Defenders of Wildlife, 504 U.S. 555, 560 (1992); Allen v. Wright, 468 U.S. 737, 751 (1984).

65. See Raines v. Byrd, 521 U.S. 811, 820–21 (1997). In limiting such "legislative standing," the Court emphasized the lack of historical practice involving such suits. See id. at 826. For a lower court decision relying on *Raines* to deny standing to members of Congress challenging presidential military action, see Campbell v. Clinton, 203 F.3d 19 (D.C. Cir. 2000). See also Clapper v. Amnesty International USA, 568 U.S. 398, 409 (2013) ("We have often found a lack of standing in cases in which the Judiciary has been requested to review actions of the political branches in the fields of intelligence gathering and foreign affairs.").

66. 369 U.S. 186 (1962).

67. See Curtis A. Bradley, The Political Question Doctrine and International Law, 91 Geo. Wash. L. Rev. 1555 (2023) (symposium contribution); Edwin D. Dickinson, The Law of Nations as National Law: "Political Questions," 104 U. Pa. L. Rev. 451, 453–54 (1952); see also, e.g., Jones v. United States, 137 U.S. 202, 221 (1890) ("Who is the sovereign, *de jure* or *de facto*, of a territory is not a judicial, but a political question, the determination of which by the legislative and executive departments of any government conclusively binds the judges, as well as all other officers, citizens and subjects of that government."). Cf. Tara Leigh Grove, The Lost History of the Political Question Doctrine, 90 N.Y.U. L. Rev. 1908, 1911 (2015) ("The courts treated the political branches' determination as a (factual) rule of decision for the case.").

68. 566 U.S. 189, 195 (2012).

69. Hernandez v. Mesa, 140 S. Ct. 735, 744 (2020) (quoting Jesner v. Arab Bank PLC, 138 S. Ct. 1386, 1403 (2018)). For a defense of broad judicial abstention in cases involving claims of presidential authority that do not conflict with statutes, including in foreign affairs, see Jesse H. Choper, Judicial Review and the National Political Process: A Functional Reconsideration of the Role of the Supreme Court 319–20, 356–57 (1980). For a lower court decision (written by Judge Augustus Hand) that appeared to endorse judicial deference under such circumstances and that appears to have been an influence on Justice Jackson in drafting his concurrence in *Youngstown*, see United States v. Western Union Tel. Co., 272 F. 311, 318–19 (S.D.N.Y. 1921), aff'd, 272 F. 893 (2d Cir. 1921), rev'd based on settlement, 260 U.S. 754 (1922). See also Adam J. White, Justice Jackson's Draft Opinions in *The Steel Seizure Cases*, 69 Albany L. Rev. 1107, 1112 (2006).

70. See Curtis A. Bradley & Eric A. Posner, The Real Political Question Doctrine, 75 Stan. L. Rev. 1031 (2023).

71. See, e.g., Doe v. Bush, 323 F.3d 133, 139 (1st Cir. 2003); Dellums v. Bush, 752 F. Supp. 1141, 1150 (D.D.C. 1990). See also David M. Driesen, The Political Remedies Doctrine, 71 Emory L.J. 1 (2021).

72. 444 U.S. at 998 (Powell, J., concurring).

73. Jama v. Immigration and Customs Enforcement, 543 U.S. 335, 368 (2005). For an argument that judicial deference in foreign affairs should become more context dependent, see Elad Gil, Rethinking Foreign Affairs Deference, 64 B.C. L. Rev. 1603 (2022). For an argument that courts should play a more active role in resolving foreign relations disputes, see Martin S. Flaherty, Restoring the Global Judiciary: Why the Supreme Court Should Rule in Foreign Affairs (2019).

74. See, e.g., Water Splash Inc. v. Menon, 581 U.S. 271, 281 (2017); Abbott v. Abbott, 560 U.S. 1, 15 (2010); Medellin v. Texas, 552 U.S. 491, 513 (2008).

75. Compare, for example, Ganesh Sitaraman & Ingrid Brunk Wuerth, The Normalization of Foreign Relations Law, 128 Harv. L. Rev. 1897 (2015), with Curtis A. Bradley, Foreign Relations Law and the Purported Shift Away from "Exceptionalism," 128 Harv. L. Rev. F. 294 (2015), and Carlos M. Vazquez, The Abiding Exceptionalism of Foreign Relations Doctrine, 128 Harv. L. Rev. F. 305 (2015).

76. In the 1990s, I coined the term "foreign affairs exceptionalism" to refer to "the view that the federal government's foreign affairs powers are subject to a different, and generally more relaxed, set of constitutional restraints than those that govern its domestic powers." Curtis A. Bradley, A New American Foreign Affairs Law?, 70 U. Colo. L. Rev. 1089, 1096 (1999). But the term has been used since then to refer more generally to differential legal treatment between domestic and foreign affairs.

77. See, e.g., Sitaraman & Wuerth, supra note 76, at 1901.

78. See, e.g., Biden v. Texas, 142 S. Ct. 2528, 2543 (2022) (immigration); Egbert v. Boule, 142 S. Ct. 1793, 1804–5 (2022) (constitutional tort); Hernandez v. Mesa, 140 S. Ct. 735, 744 (2020) (same); Trump v. Hawaii, 138 S. Ct. 2392, 2419 (2018) (immigration); Jesner v. Arab Bank, 138 S. Ct. 1386, 1403 (2018) (human rights litigation); Ziglar v. Abbasi, 582 U.S. 120, 142 (2017) (constitutional tort).

3. The Recognition Power

1. Presidential Proclamation Recognizing Jerusalem as the Capital of the State of Israel and Relocating the United States Embassy to Israel to Jerusalem (Dec. 6, 2017).

2. Proclamation on Recognizing the Golan Heights as Part of the State of Israel (Mar. 25, 2019).

3. For accounts of the history of the U.S. recognition policy, see Taylor Cole, The Recognition Policy of the United States Since 1901 (1928); L. Thomas Galloway, Recognizing Foreign Governments: The Practice of the United States (1977); Julius Goebel, The Recognition Policy of the United States (1915); 1 Green Haywood Hackworth, Digest of International Law §§ 35–51, at 195–318 (1940); 1 John Bassett Moore, A Digest of International Law §§ 27–58, at 72–164 (1906); 2 Marjorie M. Whiteman, Digest of International Law §§ 6–64, at 133–467 (1963); State Department Research Memorandum, The Problem of Recognition in American Foreign Policy (Aug. 1950) (on file with author); Donald Paul Bakker, Congress and the Power to Recognize, in 3 Columbia Essays in International Affairs, The Dean's Papers 1967 (1968); Robert J. Reinstein, Is the President's Recognition Power Exclusive?, 86 U. Rich. L. Rev. 1 (2013).

4. 576 U.S. 1 (2015).

5. See Memorandum Opinion from Steven A. Engel, Assistant Attorney General, for the Legal Adviser to the National Security Council, Congressionally Mandated Notice Period for Withdrawing from the Open Skies Treaty, 44 Op. O.L.C. slip op. (Sept. 22, 2020).

6. See Restatement (Third) of Foreign Relations Law of the United States § 203, cmt. a, p. 84 (1987); Whiteman, supra note 3, at 1.

7. See David M. Golove & Daniel J. Hulsebosch, A Civilized Nation: The Early American Constitution, the Law of Nations, and the Pursuit of International Recognition, 85 N.Y.U. L. Rev. 932, 942 (2010).

8. See Moore, supra note 3, at 73. Recognizing a regime and conducting diplomatic relations with it are separate phenomena: it is possible to have diplomatic relations with an entity without recognizing it as a state (the Vatican, for example), and it is possible to recognize a state without having formal diplomatic relations with it (Iran, for example).

9. Zivotofsky v. Kerry, 576 U.S. 1, 11 (2015).

10. See Restatement (Third) of Foreign Relations Law, supra note 6, § 205; Pfizer Inc. v. Government of India, 434 U.S. 308, 319–20 (1978); Republic of Panama v. Republic Nat'l Bank, 681 F. Supp. 1066, 1071 (S.D.N.Y. 1988). But cf. National Petrochemical Co. v. M/T Stolt Sheaf, 860 F.2d 551, 553–54 (2d Cir. 1988) ("A break in diplomatic relations with another government does not automatically signify denial of access to federal courts"). See also P.L. 63–43, § 25(B)(3) (Dec. 23, 1913), as amended through P.L. 117–263 (Dec. 23, 2022) (tying access to foreign government property held in Federal Reserve banks to executive branch recognition).

11. See, e.g., National City Bank v. Republic of China, 348 U.S. 356, 358 (1955); Lafontant v. Aristide, 844 F. Supp. 128, 132 (E.D.N.Y. 1994). See also Knox v. PLO, 306 F. Supp. 2d 424, 430 (S.D.N.Y. 2004).

12. See Banco Nacional de Cuba v. Sabbatino, 376 U.S. 398, 400 (1964) ("The act of state doctrine in its traditional formulation precludes the courts of this country from inquiring into the validity of the public acts [that] *a recognized foreign sovereign power* committed within its own territory.") (emphasis added).

13. Oetjen v. Central Leather Co., 246 U.S. 297, 303 (1918).

14. See, e.g., Memorandum Opinion for the Counsel to the President, Constitutionality of Legislative Provision Regarding ABM Treaty, 20 Op. O.L.C. 246, 252 (June 26, 1996).

15. See Restatement (Third) of Foreign Relations Law, supra note 6, § 204, cmt. a. In *The Federalist Papers,* Alexander Hamilton described the power to receive ambassadors in narrow terms, as "more a matter of dignity than of authority" and as "without consequence in the administration of the government." The Federalist No. 69, at 420 (Clinton Rossiter ed., 1961). Hamilton later evinced a broader view. See Alexander Hamilton, Pacificus No. 1 (June 29, 1793), in 15 The Papers of Alexander Hamilton 33, 41 (Harold C. Syrett & Jacob E. Cooke eds., 1969) (contending that the Receptions Clause "includes th[e power] of judging, in the case of a revolution of government in a foreign country, whether the new rulers are competent organs of the national will, and ought to be recognised, or not"). In debating Hamilton, James Madison referred back to what Hamilton had said in *The Federalist Papers,* which Madison described as part of the "original gloss" on the Receptions Clause. See James Madison, Helvidius No. 3 (Sept. 7, 1793), in 15 The Papers of James Madison 95, 98 (Thomas A. Mason et al. eds., 1985). For arguments in favor of a narrow view of the Receptions Clause, see David Gray Adler, The President's Recognition Power: Ministerial or Discretionary?, 25 Pres. Stud. Q. 267 (1995); Robert J. Reinstein, Recognition: A Case Study in the Original Understanding of Executive Power, 45 U. Rich. L. Rev. 801, 812–16 (2011).

16. See, e.g., 3 Joseph Story, Commentaries on the Constitution of the United States § 1560, at 416 (1833).

17. See U.S. Const. art. II, § 2 ("The President shall have power to fill up all vacancies that may happen during the recess of the Senate, by granting commissions which shall expire at the end of their next session"). On the basis of longstanding practice, moreover, the diplomatic position being filled could be created in the first instance by the president. See Memorandum Opinion for the Counsel to the President, 20 Op. O.L.C. 286 (July 26, 1996). There is also a long history, dating back to near the Founding, of the president appointing diplomatic agents for particular missions without seeking the Senate's approval. See Louis Henkin, Foreign Affairs and the United States Constitution 42 (2d ed. 1996); Henry M. Wriston, Executive Agents in American Foreign Relations (1929); Ryan M. Scoville, Ad Hoc Diplomats, 68 Duke L.J. 907 (2019). In late 2021, Congress placed limitations on these appointments—requiring, for example, Senate advice and consent for long-term appointments involving the exercise of significant authority. See National Defense Authorization Act for Fiscal Year 2022, § 5105; Ryan Scoville, An Important Development in the Law of Diplomatic Appointments, Lawfare (Jan. 31, 2022).

18. See Memorandum Opinion for the Deputy Attorney General and the Associate Attorney General, Presidential Power to Expel Diplomatic Personnel from the United States, 4B Op. O.L.C. 207 (Apr. 4, 1980). An early example of a presidential exercise of expulsion authority was George Washington's demand during the Neutrality Crisis of 1793 that France recall its ambassador. See id. at 208.

19. See Clarence A. Berdahl, The Power of Recognition, 14 Am. J. Int'l L. 519, 521 (1920).

20. See Saikrishna B. Prakash & Michael D. Ramsey, The Executive Power over Foreign Affairs, 111 Yale L.J. 231, 313 (2001).

21. In Zivotofsky, 576 U.S. at 14, the Court said that, because specific clauses in the Constitution implicitly conferred the recognition power on the president, the Court "need not consider whether or to what extent the Vesting Clause . . . provides further support for the President's action here."

22. See, e.g., Guaranty Trust Co. v. United States, 304 U.S. 126, 137 (1938); Jones v. United States, 137 U.S. 202, 221 (1890); United States v. Palmer, 16 U.S. (3 Wheat.) 610, 643 (1818). See also Baker v. Carr, 369 U.S. 186, 212 (1962) (noting that "recognition of foreign governments . . . strongly defies judicial treatment").

23. See Curtis A. Bradley, The Political Question Doctrine and International Law, 91 Geo. Wash. L. Rev. 1555 (2023) (symposium contribution).

24. Letter from George Washington to Gouverneur Morris (Mar. 25, 1793), in 32 The Writings of George Washington 402 (John C. Fitzpatrick ed., 1939).

25. See Curtis A. Bradley & Martin S. Flaherty, Executive Power Essentialism and Foreign Affairs, 102 Mich. L. Rev. 545, 664–76 (2004).

26. See Letter to Gouverneur Morris (Mar. 12, 1793), in 25 Papers of Thomas Jefferson 367, 367–68 (John Catanzariti ed., 1992).

27. Alexander Hamilton, the Secretary of the Treasury, argued that Genet should be received with qualifications so that the reception would not be treated as an acceptance of the continued validity of the United States' treaties with France, but Hamilton's position did not prevail.

28. See Goebel, supra note 3, at 97–115; State Department Research Memorandum, supra note 3, at 7–8.

29. See, e.g., Letter from Thomas Jefferson to Gouverneur Morris (Nov. 7, 1792) ("It accords with our principles to acknowledge any Government to be rightful which is formed by the will of the nation, substantially declared.").

30. See State Department Research Memorandum, supra note 3, at 9 ("Jefferson's immediate successors . . . stressed his acceptance of the government de facto and they assumed that the acquiescence of the people signified the will of the nation.").

31. For an argument that the de facto approach was mandated by international law, see Adler, supra note 15. Emmerich Vattel, an international law publicist frequently invoked by the Founding generation, contended that "a sovereign can not, without urgent reasons, refuse to admit and give audience to the minister of a friendly power or of a power with which he is at peace." He also said that "foreign powers look to the sovereign in actual possession, if their interests invite them to do so," and that "there is no safer rule, nor one more in accord with the Law of Nations and the independence of States." 4 Emmerich de Vattel, The Law of Nations or the Principles of Natural Law, ch. 5, §§ 65, 68 at 364, 365–66 (1753) (Charles G. Fenwick trans., 1916). It is debatable how mandatory this framing is, and the de facto approach does not appear to have been followed by European nations when the United States adopted it. See Goebel, supra note 3, at 42, 114. But over time the U.S. practice influenced other nations in their recognition policy. See State Department Research Memorandum, supra note 3, at 5–6 (noting that "the United States played a large role in developing the theory of *de facto* recognition (i.e., the recognition of *de facto* governments), which many other states came to adopt in the course of the nineteenth century").

32. See generally Tim Mathewson, A Proslavery Foreign Policy: Haitian-American Relations during the Early Republic (2003); Robert J. Reinstein, Slavery, Executive Power and International Law: The Haitian Revolution and American Constitutionalism, 53 Am. J. Legal Hist. 141 (2013).

33. Act of Feb. 27, 1800, ch. 10, § 7, 2 Stat. 7, 10.

34. Act of Feb. 28, 1806, ch. 9, § 1, 2 Stat. 351, 351.

35. 8 U.S. (8 Cranch) 241 (1804).

36. See also Clark v. United States, 5 F. Cas. 932, 934 (C.C.D. Pa. 1811) (interpreting the 1806 statute as a congressional acknowledgment of the sovereignty of France over the island and giving it judicial deference). In 1809, the Madison administration declined to recognize Spain's ousted royal government (after France's Napoleon Bonaparte had invaded Spain and installed his brother as the king) and thus would not officially receive its ambassador, Luis de Onis, until the situation in Spain was resolved. The administration did not receive Onis as Spain's ambassador until 1815. See Moore, supra note 3, at 131–33. A few years later, the United States negotiated a treaty with Spain, known as the Adams-Onis Treaty, pursuant to which it acquired Florida.

37. 23 Annals Cong. 428 (Dec. 1811).

38. James Monroe to the Members of the Cabinet (Oct. 25 & 30, 1817), reprinted in 6 The Writings of James Monroe 31 (Stanislaus M. Hamilton ed., 1902).

39. 32 Annals Cong. 1468 (Mar. 24, 1818).

40. Id. at 1488.

41. See Bakker, supra note 3, at 412–18.

42. Id. at 1500.

43. For constitutional concerns, see, e.g., id. at 1570 (Rep. Alexander Smyth) ("The acknowledgment of the independence of a new Power is an exercise of Executive authority; consequently, for Congress to direct the Executive how he shall exercise this power, is an act of usurpation."). Cf. David P. Currie, The Constitution in Congress: The Jeffersonians, 1801–1829, at 202 (2001) (noting that "it is by no means clear that all who voted against [the proposal] believed it unconstitutional"); Goebel, supra note 3, at 142–43 (referring to a "vague feeling which prevailed that any action on the part of Congress would necessarily constitute an infringement upon executive prerogatives").

44. See Moore, supra note 3, at 79–80.

45. See Goebel, supra note 3, at 126–32. As discussed in Chapter 6, aggressive military actions by General Andrew Jackson in Florida helped incentivize Spain to conclude the treaty.

46. 37 Annals of Cong. 1055 (Feb. 26, 1821).

47. 37 Annals of Cong. 1053 (Rep. Robertson).

48. 37 Annals of Cong. 1092, 1180.

49. 4 Memoirs of John Quincy Adams, 204–7 (Charles Francis Adams ed., 1875) (describing a cabinet meeting from Jan. 1, 1819).

50. James Monroe, Message to the Senate and House of Representatives of the United States (Mar. 8, 1822).

51. Although Clay was Adams's political rival and a source of annoyance to Adams during the South American recognition debates, he later helped Adams get elected to the presidency and served as Adams's Secretary of State. After that, Clay served in the Senate and became chair of the Foreign Relations Committee. He was also a serious candidate in several presidential

elections. Abraham Lincoln greatly admired Clay and considered him an ideal statesman. See generally Harlow Giles Unger, Henry Clay: America's Greatest Statesman (2015).

52. See Act of May 4, 1822, ch. 52, 3 Stat. 678. This statute is one of countless broad delegations of discretion to the president in foreign affairs, a topic considered in Chapter 8.

53. Two years later, Monroe, after consulting with his cabinet, determined that "no message to Congress would be necessary" before the president recognized Brazil, because "the power of recognizing foreign Governments was necessarily implied in that of receiving Ambassadors and public Ministers." 6 Memoirs of John Quincy Adams, Comprising Portions of His Diary from 1795 to 1848, at 329, 348, 358–59 (Charles Francis Adams ed., 1875). For the argument that these events tend to support presidential control over recognition, see, e.g., Frederic L. Paxson, The Independence of the South American Republics: A Study in Recognition and Foreign Policy 146 (2d ed. 1916); Goebel, supra note 3, at 159. For additional discussion of these events, see Samuel Flagg Bemis, The Latin American Policy of the United States: An Historical Interpretation ch. 3 (1943).

54. In the early 1820s, the Monroe administration was also confronted with the issue of whether to recognize Greek independence from the Ottoman Empire. Daniel Webster introduced a resolution in the House calling for a diplomatic agent to be sent to Greece "whenever the President shall deem it expedient to make such appointment," but the resolution failed to pass. See Ernest R. May, The Making of the Monroe Doctrine 228–40 (1975). The United States did not recognize Greece until 1837.

55. This is one of many examples in which the issue of slavery was an important factor in U.S. foreign policy. See George C. Herring, From Colony to Superpower: U.S. Foreign Relations Since 1776, at 176–77 (2008) ("In foreign policy, as in domestic affairs, slavery dominated the politics of the antebellum era.").

56. See Daniel Walker Howe, What Hath God Wrought: The Transformation of America, 1815–1848, at 702–8 (2007).

57. S. Doc. 406, 24th Cong., 1st Sess. 3 (June 18, 1836).

58. Message to Congress Regarding Texas (Dec. 21, 1836).

59. Goebel, supra note 3, at 158.

60. Act of Mar. 3, 1837, 5 Stat. 170.

61. 4 Cong. Globe 213 (Feb. 28, 1837).

62. See John M. Belohlavek, "Let the Eagle Soar!": The Foreign Policy of Andrew Jackson 237 (1985).

63. Message from Andrew Jackson to the Senate (Mar. 3, 1837). See also Bakker, supra note 3, at 426 (noting that "neither Congress nor the President seemed to want the responsibility for acknowledging Texan independence").

64. See Galloway, supra note 3, at 19–24; Louis L. Jaffe, Judicial Aspects of Foreign Relations 107–9 (1933); State Department Research Memorandum, supra note 3, at 24–30. These normative criteria were not consistently applied. See Goebel, supra note 3, at 208–11 (noting a reversion to the de facto approach in the late nineteenth century); Cole, supra note 3, 30–34 (describing inconsistency of application).

65. See Goebel, supra note 3, at 171–92; Moore, supra note 3, at 103–5. For discussion of the international context of the Civil War, including issues of recognition, see Dean B. Mahin, One War at a Time: The International Dimensions of the American Civil War (1999); D. P. Crook, Diplomacy during the American Civil War (1976). For a decision holding that the

Confederacy was an illegal organization, in part because of the prohibition in Article I, Section 10, of the Constitution against states making treaties, see Williams v. Bruffy, 96 U.S. 176 (1877).

66. See Abraham Lincoln, First Annual Message to Congress (Dec. 3, 1861) (noting that he was "unwilling . . . to inaugurate a novel policy in regard to them without the approbation of Congress" and seeking "an appropriation for maintaining a chargé d'affaires near each of those new States").

67. See Cong. Globe, 37th Cong., 2d Sess. 1773 (Apr. 23, 1862).

68. Act of June 6, 1862, 12 Stat. 421.

69. In 1861, France, along with the United Kingdom and Spain, had invaded Mexico in an effort to pressure the country to settle its debts. After a settlement was reached, the United Kingdom and Spain withdrew their troops, but France remained.

70. Cong. Globe, 38th Cong., 1st Sess. 1408 (1864).

71. Cong. Globe, 38th Cong., 1st Sess. 2475 (1864).

72. See H. Rept. 129, 38th Cong., 1st Sess. (June 27, 1864).

73. Cong. Globe, 38th Cong., 2d Sess. 48, 65–66 (1865).

74. After the Civil War ended, the United States demanded the withdrawal of French troops from Mexico. The French troops left, Maximilian's forces were subsequently defeated by the forces of President Benito Juarez, and Maximilian was executed.

75. The Senate was initially unsure whether this process should be used for agreements with Indian tribes, but it deferred to President Washington's suggestion that the same process be used as for agreements with European nations "so that our national proceedings in this respect may become uniform and directed by fixed and stable principles." George Washington, Special Message (Sept. 17, 1789). See also Samuel B. Crandall, Treaties: Their Making and Enforcement § 66, at 133 (2d ed. 1916); Ralston Hayden, The Senate and Treaties, 1789–1816, at 11–16 (1920).

76. See 15 Stat. 7, ch. 13, § 6 (Mar. 29, 1867), repealed 15 Stat. 18, ch. 34 (July 20, 1867).

77. 16 Stat. 13, ch. 16 (Apr. 10, 1869).

78. Act of Mar. 3, 1871, ch. 120, 16 Stat. 544, 566 (Mar 3, 1871). For the current codification of this statute, see 25 U.S.C. § 71.

79. But cf. Zivotofsky, 576 U.S. at 22 ("Recognition of Indian tribes . . . is . . . a distinct issue from the recognition of foreign countries.").

80. See, e.g., Cong. Globe, 41st Cong., 3d Sess. 1824 (1871) (Sen. Casserly) ("Of course I need not remind Senators, either the lawyers here or those who are not lawyers, that the various departments of this Government, the judiciary included, follow the Executive in regard to the recognition of the existence of other States and Powers."). See also David P. Currie, Indian Treaties, 10 Green Bag 2d 445, 451 (Summer 2007) ("The entire enterprise was flatly unconstitutional, and it seems extraordinary that President Grant unblinkingly signed it into law."); David H. Moore & Michalyn Steele, Revitalizing Tribal Sovereignty in Treatymaking, 97 N.Y.U. L. Rev. 137 (2022) (contending that the 1871 law is unconstitutional). The Supreme Court had earlier suggested that Indian tribes should be thought of as more like "domestic dependent nations" rather than foreign nations. See Cherokee Nation v. State of Georgia, 30 U.S. (5 Pet.) 1, 17 (1831). See also Jones v. Meehan, 175 U.S. 1, 10 (1899) ("The Indian tribes within the limits of the United States are not foreign nations; though distinct political communities, they are in a dependent condition."). But cf. United States v. Lara, 541 U.S. 193, 215 (2004) (Thomas, J., concurring) ("In my view, the tribes either are or are not separate sovereigns, and our federal Indian law cases untenably hold both positions simultaneously.").

81. Ulysses S. Grant, Seventh Annual Message to Congress (Dec. 7, 1875).

82. See Moore, supra note 3, 107–10.

83. See Congress Powerless, N.Y. Times, Dec. 19, 1896.

84. Sen. Hale, Memorandum, Power to Recognize Independence of a New Foreign State, S. Doc. 56, 54th Cong., 2d Sess. (Jan. 11, 1897), 29 Cong. Rec. 663 (Jan. 11, 1897).

85. See 29 Cong. Rec. 682 (Jan. 11, 1897).

86. William McKinley, Message regarding Cuban Civil War (Apr. 11, 1898).

87. Act of Apr. 20, 1898, 30 Stat. 738.

88. Robert Reinstein contends that in this instance Congress "exercised the recognition power through legislation." Reinstein, supra note 3, at 41. But this appears to be an overreading of what happened. Congress decided not to include language proposed by the Senate that would have declared "that the Government of the United States hereby recognizes the Republic of Cuba as the true and lawful Government of that island." In discussing the proposal, some members of Congress expressed the view that recognition was exclusively an executive function, and other members disagreed. The executive branch, for its part, maintained that Congress could not mandate recognition. The Supreme Court later observed that the resolution that Congress actually passed "was not intended as a recognition of the existence of an organized government instituted by the people of that island in hostility to the government maintained by Spain." Neely v. Henkel, 180 U.S. 109, 124 (1901). See also Edward S. Corwin, The President's Control of Foreign Relations 80–81 (1917) ("I think it is extremely doubtful whether this declaration, considered in the light of the discussion which attended its adoption, is to be regarded as a claim by Congress to the power of recognition."); Quincy Wright, The Control of American Foreign Relations 271 (1922) (contending that the congressional statement "was in fact and was understood at the time to be a declaration of intervention and not a recognition").

89. The end of the U.S. occupation, however, was based on terms set by Congress, in what was known as the Platt Amendment, which Cuba incorporated into its new constitution.

90. See Hackworth, supra note 3, at 162 ("In every instance in which recognition has been accorded by the United States since 1906, the act has been that of the President, taken solely on his responsibility.").

91. See Cole, supra note 3, at 38–42.

92. See State Department Research Memorandum, supra note 3, at 35–36. On that basis, Wilson refused, for example, to recognize the Huerta regime in Mexico in 1913.

93. See State Department Research Memorandum, supra note 3, at 60–62. See also Quincy Wright, The Stimson Note of January 7, 1932, 26 Am. J. Int'l L. 342 (1932); David Turns, The Stimson Doctrine of Non-Recognition: Its Historical Genesis and Influence on Contemporary International Law, 2 Chinese J. Int'l L. 105 (2003).

94. S.J. Res. (Jan. 2, 1913).

95. See Hackworth, supra note 3, at 163–64.

96. 59 Cong. Rec. 73 (Dec. 3, 1919).

97. Letter from Wilson to Sen. Fall (Dec. 8, 1919), in S. Doc. No. 285, 66th Cong., 2d Sess. 843D (1920). See also Wilson Rebuffs Senate on Mexico, N.Y. Times, Dec. 8, 1919.

98. For an account of the agreements reflected in the notes, see Donald G. Bishop, The Roosevelt-Litvinov Agreements: The American View 15–22 (1965). As discussed in Chapter 4, the agreements were concluded as "sole executive agreements"—that is, by the executive without authorization or approval by Congress.

99. On May 14, 1948, Truman recognized the provisional Jewish government as the de facto authority in the state of Israel. Statement by the President Announcing Recognition of the State of Israel, 1 Pub. Papers 258 (May 14, 1948). He extended de jure recognition to the government on January 31, 1949.

100. See Whiteman, supra note 3, at 45.

101. See United States v. Belmont, 301 U.S. 324 (1937); United States v. Pink, 315 U.S. 203 (1942).

102. Pink, 315 U.S. at 229. Cf. Goldwater v. Carter, 444 U.S. 996, 1007 (1979) (Brennan, J., dissenting) (arguing that the recognition power gives the president the authority to terminate a treaty when such an action is a "necessary incident" to the recognition).

103. Joint Communique of the United States of America and the People's Republic of China (effective Jan. 1, 1979); Terrance Smith, Link to Taiwan Ends, N.Y. Times (Dec. 16, 1978).

104. See Reinstein, supra note 3, at 46.

105. See Taiwan Relations Act, 93 Stat. 14 (1979), codified as amended at 22 U. S. C. §§ 3301–16. Cf. 125 Cong. Rec. 6709 (1979) (Sen. Jacob Javits) ("Neither bill [proposed by the House and Senate] sought to reestablish official relations between the United States and the Republic of China on Taiwan; Congress . . . does not have the authority to do that even if it wanted to do so.").

106. Michael Crowley, One of the Most Influential Ambassadors in Washington Isn't One, N.Y. Times (Jan. 21, 2023).

107. See Hearings on Taiwan Legislation before the House Committee on Foreign Affairs, 96th Cong., 1st Sess., 14–15, 27 (1979) (statement of Warren Christopher, Deputy Secretary of State).

108. In the 1972 Shanghai Communique, the United States had acknowledged that "all Chinese on either side of the Taiwan Strait maintain there is but one China."

109. See 108 Stat. 395, §132, as amended by 108 Stat. 4302, § 1(r).

110. See, e.g., Diplomatic Relations: A Foreign Relations Outline, 77 Dep't St. Bull. 462 (1977); Galloway, supra note 3, at 139–43. In 1969, the Senate, with the support of the State Department, issued a nonbinding resolution stating that it was "the sense of the Senate that when the United States recognizes a foreign government and exchanges diplomatic representatives with it, this does not of itself imply that the United States approves of the form, ideology, or policy of that foreign government." S. Res. 205 (Sept. 25, 1969). The senator who proposed the resolution contended that this "would return America to its original recognition policy, the policy that our Nation followed with great success in the days of Jefferson, Madison, Monroe, and Adams."

111. Proclamation on Recognizing the Sovereignty of the Kingdom of Morocco over the Western Sahara (Dec. 10, 2020).

112. The subsequent Biden administration eventually decided not to continue recognizing Guaido.

113. See, e.g., Scott R. Anderson, History and the Recognition of the Taliban, Lawfare (Aug. 26, 2021).

114. 109 Stat. 398, § 3(a) (Nov. 8, 1995).

115. Bill to Relocate United States Embassy from Tel Aviv to Jerusalem, 19 Op. O.L.C. 123 (1995).

116. Foreign Relations Authorization Act, Fiscal Year 2003 (Act), § 214, Pub. L. No. 107–228, 116 Stat. 1350, 1365.

117. Statement on Signing the Foreign Relations Authorization Act, Fiscal Year 2003 (Sept. 30, 2002).

118. See Zivotofsky v. Secretary of State, 444 F.3d 614 (D.C. Cir. 2006). The Supreme Court never addressed the standing issue.

119. Zivotofsky v. Clinton, 566 U.S. 189, 196 (2012).

120. See Zivotofsky v. Kerry, 576 U.S. 1 (2015).

121. As noted at the outset of this chapter, President Trump changed course and recognized Israeli sovereignty over Jerusalem in 2017. In 2020, the State Department announced that U.S. citizens born in Jerusalem could choose to list their place of birth as either Jerusalem or Israel.

122. See, e.g., Reinstein, supra note 3, at 50 ("The repeated exercise of this power by the Executive and its acquiescence by Congress has placed a 'gloss' on the separation of powers.").

123. See Reinstein, supra note 3.

124. Story, supra note 16, at 417 ("That a power, so extensive in its reach over our foreign relations, could not be properly conferred on any other, than the executive department, will admit of little doubt."). But see William Rawle, A View of the Constitution of the United States of America 195 (2d ed. 1829) ("The legislature indeed possesses a superior power, and may declare its dissent from the executive recognition or refusal, but until that sense is declared, the act of the executive is binding.").

125. See Corwin, supra note 88, at 82 ("Recognition, as it is known to International Law, belongs, it seems clear, to the President alone, or to the President in conjunction with the Senate.").

126. See Wright, supra note 88, at 272–73 (arguing that the "better opinion" is that the president's recognition power is exclusive). See also John Mabry Mathews, The Conduct of American Foreign Relations 124–26 (1922) (arguing that the president's recognition power should be considered exclusive); 1 Westel Woodbury Willoughby, The Constitutional Law of the United States 462 (1910) ("The legislature may express its wishes or opinions [about recognition], but may not command.").

127. Restatement (Third) of the Foreign Relations Law of the United States § 204, at 89 (1987) ("Under the Constitution of the United States the President has exclusive authority to recognize or not to recognize a foreign state or government.").

128. See, e.g., Banco Nacional de Cuba v. Sabbatino, 376 U.S. 398, 410 (1964) ("Political recognition is exclusively a function of the Executive.").

129. But see Myers v. United States, 272 U.S. 52, 163 (1926) (relying in part on congressional acquiescence in support of an exclusive presidential power of removal of executive officers).

130. Cf. 576 U.S. at 17 (noting that, "until today, the political branches have resolved their disputes over questions of recognition").

131. See National Defense Authorization Act for Fiscal Year 2016 § 1245.

132. 576 U.S. at 30.

133. Youngstown Sheet & Tube Co. v. Sawyer, 343 U.S. 579, 638 (Jackson, J., concurring). Cf. Laurence H. Tribe, American Constitutional Law 636 (3d ed. 2000) ("Because acquired executive power may be exercised only so long as Congress does not object, Congress retains the power to limit executive action in areas that were previously wholly discretionary with the Executive, so long as Congress acts within its constitutional grants of enumerated authority.").

134. There were reasonable arguments in *Zivotofsky* that the statute in question was not itself a regulation of recognition. See, e.g., 576 U.S. at 64 (Roberts, C.J., dissenting). The majority was concerned, however, that Congress was in effect forcing the executive branch to speak in a manner inconsistent with its recognition policy. See id. at 29 ("If Congress could command the President to state a recognition position inconsistent with his own, Congress could override the President's recognition determination.").

135. See Jack Goldsmith, Zivotofsky II as Precedent in the Executive Branch, 113 Harv. L. Rev. 112, 134 (2015).

136. Memorandum Opinion from Steven A. Engel, Assistant Attorney General, for the Legal Advisor to the National Security Council, Congressionally Mandated Notice Period for Withdrawing from the Open Skies Treaty, 44 Op. O.L.C. slip op. (Sept. 22, 2020).

4. Making International Agreements

1. See Made in the USA Foundation v. United States, 242 F.3d 1300 (11th Cir. 2001). The court expressed the view that historical practice was relevant to its political question analysis "inasmuch as it fleshes out the manner in which the executive and legislative branches have sought to exercise and accommodate their textually committed foreign affairs powers over time." Id. at 1311 n.27.

2. Whether Uruguay Round Agreements Required Ratification as a Treaty, 18 Op. O.L.C. 232, 233 (1994).

3. See Ralston Hayden, The Senate and Treaties, 1789–1817, at 105–6 (1920); Curtis A. Bradley & Martin S. Flaherty, Executive Power Essentialism and Foreign Affairs, 102 Mich. L. Rev. 545, 626–36 (2004).

4. 2 Emmerich de Vattel, The Law of Nations or the Principles of Natural Law, ch. 12, § 153 (1753) (Charles G. Fenwick trans., 1916).

5. See, e.g., Abraham C. Weinfeld, What Did the Framers of the Federal Constitution Mean by "Agreements or Compacts"?, 3 U. Chi. L. Rev. 453, 457–60 (1936).

6. Wallace McClure, International Executive Agreements: Democratic Procedure under the Constitution of the United States 4 (1941). Part of McClure's book-length study of executive agreements was focused on the general phenomenon of "Constitutional Development through Usage"—that is, historical gloss. See id. at 191–252.

7. See Congressional Research Service, Treaties and Other International Agreements: The Role of the United States Senate, S. Prt. 106–71, 106th Cong., 2d Sess. at 39 (Comm. Print 2001) [hereinafter CRS Study].

8. See Glen S. Krutz & Jeffrey S. Peake, Treaty Politics and the Rise of Executive Agreements (2011); Oona A. Hathaway, Presidential Power over International Law: Restoring the Balance, 119 Yale L.J. 140 (2009).

9. See Curtis A. Bradley, Jack Goldsmith, and Oona A. Hathaway, The Rise of Nonbinding International Agreements: An Empirical, Comparative, and Normative Analysis, 90 U. Chi. L. Rev. 1281 (2023).

10. See Curtis A. Bradley & Jack L. Goldsmith, Presidential Control over International Law, 131 Harv. L. Rev. 1201, 1213 (2018).

11. See, e.g., Restatement (Third) of the Foreign Relations Law of the United States § 303, cmt. f (1987); CRS Study, supra note 7, at 86.

12. See Samuel B. Crandall, Treaties: Their Making and Enforcement 119 & n.54 (2d ed. 1916).

13. See Crandall, supra note 12, at 117–18.

14. The Supreme Court gave effect to such an agreement in Wilson v. Girard, 354 U.S. 524 (1957).

15. See Bradley & Goldsmith, supra note 10, at 1268–69.

16. See Chandler P. Anderson, The Senate and Obligatory Arbitration Treaties, 26 Am. J. Int'l L. 328 (1932).

17. See 2 George H. Haynes, The Senate of the United States: Its History and Practice 614–17 (1938).

18. See Sean D. Murphy, The United States and the International Court of Justice: Coping with Antinomies, in The Sword and the Scales: The United States and International Courts and Tribunals (Cesare P. R. Romano ed., 2009).

19. See S. Rep. No. 632, 92d Cong., 2d Sess. 6 (1972). The Senate recommended that the agreement be submitted as a treaty. See S. Res. 214, 92d Cong., 2d Sess., 118 Cong. Rec. 6870 (1972). But the executive branch declined to do so, noting that the agreement had already been concluded.

20. Act of Feb. 20, 1792, ch. 7, § 26, 1 Stat. 232, 239.

21. Congress gave more general authorization of such executive agreements in an 1872 revision of the statute, which stated that the postmaster general could conclude "postal treaties or conventions" "with the advice and consent *of the President*." 17 Stat. 283 (1872) (emphasis added).

22. Postal Conventions with Foreign Countries, 19 Op. Att'y Gen. 513, 515 (1890).

23. See McClure, supra note 6, at 62–68.

24. See id. at 15. See also David H. Moore & Michalyn Steele, Revitalizing Tribal Sovereignty in Treatymaking, 97 N.Y.U. L. Rev. 137, 145 (2022).

25. See 3 Stat. 224 (1815).

26. See Crandall, supra note 12, at 121.

27. See 30 Stat. 151, 203, ch. 11, § 3 (July 24, 1897).

28. 143 U.S. 649 (1892).

29. 224 U.S. 583 (1912).

30. 37 Stat. 560, § 6 (1912).

31. See 40 Stat. 35, § 2 (1917).

32. In 1922, Congress had directed the establishment of a five-member commission, consisting of the Secretary of the Treasury and four members to be appointed by the president, to negotiate the agreements, and it had directed that the agreements were to be transmitted to Congress for approval. See Act of Feb. 9, 1922, ch. 47, 42 Stat. 363; Act of Feb. 28, 1923, ch. 146, 42 Stat. 1325.

33. 48 Stat. 943 (1934). For a decision holding that this statute did not constitute an unlawful delegation of authority to the executive branch, see Star-Kist Foods Inc. v. United States, 275 F.2d 472 (C.C.P.A. 1959).

34. Green H. Hackworth, Legal Aspects of the Trade Agreements Act of 1934, 21 A.B.A. J. 570, 571 (1935).

35. See 48 Stat. 1182 (1934).

36. 5 Green Haywood Hackworth, Digest of International Law 407 (1943).

37. See, e.g., James W. Garner, Acts and Joint Resolutions of Congress as Substitutes for Treaties, 29 Am. J. Int'l L. 482 (1935).

38. Years later, when interpreting a statute that disallows discrimination against U.S. citizens on military bases except as permitted by treaty, the Supreme Court interpreted the word "treaty" as encompassing executive agreements. See Weinberger v. Rossi, 456 U.S. 25 (1982).

39. See Joel R. Paul, The Geopolitical Constitution: Executive Expediency and Executive Agreements, 86 Calif. L. Rev. 671, 742 (1998) ("During FDR's thirteen years in office, he signed 609 executive agreements, almost doubling the number of agreements signed by all his predecessors combined.").

40. 88 Cong. Rec. 9276 (1942). See also Herbert W. Briggs, Treaties, Executive Agreements, and the Panama Joint Resolution of 1943, 37 Am. Pol. Sci. Rev. 686 (1943).

41. See Herbert W. Briggs, The UNRRA Agreement and Congress, 38 Am. J. Int'l L. 650 (1944).

42. 89 Cong. Rec. 7728 (1943).

43. Resolution of Nov. 5, 1943, 78th Cong., 1st Sess., 89 Cong. Rec. 9222 (1943).

44. See, e.g., Edward S. Corwin, The Constitution and World Organization 44 (1944); McClure, supra note 6; Quincy Wright, The United States and International Agreements, 38 Am. J. Int'l L. 341 (1944).

45. See, e.g., Edwin Borchard, Shall the Executive Agreement Replace the Treaty?, 53 Yale L.J. 663 (1944).

46. Myres S. McDougal & Asher Lans, Treaties and Congressional-Executive or Presidential Agreements: Interchangeable Instruments of National Policy, 54 Yale L.J. 181 (1945).

47. See 91 Cong. Rec. 4367 (1945).

48. See 59 Stat. 1031 (Aug. 4, 1947).

49. See 59 Stat. 512 (July 31, 1945).

50. This action was controversial in Congress. When enacting extensions of the Reciprocal Trade Agreements Act in the 1950s, Congress stated that the extensions "shall not be construed to determine or indicate the approval or disapproval by the Congress of the Executive Agreement known as the General Agreement on Tariffs and Trade." See, e.g., Trade Agreements Extension Act of June 16, 1951, Pub. L. 82–50, § 10, 65 Stat. 72, 75 (1951).

51. 68 Stat. 454, § 101 (July 10, 1954).

52. 75 Stat. 424, §§ 202(b), 503 (Sept. 4, 1961).

53. See Duane Tananbaum, The Bricker Amendment Controversy (1988); Loch K. Johnson, The Making of International Agreements: Congress Confronts the Executive ch. 4 (1984).

54. See John Foster Dulles, The Making of Treaties and Executive Agreements, 28 Dep't State Bull. 594 (Apr. 20, 1953); Treaties and Executive Agreements: Hearings on S.J. Res. 1 and S.J. Res. 43 before a Subcommittee of the Senate Committee on the Judiciary, 83d Cong. 825 (1953).

55. See U.S. Dep't of State, Foreign Affairs Manual, 11 FAM 723.3.

56. See Restatement (Third), supra note 11, § 303, cmt. c. See also, e.g., Louis Henkin, Foreign Affairs and the Constitution 175 (1972); Bruce Ackerman & David Golove, Is NAFTA Constitutional?, 108 Harv. L. Rev. 799, 896 (1995).

57. See Phillip R. Trimble & Jack S. Weiss, The Role of the President, Senate and Congress with Respect to Arms Control Treaties Concluded by the United States, 67 Chi-Kent L. Rev. 645, 659 (1991).

58. S. Exec. Rept. No. 102–22, at 81 (1991).

59. See Trimble & Weiss, supra note 57, at 662.

60. For criticism of Clinton's concession to the Senate, see Phillip R. Trimble & Alexander W. Koff, All Fall Down: The Treaty Power in the Clinton Administration, 16 Berkeley J. Int'l L. 55 (1998).

61. See David E. Sanger, Obama to Seek Ratification of Nuclear Test Ban Treaty, N.Y. Times (Feb. 18, 2010).

62. See Thom Shanker, Senators Insist on Role in Nuclear Arms Deals, N.Y. Times (Mar. 17, 2002).

63. The Senate has insisted on the use of the treaty process for arms control agreements even though a 1961 statute, the Arms Control and Disarmament Act, seemed to accept the possibility of concluding such agreements with the approval of Congress. See Pub. L. No. 87–297, § 33, 75 Stat. 631, 634 (prohibiting the executive branch from obligating the United States to disarm or reduce its armaments "except pursuant to the treaty making power of the President under the Constitution or unless authorized by further affirmative legislation by the Congress of the United States").

64. See Albert R. Hunt, On Disabilities Treaty, the Right Fights with the Right, N.Y. Times (Feb. 23, 2014).

65. In upholding an extradition under one of these agreements, a federal court of appeals concluded that an Article II treaty was not required, stating that the court was "unconvinced that the President's practice of usually submitting a negotiated treaty to the Senate reflects a historical understanding that a treaty is required to extradite." Ntakirutimana v. Reno, 184 F.3d 419, 416 (5th Cir. 1999).

66. The federal extradition statute allows the executive branch to extradite non-U.S. nationals under some circumstances without an agreement in place with the requesting country. See 18 U.S.C. § 3181(b).

67. Agreements relating to "private international law" topics such as choice of law, the enforcement of judgments, wills and trusts, and family law, which are primarily matters of state law in the United States, have also generally been concluded through the Article II treaty process. As a general matter, the Article II treaty process, with its supermajority Senate protection of state interests, may be needed for agreements that regulate domestic matters falling outside of what Congress could regulate in the absence of a treaty. That is, it may be that only Article II treaties benefit from the holding of *Missouri v. Holland*. See, e.g., Oona A. Hathaway, Treaties' End: The Past, Present, and Future of International Lawmaking in the United States, 117 Yale L.J. 1236, 1340–49 (2009); David Sloss, International Agreements and the Political Safeguards of Federalism, 55 Stan. L. Rev. 1963, 1975 (2003).

68. See Settlement of the Case of the Schooner "Wilmington Packet," U.S.-Neth., Dec. 12, 1799, reprinted in 5 Treaties and Other International Acts of the United States of America 1075 (Hunter Miller ed., 1937). Two sole executive agreements relating to the slave revolt in Saint-Domingue (present-day Haiti) predated the *Wilmington Packet* agreement. These agreements were made in secret, in coordination with Great Britain. See Robert J. Reinstein, Slavery, Executive Power, and International Law: The Haitian Revolution and American Constitutionalism, 53 Am. J. Leg. Hist. 141, 166–70 (2013).

69. See McClure, supra note 6, at 44 ("The case of the 'Wilmington Packet' set a precedent which was to be followed in a long line of subsequent claims, settlement of which has been sought by the authority of the Executive alone."). See also Evan T. Bloom, Note, The Executive

Claims Settlement Power: Constitutional Authority and Foreign Affairs Applications, 85 Colum. L. Rev. 155 (1985).

70. See Crandall, supra note 12, at 108.

71. See James Barnett, International Agreements without the Advice and Consent of the Senate, 15 Yale L.J. 20, 77–78 (1905–1906). See also Ingrid Brunk Wuerth, The Dangers of Deference: International Claims Settlement by the President, 44 Harv. Int'l L.J. 1, 27 (2003).

72. See Memorandum from Solicitor for the Department of State (Apr. 5, 1909), excerpted in 5 Hackworth Digest, supra note 36, at 403–4.

73. See 5 Hackworth Digest, supra note 36, at 404; 79 Cong. Rec. 968–69 (Jan. 25, 1935) (listing forty agreements to arbitrate not submitted to the Senate). It is well settled that a federal statute is required for appropriations and that a treaty by itself cannot accomplish this. Starting with the 1794 Jay Treaty, Congress has long insisted that it has the discretion not to make an appropriation promised in a treaty.

74. McClure, supra note 6, at 53.

75. See Thomas M. Franck & Edward Weisband, Foreign Policy by Congress 145 n.81 (1979).

76. Crandall, supra note 12, at 108.

77. 453 U.S. 654 (1983).

78. 539 U.S. 396 (2003).

79. For an argument that historical practice did not support the Clinton administration's settlement of claims against private actors, see Wuerth, supra note 71, at 19–41. For criticism of the Court's broad endorsement of executive agreements and its suggestion that executive branch foreign policy might preempt state law even in the absence of international agreements, see Brannon P. Denning & Michael D. Ramsey, American Insurance Association v. Garamendi and Executive Preemption in Foreign Affairs, 46 Wm. & Mary L. Rev. 825 (2004).

80. See 539 U.S. at 436 (Ginsburg, J., dissenting).

81. 552 U.S. 491 (2008).

82. Cartel for the Exchange of Prisoners of War, U.S.-G.B., May 12, 1813, 2 Treaties and Other International Acts of the United States of America 558 (Hunter Miller ed., 1937).

83. Exchange of Notes Relative to Naval Forces on the American Lakes, U.S.-G.B., Apr. 29, 1817.

84. Message from President James Monroe to the Senate of the United States (Apr. 6, 1818).

85. See McClure, supra note 6, at 49 (describing this agreement as "by far the most famous and significant of the early executive agreements").

86. See 3 Stat. 217 (Feb. 27, 1815).

87. Tucker v. Alexandroff, 183 U.S. 424, 435 (1902).

88. See Restatement (Second) of the Foreign Relations Law of the United States § 121, cmt. b (1965).

89. Protocol of Agreement between the United States and Spain, Embodying the Terms of a Basis for the Establishment of Peace between the Two Countries, Aug. 12, 1898, U.S.-Spain, 30 Stat. 1742.

90. 42 Stat. 105 (1921).

91. See Agreement on Ending the War and Restoring Peace in Viet-Nam, Jan. 27, 1973, 24 U.S.T. 115, 935 U.N.T.S. 2.

92. See David Zucchino, The U.S. War in Afghanistan: How It Started, How It Ended, N.Y. Times (Oct. 7, 2021).

93. John W. Foster, The Practice of Diplomacy 318 (1906).

94. 39 Op. Att'y Gen. 484, 487 (1941).

95. For additional defense of the constitutionality of using an executive agreement in this instance, see Quincy Wright, The Transfer of Destroyers to Great Britain, 34 Am. J. Int'l L. 680 (1940). For criticism, see Edwin Borchard, The Attorney General's Opinion and the Exchange of Destroyers for Naval Bases, 34 Am. J. Int'l L. 690 (1940). For further discussion of the historical context, see William R. Casto, Advising Presidents: Robert Jackson and the Destroyers-for-Bases Deal, 52 Am. J. Leg. Hist. 1 (2012).

96. See Michael J. Glennon, Assistant Counsel, Senate Office of Legislative Counsel, Memorandum of Law (submitted Sept. 24, 1975), 121 Cong. Rec. 36724 (Nov. 14, 1975).

97. Monroe Leigh, Department of State Legal Adviser's Reply to Senate Office of Legislative Counsel, Memorandum on Certain Middle East Agreements (submitted Oct. 8, 1975), 121 Cong. Rec. 36718 (Nov. 14, 1975).

98. For accounts of the agreement, see Donald G. Bishop, The Roosevelt-Litvinov Agreements (1965); Stephen M. Millett, The Constitutionality of Executive Agreements: An Analysis of United States v. Belmont (1990).

99. 301 U.S. 324 (1937). The decision was authored by Justice Sutherland, who also authored the decision in *United States v. Curtiss-Wright Export Corporation,* which is discussed in various places in this book.

100. The Court reaffirmed this analysis in another case involving the Roosevelt-Litvinov Agreement, United States v. Pink, 315 U.S. 203 (1942). The Court emphasized that "we are dealing with an exclusive federal function. If state laws and policies did not yield before the exercise of the external powers of the United States, then our foreign policy might be thwarted." Id. at 232.

101. Watts v. United States, 1 Wash. Terr. 288, 293–94 (1870).

102. See Crandall, supra note 12, at 112–13.

103. See John Bassett Moore, Treaties and Executive Agreements, 20 Pol. Sci. Q. 385, 398 (1905); see also William Hays Simpson, Use of Modi Vivendi in Settlement of International Disputes, 11 Rocky Mtn. L. Rev. 89, 100 (1938) (describing how modi vivendi have addressed a wide variety of subject matters).

104. See Theodore Roosevelt, An Autobiography 552 (1920).

105. See 40 Cong. Rec. 433, 1173, 1417, 2125 (1905–1906).

106. William Howard Taft, Our Chief Magistrate and His Powers 111–12 (1916). The modus vivendi was negotiated under the auspices of the 1903 Hay-Varilla Treaty with Panama and thus was arguably a treaty-based executive agreement. See CRS Study, supra note 7, at 86.

107. See Daniel Bodansky & Peter Spiro, Executive Agreement+, 49 Vand. J. Transnat'l L. 885 (2016).

108. Id. at 890. But cf. David A. Wirth, Executive Agreements Relying on Implied Statutory Authority: A Response to Bodansky and Spiro, 50 Vand. J. Transnat'l L. 741 (2017) (contending that this is not a new phenomenon).

109. Letter from Sen. Ron Wyden to Pres. Barack Obama (Oct. 12, 2011).

110. See Letter from Harold Koh, Legal Adviser, to Sen. Ron Wyden (Mar. 6, 2012).

111. See Letter from Legal Academics to Members of United States Senate Committee on Finance (May 16, 2012).

112. See Letter from Sen. Ron Wyden to Legal Adviser Harold Koh (July 25, 2012).

113. Harold Hongju Koh, Twenty-First-Century International Lawmaking, 101 Georgetown L.J. Online 1, 8 (2012).

114. Harold Hongju Koh, Triptych's End: A Better Framework to Evaluate 21st Century International Lawmaking, 126 Yale L.J.F. 338 (2017).

115. See also Jean Galbraith, From Treaties to International Commitments: The Changing Landscape of Foreign Relations Law, 84 U. Chi. L. Rev. 1675 (2017).

116. Cf. Louis Henkin, Foreign Affairs and the United States Constitution 222 (2d ed. 1996) (noting that full interchangeability of sole executive agreements and Article II treaties would be "unacceptable, for it would wholly remove the 'check' of Senate consent which the Framers struggled and compromised to write into the Constitution").

117. See Oona A. Hathaway, Curtis A. Bradley, and Jack L. Goldsmith, The Failed Transparency Regime for Executive Agreements: An Empirical and Normative Analysis, 134 Harv. L. Rev. 629, 712 (2020).

118. S. Res. 85, 91st Cong., 1st Sess. (June 25, 1969). See Ellen C. Collier, The National Commitments Resolution of 1969: Background and Issues (Library of Congress, Legislative Reference Service, May 11, 1970).

119. S. Rpt. 91–129, 91st Cong., 1st Sess. 26 (Apr. 16, 1969). The initial version of the resolution did not define "national commitment" and thus might have covered all international agreements, even nonbinding ones, but its scope was narrowed in response to executive branch objections. As passed by the Senate, the resolution defined national commitment as "the use of the armed forces on foreign territory, or a promise to assist a foreign country, government or people by the use of the armed forces or financial resources of the United States, either immediately or upon the happening of certain events."

120. See CRS Study, supra note 7, at 43–49; Michael J. Glennon, Constitutional Diplomacy 183–89 (1990).

121. S. Res. 214 (1972).

122. 1 U.S.C. § 112b.

123. Hearing, Subcommittee on Separation of Powers, Senate Judiciary Committee, Congressional Oversight of Executive Agreements, 92d Cong., 2d Sess. 1 (1972).

124. See Hathaway, Bradley, and Goldsmith, supra note 117, at 645–54.

125. See H.R. 7776, National Defense Authorization Act for Fiscal Year 2023, § 5947. These reforms implement a number of the proposals that my coauthors and I had made in Hathaway, Bradley, and Goldsmith, supra note 117.

126. See Curtis A. Bradley, Reassessing the Legislative Veto: The Statutory President, Foreign Affairs, and Congressional Workarounds, 13 J. Leg. Analysis 439, 460 (2021). To take one example, Congress has imposed extensive procedural hurdles, including a waiting period, for the executive branch's negotiation and conclusion of nuclear cooperation agreements. See id. at 460.

127. See Bradley, Goldsmith, and Hathaway, supra note 9.

128. National Defense Authorization Act for Fiscal Year 2023, § 5947. The act also requires the reporting of nonbinding agreements that are specifically requested by the chairs or ranking members of Congress's foreign affairs committees. In October 2023, the U.S. State Department issued regulations implementing the new requirements. See, e.g., 22 C.F.R. § 181.4(b) (listing factors to be considered in deciding whether a nonbinding agreement meets the significance threshold).

129. See Roosevelt, supra note 104, at 551; Investigation of Panama Canal Matters: Hearing before the Senate Committee on Interoceanic Canals, 59th Cong. 2590 (1907) (cable of Secretary of War William Howard Taft to Secretary of State John Hay).

130. Treaty of Peace with Germany: Hearing before the Senate Committee on Foreign Relations, 66th Cong. 219 (1919) (testimony of Secretary of State Robert Lansing). President Harding later described the "so-called Lansing-Ishii agreement" as an "exchange of notes [that], in the nature of things, did not constitute anything more than a declaration of Executive policy." 5 Hackworth Digest, supra note 36, at 431.

131. See Letter from Sec'y of State Gresham to Mr. Mendonca (Oct. 26, 1894), excerpted in V John Bassett Moore, A Digest of International Law 361–62 (1906). Professors Bruce Ackerman and David Golove generalize from examples like this one to suggest that executive agreements were viewed by the United States as nonbinding at that time. See Ackerman & Golove, supra note 56, at 823–24. This claim is an overstatement; even the Brazil agreement was treated as binding until Congress repealed the delegation. See also Michael D. Ramsey, Executive Agreements and the (Non)Treaty Power, 77 N.C. L. Rev. 133, 190 (1998); Peter J. Spiro, Treaties, Executive Agreements, and Constitutional Method, 79 Tex. L. Rev. 961, 986 (2001).

132. See Oscar Schachter, The Twilight Existence of Nonbinding International Agreements, 71 Am. J. Int'l L. 296, 297–98 (1977).

133. To help monitor compliance with the accords, Congress created the Commission on Security and Cooperation in Europe, also known as the Helsinki Commission. See 90 Stat. 661 (1976).

134. Statement by Secretary of State Cyrus Vance (Sept. 23, 1977), 77 Dep't St. Bull. 642 (1977).

135. See Letter from Herbert J. Hansell, State Department Legal Adviser, to John J. Sparkman, Chairman, Senate Foreign Relations Committee, Sept. 28, 1977, reprinted in S. Rep. No. 499, 95th Cong., 1st Sess. (1977).

136. See Bradley, Goldsmith, and Hathaway, supra note 9, at 1307. Despite the requirement in the Constitution of congressional approval of any "agreement or compact" made by a U.S. state with a foreign power (see U.S. Const. art. I, § 10), states often make agreements with foreign governments without seeking congressional approval, and many of these agreements are nonbinding. See Michael J. Glennon & Robert D. Sloane, Foreign Affairs Federalism: The Myth of National Exclusivity ch. 8 (2016); Ryan M. Scoville, The International Commitments of the Fifty States, 70 UCLA L. Rev. 310 (2023); Curtis A. Bradley, State International Agreements: The United States, Canada, and Constitutional Evolution, 60 Can. Y.B. Int'l L. 6 (2023).

137. See, e.g., Ramsey, supra note 131.

138. See, e.g., Dole v. Carter, 569 F.2d 1109, 1110 (10th Cir. 1977) ("We decline to enter into any controversy relating to distinctions which may be drawn between executive agreements and treaties.").

139. See 22 U.S.C. § 7401(a) ("The United States shall not become a party to the International Criminal Court except pursuant to a treaty made under Article II, section 2, clause 2 of the Constitution of the United States on or after November 29, 1999.").

140. See Ackerman & Golove, supra note 56.

141. See Bradley & Goldsmith, supra note 10, at 1212 n.26.

142. For additional reasons to doubt the constitutional moment account of the rise of executive agreements, see Paul, supra note 39, at 742–46; Spiro, supra note 131, at 992–93; John C. Yoo, Laws as Treaties? The Constitutionality of Congressional-Executive Agreements, 99 Mich. L. Rev. 757, 782–88 (2001). See also Laurence H. Tribe, Taking Text and Structure Seriously: Reflections on Free-Form Method in Constitutional Interpretation, 108 Harv. L. Rev. 1221 (1995).

5. Terminating Treaties and Executive Agreements

1. Joint Communique of the United States of America and the People's Republic of China (effective Jan. 1, 1979); Terrance Smith, Link to Taiwan Ends, N.Y. Times (Dec. 16, 1978).

2. Mutual Defense Treaty between the United States and the Republic of China, U.S.-Rep. of China, art. V, Dec. 2, 1954, 6 U.S.T. 433. The implications of such mutual defense pacts for the U.S. law of war powers are considered in Chapter 6.

3. See International Security Assistance Act, Pub. L. 95–438, 92 Stat. 730, § 26(b) (Sept. 26, 1978).

4. Memorandum from Herbert J. Hansell, Legal Adviser, U.S. Dep't of State, to the Secretary of State, President's Power to Give Notice of Termination of U.S.-ROC Mutual Defense Treaty (Dec. 15, 1978).

5. Pub. L. No. 96–8, 93 Stat. 14 (Apr. 10, 1979), codified at 22 U.S.C. § 3301 et seq.

6. For accounts of the history of U.S. treaty terminations, see David Gray Adler, The Constitution and the Termination of Treaties (1986); Curtis A. Bradley, Treaty Termination and Historical Gloss, 92 Tex. L. Rev. 773 (2014); 5 Green Haywood Hackworth, Digest of International Law 319–42 (1943).

7. See Louis Henkin, Foreign Affairs and the United States Constitution 211 (2d ed. 1996) (noting that "the Constitution tells us only who can make treaties for the United States; it does not say who can unmake them").

8. See, e.g., Michael D. Ramsey, The Constitution's Text in Foreign Affairs 158 (2007).

9. See U.S. Const. art. I, § 7; Clinton v. City of New York, 524 U.S. 417, 438 (1998) ("There is no provision in the Constitution that authorizes the President to enact, to amend, or to repeal statutes."); INS v. Chadha, 462 U.S. 919, 954 (1983) ("Repeal of statutes, no less than enactment, must conform with Art. I."). A statute might, however, terminate by its terms—for example, pursuant to a sunset provision.

10. See Zivotofsky v. Kerry, 576 U.S. 1, 13 (2015) (noting that "the Senate may not conclude or ratify a treaty without Presidential action").

11. See Louis Henkin, Litigating the President's Power to Terminate Treaties, 73 Am. J. Int'l L. 647, 653 (1979) (arguing that "termination of a treaty by the President is not 'repeal' of a 'law'; it is an international act terminating an international legal obligation of the United States").

12. See Myers v. United States, 272 U.S. 52 (1926).

13. See 2 Emmerich de Vattel, The Law of Nations or the Principles of Natural Law bk. 3, § 175 (1758) (Charles G. Fenwick trans., 1916) (noting that "conventions and treaties are broken or annulled when war breaks out between the contracting parties"); William Rawle, A View of the Constitution of the United States of America 68 (2d ed. 1829) ("Congress alone possesses the right to declare war; and the right to qualify, alter, or annul a treaty being of a tendency to produce war, is an incident to the right of declaring war."). See also Daniel J. Hessel, Note, Founding-Era Jus Ad Bellum and the Domestic Law of Treaty Withdrawal, 125 Yale L.J. 2394 (2016).

14. Cf. Head Money Cases, 112 U.S. 580, 599 (1884) ("So far as a treaty made by the United States with any foreign nation can become the subject of judicial cognizance in the courts of this country, it is subject to such acts as Congress may pass for its enforcement, modification, or repeal.").

15. Act of July 7, 1798, ch. 67, 1 Stat. 578, 578.

16. Thomas Jefferson, A Manual of Parliamentary Practice § 51 (Samuel Harrison Smith ed., 1801) ("Treaties being declared, equally with the laws of the U[nited] States, to be the supreme law of the land, it is understood that an act of the legislature alone can declare them infringed and rescinded. This was accordingly the process adopted in the case of France in 1798.").

17. James K. Polk, First Annual Message (Dec. 2, 1845), in 5 A Compilation of the Messages and Papers of the Presidents 2235, 2245 (James D. Richardson ed., 1897).

18. Joint Resolution of Apr. 27, 1846, 9 Stat. 109.

19. See Cong. Globe, 29th Cong., 1st Sess. 635 (1846). See also David P. Currie, The Constitution in Congress: Descent into the Maelstrom, 1829–1861, at 78–80 (2005).

20. H.R. Rep. No. 29–34, at 1–3 (1984).

21. S. Doc. No. 29–489, at 15 (1st Sess. 1846).

22. Before signing the new treaty, Polk sought the Senate's advice about whether he should do so, even though (as noted in Chapter 7) presidents had by that point generally moved away from giving the Senate a formal advice role in the treaty process.

23. Joint Resolution of Jan. 18, 1865, 13 Stat. 566 (1865).

24. See Letter from Charles Francis Adams, Minister to the U.K., to William H. Seward, U.S. Sec'y of State (Mar. 23, 1865), in Papers Relating to Foreign Affairs, pt. 1, at 258 (1866); Letter from William H. Seward, U.S. Sec'y of State, to Charles Francis Adams, Minister to the U.K. (Jan. 18, 1865), in Papers Relating to Foreign Affairs, pt. 1, at 93.

25. See Joint Resolution of June 17, 1874, 18 Stat. 287; Letter from Hamilton Fish, U.S. Sec'y of State, to J. R. Jones, Minister to Belgium (June 17, 1874), in Papers Relating to the Foreign Relations of the United States 64 (1874); see also Ulysses S. Grant, Sixth Annual Message (Dec. 7, 1874), in 10 A Compilation of the Messages and Papers of the Presidents 4238, 4242 (reporting that "the notice directed by the resolution of Congress of June 17, 1874, to be given to terminate the convention of July 17, 1858, between the United States and Belgium has been given, and the treaty will accordingly terminate on the 1st day of July, 1875").

26. Joint Resolution of Mar. 3, 1883, 22 Stat. 641; Letter from Frederick T. Frelinghuysen, U.S. Sec'y of State, to J. R. Lowell, Minister to the U.K. (Apr. 5, 1883), in Papers Relating to the Foreign Relations of the United States 413, 413–14 (1884).

27. 38 Stat. 1164, 1184 (1915); Circular from William Jennings Bryan, U.S. Sec'y of State, to Ambassador Page (May 29, 1915), in Papers Relating to the Foreign Relations of the United States 3 (1924).

28. Franklin Pierce, Second Annual Message (Dec. 4, 1854), in 7 A Compilation of the Messages and Papers of the Presidents 2806, 2812.

29. Franklin Pierce, Third Annual Message (Dec. 31, 1855), in 7 A Compilation of the Messages and Papers of the Presidents, at 2860, 2867.

30. S. Rep. No. 97, 34th Cong., 1st Sess. (Apr. 7, 1856). Some years earlier, Secretary of State James Buchanan had informed Denmark that, in order for the United States to withdraw from the treaty, "an Act must first pass Congress to enable the President to give the required notice." Letter from James Buchanan, Sec'y of State, to Robert P. Flenniken, Minister to Den. (Oct. 14, 1848), in 8 The Works of James Buchanan 220, 224 (John Bassett Moore ed., 1909).

31. Another example is President Wilson's termination of an international sanitary convention in 1921 with the Senate's advice and consent. See V Hackworth, supra note 6, at 322.

32. Rutherford B. Hayes, Veto of the Chinese Immigration Bill, H.R. Exec. Doc. No. 45–102, at 5 (3d Sess. 1879). It is possible that Hayes was referring to Congress's authority to override

the domestic effects of a treaty rather than its authority to terminate a treaty internationally. See Adler, supra note 6, at 175–76.

33. Merchant Marine (Jones) Act, ch. 250, § 34, 41 Stat. 988, 1007 (1920).

34. U.S. Dep't of State, Press Release 2–3 (Sept. 6, 1920) (on file with author); see also President Won't Denounce Treaties; Defies Congress, N.Y. Times (Sept. 25, 1920); Jesse S. Reeves, The Jones Act and the Denunciation of Treaties, 15 Am. J. Int'l L. 33 (1921).

35. See Statement by State Department (Sept. 24, 1920), in 17 A Compilation of the Messages and Papers of the Presidents 8871 (1927). The next year, Secretary of State Charles Evans Hughes similarly advised President Harding that, "as the existing treaties do not permit such partial termination by notice, it follows that Congress has failed to give a mandate on which the President can act." Memorandum for President Harding, Oct. 8, 1925, Dep't of State, file 195/389, reprinted in 5 Hackworth, supra note 6, at 326.

36. As discussed in Chapter 4, the agreement was concluded unilaterally by President Monroe, but a year later he sent it to the Senate, where it was approved (after it had already taken effect).

37. Joint Resolution of Feb. 9, 1865, 13 Stat. 568.

38. See, e.g., 35 Cong. Globe 313 (1865) (Sen. Davis) ("It is indispensably incumbent and necessary, in order to secure the termination of this treaty, that it shall be terminated, not by the action of the President, but by the action of Congress.").

39. Letter from Ulysses S. Grant to the Senate and House of Representatives (June 20, 1876), in 10 A Compilation of the Messages and Papers of the Presidents 4324, 4327.

40. 48 Cong. Rec. 453 (1911).

41. Joint Resolution of Dec. 21, 1911, 37 Stat. 627 (1911).

42. See, e.g., John L. Cadwalader, Digest of the Published Opinions of the Attorneys General, and of the Leading Decisions of the Federal Courts with Reference to International Law, Treaties, and Kindred Subjects §§ 48–50, at 234 (rev. ed. 1877) (discussing the principles of treaty abrogation but making no mention of abrogation by the executive branch); 2 Francis Wharton, A Digest of the International Law of the United States § 137(a), at 58–65 (2d ed. 1887) (same); see also David A. Schnitzer, Note, Into Justice Jackson's Twilight: A Constitutional and Historical Analysis of Treaty Termination, 101 Geo. L.J. 243, 265–66 (2012) (surveying the digests' treatment of treaty abrogation).

43. 2 Charles Henry Butler, The Treaty-Making Power of the United States § 384, at 129 (1902).

44. Edward S. Corwin, The President's Control of Foreign Relations 115 (1917). An early break from the scholarly consensus occurred in 1910, when the constitutional law scholar Westel Willoughby stated without discussion that "though the Senate participates in the ratification of treaties, the President has the authority, without asking for senatorial advice and consent, to denounce an existing treaty and to declare it no longer binding upon the United States." 1 Westel Woodbury Willoughby, The Constitutional Law of the United States § 223 (1910). Other scholars followed in the 1920s. See, e.g., John Mabry Mathews, The Conduct of American Foreign Relations 251 (1922) (contending that "it cannot be maintained . . . that law and practice bear out [Corwin's] sweeping statement").

45. Quincy Wright, The Control of American Foreign Relations 260 (1922).

46. See Letter from John Hay, U.S. Sec'y of State, to Ambassador Leishman (Mar. 8, 1899), in Papers Relating to the Foreign Relations of the United States 753, 753–54 (1901).

47. In Van der Weyde v. Ocean Transport Co., 297 U.S. 114 (1936), the Supreme Court avoided deciding whether the executive had the authority, "in the absence of congressional

action, or of action by the treaty-making power, to denounce a treaty of the United States." But it upheld the validity of executive termination of certain provisions of a treaty with Norway that the president considered to be in conflict with the 1915 Seaman's Act, stating that "it was incumbent upon the President, charged with the conduct [of] negotiations with foreign governments and also with the duty to take care that the laws of the United States are faithfully executed, to reach a conclusion as to the inconsistency between the provisions of the treaty and the provisions of the new law."

48. Memorandum from James Brown Scott, Solicitor, U.S. Dep't of State, to President Wilson (June 12, 1909) (on file with author).

49. Telegram from Frank B. Kellogg, U.S. Sec'y of State, to Ambassador Sheffield (Mar. 21, 1927), in 3 Papers Relating to the Foreign Relations of the United States, 1927, at 230, 230–31 (1942).

50. U.S. Dep't of State, Press Release, Withdrawal of United States from International Convention for the Abolition of Import and Export Prohibitions and Restrictions (July 5, 1933), reprinted in Dep't of State, Press Releases, July 1–December 30, 1933, at 18.

51. See 2 Foreign Relations of the United States: Diplomatic Papers, 1933, at 552–69 (1949).

52. Memorandum from R. Walton Moore, Acting U.S. Sec'y of State, to President Roosevelt (Nov. 9, 1936) (on file with author). The State Department Legal Adviser had prepared a memorandum earlier that year contending that, regardless of whether the president has a general power to terminate treaties unilaterally, it seems "that little doubt could arise when, as in the case of the Seaman's Act, he is called upon to terminate provisions of treaties inconsistent with an Act of Congress and when failure to do so would place this Government in the position of failing to observe its treaty obligations." Memorandum from Green Haywood Hackworth, Legal Adviser of the Dep't of State, Abrogation of Treaties (Jan. 27, 1936), quoted in 5 Hackworth, supra note 6, at 328.

53. 5 Hackworth, supra note 6, at 331–32 (excerpting State Department memorandum).

54. Int'l Load Line Convention, 40 Op. Att'y Gen. 119, 123 (1941).

55. Treaty Information, 11 Dep't St. Bull. 442 (1944).

56. See, e.g., Wallace McClure, International Executive Agreements: Democratic Procedure under the Constitution of the United States 306 (1941) (claiming that "in treaty making[,] . . . negative action, not being feared by the constitution makers, was left to the repository of general executive power"); Myres S. McDougal & Asher Lans, Treaties and Congressional-Executive or Presidential Agreements: Interchangeable Instruments of National Policy: I, 54 Yale L.J. 181, 336–37 (1945) (asserting that termination of both executive agreements and treaties can be "effected by executive denunciation, with or without prior Congressional authorization").

57. Treaty Information, 32 Dep't St. Bull. 906 (1955); Treaty Information, 38 Dep't St. Bull. 238 (1958).

58. Cape Spartel Light: Transfer of Management to Morocco; Termination of Convention of May 31, 1865, Mar. 31, 1958, 9 U.S.T. 527, 532.

59. Memorandum from William Whittington, Termination of Treaties: International Rules and Internal United States Procedure 3 (Feb. 10, 1958) (on file with author).

60. Proclamation No. 3447, Embargo on All Trade with Cuba, 27 Fed. Reg. 1085 (Feb. 7, 1962), reprinted in 76 Stat. 1446 (1962).

61. Treaty Information, 53 Dep't St. Bull. 923, 924 (1965). See also John H. Riggs Jr., Termination of Treaties by the Executive without Congressional Approval: The Case of the Warsaw Convention, 32 J. Air L. & Comm. 526 (1966); Comment, Presidential Amendment and Termination of Treaties: The Case of the Warsaw Convention, 34 U. Chi. L. Rev. 580 (1967).

62. 125 Cong. Rec. 13,685 (1979). For the hearings held on this proposed resolution, see Hearings before the Senate Committee on Foreign Relations on S. Res. 15, Resolution concerning Mutual Defense Treaties, 96th Cong., 1st Sess. (1979) [hereinafter Treaty Termination Hearings].

63. See S. Rep. No. 96–7 (1979).

64. 125 Cong. Rec. 13,695–96 (1979).

65. Goldwater v. Carter, 481 F. Supp. 949, 965 (D.D.C. 1979). As noted in Chapter 1, it is unlikely that a case brought in this posture today would be able to overcome limits on legislative standing.

66. Goldwater v. Carter, 617 F.2d 697 (D.C. Cir. 1979) (per curiam).

67. Justice Brennan reasoned that the termination was lawful because it was "a necessary incident" to President Carter's recognition of mainland China, which fell within his constitutional authority. Id. at 1007 (Brennan, J., dissenting). (The president's recognition power is considered in detail in Chapter 3.) Justices Blackmun and White wanted to hold oral argument before making a decision. Id. at 1006 (Blackmun & White, JJ., dissenting in part).

68. Several years later, in the mid-1980s, Goldwater introduced a resolution stating that it was the sense of the Senate that, unless otherwise provided in a treaty, termination required either the advice and consent of the Senate or congressional approval. S. Res. 40, 99th Cong., 131 Cong. Rec. 678 (1985). But the Senate never voted on the resolution.

69. 22 U.S.C. § 3303(c).

70. 22 U.S.C. § 3302(a).

71. In 2022, President Biden seemed to deviate from the strategic ambiguity approach by suggesting more directly that the United States would come to Taiwan's aid if it were attacked, but other officials insisted that he was not changing the U.S. approach. See Zolan Kanno-Youngs & Peter Baker, Biden Pledges to Defend Taiwan If It Faces a Chinese Attack, N.Y. Times (May 23, 2022); Amy B. Wang, Biden Says U.S. Troops Would Defend Taiwan in Event of Attack by China, Wash. Post (Sept. 18, 2022). A potential advantage of the strategic ambiguity approach is that it may deter Taiwan from being too aggressive, since it cannot be entirely sure of how much protection the United States will provide. See Brett V. Benson, Why It Makes Sense for the U.S. to Not Commit to Defending Taiwan, Wash. Post (May 25, 2022). For consideration of whether the president has the constitutional authority to use force to protect Taiwan in the event of an attack by mainland China, see Scott R. Anderson, Taiwan, War Powers, and Constitutional Crisis, 64 Va. J. Int'l L. 171 (2023).

72. See 118 Stat. 656 (June 14, 2004). In signing this legislation, President George W. Bush stated that, "consistent with the President's constitutional authority to conduct the Nation's foreign affairs, the Executive shall construe the Act to be consistent with the 'one China' policy of the United States, which remains unchanged, and determine the measures best suited to advance the overall goal of Taiwan participation in the World Health Organization." Statement on Signing Legislation Supporting the Participation of Taiwan in the World Health Organization (June 14, 2004).

73. See H.R. 4004, United States–Taiwan Initiative on 21st-Century Trade First Agreement Implementation Act. In signing this legislation, President Biden issued a statement contending that the section of the law concerning the negotiation of trade agreements raised constitutional concerns and that "in cases where the requirements [of this section] would impermissibly infringe upon my constitutional authority to negotiate with a foreign partner, my Administration will treat them as non-binding." Statement from President Biden (Aug. 7, 2023).

74. Economic Sanctions against Nicaragua, 85 Dep't St. Bull. 74, 74–75 (1985). A federal district court subsequently applied the political question doctrine to dismiss a challenge to this termination. See Beacon Prods. Corp. v. Reagan, 633 F. Supp. 1191, 1198–99 (D. Mass. 1986).

75. See Dep't of the Treasury, United States Terminates Tax Treaty with Malta, Treas. RR-717 (Nov. 20, 1995).

76. Office of Legal Adviser, U.S. Dep't of State, 2002 Digest of United States Practice in International Law 2002, at 202–6 (Sally J. Cummins & David P. Stewart eds., 2002).

77. See Terence Neilan, Bush Pulls Out of ABM Treaty, Putin Calls Move a Mistake, N.Y. Times (Dec. 13, 2001).

78. Bruce Ackerman, Op-Ed, Treaties Don't Belong to Presidents Alone, N.Y. Times (Aug. 29, 2001). With respect to historical practice, Ackerman mentioned Congress's 1798 termination of the French treaties and President Polk's solicitation of congressional authorization to terminate the Oregon Territory Treaty in 1846 and then asserted that "the big change occurred in 1978, when Jimmy Carter unilaterally terminated our mutual defense treaty with Taiwan." This is, needless to say, a very partial account of the history (as might be expected in an op-ed format).

79. See Kucinich v. Bush, 236 F. Supp. 2d 1 (D.D.C. 2002).

80. Memorandum from John C. Yoo & Robert J. Delahunty for John Bellinger III, Authority of the President to Suspend Certain Provisions of the ABM Treaty (Nov. 15, 2001).

81. The memorandum asserted that presidents could terminate treaties even when termination was not allowed by international law. See id. at 12. OLC later disavowed this and another opinion "to the extent they suggested that the President has unlimited authority to suspend a treaty beyond the circumstances traditionally recognized." Memorandum of Steven G. Bradbury, Principal Deputy Assistant Att'y Gen., for the Files, Status of Certain OLC Opinions Issued in the Aftermath of the Terrorist Attacks of September 11, 2001, at 9 (Jan. 15, 2009).

82. Frederic L. Kirgis, President Bush's Determination regarding Mexican Nationals and Consular Convention Rights, ASIL Insights (Mar. 2005); U.S. Dep't of the Treasury, Press Release, United States Terminates Estate and Gift Tax Treaty with Sweden (June 15, 2007).

83. See U.S. Dep't of State, Digest of United States Practice in International Law 2016, at 149–50 (CarrieLyn D. Guymon ed., 2016).

84. The five Senate-approved treaties were the Intermediate-Range Nuclear Forces Treaty, a treaty of amity with Iran, a protocol to the Vienna Convention on Diplomatic Relations allowing for adjudication in the International Court of Justice, the Open Skies Treaty, and a prisoner transfer agreement with Hong Kong.

85. Press Statement, U.S. Dep't of State, Suspending and Terminating the Asylum Cooperative Agreements with the Governments of El Salvador, Guatemala, and Honduras (Feb. 6, 2021).

86. Jeff Stein, U.S. to Terminate Treaty with Hungary over Resistance to Global Tax, Wash. Post (July 9, 2022).

87. Fishery Conservation and Management Act of 1976, Pub. L. No. 94–265, § 202(b), 90 Stat. 331, 340–41.

88. Comprehensive Anti-Apartheid Act of 1986, Pub. L. No. 99–440, § 306(b)(1), § 313, 100 Stat. 1086, 1100, 1104. Although Reagan's veto message did not refer specifically to the provisions in the act relating to treaty termination, it did state generally that the act "contains provisions that infringe on the President's constitutional prerogative to articulate the foreign policy of the United States." Ronald Reagan, Message to the House of Representatives Returning

without Approval a Bill concerning Apartheid in South Africa (Sept. 26, 1986). After Congress overrode his veto, Reagan stated that, although he "deeply regret[ted]" that it had done so, his administration "will . . . implement the law." Ronald Reagan, Statement on the Comprehensive Anti-Apartheid Act of 1986 (Oct. 2, 1986).

89. See South African Airways v. Dole, 817 F.2d 119, 121 (D.C. Cir. 1987).

90. See Restatement (Third) of the Foreign Relations Law of the United States § 339 reporters' n. 2 (1987) ("No one has questioned the President's authority to terminate sole executive agreements.").

91. See Mark Landler, Trump Abandons Iran Nuclear Deal He Long Scorned, N.Y. Times (May 8, 2018).

92. See Curtis A. Bradley, Exiting Congressional-Executive Agreements, 67 Duke L.J. 1615 (2018). See also Henkin, supra note 7, at 496 n.159 ("The question as to who has the power to terminate a Congressional-Executive agreement is unresolved, but the President's authority seems no weaker than in regard to treaties.").

93. For arguments along these lines, see Joel P. Trachtman, Power to Terminate U.S. Trade Agreements: The Presidential Dormant Commerce Clause versus an Historical Gloss Half Empty, 51 Int'l Lawyer 445 (2018).

94. See, e.g., Reciprocal Trade, Costa Rica-U.S., Apr. 3, 1951, T.I.A.S. No. 2237 (terminating Reciprocal Trade, Costa Rica-U.S., Nov. 28, 1936, 50 Stat. 1582).

95. See Proclamation No. 3111 (Aug. 27, 1955).

96. See Proclamation No. 4993 (Oct. 29, 1982).

97. See Diplomatic Note to the Ministry of Foreign Affairs of Japan from the U.S. Embassy (Dec. 17, 2004); U.S. Trade Representative, Press Release, U.S. Files WTO Case against EU over Unfair Airbus Subsidies (Oct. 10, 2004).

98. See U.S. Dep't of State, Digest of United States Practice in International Law 1975, at 70–73 (Eleanor C. McDowell ed., 1976); U.S. Dep't of State, Digest of United States Practice in International Law 1980, at 76–78 (Marian Nash Leich ed., 1986).

99. See U.S. Dep't of State, Cumulative Digest of United States Practice in International Law 1981–1988, at 405–9 (Marian Nash [Leich] ed., 1993).

100. U.S. Dep't of State, Digest of United States Practice in International Law 2003, at 421–23 (Sally J. Cummins & David P. Stewart eds., 2004); U.S. Dep't State, Press Release, The United States Withdraws from UNESCO (Oct. 12, 2017).

101. See Christina Morales, Biden Restores Ties with the World Health Organization That Were Cut by Trump, N.Y. Times (Jan. 20, 2021).

102. 36 Stat. 11, 83, Sec. 4 (1909).

103. 42 Stat. 1225 (1923). See McClure, supra note 56, at 29.

104. See Pub. L. No. 82–50, § 5, 65 Stat. 72, 73 (1951). The Truman administration relied on this law in terminating congressional-executive agreements with the Soviet Union and several Soviet satellite countries. Dep't of State, Office of the Historian, Foreign Relations of the United States, 1951, Europe: Political and Economic Developments, vol. 4, pt. 2.

105. See Trade Expansion Act of 1962, Pub. L. 87–794, § 255(a).

106. See also Randall H. Nelson, The Termination of Treaties and Executive Agreements by the United States: Theory and Practice, 42 Minn. L. Rev. 879, 882–83 (1958) (noting that "the United States treats executive agreements and treaties in precisely the same manner when effecting their termination").

107. See, e.g., Julian Ku & John Yoo, Trump Might Be Stuck with NAFTA, L.A. Times (Nov. 29, 2016); John C. Yoo, Laws as Treaties? The Constitutionality of Congressional-Executive Agreements, 99 Mich. L. Rev. 757, 815 (2001).

108. See Edwards v. Carter, 580 F.2d 1055, 1057–58 (D.C. Cir. 1978) ("Many of the powers thereafter enumerated in [Article I,] § 8 involve matters that were at the time the Constitution was adopted, and that are at the present time, also commonly the subject of treaties. The most prominent example of this is the regulation of commerce with foreign nations.").

109. John Yoo's argument against a presidential power to terminate congressional-executive agreements connects to his narrow originalist conception of the Article II treaty power, pursuant to which treaties could never be self-executing for matters falling within Congress's Article I powers. See John C. Yoo, Globalism and the Constitution: Treaties, Non-Self-Execution, and the Original Understanding, 99 Colum. L. Rev. 1955 (1999). This conception is at odds with the understandings and practices that have prevailed since the Founding. See Carlos Manuel Vázquez, Laughing at Treaties, 99 Colum. L. Rev. 2154, 2191 (1999).

110. Ana Swanson, Trump's Tough Talk on NAFTA Raises Prospects of Pact's Demise, N.Y. Times (Oct. 11, 2017).

111. Memorandum Opinion for the Counsel to the President, Authority to Withdraw from the North American Free Trade Agreement, 42 Op. O.L.C. slip op. at 11 (Oct. 17, 2018) [hereinafter NAFTA Memorandum].

112. The memorandum notes that OLC had solicited and considered the views of the State Department Legal Adviser's Office, and it refers to a 2017 memorandum prepared by that office, which has not been publicly released.

113. See Bradley, supra note 92, at 1635–36. These sunset provisions are further evidence of congressional acquiescence in a presidential termination authority. They could also be viewed as implicit delegations of termination authority. See Timothy Meyer & Ganesh Sitaraman, Trade and the Separation of Powers, 107 Calif. L. Rev. 583, 656 (2019). The topic of congressional delegation of foreign affairs authority to the executive branch is addressed in Chapter 8.

114. See Julian E. Barnes & Helene Cooper, Trump Discussed Pulling U.S. from NATO, Aides Say Amid New Concerns Over Russia, N.Y. Times (Jan. 14, 2019); Mariano Alfaro, Bolton Says Trump Might Have Pulled the U.S. Out of NATO If He Had Been Reelected, Wash. Post (Mar. 4, 2022).

115. National Defense Authorization Act for FY2020, § 1242.

116. National Defense Authorization Act for FY2020, § 1234(a), 22 U.S.C. § 2593a note.

117. Donald J. Trump, Statement on Signing the National Defense Authorization Act for Fiscal Year 2020 (Dec. 20, 2019).

118. Memorandum Opinion from Steven A. Engel, Assistant Attorney General, for the Legal Adviser to the National Security Council, Congressionally Mandated Notice Period for Withdrawing from the Open Skies Treaty, 44 Op. O.L.C. slip op. (Sept. 22, 2020).

119. For a critique of OLC's tendency to overargue the implications of presidential authority relating to diplomacy, see Jean Galbraith, The Runaway Presidential Power over Diplomacy, 108 Va. L. Rev. 81 (2022).

120. This was true even though Reagan's Office of Legal Counsel had apparently concluded that Congress could not constitutionally compel the president to terminate a treaty. See Memorandum Opinion, supra note 119, at 27–28 (quoting from an unpublished OLC opinion from 1986 to this effect).

121. See NAFTA Memorandum, supra note 112, at 5 ("Where an international agreement contains defined procedures for termination or withdrawal and Congress approves the agreement *without limiting those procedures,* the President may invoke the right of the United States to terminate or withdraw under those procedures without the need for additional congressional authorization.") (emphasis added).

122. Youngstown Sheet & Tube Co. v. Sawyer, 343 U.S. 579, 640 (1952) (Jackson, J., concurring). See also Scott R. Anderson & Pranay Vaddi, When Can the President Withdraw from the Open Skies Treaty?, Lawfare (Apr. 22, 2020).

123. See Curtis Bradley & Jack Goldsmith, Constitutional Issues Relating to the NATO Support Act, Lawfare (Jan. 28, 2019).

124. See also Catherine Amirfar & Ashika Singh, The Trump Administration and the "Unmaking" of International Agreements, 59 Harv. Int'l L.J. 443, 456 (2018) ("If the Executive may not make agreements on subjects within Article I's domain that conflict with the will of Congress, as expressed through a constitutionally-mandated process such as a statute, it is difficult to see why the Executive should be constitutionally able to unmake agreements in the same circumstances."); Kristen E. Eichensehr, Treaty Termination and the Separation of Powers, 53 Va. J. Int'l L. 247, 279–86 (2013) (arguing that "for cause" limitations imposed by the Senate on the president's treaty termination power would be constitutional).

125. In the congressional hearings on President Carter's termination of the Taiwan mutual defense treaty, there was discussion of whether and to what extent Congress or the Senate could limit the president's termination authority, and an official from OLC expressed the view that the Senate could not do so through reservations to its advice and consent. See Treaty Termination Hearings, supra note 62, at 218 (statement of Larry A. Hammond, Deputy Assist. Att'y Gen., Office of Legal Counsel). By contrast, the Senate Foreign Relations Committee insisted that it was "clear beyond question" that the Senate could validly limit the president's authority to terminate a treaty by placing a condition on such termination in the Senate's advice and consent to the treaty. See S. Rep. No. 96–119, at 11 (1979).

126. See National Defense Authorization Act for Fiscal Year 2024, § 1250A (Dec. 22, 2023) (stating "the President shall not suspend, terminate, denounce, or withdraw the United States from the North Atlantic Treaty, done at Washington, DC, April 4, 1949, except by and with the advice and consent of the Senate, provided that two-thirds of the Senators present concur, or pursuant to an Act of Congress"). President Biden issued a signing statement that raised constitutional concerns about other sections in the act, but not this section. See Statement from President Joe Biden on H.R. 2670 (Dec. 22, 2023).

127. This is not to suggest that everyone agrees. For a contrary view, see Harold Hongju Koh, Presidential Power to Terminate International Agreements, 128 Yale L.J. F. 432 (Nov. 12, 2018).

128. The Restatement (Fourth) of the Foreign Relations Law of the United States § 313 (2018), for which I served as a Reporter, concludes that, "according to established practice, the President has the authority to act on behalf of the United States in suspending or terminating U.S. treaty commitments and in withdrawing the United States from treaties." Its position is similar to that taken by the Restatement (Third), published in 1987, see § 339, and the Restatement (Second), published in 1965, see § 163. (There was no Restatement (First) of Foreign Relations Law.)

129. Cf. Eric A. Posner & Adrian Vermeule, Constitutional Showdowns, 156 U. Pa. L. Rev. 991 (2008).

130. See also G. Edward White, The Transformation of the Constitutional Regime of Foreign Relations, 85 Va. L. Rev. 1, 146 (1999) ("The dominance of the principle of national executive discretion in foreign affairs had come incrementally.").

131. See Jean Galbraith, Treaty Termination as Foreign Affairs Exceptionalism, 92 Tex. L. Rev. See Also 121 (2014). The United States is hardly alone in allowing its executive to withdraw from treaties; that is in fact the norm in a large majority of countries. See Laurence R. Helfer, Treaty Exit and Intra-Branch Conflict at the Interface of International and Domestic Law, in The Oxford Handbook of Foreign Relations Law 355, 357 (Curtis A. Bradley ed., 2019).

6. Using Military Force

1. Barack Obama's Q&A, Boston Globe (Dec. 20, 2007).

2. Caroline D. Krass, Memorandum Opinion for the Attorney General, Authority to Use Military Force in Libya, 35 Op. O.L.C. 20, 29 (Apr. 1, 2011).

3. Barack Obama, Remarks by the President in Address to the Nation on Syria (Sept. 10, 2013). For an insider's account of Obama's decision, see Ben Rhodes, Inside the White House During the Syrian "Red Line" Crisis, Atlantic (June 3, 2018). See also Charlie Savage, Power Wars: Inside Obama's Post-9/11 Presidency 650–54 (2015).

4. See Steven A. Engel, Assistant Attorney General, Office of Legal Counsel, Memorandum Opinion for the Counsel to the President, April 2019 Airstrikes against Syrian Chemical-Weapons Facilities, 42 Op. O.L.C. slip op. 1 (May 31, 2018).

5. Johnson v. Eisentrager, 339 U.S. 763, 788 (1950).

6. Federalist No. 69 (Hamilton), in The Federalist Papers 418 (Clinton Rossiter ed., 1961).

7. Id. (emphasis in original). See also Youngstown Sheet & Tube Co. v. Sawyer, 343 U.S. 579, 641 (1952) (Jackson, J., concurring) ("These cryptic words [of the Commander in Chief Clause] have given rise to some of the most persistent controversies in our constitutional history.").

8. Although typically described as a declared war, Congress in the Mexican-American War did not say that it was declaring war; rather, it simply said that "a state of war exists" between Mexico and the United States.

9. 2 The Records of the Federal Convention of 1787, at 318–19 (Max Farrand ed., 1911).

10. James Madison, Letters of Helvidius No. 1 (Aug. 24, 1793), reprinted in 15 The Papers of James Madison 66, 69 (Thomas A. Mason et al. eds., 1985).

11. Alexander Hamilton, Letters of Pacificus No. 1 (June 29, 1793), reprinted in 15 The Papers of Alexander Hamilton 33, 40 (Harold C. Syrett & Jacob E. Cooke eds., 1969).

12. John Quincy Adams, An Eulogy on the Life and Character of James Madison (Sept. 27, 1836).

13. For general accounts of the history of presidential uses of force, see Louis Fisher, Presidential War Power (3d ed. 2014); Arthur M. Schlesinger Jr., The Imperial Presidency (1973) (2004 ed.); Francis D. Wormuth & Edwin B. Firmage, To Chain the Dog of War: The War Powers of Congress in History and Law (1986); Curtis A. Bradley & Jean Galbraith, Presidential War Powers as an Interactive Dynamic: International Law, Domestic Law, and Practice-Based Legal Change, 91 N.Y.U. L. Rev. 689 (2016).

14. Letter from George Washington to Governor William Moultrie, Aug. 28, 1793, in 33 The Writings of George Washington 73 (John C. Fitzpatrick ed., 1939). As Louis Fisher has noted, however, "as the years progressed, the distinction between defensive and offensive actions on Indian policy gradually blurred," and "presidential policies of restraint carried only

so much weight in a country that was expanding in size and highly decentralized." Fisher, supra note 13, at 20.

15. See, e.g., 1 Stat. 578 (July 9, 1798). See generally Alexander DeConde, The Quasi-War: The Politics and Diplomacy of the Undeclared War with France, 1797–1801 (1966); Dean Alfange Jr., The Quasi-War and Presidential Warmaking, in The Constitution and the Conduct of American Foreign Policy (David Gray Adler & Larry N. George eds., 1996).

16. See Bas v. Tingy, 4 U.S. (4 Dall.) 37 (1800); Little v. Barreme, 6 U.S. (1 Cranch) 170 (1804). For an account of the early post-Founding history of war powers, including Congress's actions in the Quasi-War, see Abraham D. Sofaer, War, Foreign Affairs, and Constitutional Power (1976).

17. Talbot v. Seeman, 5 U.S. (1 Cranch) 1, 28 (1801). For an argument that the Adams administration "took an impressive number of actions without—or in violation of—statutory authorization," see Robert J. Reinstein, Slavery, Executive Power and International Law: The Haitian Revolution and American Constitutionalism, 53 Am. J. Leg. Hist. 141, 180 (2013).

18. See David P. Currie, The Constitution in Congress: The Federalist Period, 1789–1801, at 84 (1997).

19. Letter from Alexander Hamilton to James McHenry (May 17, 1798), in 21 The Papers of Alexander Hamilton 461–62 (Harold C. Syrett ed., 1974). Hamilton had served as Secretary of the Treasury under Washington but at this point was back in private practice as a lawyer in New York, although he was in frequent contact with the Adams administration.

20. See Max Boot, The Savage Wars of Peace: Small Wars and the Rise of American Power 3–29 (rev. ed. 2014); Sofaer, supra note 16, at 208–24.

21. 2 Stat. 101 (1801).

22. Thomas Jefferson, First Annual Message (Dec. 8, 1801), in 1 A Compilation of the Messages and Papers of the Presidents 314, 315 (James D. Richardson ed., 1899). Jefferson's account of his own authority was narrower than the directions he had given to the navy. See Montgomery N. Kosma, Our First Real War, 2 Green Bag 2d 169 (1999).

23. Alexander Hamilton, The Examination No. 1 (Dec. 17, 1801), in 25 The Papers of Alexander Hamilton 444, 455–56 (Harold C. Syrett ed., 1977).

24. Among the scholars today who insist that the president cannot initiate wars without congressional authorization, there is debate about how far the president can go in responding to attacks. Compare Saikrishna Prakash, Unleashing the Dogs of War: What the Constitution Means by "Declare War," 93 Cornell L. Rev. 45 (2007) (narrow view), with Michael D. Ramsey, The President's Power to Respond to Attacks, 93 Cornell L. Rev. 169 (2007) (broad view).

25. 2 Stat. 129, 130, § 2 (Feb. 6, 1802).

26. James Monroe, Message to Congress (Mar. 25, 1818). He contended that Spain was bound under a 1795 treaty to restrain the Indians from committing hostilities against the United States.

27. See 2 Messages and Papers of the President 1789–1897, at 31–32 (James Richardson ed., 1987).

28. See Daniel Walker Howe, What Hath God Wrought: The Transformation of America, 1815–1848, at 98–104 (2007).

29. 33 Annals of Cong. 268 (1819).

30. Letter from James Monroe to Andrew Jackson (July 19, 1818).

31. Memoirs of John Quincy Adams (July 15, 1818). For discussion of the constitutional debate in Congress concerning Jackson's actions, see David P. Currie, Rumors of Wars: Presidential and Congressional War Powers, 1809–1829, 67 U. Chi. L. Rev. 1, 13–16 (2000).

32. See Milton Offutt, The Protection of Citizens Abroad by the Armed Forces of the United States 1 (1928).

33. Andrew Jackson, Third Annual Message (Dec. 6, 1831).

34. See Henry Bartholomew Cox, War, Foreign Affairs, and Constitutional Power, 1829–1901, at 61 (1984). See also Julius Goebel Jr., The Struggle for the Falkland Islands: A Study in Legal and Diplomatic History 438–46 (1927).

35. Andrew Jackson, Fourth Annual Message (Dec. 4, 1832).

36. See Offutt, supra note 32, at 7.

37. Letter from William L. Marcy to Chevalier Hulsemann (Sept. 26, 1853), in Correspondence Between the Secretary of State and Charge D'Affaires of Austria Relative to the Case of Martin Koszta 8, 27 (1853).

38. 135 U.S. 1 (1890).

39. For a general account of the Greytown incident, see 7 John Bassett Moore, A Digest of International Law § 1168, at 346–54 (1906). See also David P. Currie, The Constitution in Congress: Descent into the Maelstrom, 1829–1861, at 117–21 (2005).

40. Franklin Pierce, Second Annual Message to Congress (Dec. 4, 1854).

41. See, e.g., Cong. Globe, 33d Cong., 2d Sess. 951 (1855) (Rep. Peckham); id. at app. 71 (Rep. Cox).

42. Durand v. Hollins, 8 F. Cas. 111 (C.C.S.D.N.Y. 1860). See also Perrin v. United States, 4 Ct. Cl. 543, 547 (1868) (describing claims stemming from the bombardment of Greytown as "international political questions, which no court of this country in a case of this kind is authorized or empowered to decide").

43. President Buchanan, however, evinced a narrower view of presidential war powers. See, e.g., 28 Cong. Globe Appendix 5 (stating that the president "cannot legitimately resort to force, without the direct authority of Congress except in resisting and repelling hostile attacks").

44. James Buchanan, Second Annual Message to Congress on the State of the Union (Dec. 6, 1858).

45. Letter from Lewis Cass to Lord Napier (Apr. 10, 1857).

46. Perry had been instructed to "do everything to impress [the Japanese] with a just sense of the power and greatness of this country" but not to resort to force except in self-defense. Congress did not object to Perry's actions and in fact awarded him $20,000 for his efforts.

47. See 7 Moore, supra note 39, § 1093, at 116–17.

48. See Boot, supra note 20, at 58–59.

49. As discussed in Chapter 4, the Senate rejected the treaty, and Tyler subsequently concluded the annexation through a statute instead.

50. Cong. Globe, 42d Cong., 1st Sess., at 294 (Mar. 27, 1871) (fifth resolution).

51. Cong. Globe, 42d Cong., 1st Sess., App. at 52.

52. William Rawle, A View of the Constitution of the United States of America 109 (2d ed. 1829). See also Sofaer, supra note 16, at 93–94; Matthew C. Waxman, The Power to Threaten War, 123 Yale L.J. 1626 (2014).

53. James Monroe, Seventh Annual Message to Congress (Dec. 2, 1823).

54. Before issuing this statement, the Monroe administration had rejected a suggestion by the British that the United States and Great Britain issue a joint declaration. See Ernest R. May, The Making of the Monroe Doctrine 4–8 (1975). See also Dexter Perkins, A History of the Monroe Doctrine (rev. ed. 1955); Jay Sexton, The Monroe Doctrine: Empire and Nation in Nineteenth-Century America (2011).

55. See George Dangerfield, The Era of Good Feelings 360–65 (1952).

56. See David P. Currie, The Constitution in Congress: The Jeffersonians, 1801–1829, at 211–12, 215–16 (2001).

57. See Letter from Henry Clay to John Quincy Adams (Mar. 29, 1826).

58. See generally Amy S. Greenberg, A Wicked War: Polk, Clay, Lincoln, and the 1846 U.S. Invasion of Mexico (2012).

59. James Polk, Special Message to Congress (May 11, 1846), in 3 A Compilation of the Messages and Papers of the Presidents 2287, 2293 (James D. Richardson ed., 1897).

60. Cong. Globe, 29th Cong., 1st Sess. 799 (May 12, 1846).

61. Id. at 800.

62. Cong. Globe, 30th Cong., 1st Sess. 95 (Jan. 5, 1848).

63. Letter from Abraham Lincoln to William H. Herndon (Feb. 15, 1848), in 1 The Collected Works of Abraham Lincoln 451 (Roy B. Basler ed., 1953) (emphasis in original).

64. Letter from Daniel Webster to Luther Severance (July 14, 1851), in The Papers of Daniel Webster Digital Edition (Charles M. Wiltse ed., 2018).

65. 67 U.S. (2 Black) 635, 668 (1863).

66. William Whiting, War Powers under the Constitution of the United States 38–39 (10th ed. 1864) (emphasis in original).

67. This was the title of Woodrow Wilson's PhD thesis, which he published in 1885. Writing almost a quarter century later, Wilson struck a different tone, remarking on the president's broad control over U.S. foreign relations. See Woodrow Wilson, Constitutional Government in the United States 77–78 (1908).

68. For an account of how international law was invoked to helped justify American imperialism after the Spanish-American War, see Benjamin Allen Coates, Legalist Empire: International Law and American Foreign Relations in the Early Twentieth Century ch. 2 (2016).

69. See Boxer Movement, 5 John Bassett Moore, A Digest of International Law, §§ 808–10, at 476–533 (1906); George C. Herring, From Colony to Superpower: U.S. Foreign Relations since 1776, at 332 (2008).

70. For an account of the U.S. decision to take the Philippines during the Spanish-American War, see Philip Zelikow, Why Did America Cross the Pacific? Reconstructing the U.S. Decision to Take the Philippines, 1898–99, 1 Tex. Nat'l Sec. Rev. 36 (2017).

71. William McKinley, Message to Congress (Dec. 3, 1900), in 34 Cong. Rec. 2, 4 (1901). China subsequently agreed in a protocol to make reparations and other concessions to the allied powers.

72. 7 Moore, supra note 39, at 118. See also Schlesinger, supra note 13, at 89 ("The intervention in China marked the start of a crucial shift in the presidential employment of armed forces overseas.").

73. David Gartner, Foreign Relations, Strategic Doctrine, and Presidential Power, 63 Ala. L. Rev. 499, 527 (2012). See also Boot, supra note 20, at 129–56.

74. Theodore Roosevelt, Fourth Annual Message (Dec. 6, 1904).

75. William Howard Taft, The Boundaries Between the Executive, the Legislative and the Judicial Branches of the Government, 25 Yale L.J. 699, 610–11 (1916).

76. For example, a treaty between the United States and Cuba, concluded after the Spanish-American War, provided that "the Government of Cuba consents that the United States may exercise the right to intervene for the preservation of Cuban independence, and

the maintenance of a government adequate for the protection of life, property, and individual liberty." This condition was also reflected in a federal statute known as the Platt Amendment. A treaty with Haiti concluded in 1915 similarly gave the United States a right to intervene.

77. See Mariah Zeisberg, War Powers: The Politics of Constitutional Authority 116–20 (2013).

78. Clark was a prominent Mormon attorney who ended up having a long career in government service. Brigham Young University's law school, which was founded in 1973, is named after Clark.

79. 175 U.S. 677 (1900).

80. 55 Cong. Rec. 20 (Mar. 8, 1917); U.S. Dep't of State, Papers Relating to the Foreign Relations of the United States, Supp. 1, at 171 (1917).

81. See George F. Kennan, Russia Leaves the War (1958); Carl J. Richard, When the United States Invaded Russia: Woodrow Wilson's Siberian Disaster (2017).

82. 59 Cong. Rec. 4333 (1920).

83. See generally John Milton Cooper Jr., Breaking the Heart of the World: Woodrow Wilson and the Fight for the League of Nations (2001); Thomas J. Knock, To End All Wars: Woodrow Wilson and the Quest for a New World Order (new ed. 2019).

84. 22 U.S.C. § 287d.

85. S. Rep. No. 79–8, at 9 (1945).

86. See also David Golove, From Versailles to San Francisco: The Revolutionary Transformation of the War Powers, 70 U. Colo. L. Rev. 1491 (1999); Jane E. Stromseth, Rethinking War Powers: Congress, the President, and the United Nations, 81 Geo. L.J. 597 (1993).

87. Statement by the President (June 27, 1950).

88. UN Security Council Res. 83 (June 27, 1950).

89. Harry S. Truman, The President's News Conference (June 29, 1950).

90. See generally Larry Blomstedt, Truman, Congress, and Korea: The Politics of America's First Undeclared War (2016).

91. See United States v. Bolton, 192 F.2d 805 (2d Cir. 1951).

92. Dean Acheson, Present at the Creation: My Years in the State Department 414 (1969).

93. See Schlesinger, supra note 13, at 132–33.

94. See U.S. Dept. of State, Authority of the President to Repel the Attack in Korea, 23 Dep't of State Bull. 173 (July 1, 1950). As published in the *Department of State Bulletin*, the memo was redacted, leaving out introductory paragraphs that made clear that the president ordered the use of force before the UN Security Council had authorized such action. See Mary L. Dudziak, The Gloss of War, 122 Mich. L. Rev. 149 (2023).

95. The State Department included with the memorandum a list of past instances in which the United States had used military force abroad outside the context of a war. For a critical assessment of these arguments made in defense of Truman's actions, see Louis Fisher, The Korean War: On What Legal Basis Did Truman Act?, 89 Am. J. Int'l L. 21 (1995).

96. Franklin S. Pollak, Power of the President to Send Troops Abroad 34 (Apr. 27, 1951). This OLC opinion has not been publicly released, but this portion of it was quoted many years later in a publicly released opinion concerning the use of force in support of a UN operation in Somalia.

97. 96 Cong. Rec. 9322–23 (1950).

98. Henry Steele Commager, Presidential Power: The Issue Analyzed, N.Y. Times Magazine 11 (Jan. 14, 1951). Commager later evinced a narrower view of presidential war powers

during the Vietnam War. See Hearings on S.J. 731, S.J. Res. 18 and S.J. Res. 59, 92d Cong., 1st Sess. 7–27 (1971).

99. Arthur Schlesinger Jr., Presidential Power: Taft Statement on Troops Opposed, Actions of Past Presidents Cited, N.Y. Times 28 (Jan. 9, 1951).

100. Cf. Schlesinger, supra note 13, at 139 (referring to his earlier remark as "hyperbole").

101. H.R. Rep. No. 82–127, Background Information on the Use of United States Armed Forces in Foreign Countries, 82d Cong., 1st Sess. (Feb. 20, 1951).

102. Powers of the President to Send the U.S. Armed Forces Outside the United States, 82d Cong., 1st Sess. (Comm. Print Feb. 28, 1951).

103. S. Res. 99, 82d Cong. (1951).

104. 343 U.S. 579 (1952).

105. See id. at 642 (Jackson, J., concurring).

106. See 69 Stat. 7 (1955); 71 Stat 5 (1957). The Taiwan authorization was repealed in 1974, but the Middle East authorization is still in effect today. See Matthew Waxman, Remembering Eisenhower's Middle East Force Resolution, Lawfare (Mar. 9, 2019). Its scope is uncertain, however—it states vaguely that the use of force "shall be consonant with the treaty obligations of the United States and with the Constitution of the United States."

107. Message from the President to the Congress (Jan. 24, 1955).

108. Statement by the President following the Landing of United States Marines at Beirut (July 15, 1958).

109. For accounts of the crisis, see, e.g., Robert F. Kennedy, Thirteen Days: A Memoir of the Cuban Missile Crisis (1969); Max Hastings, The Abyss: Nuclear Crisis Cuba 1962 (2022); Serhii Plokhy, Nuclear Folly: A History of the Cuban Missile Crisis (2021).

110. See S.J. Res. 230, Pub. L. No. 87–733 (Oct. 3, 1962). See also Patrick Hulme, Remembering the Cuban Missile Crisis: Executive Unilateralism or Congressional Drive toward the Brink?, Lawfare (Oct. 24, 2023).

111. Pub. L. No. 88–408, § 1, 78 Stat. 384 (1964).

112. Lyle Denniston, The Vietnam War and Its Constitutional Legacy—Part I, National Constitution Center (Sept. 19, 2017).

113. See, e.g., Massachusetts v. Laird, 451 F.2d 26 (1st Cir. 1971); Orlando v. Laird, 443 F.2d 1039 (2d Cir. 1971). In one case, a district court judge enjoined U.S. bombing in Cambodia. The injunction, however, was stayed by the appeals court. Although Justice Douglas on the Supreme Court briefly lifted the stay, his order was quickly overturned by Justice Marshall, in a ruling supported by the rest of the justices. The appeals court then overturned the district court's injunction on the basis of the political question doctrine. See Holtzman v. Schlesinger, 484 F.2d 1307 (2d Cir. 1973).

114. Leonard C. Meeker, The Legality of United States Participation in the Defense of Viet-Nam, 54 Dep't of State Bull. 474 (1966).

115. In fact, as discussed earlier in this chapter, Congress authorized most of the military actions in the war with France.

116. Memorandum from William H. Rehnquist, Assistant Attorney General, Office of Legal Counsel, Presidential Authority to Permit Incursion into Communist Sanctuaries in the Cambodian Border Area (May 14, 1970).

117. Memorandum from William H. Rehnquist, Assistant Attorney General, to Charles W. Colson, Special Counsel to the President, The President and the War Power: South Vietnam and the Cambodian Sanctuaries (May 22, 1970).

118. Pub. L. No. 93–148 (1973), codified at 50 U.S.C. §§ 1541–1548. In his veto message, Nixon argued, among other things, that the Resolution "would attempt to take away, by a mere legislative act, authorities which the President has properly exercised under the Constitution for almost 200 years."

119. See Memorandum from John M. Harmon, Office of Legal Counsel, to the Attorney General, Presidential Power to Use the Armed Forces without Statutory Authorization, 4A Op. O.L.C. 185, 196 (Feb. 12, 1980); Hearing on Libya and War Powers, Senate Committee on Foreign Relations, 112th Cong., 1st Sess. 53 (statement of Harold Hongju Koh, Legal Adviser, Dep't of State).

120. See, e.g., Randolph D. Moss, Assistant Attorney General, Authorization for Continuing Hostilities in Kosovo, 24 Op. O.L.C. 327 (2000); Hearing on Libya and War Powers, supra note 119, at 9 (testimony by Harold Koh).

121. See Cong. Res. Serv., The War Powers Resolution: Concepts and Practice, Appendix A (updated Mar. 8, 2019).

122. See, e.g., Deployment of U.S. Armed Forces into Haiti, 18 Op. O.L.C. 172, 175–76 (1994) ("The structure of the War Powers Resolution ('WPR') recognizes and presupposes the existence of unilateral presidential authority to deploy armed forces.").

123. Memorandum from John M. Harmon, supra note 119, at 187.

124. See Scott R. Anderson, Taiwan, War Powers, and Constitutional Crisis, 64 Va. J. Int'l L. 171, 204–18 (2023) (reviewing the development of this test and considering why the executive branch appears to be inconsistent in committing to it).

125. Memorandum Opinion from Timothy E. Flanigan for the Attorney General, Authority to Use U.S. Military Forces in Somalia (Dec. 4, 1992), 16 Op. Off. Legal Counsel 6, 8 (1992).

126. Letter from the President Regarding the Commencement of Operations in Libya (Mar. 21, 2011).

127. Memorandum Opinion for the Attorney General, Authority to Use Military Force in Libya, 35 Op. O.L.C. 20 (Apr. 1, 2011).

128. For a critique of OLC's analysis, including what it gleaned from the historical practice, see Michael J. Glennon, The Cost of "Empty Words": A Comment on the Justice Department's Libya Opinion, Harv. Nat'l Security J. F. (2011) (online).

129. For an argument that OLC's national interests test is an empty limitation, see Curtis Bradley & Jack Goldsmith, OLC's Meaningless "National Interests" Test for the Legality of Presidential Uses of Force, Lawfare (June 5, 2018).

130. See Curtis A. Bradley & Jack L. Goldsmith, Congressional Authorization and the War on Terrorism, 118 Harv. L. Rev. 2047 (2005). See also, e.g., William Michael Treanor, The War Powers outside the Courts, in The Constitution in Wartime: Beyond Alarmism and Complacency 144 (2005) ("It is hard for me to see that this is actually a difficult issue.").

131. See John Hart Ely, War and Responsibility: Constitutional Lessons of Vietnam and Its Aftermath 117 (1993).

132. See Richard F. Grimmett, Congressional Use of Funding Cutoffs Since 1970 Involving U.S. Military Forces and Overseas Deployments, at 3 (Cong. Res. Serv., Jan. 16, 2007). See also Memorandum from John M. Harmon, supra note 119, at 187; Fisher, supra note 13, at 44.

133. See Scott R. Anderson, The Underappreciated Legacy of the War Powers Resolution, Lawfare (Nov. 9, 2023); Jane C. Stromseth, Understanding Constitutional War Powers Today: Why Methodology Matters, 106 Yale L.J. 845, 883 (1996) (reviewing Louis Fisher, Presidential War Power [1995]).

134. See also Zeisberg, supra note 77, at 7; Peter J. Spiro, War Powers and the Sirens of Formalism, 68 N.Y.U. L. Rev. 1338, 1340 (1993) (reviewing Ely, supra note 131). Many scholars have argued that the Constitution's original understanding was that the president would not have the authority to initiate even smaller-scale hostilities. See, e.g., Ely, supra note 131, at 3; Michael D. Ramsey, Textualism and War Powers, 69 U. Chi. L. Rev. 1543, 1547 (2002).

135. See, e.g., David Gray Adler, The Constitution and Presidential Warmaking, in The Constitution and the Conduct of American Foreign Policy 183 (David Gray Adler & Larry N. George eds., 1996); Francis D. Wormuth & Edwin B. Firmage, To Chain the Dog of War: The War Powers of Congress in History and Law 28 (2d ed. 1989). See also Stephen M. Griffin, Long Wars and the Constitution 32 (2013) (referring to the "1950 thesis").

136. Contrary to what Professor Stephen Griffin has suggested, the fact that some historic uses of force were carried out pursuant to problematic foreign policies (such as gunboat diplomacy) does not make them irrelevant as precedent: these historic actions contributed to an understanding that presidents could use force in some instances without congressional authorization (a legal question), even if we might reject today some of the foreign policy rationales for those actions (a policy question). Cf. Stephen M. Griffin, Against Historical Practice: Facing Up to the Challenge of Informal Constitutional Change, 35 Const. Comm. 79, 94–95 (2020).

7. Congress's Gloss-Based Authority

1. Military Order, Detention, Treatment, and Trial of Certain Non-Citizens in the War Against Terrorism (Nov. 13, 2021).

2. Brief for Respondents, Hamdan v. Rumsfeld, No. 05–184, at 8 (Feb. 2006).

3. Id. at 22. The Justice Department's Office of Legal Counsel also took the position that Congress could not regulate the presidential use of military commissions. See Memorandum for Daniel J. Bryant, Assistant Attorney General, Office of Legislative Affairs, from Patrick F. Philbin, Deputy Assistant Attorney General, Office of Legal Counsel, Re: Swift Justice Authorization Act at 2, 12 (Apr. 8, 2002).

4. 548 U.S. 557 (2006).

5. See 10 U.S.C. § 836(b). For disagreement with the Court's reading of the statute, see 548 U.S. at 711–12 (Thomas, J., dissenting).

6. Id. at 593 n.23.

7. See, e.g., id. at 593 & n.22 (noting that the reference could be traced back to the 1916 Articles of War). See also id. at 595 (plurality opinion) ("The common law governing military commissions may be gleaned from past practice and what sparse legal precedent exists.").

8. See Military Commissions Act of 2006, Pub. L. 109–366, 120 Stat. 2600 (Oct. 16, 2006).

9. See, e.g., Stewart Jay, The Status of the Law of Nations in Early American Law, 42 Vand. L. Rev. 819, 846 (1989).

10. 1 Stat. 381 (June 5, 1794). For the current version of the Neutrality Act, see 18 U.S.C. §§ 958–60.

11. The shift away from a formal "advice" role for the Senate in the treaty process, which began during the George Washington administration and was eventually accepted by the Senate, is another element of the constitutional law of foreign relations that is rooted in historical practice. See Samuel B. Crandall, Treaties: Their Making and Enforcement 70–71 (2d

ed. 1916); Charles C. Tansill, The Treaty-Making Powers of the Senate, 18 Am. J. Int'l L. 459 (1924).

12. See Sen. Exec. J., 4th Cong., Special Sess., June 14, 1795, at 186.

13. See Abraham D. Sofaer, War, Foreign Affairs and Constitutional Power 96 (1976). After deciding to accept the Senate's condition, Washington concluded (after getting advice from his cabinet) that he did not need to resubmit the treaty to the Senate for its approval, "thus setting a precedent which has been followed ever since." 2 George H. Haynes, The Senate of the United States: Its History and Practice 607 (1938).

14. See 5 John Bassett Moore, A Digest of International Law 199–201 (1906); William W. Bishop Jr., Reservations to Treaties, 103 Recueil des Cours 245, 266–67 (1961).

15. See Ralston Hayden, The Senate and Treaties, 1789–1817, at 150 (1920).

16. See, e.g., Haynes, supra note 13, at 613. The international law rules governing conditions attached to multilateral treaties are more complicated, but in general international law permits them unless they are expressly or implicitly prohibited by the treaty. See Vienna Convention on the Law of Treaties, arts. 19–23, May 23, 1969, 1155 U.N.T.S. 331.

17. For a collection of examples up through the early twentieth century, see David Hunter Miller, Reservations to Treaties: Their Effect, and the Procedure in Regard Thereto (1919).

18. Cong. Res. Serv., 106th Cong., Treaties and Other International Agreements: The Role of the United States Senate 125–26 (Comm. Print 2001) [hereinafter CRS Study].

19. Restatement (Fourth) of the Foreign Relations Law of the United States § 305(2) (2018); CRS Study, supra note 18, at 124. The conditions are binding—that is, as long as they relate to the treaty and do not conflict with the Constitution. See Restatement (Fourth), supra, § 305(1); H. Jefferson Powell, The President's Authority over Foreign Affairs: An Executive Branch Perspective, 67 Geo. Wash. L. Rev. 527, 562 (1999); Constitutionality of Proposed Conditions to Senate Consent to the Interim Convention on Conservation of North Pacific Fur Seals, 10 Op. O.L.C. 12, 17–18 (1986).

20. As discussed in Chapter 4, for example, the Theodore Roosevelt administration initially declined to conclude arbitration treaties because of conditions imposed by the Senate. See also Chandler P. Anderson, The Senate and Obligatory Arbitration Treaties, 26 Am. J. Int'l L. 328 (1932).

21. Kevin C. Kennedy, Conditional Approval of Treaties by the U.S. Senate, 19 Loy. L.A. Int'l & Comp. L.J. 89 (1996). See also Stefan A. Riesenfeld & Frederick M. Abbott, The Scope of U.S. Senate Control over the Conclusion and Operation of Treaties, 67 U. Chi.-Kent L. Rev. 571, 586 (1991) (calculating that 17.5 percent of treaties ratified by the United States from 1970 to 1987 were subject to conditions).

22. See David P. Currie, The Constitution in Congress: The Federalist Period, 1789–1801, at 211 (1997).

23. See, e.g., Michael J. Glennon, Constitutional Diplomacy 68 (1990); Riesenfeld & Abbott, supra note 21, at 584–85; John Bassett Moore, Treaties and Executive Agreements, 20 Pol. Sci. Q. 385, 417 (1905).

24. See Curtis A. Bradley & Jack L. Goldsmith, Treaties, Human Rights, and Conditional Consent, 149 U. Pa. L. Rev. 399, 408 (2000).

25. See, e.g., Riesenfeld & Abbott, supra note 21, at 599.

26. When suggesting the use of non-self-execution declarations in connection with human rights treaties it submitted to the Senate in the 1970s, the Carter administration explained that

the rights guaranteed by the treaties were generally protected under existing U.S. law and that it was "preferable to leave any further implementation that may be desired to the domestic legislative and judicial process." Message from the President Transmitting Four Treaties Pertaining to Human Rights, 92d Cong., 2d Sess. viii (Feb. 23, 1978).

27. See Sosa v. Alvarez-Machain, 542 U.S. 692, 735 (2004) (noting that the United States ratified the International Covenant on Civil and Political Rights "on the express understanding that it was not self-executing and so did not itself create obligations enforceable in the federal courts").

28. See, e.g., Renkel v. United States, 456 F.3d 640, 644 (6th Cir. 2006) ("We, along with several of our sister courts, have given judicial effect to the Senate's declaration."). For a decision that raised constitutional questions about a reservation that was akin to a non-self-execution declaration, see Power Authority of New York v. Federal Power Commission, 247 F.3d 538 (D.C. Cir. 1957), vacated and remanded with directions to dismiss as moot, 355 U.S. 64 (1957). For an argument that the reservation in that case was not constitutionally problematic, see Louis Henkin, The Treaty Makers and the Law Makers: The Niagara Reservation, 56 Colum. L. Rev. 1151 (1956).

29. Zivotofsky v. Kerry, 576 U.S. 1 (2015).

30. See Jack Goldsmith, How the Supreme Court Should Resolve Zivotofsky, Lawfare (Oct. 30, 2014); Marty Lederman, The Article I Argument in Zivotofsky, Just Security (Oct. 30, 2014); Michael Ramsey, Zivotofsky on Monday, Originalism Blog (Aug. 31, 2014). But see Eugene Kontorovich, The Article I Power in Zivotofsky v. Kerry, Volokh Conspiracy (Oct. 30, 2014).

31. 576 U.S. 1, 45 (2015) (Thomas, J., concurring in the judgment and dissenting in part).

32. Id. at 83 (Scalia, J., dissenting).

33. See Brief for the United States Senate as Amicus Curiae Supporting Petitioner, Zivotofsky v. Kerry, No. 13–628 (July 22, 2014).

34. See U.S. Dep't of State, The American Passport: Its History and a Digest of Laws, Rulings and Regulations Governing Its Issuance 3–4 (1898).

35. Urtetiqui v. D'Arcy, 34 U.S. 692, 699 (1835).

36. 2 Stat. 203, 205 (Feb. 28, 1803).

37. 3 Stat. 195, 199 (Jan. 30, 1815).

38. See 34 U.S. at 699 ("There is no law of the United States in any manner regulating the issuing of passports, or directing upon what evidence it may be done, or declaring their legal effect. It is understood as matter of practice that some evidence of citizenship is required by the Secretary of State before issuing a passport. This, however, is entirely discretionary with him."). See also Haig v. Agee, 453 U.S. 280, 294 (1981) (noting that, before 1856, "the common perception was that the issuance of a passport was committed to the sole discretion of the Executive and that the Executive would exercise this power in the interests of the national security and foreign policy of the United States").

39. 11 Stat. 52, 60 (Aug. 18, 1856). See also Craig Robertson, The Passport in America: The History of a Document 141 (2010).

40. See, e.g., 22 U.S.C. § 2714 (drug traffickers); 22 U.S.C. § 2121a (sex tourists).

41. 108 Stat. 395, § 132 (Apr. 30, 1994).

42. See U.S. Dep't of State, 8 Foreign Affairs Manual § 403.4–4(D). Justice Thomas claimed that "the President's decision to adopt [the allowance called for by the Taiwan statute] . . . says nothing about the constitutionality of the Taiwan provision in the first place." 576 U.S. at 52.

But it is relevant if one is willing to credit historical gloss. That does not mean, however, that the Jerusalem passport statute was valid. As discussed in Chapter 3, the Taiwan statute did not directly conflict with presidential recognition policy concerning Taiwan (since the passport designation did not say that Taiwan was an independent nation), so this example does not necessarily support a claim that Congress has authority over the issue of recognition, which was another issue in *Zivotofsky.*

43. 576 U.S. at 84 (Scalia, J., dissenting).

44. Cf. id. at 82 (Scalia, J., dissenting) ("To be sure, early Presidents granted passports without express congressional authorization. But this point establishes Presidential authority over passports in the face of congressional *silence,* not Presidential authority in the face of congressional *opposition.*").

45. Bill to Relocate United States Embassy from Tel Aviv to Jerusalem, 19 Op. O.L.C. 123, 124 (1995).

46. Legislation Prohibiting Spending for Delegations to U.N. Agencies Chaired by Countries That Support Int'l Terrorism, 33 Op. O.L.C. 221, 231 (2009).

47. See Congressionally Mandated Notice Period for Withdrawing from the Open Skies Treaty, 44 Op. O.L.C., slip op. (2020). I critique that particular claim in Chapter 5.

48. See generally Jean Galbraith, The Runaway Presidential Power over Diplomacy, 108 Va. L. Rev. 81 (2022). See also, e.g., Eli E. Nobleman, Financial Aspects of Congressional Participation in Foreign Relations, 289 Annals Am. Acad. Pol. & Soc. Sci. 145 (1953).

49. See 576 U.S. at 21 ("In a world that is ever more compressed and interdependent, it is essential the congressional role in foreign affairs be understood and respected. For it is Congress that makes laws, and in countless ways its laws will and should shape the Nation's course.").

50. See David E. Sanger & Matt Flegenheimer, Congress Set to Prod Trump, Who Denies Russia Meddled, to Punish Moscow, N.Y. Times (June 13, 2017).

51. See Jennifer Steinhauer, Mark Mazzetti, and Julia Hirschfield Davis, Congress Votes to Override Obama Veto on 9/11 Victims Bill, N.Y. Times (Sept. 28, 2016). Since 1976, Congress has comprehensively regulated foreign sovereign immunity in U.S. courts and in the Foreign Sovereign Immunities Act and on a number of occasions has adopted amendments to the Act over objections from the executive branch. This is true even though, before the enactment of the statute, the executive branch had significant control over immunity determinations.

52. See David H. Moore, The Missing D in U.S. Foreign Relations Law, 109 Geo. L.J. 1139 (2021); see also Edward Wong, Annie Karni, and Emily Cochrane, Trump Administration Drops Proposal to Cut Foreign Aid after Intense Debate, N.Y. Times (Aug. 22, 2019).

53. See Eric Schmitt, Senate Kills Test Ban Treaty in Crushing Loss for Clinton; Evokes Versailles Pact Defeat, N.Y. Times (Oct. 14, 1999).

54. See American Servicemembers' Protection Act, P.L. 107–206, title II, 116 Stat. 889 (2002), codified at 22 U.S.C. §§ 7421 *et seq.*

55. See Restatement (Fourth) of the Foreign Relations Law of the United States § 441(1) (2018); see also, e.g., Banco Nacional de Cuba v. Farr, 383 F.2d 166, 182 (2d Cir. 1967) ("Since Congress thus clearly possesses a constitutional interest in the problem involved in this case, it was entitled to make its will known by means of a statute.").

56. See generally Elmer Plischke, U.S. Department of State: A Reference History (1999); Graham Henry Stuart, The Department of State: A History of Its Organization, Procedure and

Personnel (1949); Gaillard Hunt, The Department of State of the United States: Its History and Functions (1914).

57. Congress initially established a Department of Foreign Affairs but then quickly changed its name to the Department of State because it was assigning it some domestic duties (such as dealing with patents, managing the mint, and conducting the census). See 1 Stat. 28 (July 27, 1789); 1 Stat. 68 (Sept. 15, 1789).

58. See 22 U.S.C. § 2651a.

59. See 1 U.S.C. § 112a; 1 U.S.C. § 112b. The publication statute dates back to 1950, and the reporting statute dates back to 1972. See Oona A. Hathaway, Curtis A. Bradley, and Jack L. Goldsmith, The Failed Transparency Regime for Executive Agreements: An Empirical and Normative Analysis, 134 Harv. L. Rev. 629, 645–51 (2020).

60. See 22 U.S.C. § 2656f.

61. These reports are required by, among other things, the Foreign Assistance Act of 1961. See 22 U.S.C. § 2304(b).

62. See National Defense Authorization Act for Fiscal Year 2022, § 5105 (requiring, among other things, Senate advice and consent for long-term appointments involving the exercise of significant authority, and imposing various reporting requirements); Ryan Scoville, An Important Development in the Law of Diplomatic Appointments, Lawfare (Jan. 31, 2022).

63. See 22 U.S.C. § 3903 *et seq.* See generally Harry W. Kopp, The Voice of the Foreign Service: A History of the American Foreign Service Association (2015).

64. See Ryan M. Scoville, Unqualified Ambassadors, 69 Duke L.J. 71, 164–66 (2019).

65. See 22 U.S.C. § 6085(c)(1)(b). Until President Trump stopped doing so in 2019, presidents had consistently invoked the suspension provision. See Niraj Chokshi & Frances Robles, Trump Administration Announces New Restrictions on Dealing with Cuba, N.Y. Times (Apr. 17, 2019). Presidents are not allowed to suspend already-pending claims. See 22 U.S.C. § 6082(h)(2).

66. 110 Stat. 3009–116 (Sept. 30, 1996).

67. See 22 U.S.C. § 2371(c).

68. Iran Nuclear Agreement Review Act of 2015, Pub. L. No. 114–17, § 135(d)(6).

69. See 130 Stat. 93 (Feb. 18, 2016).

70. See Mark A. Chinen, Presidential Certifications in U.S. Foreign Policy Legislation, 31 Int'l L. & Pol. 217, 219 (1999) ("Certification requirements—laws that require the President to certify as to particular conditions before acting—appear throughout U.S. foreign policy legislation."). See also David Manners-Weber, Comment, Certification as Sabotage: Lessons from Guantanamo Bay, 127 Yale L.J. 1416 (2018).

71. See 22 U.S.C. § 5811 note. The act extended and made global a 2012 statute that imposed sanctions on individuals involved in the detention, abuse, or death of Sergei Magnitsky, a Russian accountant who exposed Russian government corruption. See Cong. Res. Serv., The Global Magnitsky Human Rights Accountability Act (Dec. 3, 2021).

72. See § 1263(d) of the Act.

73. President Barack Obama, Statement on Signing the National Defense Authorization Act for Fiscal Year 2017 (Dec. 23, 2016).

74. Despite imposing sanctions, the Trump administration declined to report to Congress within 120 days as called for by the Act. A potential constitutional problem with the reporting requirement is that it is triggered by congressional action that does not involve the enactment

of a statute and thus might run afoul of the Supreme Court's decision in INS v. Chadha, 462 U.S. 919 (1983). See Ryan Goodman, Trump's Invoking Obama Signing Statement as Reason Not to Report to Congress on Khashoggi Murder: A Roundup of Expert Views, Just Security (Feb. 28, 2019).

75. See Paul Mozur, Amy Chang Chien, and Michael D. Shear, Nancy Pelosi Arrives in Taiwan, Drawing a Sharp Response from Beijing, N.Y. Times (Aug. 2, 2022).

76. See David Stout & Hassan M. Fattah, Bush Assails Pelosi's Trip to Syria, N.Y. Times (Apr. 3, 2007).

77. See Julie Hirschfield Davis, White House, Citing Israeli Election, Says Obama and Netanyahu Won't Meet, N.Y. Times (Jan. 22, 2015); Helene Cooper, Invitation to Israeli Leader Puts Obama on the Spot, N.Y. Times (Apr. 20, 2011). For examples of nonexecutive diplomacy from the early twentieth century, see Edward S. Corwin, The President: Office and Powers 184 (4th ed. 1957); Haynes, supra note 13, at 680–85. For later examples, see Ryan Scoville, Legislative Diplomacy, 112 Mich. L. Rev. 331, 351–54 (2013).

78. U.S. Senate, An Open Letter to the Leaders of the Islamic Republic of Iran (Mar. 9, 2015). Some of the reasoning in the letter seemed confused about constitutional practice with respect to both treaties and executive agreements. See Curtis A. Bradley, Republicans Fail in an Attempt at a Civics Lecture to Iranian Leaders, Conversation (Mar. 11, 2015).

79. See Steven V. Roberts, Letter to Nicaragua: "Dear Commandante," N.Y. Times (Apr. 24, 1984).

80. See Scoville, supra note 77.

81. The Logan Act, which has been around since 1799, provides for criminal punishment of "any citizen . . . who, without authority of the United States, directly or indirectly commences or carries on any correspondence or intercourse with any foreign government or any officer or agent thereof, with intent to influence the measures or conduct of any foreign government or of any officer or agent thereof, in relation to any disputes or controversies with the United States, or to defeat the measures of the United States." 18 U.S.C. § 953. The Act was passed after a private citizen traveled to France while the United States was preparing for hostilities against that country and attempted to negotiate a peace settlement. No one has ever been convicted of violating the act (although there were a couple of indictments under the act during the nineteenth century), and there are questions about whether the Act is constitutional and whether and to what extent it applies to members of Congress. The Act has nevertheless been invoked at various times by the executive branch—for example, to advise people not to engage in particular conduct and to provide a basis for passport restrictions. There are also periodic allegations that individuals—including sometimes members of Congress—have violated the Act as a result of their interactions with foreign officials. For discussions of the Act and its implications, see Daniel B. Rice, Nonenforcement by Accretion: The Logan Act and the Take Care Clause, 55 Harv. J. Legis. 443 (2018); Detlev F. Vagts, The Logan Act: Paper Tiger or Sleeping Giant?, 60 Am. J. Int'l L. 268 (1966); Daniel J. Hemel & Eric A. Posner, The Logan Act and Its Limits, Lawfare (Dec. 7, 2017); Cong. Res. Serv., Conducting Foreign Relations without Authority: The Logan Act (Mar. 11, 2015).

82. Although the topic is beyond the scope of this book, U.S. states and municipalities have also long engaged in diplomacy. See, e.g., Michael J. Glennon & Robert D. Sloane, Foreign Affairs Federalism: The Myth of National Exclusivity (2016); Curtis A. Bradley, State International Agreements: The United States, Canada, and Constitutional Evolution, 60 Can.

Y.B. Int'l L. 6 (2023); Ryan M. Scoville, The International Commitments of the Fifty States, 70 UCLA L. Rev. 310 (2023); Julian G. Ku, Gubernatorial Foreign Policy, 115 Yale L.J. 2380 (2006).

83. 22 U.S.C. § 287a.

84. See 552 U.S. 491, 527 (2008).

85. See Katie Rogers & Apoorva Mandivilli, Trump Administration Signals Formal Withdrawal from W.H.O., N.Y. Times (July 7, 2020). When President Biden took office in January 2021, the one-year period had not yet elapsed, and he immediately revoked the notice of withdrawal. See Christina Morales, Biden Restores Ties with the World Health Organization That Were Cut by Trump, N.Y. Times (Jan. 20, 2021).

86. See Christopher Marquis, Satisfied with UN Reforms, Helms Relents on Back Dues, N.Y. Times (Jan. 10, 2001).

87. Kristina Daugirdas, Congress Underestimated: The Case of the World Bank, 107 Am. J. Int'l L. 517, 519, 561 (2013).

88. 88 Stat. 445 (1974).

89. 110 Stat. 785 § 105 (Mar. 12, 1996).

90. William J. Clinton, Statement on Signing the Cuban Liberty and Democratic Solidarity (Libertad) Act of 1996 (Mar. 12, 1996). For an appeals court decision holding that a statutory mandate telling the executive to initiate treaty negotiations concerning the protection of sea turtles unconstitutionally infringed on executive power, see Earth Island Institute v. Christopher, 6 F.3d 648, 650 (9th Cir. 1993). The executive branch nevertheless negotiated a treaty protecting sea turtles, which it ratified in 1998. See Inter-American Convention for the Protection and Conservation of Sea Turtles (entered into force on May 22, 1998). In its submission of the treaty to the Senate, the executive branch noted that Congress had called for the negotiation of such a treaty. See William J. Clinton, Letter of Transmittal (May 22, 1998).

91. 123 Stat. 524.

92. Statement on Signing the Omnibus Appropriations Act (Mar. 11, 2009).

93. See Legislation Prohibiting, supra note 46.

94. See Galbraith, supra note 48, at 89 ("While historical practice is often thought to be a tool of presidential power, it is notable how much historical practice there is—albeit uncited by OLC—that supports Congress's authority to issue mandates with respect to international engagement.").

95. Application of the Anti-Terrorism Act of 1987 to Diplomatic Visit of Palestinian Delegation, 46 Op. O.L.C., slip op. at 7 (Oct. 28, 2022); see also Statement from President Joe Biden on H.R. 2670 (Dec. 22, 2023) (statement by the president that he "recognize[s] that '[i]t is not for the President alone to determine the whole content of the Nation's foreign policy' [*Zivotofsky v. Kerry*]"). A 1913 statute, which is still on the books, says that the executive branch "shall not extend or accept any invitation to participate in any international congress, conference, or like event, without first having specific authority of law to do so." 37 Stat. 913 (1913). The executive branch does not follow this statute, and its failure to do so does not appear to have generated controversy. See Louis Henkin, Foreign Affairs and the United States Constitution 118 (2d ed. 1996) (referring to the law as a "known dead letter"). See also Henry M. Wriston, American Participation in International Conferences, 20 Am. J. Int'l L. 33 (1926) (criticizing the statute).

96. See Daugirdas, supra note 87, at 545 (noting that, for the World Bank, "there is no indication that Congress began to doubt its constitutional authority; Congress continued to

legislate negotiation and voting instructions; and individual members continued to threaten funding cuts").

97. See 576 U.S. at 13 (noting that "the President has the sole power to negotiate treaties"); United States v. Curtiss-Wright Export Corp., 299 U.S. 304, 319 (1936) (noting that the president "makes treaties with the advice and consent of the Senate; but he alone negotiates").

98. See Galbraith, supra note 48, at 100–101.

99. 110 Stat. 3009, 3009–166 (Sept. 30, 1996).

100. See Crosby v. National Foreign Trade Council, 530 U.S. 363, 381 (2000).

101. See 129 Stat. 201 (May 22, 2015), codified at 42 U.S.C. § 2160e.

102. Congress has also long regulated information disclosure by the executive branch, including for materials relating to foreign affairs, through statutes such as the Freedom of Information Act and the Classified Information Procedures Act. See Jared Cole, Note, Historical Gloss and Congressional Power: Control over Access to National Security Secrets, 99 Va. L. Rev. 1855 (2013). Although not explored in this book, arguments about the scope of "executive privilege"—that is, the right of the executive branch to withhold certain materials from the other branches of government—have been heavily informed by historical practice, and this has been true since shortly after the Founding. In 1796, in refusing to turn over to the House of Representatives negotiation materials concerning the Jay Treaty, George Washington appealed to historical practice. See George Washington, Message to the House regarding Documents Relative to the Jay Treaty (Mar. 30, 1796) ("In this construction of the Constitution every House of Representatives has heretofore acquiesced, and until the present time not a doubt or suspicion has appeared, to my knowledge, that this construction was not the true one."). See also Jean Galbraith, Getting the Jay Treaty Right on "Executive Privilege," Just Security (Oct. 4, 2019).

103. Youngstown Sheet & Tube Co. v. Sawyer, 343 U.S. 579, 641 (1952) (Jackson, J., concurring).

104. See, e.g., Swaim v. United States, 28 Ct. Cl. 173, 221 (1893) ("Congress may increase the Army, or reduce the Army, or abolish it altogether; but so long as we have a military force Congress can not take away from the President the supreme command."), aff'd, 165 U.S. 553 (1897).

105. Placing of United States Armed Forces Under United Nations Operational or Tactical Control, 20 Op. O.L.C. 182 (May 8, 1996). The bill would have allowed for a presidential waiver of the restriction if the president certified to Congress fifteen days in advance of the placement that it was "in the national security interests of the United States to place any element of the armed forces under United Nations operational or tactical control" and provided a detailed report to Congress containing specific types of information.

106. 1 Stat. 613 (Feb. 9, 1799) (emphasis added).

107. Little v. Barreme, 6 U.S. (2 Cranch) 170 (1804). For an account of the decision, see Michael J. Glennon, Two Views of Presidential Foreign Affairs Power: Little v. Barreme or Curtiss-Wright?, 13 Yale J. Int'l L. 5 (1988).

108. Marshall also noted that he had initially been of the view that the captain should not be personally liable since the captain had merely been following instructions. But Marshall said that he had been convinced that he was mistaken and that "the instructions cannot change the nature of the transaction or legalize an act which without those instructions would have been a plain trespass." After this decision, Congress enacted a statute indemnifying the captain for the damage award. See 6 Stat. 63 (1807).

109. 12 U.S. (8 Cranch) 110 (1814).

110. Justice Story dissented, arguing that the declaration of war should be construed as conveying to the president the power to take all wartime actions allowed by the international laws of war, including seizing enemy property. Story acknowledged, however, that "if, indeed, there be a limit imposed [by Congress] as to the extent to which hostilities may be carried by the executive, . . . the executive cannot lawfully transcend that limit."

111. See Curtis A. Bradley & Jack L. Goldsmith, Congressional Authorization and the War on Terrorism, 118 Harv. L. Rev. 2047, 2093–94 (2005).

112. 1 Stat. 381, 384 § 8 (June 5, 1794).

113. 1 Stat. 424, 424 (Feb. 2, 1795).

114. Bradley & Goldsmith, supra note 111, at 2072.

115. See David J. Barron & Martin S. Lederman, The Commander in Chief at the Lowest Ebb—A Constitutional History, 121 Harv. L. Rev. 941, 958–60, 973–74 (2008). Under the Antideficiency Act, the first version of which dates back to 1870, a federal officer or employee "may not make or authorize an expenditure or obligation exceeding an amount available in an appropriation or fund for the expenditure or obligation," and violations are subject to possible criminal punishment. 31 U.S.C. § 1341.

116. See Barron & Lederman, supra note 115, at 1041–47.

117. See, e.g., Clarence A. Berdahl, War Powers of the Executive of the United States 231 (1921). But see Edward S. Corwin, The Power of Congress to Declare Peace, 18 Mich. L. Rev. 669, 675 (1920). See also Avery C. Rasmussen & Saikrishna Bangalore Prakash, The Peace Powers: How to End a War, 170 U. Pa. L. Rev. 717 (2022).

118. The Quasi-War ended with the Convention of 1800, the Barbary wars ended through the 1805 Treaty of Tripoli and the 1815 Algerian Treaty, the War of 1812 ended with the 1815 Treaty of Ghent, the Mexican-American War ended with the 1848 Treaty of Guadalupe Hidalgo, and the Spanish-American War ended with the 1898 Treaty of Paris.

119. 42 Stat. 105 (July 2, 1921). Harding then negotiated treaties giving effect to what Congress had done.

120. 65 Stat. 451 (Oct. 19, 1951).

121. 84 Stat. 2053 (Jan. 12, 1971).

122. 84 Stat. 1942 (Jan. 5, 1971).

123. See generally Cong. Res. Serv., Congressional Restrictions on U.S. Military Operations in Vietnam, Cambodia, Laos, Somalia, and Kosovo: Funding and Non-Funding Approaches (Jan. 16, 2007).

124. See S.J. Res. 159, 97 Stat. 805 (1983).

125. See 107 Stat. 1418, 1475–77 (Nov. 11, 1993).

126. See S.J. Res. 7, 116th Cong. (2019).

127. Presidential Veto Message to the Senate to Accompany S.J. Res. 7 (Apr. 16, 2019).

128. 33 U.S.C. §§ 1541–50.

129. The period can be extended by an additional thirty days if the president certifies to Congress that "unavoidable military necessity respecting the safety of United States Armed Forces requires the continued use of such armed forces in the course of bringing about a prompt removal of such forces."

130. See, e.g., David P. Auerswald & Peter F. Cowhey, The War Powers Resolution and the Use of Force, 41 Int'l Stud. Q. 505 (1997) (finding that presidents limit the duration of the use

of force in response to the War Powers Resolution). See also Louis Fisher, Presidential War Power 150 (3d ed. 2013) (observing that "military operations in Grenada and Panama were conducted as though the 60-day limit was enforceable—if not legally, then politically").

131. See generally Matthew C. Weed, The War Powers Resolution: Concepts and Practice (Cong. Res. Serv., Mar. 8, 2019).

132. See Memorandum from John C. Yoo, Deputy Assistant Attorney General, to Daniel J. Bryant, Assistant Attorney General, Office of Legislative Affairs, Applicability of 18 U.S.C. § 4001(a) to Military Detention of United States Citizens 10 (June 27, 2002) ("Congress may no more regulate the President's ability to detain enemy combatants than it may regulate his ability to direct troop movements on the battlefield."). Like many of the war on terror memos, this one was overargued. It was addressing the issue of whether 18 U.S.C. § 4001(a), which states that "no citizen shall be imprisoned or otherwise detained by the United States except pursuant to an Act of Congress," applies to wartime detentions. There are reasonable arguments that the statute was not meant to apply in that context and that in any event Congress's post–September 11 authorization of force was sufficient to meet the statutory requirement. See Curtis A. Bradley & Jack L. Goldsmith, Congressional Authorization and the War on Terrorism, 118 Harv. L. Rev. 2047, 2106 (2005); Hamdi v. Rumsfeld, 542 U.S. 507, 517–19 (2004) (plurality opinion). Thus, there was no need to argue that Congress lacks the authority to regulate such detentions.

133. See Memorandum from Jay S. Bybee, Assistant Attorney General, for William J. Haynes II, General Counsel, Department of Defense, The President's Power as Commander in Chief to Transfer Captured Terrorists to the Control and Custody of Foreign Nations (Mar. 13, 2002); Memorandum from Jay S. Bybee to Alberto R. Gonzales, Standards of Conduct for Interrogation under 18 U.S.C. §§ 2340–2340A (Aug. 1, 2002). Once again, OLC overargued the memo. OLC took the position not only that the Bush administration's interrogation practices did not violate an anti-torture statute but that "any effort by Congress to regulate the interrogation of battlefield combatants would violate the Constitution's sole vesting of the Commander-in-Chief authority in the President." OLC also advocated in this memo a very narrow view of what constitutes torture, a position that it repudiated two years later.

134. 1 Stat. 95, 96 (Sept. 29, 1789).

135. See John Fabian Witt, Lincoln's Code: The Laws of War in American History (2012); see also Curtis A. Bradley, The Story of Ex Parte Milligan: Military Trials, Enemy Combatants, and Congressional Authorization, in Presidential Power Stories 99 (Christopher H. Schroeder & Curtis A. Bradley eds., 2009).

136. See 1 Stat. 624 (Feb. 28, 1799) (giving the president the power to "exchange or send away" French prisoners taken from captured vessels "as he may deem proper and expedient"); 1 Stat. 743 (1799) (authorizing and directing the president to retaliate against French prisoners if he learns that France has mistreated Americans who have been impressed into service). See also Ingrid Brunk Wuerth, The Captures Clause, 76 U. Chi. L. Rev. 1683, 1734 (2009).

137. 2 Stat. 777 (July 6, 1812).

138. See 2 Stat. 829 (Mar. 3, 1813).

139. For an argument that presidents are obligated to comply with the Geneva Conventions unless Congress provides otherwise, see Derek Jinks & David Sloss, Is the President Bound by the Geneva Conventions, 99 Cornell L. Rev. 97 (2004).

140. 18 U.S.C. § 2441.

141. Statement on Signing the War Crimes Act of 1996 (Aug. 21, 1996). Congress extended the jurisdictional reach of the statute in early 2023. See S. 4240, Pub. L. 117–351 (signed Jan. 5, 2023).

142. See 548 U.S. at 630–31.

143. Public Law 109–148, approved Dec. 30, 2005. See also Eric Lichtblau, Congress Adopts Restriction on Treatment of Detainees, N.Y. Times (May 11, 2005).

144. See, e.g., Guy Dinmore, CIA Forced Bush Hand on Secret Prisons, Financial Times (Sept. 21, 2006), at 1 (explaining that the Central Intelligence Agency largely halted its overseas interrogation program for high-level terrorist suspects).

145. See 18 U.S.C. § 2340A.

146. See Memorandum from Daniel Levin to James B. Comey, Deputy Att'y Gen., Legal Standards Applicable under 18 U.S.C. §§ 2340–2340A (Dec. 30, 2004) (analyzing the meaning of the statute but not suggesting that it is inapplicable to war on terror interrogations).

147. See Military Commissions Act of 2006, 120 Stat. 2632 (Oct. 17, 2006); Military Commissions Act of 2009, 123 Stat. 2190 (Oct. 28, 2009).

148. Memorandum from Daniel Levin, supra note 146. See also Curtis A. Bradley, The Bush Administration and International Law: Too Much Lawyering and Too Little Diplomacy, 4 Duke J. Const. L. & Pub. Pol'y 57, 70–71 (2009).

149. Memorandum for the Files, Status of Certain OLC Opinions Issued in the Aftermath of the Terrorist Attacks of September 11, 2001, at 2 (Jan. 15, 2009).

150. See 124 Stat. 4137, 4352 (Jan. 7, 2011).

151. Statement by the President on H.R. 1540 (Dec. 31, 2011).

152. For an argument that Obama had the constitutional authority to disregard the restriction, see Greg Craig & Cliff Sloan, The President Doesn't Need Congress's Permission to Close Guantanamo, Wash. Post (Nov. 6, 2015). For criticism of this argument, see Marty Lederman, The Insoluble Guantanamo Problem (Part Three: Executive Disregard of the GTMO-to-U.S. Relocation Prohibition Is Not a Solution), Just Security (Nov. 13, 2015).

153. See Letter from Susan A. Poling, Government Accountability Office, to Sen. Mitch McConnell et al. (Aug. 21, 2014). For an argument that the statutory restriction was likely unconstitutional because it related to "the immediate management of the war effort," see Michael Ramsey, The President's Power over Prisoners of War, Originalism Blog (June 2, 2014).

154. When presidents issue constitutional signing statements, this does not necessarily mean that they will fail to comply with a statutory provision. Often these objections appear to be raised merely to avoid the claim that the executive branch has acquiesced in a congressional assertion of authority. See Curtis A. Bradley & Eric A. Posner, Presidential Signing Statements and Executive Power, 23 Const. Comm. 307, 343 (2006).

8. Delegations of Authority

1. 48 Stat. 811 (May 28, 1934).

2. Presidential Proclamation 2087, Forbidding the Shipment of Arms to the Combatants in the Chaco (May 28, 1934).

3. United States v. Curtiss-Wright Export Corp., 14 F. Supp. 230 (S.D.N.Y. 1936). The district court reasoned that the executive branch, rather than Congress, was making the predictive evaluation about whether an arms embargo would contribute to peace. This was

constitutionally problematic, thought the court, because it is "the duty of Congress alone to conclude whether a given law will work."

4. In its brief before the Supreme Court, the U.S. government began its argument by contending: "From the beginning of the government, in the conduct of our foreign relations, Congress has followed the practice of conferring upon the President power similar to that conferred by the present resolution." Brief for the United States, United States v. Curtiss-Wright Export Co., No. 98, at 7 (Oct. 1936).

5. See Eric A. Posner & Adrian Vermeule, Interring the Nondelegation Doctrine, 69 U. Chi. L. Rev. 1721 (2002) (making this argument).

6. Cf. Wayman v. Southard, 23 U.S. 1, 43 (1825) (Marshall, C.J.) ("The line has not been exactly drawn which separates those important subjects which must be entirely regulated by the legislature itself from those of less interest in which a general provision may be made and power given to those who are to act under such general provisions to fill up the details.").

7. See, e.g., Mistretta v. United States, 488 U.S. 361, 372 (1989) ("Our jurisprudence has been driven by a practical understanding that, in our increasingly complex society, replete with ever-changing and more technical problems, Congress simply cannot do its job absent an ability to delegate power under broad general directives.").

8. 2 Westel Woodbury Willoughby, The Constitutional Law of the United States 1321 (1910).

9. See A. L. A. Schechter Poultry Corp. v. United States, 295 U.S. 495 (1935); Panama Refining Co. v. Ryan, 293 U.S. 388 (1935). These applications of the nondelegation doctrine to invalidate legislation both occurred in 1935. As one commentator quipped, the nondelegation doctrine "had one good year." Cass R. Sunstein, Nondelegation Canons, 67 U. Chi. L. Rev. 315, 322 (2000).

10. Panama Refining, 293 U.S. at 421.

11. J. W. Hampton Jr. & Co. v. United States, 276 U.S. 394, 409 (1928).

12. Whitman v. American Trucking Associations, 531 U.S. 457, 474 (2001).

13. See Gundy v. United States, 139 S. Ct. 2116, 2135–37 (2019) (Gorsuch, J., dissenting, joined by Chief Justice Roberts and Justice Thomas); id. at 2130–31 (Alito, J., concurring in the judgment); Paul v. United States, 140 S. Ct. 342, 342 (2019) (Kavanaugh, J., respecting the denial of certiorari).

14. See, e.g., West Virginia v. EPA, 142 S. Ct. 2587 (2022).

15. See, e.g., Gundy, 139 S. Ct. at 2144 (Gorsuch, J., dissenting); Department of Transp. v. Association of American Railroads, 575 U.S. 43, 80 n.5 (2015) (Thomas, J., concurring). A number of scholars have also made this distinction between delegations of domestic and foreign affairs authority. See, e.g., Michael W. McConnell, The President Who Would Not Be King 328–29 (2020); Michael B. Rappaport, The Selective Nondelegation Doctrine and the Line Item Veto: A New Approach to the Nondelegation Doctrine and Its Implications for Clinton v. City of New York, 76 Tul. L. Rev. 265, 352–53 (2001); David Schoenbrod, The Delegation Doctrine: Could the Court Give It Substance?, 83 Mich. L. Rev. 1223, 1260–65 (1985). For criticism of the distinction, see Note, Nondelegation's Unprincipled Foreign Affairs Exceptionalism, 134 Harv. L. Rev. 1132 (2021).

16. For skepticism about whether originalism supports a nondelegation doctrine, see, e.g., Julian Davis Mortenson & Nicholas Bagley, Delegation at the Founding, 121 Colum. L. Rev. 277 (2021); Nicholas R. Parrillo, A Critical Assessment of the Originalist Case against Administrative Regulatory Power: New Evidence from the Federal Tax on Private Real Estate in the

1790s, 130 Yale L.J. 1288 (2021); Christine Kexel Chabot, The Lost History of Delegation at the Founding, 56 Ga. L. Rev. 81 (2021). For the view that originalism supports meaningful nondelegation constraints, see, e.g., Gary Lawson, Delegation and Original Meaning, 88 Va. L. Rev. 327 (2002); Ilan Wurman, Nondelegation at the Founding, 130 Yale L.J. 1490 (2021).

17. 1 Stat. 372 (June 4, 1794). See also Louis Fisher, Delegating Power to the President, 19 Emory J. Pub. L. 251, 253 (1970) ("In the early days of the Republic . . . [congressional] sessions often lasted but a few months, and Congress found it necessary to delegate to the executive branch certain programs and policies that required continuous administration.").

18. For discussion of the historical context of the 1794 embargo statute, see Nicholas R. Parrillo, Nondelegation, Original Meaning, and Foreign Affairs: Congress's Delegation of Power to Lay Embargoes in 1794, 172 U. Pa. L. Rev. (forthcoming 2024).

19. 1 Stat. 613, 615 (Feb. 9, 1799).

20. Act of Apr. 22, 1808, ch. 52, 2 Stat. 490 (repealed 1809). See, e.g., 18 Annals of Cong. 2125 (1808) (Rep. Key); id. at 2236 (Rep. Rowan).

21. 2 Stat. 605 (May 1, 1810).

22. 11 U.S. (7 Cranch) 382 (1813). For an earlier lower court decision assuming the validity of a similar delegation, see The Orono, 18 F. Cas. 830, No. 10,585 (C.C.D. Mass. 1812) (Story, Circuit Justice).

23. See, e.g., William Rawle, A View of the Constitution of the United States 196 (2d ed. 1829).

24. 3 Stat. 224 (Mar. 3, 1815).

25. 26 Stat. 567, 612, § 3 (Oct. 1, 1890).

26. 143 U.S. 649 (1892).

27. See 30 Stat. 151, 203, ch. 11, § 3 (July 24, 1897).

28. 29 Stat. 604, 605, § 3 (Mar. 2, 1897).

29. 192 U.S. 470, 496 (1904).

30. 48 Stat. 943 (1934). For a decision holding that this statute did not constitute an unlawful delegation of authority to the executive branch, see Star-Kist Foods Inc. v. United States, 169 F. Supp. 268 (Cust. Ct. 1958), aff'd, 275 F.2d 472 (C.C.P.A. 1959). See also Francis B. Sayre, The Constitutionality of the Trade Agreements Act, 39 Colum. L. Rev. 751 (1939); Green H. Hackworth, Legal Aspects of the Trade Agreements Act of 1934, 21 A.B.A. J. 570 (1935).

31. See Timothy Meyer & Ganesh Sitaraman, Trade and the Separation of Powers, 107 Calif. L. Rev. 583, 597 (2019) (noting that "while the central shift from congressional power to presidential authority [over trade] was during the presidency of Franklin Roosevelt, the origins of congressional efforts to delegate power to the President began prior to the New Deal").

32. 296 U.S. 304 (1928). Under the Smoot-Halley Tariff Act of 1930, Congress set tariff rates itself. In part because of logrolling in Congress, this approach resulted in highly protectionist trade laws. See Harold Hongju Koh, Congressional Controls in Presidential Trade Policy-making After I.N.S. v. Chadha, 18 N.Y.U. J. Int'l L. & Pol. 1191, 1194 (1986).

33. 19 U.S.C. § 1862(b), (c).

34. See Federal Energy Admin. v. Algonquin SNG Inc., 426 U.S. 548, 559–60 (1976).

35. See Am. Inst. Int'l Steel Inc. v. United States, 806 Fed. Appx. 982 (Fed. Cir. 2020). Another broad delegation that the Trump administration relied on is Section 301 of the Trade Act of 1974, which allows the U.S. Trade Representative to impose a variety of trade-related sanctions after determining that a foreign government is violating a trade agreement with the United States or is engaged in actions that unjustifiably burden or restrict U.S. commerce. See 19 U.S.C. § 2411.

36. See generally Stephen I. Vladeck, Note, Emergency Power and the Militia Acts, 114 Yale L.J. 149 (2004); see also David J. Barron & Martin S. Lederman, The Commander in Chief at the Lowest Ebb—A Constitutional History, 121 Harv. L. Rev. 941, 961 (2008).

37. 1 Stat. 95, 96 (Sept. 29, 1789). See also 1 Stat. 119, 121 (Apr. 30, 1790).

38. 1 Stat. 424 (Feb. 28, 1795). The statute also allowed for the use of the militia to execute the laws when there was obstruction to such execution "by combinations too powerful to be suppressed by the ordinary course of judicial proceedings, or by the powers vested in the marshals." An earlier statute had allowed for this but had required a judicial certification of the condition. See 1 Stat. 264 (May 2, 1792).

39. See Martin v. Mott, 25 U.S. (12 Wheat.) 19, 30 (1827). The case involved the court-martial of an individual for failing to serve in a state militia after it was called up by President Madison during the War of 1812.

40. 1 Stat. 222, 223 (Mar. 3, 1791) (repealed 1795).

41. 1 Stat. 241, 242 (May 5, 1792) (repealed 1795).

42. See 4 Annals Cong. 735, 738 (1794).

43. 1 Stat. 376 (June 5, 1794).

44. 7 Annals of Cong. 283 (1797).

45. See David P. Currie, The Constitution in Congress: The Federalist Period, 1789–1801, at 244–45 (1997).

46. 8 Annals of Cong. 1525.

47. See Currie, supra note 45, at 244–48; Mortenson & Bagley, supra note 16, at 360–64. See also Richard H. Kohn, Eagle and Sword: The Beginnings of the Military Establishment in America 224 (1975) (describing the debate as "the lengthiest and most all-encompassing debate on national defense since the revolution").

48. 8 Annals of Cong. 1526.

49. See, e.g., id. at 1535 (Rep. Craik); id. at 1635 (Rep. Sewall); id. at 1637 (Rep. Dana); id. at 1642 (Rep. Otis); id. at 1655 (Rep. Brooks); id. at 1678 (Rep. Dayton). See also Currie, supra note 47, at 245 ("For the most part, the bill's defenders relied on precedent.").

50. Id. at 1660.

51. See, e.g., 8 Annals of Cong. 1541 (Rep. Nicholas); 8 Annals of Cong. 1656 (Rep. Gallatin).

52. See, e.g., id. at 1638 (Rep. Brent); id. at 1665 (Rep. Sumter); see also id. at 1538 (Rep. Gallatin) ("If these precedents deserved all the weight [the proponents of the bill] wished to give them, they would only show the danger of setting bad precedents."); id. at 1541 (Rep. Nicholas) (noting that "some" of the precedents "were in point" but that "he was not for being bound by precedent").

53. Id. at 1656. See also id. at 1638 (Rep. Brent) (arguing that the reasoning in favor of allowing this delegation would also allow for delegating the power to declare war, something that "would meet with immediate opposition").

54. Id. at 1678.

55. See id. at 1631. See also 1 Stat. 558 (May 28, 1798). Mortenson and Bagley characterize the revised bill as having "only slightly" narrowed the original one; see Mortenson & Bagley, supra note 47, at 363, but this understates the change. Cf. Currie, supra note 47, at 247 (noting that the revised bill contained "significant limitations on executive discretion").

56. 8 Annals of Cong. 1632.

57. 2 Stat. 443 (Mar. 3, 1807).

58. 12 Stat. 281 (July 29, 1861).

59. 10 U.S.C. § 252. This is an exception to the Posse Comitatus Act, which generally forbids the use of the armed forces for domestic law enforcement. See 18 U.S.C. § 1385.

60. See Order to General Scott (Apr. 27, 1861); Proclamation 94 (Sept. 24, 1862). For a decision holding that Lincoln lacked the authority to suspend the writ, see United States v. Merryman, 17 F. Cas. 144 (C.C.D. Md. 1861). For an argument that Congress's delegation to the president of authority over calling up the militia gave him some authority to suspend habeas corpus as well, see Vladeck, supra note 36, at 177.

61. 12 Stat. 755 (Mar. 3, 1863).

62. See Amy Coney Barrett, Suspension and Delegation, 99 Cornell L. Rev. 251, 252 (2014).

63. See Boumediene v. Bush, 553 U.S. 732 (2008). For a war on terror decision in which all the justices appeared to assume that the president could not suspend the writ on his own authority, see Hamdi v. Rumsfeld, 452 U.S. 507 (2004).

64. 40 Stat. 411 (Oct. 6, 1917).

65. 48 Stat. 1 (1933).

66. 90 Stat. 1255 (Sept. 14, 1976).

67. See 59 U.S.C. §1622(b).

68. See 91 Stat. 1626 (Oct. 28, 1977). See Cong. Res. Serv., The International Emergency Economic Powers Act: Origins, Evolution, and Use (updated Mar. 25, 2022).

69. See 50 U.S.C. § 1702.

70. 50 U.S.C. § 1701(a). The Act contains various consultation and reporting requirements. See 50 U.S.C. § 1703.

71. See Elizabeth Goitein, The Alarming Scope of the President's Emergency Powers, Atlantic (Jan./Feb. 2019).

72. See, e.g., United States v. Mirza, 454 Fed. Appx. 249, 255–56 (5th Cir. 2011); United States v. Amirnazmi, 645 F.3d 564, 575–77 (3d Cir. 2011); United States v. Dhafir, 461 F.3d 211, 215–17 (2d Cir. 2006); United States v. Arch Trading Co., 987 F.2d 1087, 1092–94 (4th Cir. 1993). While IEEPA is the most frequently invoked statutory source of emergency power, over a hundred statutory provisions are triggered by a presidential declaration of an emergency. See Cong. Res. Serv., National Emergency Powers (updated Nov. 19, 2021); Brennan Center, A Guide to Emergency Powers and Their Use (updated Feb. 8, 2023).

73. 22 U.S.C. § 2778.

74. See, e.g., United States v. Henry, 888 F.3d 589 (2d Cir. 2018); United States v. Kuok, 671 F.3d 931 (9th Cir. 2012).

75. 6 Stat. 798, codified as amended at 50 U.S.C. §§ 4501–68. See also Cong. Res. Serv., The Defense Production Act of 1950: History, Authorities, and Considerations for Congress (Mar. 2, 2020).

76. 1 Stat. 577 (July 6, 1798).

77. See, e.g., 8 Annals of Cong. 2007–8 (1798) (Rep. Livingston) (arguing that the act unconstitutionally combined "Legislative, Executive, and Judicial powers"). See also Mortenson & Bagley, supra note 16, at 364–65 (describing nondelegation concerns raised by James Madison).

78. 1 Stat. 577 (July 6, 1798).

79. See 50 U.S.C. § 21.

80. See Adam B. Cox & Cristina M. Rodriguez, The President and Immigration Law 21–27 (2020); Gerald L. Neuman, Strangers to the Constitution: Immigrants, Borders, and Fundamental Law (1996).

81. See 22 Stat. 58 (May 6, 1882).

82. See 40 Stat. 559 (May 22, 1918).

83. 55 Stat. 252 (June 21, 1941).

84. 338 U.S. 537 (1950).

85. 8 U.S.C. § 1182(f).

86. Proclamation No. 9645, Enhancing Vetting Capabilities and Processes for Detecting Attempted Entry into the United States by Terrorists or Other Public-Safety Threats, 82 Fed. Reg. 45161.

87. 138 S. Ct. 2392 (2018).

88. In a concurrence, Justice Thomas argued that the statute "does not set forth any judicially enforceable limits that constrain the President" and contended that this was proper because "the President has *inherent* authority to exclude aliens from the country." Id. at 2424 (emphasis added). One of the lower court judges in the cases challenging the Trump policy expressed nondelegation concerns about the statute and argued that it should be construed in a manner to avoid these concerns. See International Refugee Assistance Project v. Trump, 883 F.3d 233, 293–96 (4th Cir. 2018) (Gregory, C.J., concurring).

89. 11 Stat. 52, 60, § 23 (Aug. 18, 1856). See also Craig Robertson, The Passport in America: The History of a Document 141 (2010).

90. The 1952 statute allowed the president to make passports mandatory by proclaiming a national emergency. See 66 Stat. 163, 190 (1952). Soon thereafter, President Truman issued the required proclamation. See 67 Stat. C31 (Jan. 17, 1953). For discussion of the implications of this shift, see Louis L. Jaffe, The Right to Travel: The Passport Problem, Foreign Affairs (Oct. 1956). In 1978, Congress made mandatory passports the norm, stating that "except as otherwise provided by the President and subject to such limitations and exceptions as the President may authorize and prescribe, it shall be unlawful for any citizen of the United States to depart from or enter, or attempt to depart from or enter, the United States unless he bears a valid passport." 92 Stat. 993 (Oct. 7, 1978).

91. 357 U.S. 116 (1958).

92. 381 U.S. 1 (1965).

93. 453 U.S. 280 (1981). For a critique of the decision, see Daniel A. Farber, National Security, the Right to Travel, and the Court, 1981 Sup. Ct. Rev. 263.

94. The Court's emphasis on historical practice in discerning what Congress had authorized is similar to the analysis in Dames & Moore v. Regan, 453 U.S. 654 (1981), a decision (discussed in Chapter 4) that upheld an executive agreement that suspended billions of dollars of U.S. claims and created a new arbitral institution in The Hague to address the claims.

95. See also Patricia L. Bellia, Executive Power in Youngstown's Shadows, 19 Const. Comm. 87, 130 (2002) (noting that these passport decisions illustrate that "questions about the scope of a congressional delegation and the scope of the President's constitutional powers in foreign affairs are closely intertwined").

96. Modern international law, by outlawing the use of force except in self-defense or pursuant to authorization from the UN Security Council and by disallowing the changing of legal entitlements through war, has made declarations of war much less relevant than they once were. See, e.g., Paul Kahn, War Powers and the Millennium, 34 Loy. L.A. L. Rev. 11 (2000).

97. See Jennifer K. Elsea & Matthew C. Weed, Declarations of War and Authorizations for the Use of Military Force: Historical Background and Legal Implications, Appendix A (Cong. Res. Serv., Apr. 18, 2014); Curtis A. Bradley & Jack L. Goldsmith, Congressional Authorization

and the War on Terrorism, 118 Harv. L. Rev. 2047, 2062–66 (2005). The authorization in connection with the Mexican-American War limited to 50,000 the number of volunteer soldiers that the president could employ in the conflict but did not otherwise direct how forces should be used.

98. For a collection of some of the most significant congressional authorizations of force throughout U.S. history, see Elsea & Weed, supra note 97.

99. See Currie, supra note 47, at 244 ("The bellicose legislation of the Fifth Congress was riddled with broad delegations of authority.").

100. 1 Stat. 578 (July 9, 1798).

101. See Bas v. Tingy, 4 U.S. (4 Dall.) 37 (1800); Little v. Barreme, 6 U.S. (1 Cranch) 170 (1804).

102. 2 Stat. 129 (Feb. 6, 1802) (emphasis added). As discussed in Chapter 6, President Jefferson had earlier suggested that, without a congressional authorization, he was limited to using force purely in defense against the Barbary pirates.

103. 3 Stat. 230 (Mar. 3, 1815).

104. Act of Mar. 3, 1839, § 1, 5 Stat. 355. See also Henry Bartholomew Cox, War, Foreign Affairs, and Constitutional Power 21 (1984) (describing the statute as "one of the broadest [delegations of war power] accorded any nineteenth century president" that "would have permitted Van Buren to go to war before the British attacked U.S. positions").

105. 11 Stat. 370 (June 2, 1858).

106. See Cox, supra note 104, at 230–31.

107. Report of Senate Foreign Relations Committee, 23d Cong., 2d Sess. (Jan. 6, 1835).

108. See Cox, supra note 104, at 195–99; David P. Currie, The Constitution in Congress: Descent into the Maelstrom, 1829–1861, at 127–30 (2005); Francis D. Wormuth & Edwin B. Firmage, To Chain the Dog of War: The Power of Congress in History and Law 204–7 (1989). As noted in Chapter 6, President Buchanan had a narrow view of presidential war powers, pursuant to which presidents could "not legitimately resort to force without the direct authority of Congress, except in resisting and repelling hostile attacks." James Buchanan, Second Annual Message (Dec. 6, 1858).

109. Cong. Globe, 35th Cong., 2d Sess., pt. 2, at 1120 (1859).

110. 67 U.S. 635 (1863).

111. See Arthur M. Schlesinger Jr., The Imperial Presidency 57 (1973) (2004 ed.). As discussed in Chapter 6, an especially noteworthy military campaign that was not authorized by Congress was U.S. participation in a multinational coalition to address the Boxer Rebellion in China in 1900.

112. See Bradley & Goldsmith, supra note 97, at 2072–78.

113. Joint Resolution of Jan. 29, 1955, Pub. L. No. 4, 69 Stat. 7.

114. 71 Stat. 5 (Mar. 9, 1957). See also Matthew Waxman, Remembering Eisenhower's Middle East Force Resolution, Lawfare (Mar. 9, 2019) (describing this as "perhaps the most open-ended force resolution in American history").

115. See, e.g., 85 Cong. Rec. 2712 (1957) (Sen. Morse) (describing the resolution as "an unconstitutional delegation of the power to declare war").

116. 78 Stat. 384 (Aug. 10, 1964) (emphasis added).

117. See, e.g., Alexander M. Bickel, Congress, the President, and the Power to Wage War, 48 Chi-Kent L. Rev. 131, 137 (1971); Francis D. Wormuth, The Nixon Theory of the War Power: A

Critique, 60 Calif. L. Rev. 623, 692 (1972); William Van Alstyne, Congress, the President, and the Power to Declare War: A Requiem for Vietnam, 121 U. Pa. L. Rev. 1, 16 (1972).

118. William H. Rehnquist, The Constitutional Issues—Administration Position, 45 N.Y.U. L. Rev. 628, 637 (1970).

119. See John Hart Ely, War and Responsibility: Constitutional Lessons of Vietnam and Its Aftermath 26 (1993).

120. See 105 Stat. 3 (Jan. 14, 1991).

121. Pub. L. 107–243 (Oct. 6, 2002) (emphasis added).

122. S.J. Res. 23 (Sept. 18, 2001) (emphasis added).

123. For discussion of how uses of the Authorization for Use of Military Force evolved over time, in both Democratic and Republican administrations, see Curtis A. Bradley & Jack L. Goldsmith, Obama's AUMF Legacy, 110 Am. J. Int'l L. 628 (2016).

124. In the September 11 authorization, Congress stated that "the President has authority under the Constitution to take action to deter and prevent acts of international terrorism against the United States." S.J. Res 23, supra note 122.

125. During the debates over whether to approve the treaty, a majority of the Senate voted in favor of this reservation. See 59 Cong. Rec. 4333 (1920) (recording a vote of 56–26).

126. See UN Participation Act of 1945, § 6, 22 U.S.C. § 287d.

127. S. Rep. No. 79–8, at 9 (1945).

128. See, e.g., 96 Cong. Rec. S9540 (1950) (Sen. Knowland).

129. For scholarly debate over whether treaties can authorize presidential uses of force that would otherwise require congressional authorization, compare, e.g., Thomas M. Franck & Faiza Patel, UN Police Action in Lieu of War: "The Old Order Changeth," 85 Am. J. Int'l L. 63 (1991), and David Golove, From Versailles to San Francisco: The Revolutionary Transformation of the War Powers, 70 U. Colo. L. Rev. 1491 (1999), with Michael J. Glennon, The Constitution and Chapter VII of the United Nations Charter, 85 Am. J. Int'l L. 74 (1991), and Jane E. Stromseth, Rethinking War Powers: Congress, the President, and the United Nations, 81 Geo. L.J. 597 (1993).

130. 299 U.S. at 319–20.

131. 343 U.S. at 635.

132. 517 U.S. 748 (1996).

133. This independent authority idea has also been applied to delegations to Indian tribes. See United States v. Mazurie, 419 U.S. 544, 556–57 (1974). See also Alexander Volokh, Judicial Non-Delegation, the Inherent-Powers Corollary, and Federal Common Law, 66 Emory L.J. 1391, 1398–1403 (2017).

134. See Oona A. Hathaway, Treaties' End: The Past, Present, and Future of International Lawmaking in the United States, 117 Yale L.J. 1236, 1258 (2009). Although Congress has the authority to regulate these subjects, it is not entirely clear where it gets the authority to delegate the agreement-making power relating to them. See Louis Henkin, Foreign Affairs and the United States 216 (2d ed. 1996). It may be that Congress's regulatory authority (perhaps along with its Necessary and Proper Clause authority) can be linked with the president's agreement-negotiation authority to allow for these delegations.

135. See Abraham D. Sofaer, War, Foreign Affairs and Constitutional Power 74 (1976).

136. See also Kevin Arlyck, Delegation, Administration, and Improvisation, 97 Notre Dame L. Rev. 243, 289 (2021); Note, supra note 15, at 1139.

137. See, e.g., Michael D. Ramsey & Matthew C. Waxman, Delegating War Powers, 96 So. Cal. L. Rev. 741 (2023) (describing delegation concerns that have been raised at times with respect to decisions about whether to initiate hostilities). In domestic affairs, an early example of a proposal that prompted nondelegation objections by some members of Congress (including James Madison) concerned legislation that would have delegated to the president the authority to determine postal routes. See Mortenson & Bagley, supra note 16, at 350–56.

138. For an argument along these lines, see Curtis Bradley & Jack Goldsmith, Foreign Affairs, Nondelegation, and the Major Questions Doctrine, 172 U. Pa. L. Rev. (forthcoming 2024).

139. See, e.g., Cass R. Sunstein, There Are Two "Major Questions" Doctrines, 73 Admin. L. Rev. 475 (2021); Cass R. Sunstein, Nondelegation Canons, 67 U. Chi. L. Rev. 315 (2000); John F. Manning, The Nondelegation Doctrine as a Canon of Avoidance, 2000 Sup. Ct. Rev. 223.

140. West Virginia v. EPA, 142 S. Ct. 2587, 2609 (2022).

141. See, e.g., Dames & Moore, 453 U.S. 654, 678 (1981); 381 U.S. at 17.

142. For an argument that, in part for this reason, the major questions doctrine threatens to reduce the economic leverage that presidents can employ as part of foreign policy, including as an alternative to the use of military force, see Timothy Meyer & Ganesh Sitaraman, The National Security Consequences of the Major Questions Doctrine, 122 Mich. L. Rev. 55 (2023).

143. See, e.g., Hamdi v. Rumsfeld, 542 U.S. 507, 519 (2004) (plurality opinion); Dames & Moore v. Regan, 453 U.S. 654, 677 (1981); 381 U.S. at 11–12.

144. Edward S. Corwin, The President: Office and Powers, 1787–1957, at 171 (1957).

145. See, e.g., David H. Moore, Taking Cues from Congress: Judicial Review, Congressional Authorization, and the Expansion of Presidential Power, 90 Notre Dame L. Rev. 1019 (2015).

146. See, e.g., Rebecca Ingber, Congressional Administration of Foreign Affairs, 106 Va. L. Rev. 395 (2020).

147. The Administrative Procedure Act has been interpreted not to apply to presidential actions. See Franklin v. Massachusetts, 505 U.S. 788 (1992). In addition, the Act's process requirements for rule making do not apply to "a military or foreign affairs function of the United States." 5 U.S.C. § 553(a)(1). See also Kathryn M. Kovacs, Constraining the Statutory President, 98 Wash. U. L. Rev. 63 (2020).

148. One potential check on congressional delegations, which is no longer available, is the use of a "legislative veto" provision pursuant to which one or both houses of Congress could overturn executive branch actions without having to enact a new statute. Congress included such provisions in an array of statutes relating to foreign affairs, especially in the 1970s. However, the Supreme Court held in INS v. Chadha, 462 U.S. 919 (1983), that such provisions are unconstitutional because they allow Congress to legislate without going through the full legislative process required by the Constitution. (As noted in Chapter 1, the Court reached this conclusion despite the extensive practice since the 1930s of congressional enactment of legislative veto provisions.) Some commentators have suggested that the Court's invalidation of legislative vetoes has sharply reduced Congress's ability to control its delegations, including in foreign affairs. The critique is probably overstated, given the infrequency of Congress's use of the veto before *Chadha* and the workarounds that Congress has developed since the decision. See Curtis A. Bradley, Reassessing the Legislative Veto: The Statutory President, Foreign Affairs, and Congressional Workarounds, 13 J. Leg. Anal. 439 (2021).

Conclusion

1. See Daryl J. Levinson, Parchment and Politics: The Positive Puzzle of Constitutional Commitment, 124 Harv. L. Rev. 657, 661 (2011) ("Casting courts as constitutional enforcers merely pushes the question back to why powerful political actors are willing to pay attention to what judges say; why 'people with money and guns ever submit to people armed only with gavels.'" [quoting Matthew C. Stephenson, "When the Devil Turns . . .": The Political Foundations of Independent Judicial Review, 32 J. Legal Stud. 59, 60 (2003)]). See also Keith E. Whittington, Political Foundations of Judicial Supremacy: The President, the Supreme Court, and Constitutional Leadership in U.S. History (2007).

2. See Curtis A. Bradley & Trevor W. Morrison, Presidential Power, Historical Practice, and Legal Constraint, 113 Colum. L. Rev. 1097, 1143 (2013).

3. Federalist No. 51 (Madison), in The Federalist Papers 320 (Clinton Rossiter ed., 1961).

4. See Daryl J. Levinson & Richard H. Pildes, Separation of Parties, Not Powers, 119 Harv. L. Rev. 2311 (2006).

5. See James M. Inhofe National Defense Authorization Act for Fiscal Year 2023, Pub. L. 117–263, § 5947 (Dec. 23, 2022).

6. Moreover, although Congress has formally declared war in five conflicts, only the declarations in World War I and World War II have been viewed as relatively unproblematic. Congress's track record is not great.

Acknowledgments

For helpful comments and questions, I thank Will Baude, Dan Bodansky, Kathy Bradley, Jud Campbell, Adam Chilton, Ashley Deeks, Mary Dudziak, Jim Dwyer, Kristen Eichensehr, Martin Flaherty, Jean Galbraith, Michael Gerhardt, Tom Ginsburg, Jack Goldsmith, Jonathan Green, Monica Hakimi, Oona Hathaway, Todd Henderson, Aziz Huq, Alison LaCroix, Brian Leiter, Jonathan Masur, Henry Monaghan, Sean Murphy, Farah Peterson, Eric Posner, Mike Ramsey, Robert Reinstein, Ryan Scoville, Neil Siegel, Ed Swaine, Matt Waxman, Ilan Wurman, and participants in faculty workshops at Arizona State University's Sandra Day O'Connor College of Law, the University of Chicago Law School, and the William & Mary Law School, at a book conference at the University of Chicago Law School, and at the Virginia-Chicago Foreign Relations Law Roundtable. I also thank the two anonymous reviewers who commented on the entire manuscript as part of the publication process. For excellent research assistance, I thank Maddy Delgado, Joe Kiernan, Kira Liu, and Kelsey Roberts. I also thank my dean, Tom Miles, for his enthusiastic support and encouragement; my law school librarians for their tireless help in tracking down materials; and the University of Chicago Law School's S. Richard Fine Fund for its financial support. Finally, many of my ideas relating to this book were initially developed while I was teaching at Duke Law School, and I am greatly indebted to my deans and colleagues there.

Some of the ideas and observations in this book have been drawn from the following law review articles: Curtis A. Bradley & Trevor W. Morrison, Historical Gloss and the Separation of Powers, 126 Harv. L. Rev. 411 (2012); Curtis A. Bradley, Treaty Termination and Historical Gloss, 92 Tex. L. Rev. 773 (2014); Curtis A. Bradley & Neil S. Siegel, After Recess: Historical Practice, Textual Ambiguity, and Constitutional Adverse Possession, 2014 Sup. Ct. Rev. 1; Curtis A. Bradley & Neil S. Siegel, Constructed Constraint and the Constitutional Text, 64 Duke L.J. 1213 (2015); Curtis A. Bradley, Doing Gloss, 84 U. Chi. L. Rev. 59 (2017);

Curtis A. Bradley & Neil S. Siegel, Historical Gloss, Constitutional Conventions, and the Judicial Separation of Powers, 105 Georgetown L.J. 255 (2017); and Curtis A. Bradley & Neil S. Siegel, Historical Gloss, Madisonian Liquidation, and the Originalism Debate, 106 Va. L. Rev. 1 (2020). My thinking on these topics also benefited greatly from discussions with my students over the years and from interactions with my coauthors on the following casebook: Curtis A. Bradley, Ashley S. Deeks, and Jack L. Goldsmith, Foreign Relations Law: Cases and Materials (8th ed. 2024).

Index